CIMA

Subject P1

Management Accounting

Study Text

Published by: Kaplan Publishing UK

Unit 2 The Business Centre, Molly Millars Lane, Wokingham, Berkshire RG41 2QZ

Acknowledgements

We are grateful to the CIMA for permission to reproduce past examination questions. The answers to CIMA Exams have been prepared by Kaplan Publishing, except in the case of the CIMA November 2010 and subsequent CIMA Exam answers where the official CIMA answers have been reproduced.

Notice

British Library Cataloguing in Publication Data

A catalogue record for this book is available from the British Library.

ISBN: 978-1-78415-519-3

Printed and bound in Great Britain.

Contents

chapter Intro

Introduction

How to use the materials

These official CIMA learning materials have been carefully designed to make your learning experience as easy as possible and to give you the best chances of success in your Objective Test Examination.

The product range contains a number of features to help you in the study process. They include:

- a detailed explanation of all syllabus areas
- extensive 'practical' materials
- generous question practice, together with full solutions.

This Study Text has been designed with the needs of home study and distance learning candidates in mind. Such students require very full coverage of the syllabus topics, and also the facility to undertake extensive question practice. However, the Study Text is also ideal for fully taught courses.

The main body of the text is divided into a number of chapters, each of which is organised on the following pattern:

- **Detailed learning outcomes.** These describe the knowledge expected after your studies of the chapter are complete. You should assimilate these before beginning detailed work on the chapter, so that you can appreciate where your studies are leading.
- **Step-by-step topic coverage.** This is the heart of each chapter, containing detailed explanatory text supported where appropriate by worked examples and exercises. You should work carefully through this section, ensuring that you understand the material being explained and can tackle the examples and exercises successfully. Remember that in many cases knowledge is cumulative: if you fail to digest earlier material thoroughly, you may struggle to understand later chapters.
- **Activities.** Some chapters are illustrated by more practical elements, such as comments and questions designed to stimulate discussion.

- **Question practice.** The text contains three styles of question:
  - Exam-style objective test questions (OTQs)
  - 'Integration' questions – these test your ability to understand topics within a wider context. This is particularly important with calculations where OTQs may focus on just one element but an integration question tackles the full calculation, just as you would be expected to do in the workplace.
  - 'Case' style questions – these test your ability to analyse and discuss issues in greater depth, particularly focusing on scenarios that are less clear cut than in the Objective Test Examination, and thus provide excellent practice for developing the skills needed for success in the Operational Level Case Study Examination.
- **Solutions.** Avoid the temptation merely to 'audit' the solutions provided. It is an illusion to think that this provides the same benefits as you would gain from a serious attempt of your own. However, if you are struggling to get started on a question you should read the introductory guidance provided at the beginning of the solution, where provided, and then make your own attempt before referring back to the full solution.

If you work conscientiously through this Official CIMA Study Text according to the guidelines above you will be giving yourself an excellent chance of success in your Objective Test Examination. Good luck with your studies!

Quality and accuracy are of the utmost importance to us so if you spot an error in any of our products, please send an email to mykaplanreporting@kaplan.com with full details, or follow the link to the feedback form in MyKaplan.

Our Quality Co-ordinator will work with our technical team to verify the error and take action to ensure it is corrected in future editions.

Icon Explanations

Definition – These sections explain important areas of knowledge which must be understood and reproduced in an assessment environment.

Key point – Identifies topics which are key to success and are often examined.

Supplementary reading – These sections will help to provide a deeper understanding of core areas. The supplementary reading is **NOT** optional reading. It is vital to provide you with the breadth of knowledge you will need to address the wide range of topics within your syllabus that could feature in an assessment question. **Reference to this text is vital when self studying**.

Test your understanding – Following key points and definitions are exercises which give the opportunity to assess the understanding of these core areas.

Illustration – To help develop an understanding of particular topics. The illustrative examples are useful in preparing for the Test your understanding exercises.

Exclamation mark – This symbol signifies a topic which can be more difficult to understand. When reviewing these areas, care should be taken.

Tutorial note – Included to explain some of the technical points in more detail.

Study technique

Passing exams is partly a matter of intellectual ability, but however accomplished you are in that respect you can improve your chances significantly by the use of appropriate study and revision techniques. In this section we briefly outline some tips for effective study during the earlier stages of your approach to the Objective Test Examination. We also mention some techniques that you will find useful at the revision stage.

Planning

To begin with, formal planning is essential to get the best return from the time you spend studying. Estimate how much time in total you are going to need for each subject you are studying. Remember that you need to allow time for revision as well as for initial study of the material.

With your study material before you, decide which chapters you are going to study in each week, and which weeks you will devote to revision and final question practice.

Prepare a written schedule summarising the above and stick to it!

It is essential to know your syllabus. As your studies progress you will become more familiar with how long it takes to cover topics in sufficient depth. Your timetable may need to be adapted to allocate enough time for the whole syllabus.

Students are advised to refer to the notice of examinable legislation published regularly in CIMA's magazine (Financial Management), the students e-newsletter (Velocity) and on the CIMA website, to ensure they are up-to-date.

The amount of space allocated to a topic in the Study Text is not a very good guide as to how long it will take you. The syllabus weighting is the better guide as to how long you should spend on a syllabus topic.

Tips for effective studying

(1) Aim to find a quiet and undisturbed location for your study, and plan as far as possible to use the same period of time each day. Getting into a routine helps to avoid wasting time. Make sure that you have all the materials you need before you begin so as to minimise interruptions.

(2) Store all your materials in one place, so that you do not waste time searching for items every time you want to begin studying. If you have to pack everything away after each study period, keep your study materials in a box, or even a suitcase, which will not be disturbed until the next time.

(3) Limit distractions. To make the most effective use of your study periods you should be able to apply total concentration, so turn off all entertainment equipment, set your phones to message mode, and put up your 'do not disturb' sign.

(4) Your timetable will tell you which topic to study. However, before diving in and becoming engrossed in the finer points, make sure you have an overall picture of all the areas that need to be covered by the end of that session. After an hour, allow yourself a short break and move away from your Study Text. With experience, you will learn to assess the pace you need to work at. Each study session should focus on component learning outcomes – the basis for all questions.

(5) Work carefully through a chapter, making notes as you go. When you have covered a suitable amount of material, vary the pattern by attempting a practice question. When you have finished your attempt, make notes of any mistakes you made, or any areas that you failed to cover or covered more briefly. Be aware that all component learning outcomes will be tested in each examination.

(6) Make notes as you study, and discover the techniques that work best for you. Your notes may be in the form of lists, bullet points, diagrams, summaries, 'mind maps', or the written word, but remember that you will need to refer back to them at a later date, so they must be intelligible. If you are on a taught course, make sure you highlight any issues you would like to follow up with your lecturer.

(7) Organise your notes. Make sure that all your notes, calculations etc. can be effectively filed and easily retrieved later.

Objective Test

Objective Test questions require you to choose or provide a response to a question whose correct answer is predetermined.

The most common types of Objective Test question you will see are:

- Multiple choice, where you have to choose the correct answer(s) from a list of possible answers. This could either be numbers or text.

- Multiple choice with more choices and answers, for example, choosing two correct answers from a list of eight possible answers. This could either be numbers or text.
- Single numeric entry, where you give your numeric answer, for example, profit is $10,000.
- Multiple entry, where you give several numeric answers.
- True/false questions, where you state whether a statement is true or false.
- Matching pairs of text, for example, matching a technical term with the correct definition.
- Other types could be matching text with graphs and labelling graphs/diagrams.

In every chapter of this Study Text we have introduced these types of questions, but obviously we have had to label answers A, B, C etc rather than using click boxes. For convenience we have retained quite a few questions where an initial scenario leads to a number of sub-questions. There will be questions of this type in the Objective Test Examination but they will rarely have more than three sub-questions.

Guidance re CIMA on-screen calculator

As part of the CIMA Objective Test software, candidates are now provided with a calculator. This calculator is on-screen and is available for the duration of the assessment. The calculator is available in each of the Objective Test Examinations and is accessed by clicking the calculator button in the top left hand corner of the screen at any time during the assessment.

All candidates must complete a 15-minute tutorial before the assessment begins and will have the opportunity to familiarise themselves with the calculator and practise using it.

Candidates may practise using the calculator by downloading and installing the practice exam at www.pearsonvue.com/cima/practiceexams/.

Fundamentals of Objective Tests

The Objective Tests are 90-minute assessments comprising 60 compulsory questions, with one or more parts. There will be no choice and all questions should be attempted.

Structure of subjects and learning outcomes

Each subject within the syllabus is divided into a number of broad syllabus topics. The topics contain one or more lead learning outcomes, related component learning outcomes and indicative knowledge content.

A learning outcome has two main purposes:

(a) To define the skill or ability that a well prepared candidate should be able to exhibit in the examination.

(b) To demonstrate the approach likely to be taken in examination questions.

The learning outcomes are part of a hierarchy of learning objectives. The verbs used at the beginning of each learning outcome relate to a specific learning objective, e.g.

Calculate the break-even point, profit target, margin of safety and profit/volume ratio for a single product or service.

The verb '**calculate**' indicates a level three learning objective. The following tables list the verbs that appear in the syllabus learning outcomes and examination questions.

CIMA VERB HIERARCHY

CIMA place great importance on the definition of verbs in structuring Objective Test Examinations. It is therefore crucial that you understand the verbs in order to appreciate the depth and breadth of a topic and the level of skill required. The Objective Tests will focus on levels one, two and three of the CIMA hierarchy of verbs. However they will also test levels four and five, especially at the management and strategic levels. You can therefore expect to be tested on knowledge, comprehension, application, analysis and evaluation in these examinations.

Level 1: KNOWLEDGE

What you are expected to know.

VERBS USED	DEFINITION
List	Make a list of.
State	Express, fully or clearly, the details of/facts of.
Define	Give the exact meaning of.

For example you could be asked to make a list of the advantages of a particular information system by selecting all options that apply from a given set of possibilities. Or you could be required to define relationship marketing by selecting the most appropriate option from a list.

Level 2: COMPREHENSION

What you are expected to understand.

VERBS USED	DEFINITION
Describe	Communicate the key features of.
Distinguish	Highlight the differences between.
Explain	Make clear or intelligible/state the meaning or purpose of.
Identify	Recognise, establish or select after consideration.
Illustrate	Use an example to describe or explain something.

For example you may be asked to distinguish between different aspects of the global business environment by dragging external factors and dropping into a PEST analysis.

Level 3: APPLICATION

How you are expected to apply your knowledge.

VERBS USED	DEFINITION
Apply	Put to practical use.
Calculate	Ascertain or reckon mathematically.
Demonstrate	Prove with certainty or exhibit by practical means.
Prepare	Make or get ready for use.
Reconcile	Make or prove consistent/compatible.
Solve	Find an answer to.
Tabulate	Arrange in a table.

For example you may need to calculate the projected revenue or costs for a given set of circumstances.

Level 4: ANALYSIS

How you are expected to analyse the detail of what you have learned.

VERBS USED	**DEFINITION**
Analyse	Examine in detail the structure of.
Categorise	Place into a defined class or division.
Compare/ contrast	Show the similarities and/or differences between.
Construct	Build up or compile.
Discuss	Examine in detail by argument.
Interpret	Translate into intelligible or familiar terms.
Prioritise	Place in order of priority or sequence for action.
Produce	Create or bring into existence.

For example you may be required to interpret an inventory ratio by selecting the most appropriate statement for a given set of circumstances and data.

Level 5: EVALUATION

How you are expected to use your learning to evaluate, make decisions or recommendations.

VERBS USED	**DEFINITION**
Advise	Counsel, inform or notify.
Evaluate	Appraise or assess the value of.
Recommend	Propose a course of action.

For example you may be asked to recommend and select an appropriate course of action based on a short scenario.

Information concerning formulae and tables will be provided via the CIMA website, www.cimaglobal.com, and your ENgage login.

P1
MANAGEMENT ACCOUNTING

Syllabus overview

P1 stresses the importance of costs and the drivers of costs in the production, analysis and use of information for decision making in organisations. The time focus of P1 is the short term. It covers budgeting as a means of short-term planning to execute the strategy of organisations. In addition it provides competencies on how to analyse information on costs, volumes and prices to take short-term decisions on products and services and to develop an understanding on the impact of risk to these decisions. P1 provides the foundation for cost management and the long-term decisions covered in P2.

Summary of syllabus

Weight	Syllabus topic
30%	**A.** Cost accounting systems
25%	**B.** Budgeting
30%	**C.** Short-term decision making
15%	**D.** Dealing with risk and uncertainty

P1 – A. COST ACCOUNTING SYSTEMS (30%)

Learning outcomes On completion of their studies, students should be able to:		**Indicative syllabus content**
Lead	**Component**	
1 discuss costing methods and their results.	(a) apply marginal (or variable) throughput and absorption accounting methods in respect of profit reporting and inventory valuation	• Marginal (or variable) throughput and absorption accounting systems of profit reporting and inventory valuation, including the reconciliation of budget and actual profit using absorption and/or marginal costing principles.
	(b) compare and contrast activity-based costing with traditional marginal and absorption costing methods	• Product and service costing using an activity-based costing system. • The advantages and disadvantages of activity-based costing compared with traditional costing systems.
	(c) apply standard costing methods including the reconciliation of budgeted and actual profit margins, distinguishing between planning and operational variances	• Manufacturing standards for material, labour, variable overhead and fixed overhead. • Standards and variances in service industries, public services (e.g. health and law enforcement), and the professions (e.g. labour mix variances in consultancies). • Price/rate and usage/efficiency variances for materials, labour and variable overhead. • Subdivision of total usage/efficiency variances into mix and yield variances. • **Note:** The calculation of mix variances on both individual and average valuation bases is required. • Fixed overhead expenditure and volume variances. • Subdivision of the fixed overhead volume variance into capacity and efficiency variances. • Sales price and sales volume variances (calculation of the latter on a unit basis related to revenue, gross profit and contribution).

Learning outcomes On completion of their studies, students should be able to:		Indicative syllabus content
Lead	**Component**	
		• Sales mix and sales quantity variances. Application of these variances to all sectors including professional services and retail. • Planning and operational variances. • Variance analysis in an activity-based costing system.
	(d) interpret material, labour, variable overhead, fixed overhead and sales variances	• Interpretation of variances. • The interrelationship between variances
	(e) explain the advantages and disadvantages of standard costing in various sectors and its appropriateness in the contemporary business environment	• Criticisms of standard costing including its use in the contemporary business environment.
	(f) explain the impact of JIT manufacturing methods on cost accounting methods.	• The impact of JIT production on cost accounting and performance measurement systems.
2 discuss the role of quality costing.	(a) discuss the role of quality costing as part of a total quality management (TQM) system.	• The preparation of cost of quality reports including the classification of quality costs into prevention costs, appraisal costs, internal failure costs and external failure costs. • The use of quality costing as part of a TQM system.
3 explain the role of environmental costing.	(a) explain the role of environmental costing as part of an environmental management system.	• The classification of environmental costs using the quality costing framework. • Linking environmental costs to activities and outputs and their implication for decision making. • The difficulties in measuring environmental costs and their impact on the external environment. • The contribution of environmental costing to improved environmental and financial performance.

P1 – B. BUDGETING (25%)

Learning outcomes On completion of their studies, students should be able to:		**Indicative syllabus content**
Lead	**Component**	
1 **explain the purposes of forecasts, plans and budgets.**	(a) explain the purposes of budgets, including planning, communication, coordination, motivation, authorisation, control and evaluation, and how these may conflict.	• The role of forecasts and plans in resource allocation, performance evaluation and control. • The purposes of budgets, the budgeting process and conflicts that can arise.
2 **prepare forecasts of financial results.**	(a) calculate projected product/service volumes, revenue and costs employing appropriate forecasting techniques and taking account of cost structures.	• Time series analysis including moving totals and averages, treatment of seasonality, trend analysis using regression analysis and the application of these techniques in forecasting product and service volumes.
3 **discuss budgets based on forecasts.**	(a) prepare a budget for any account in the master budget, based on projections/forecasts and managerial targets	• The budget setting process, limiting factors, the interaction between component budgets and the master budget.
	(b) discuss alternative approaches to budgeting.	• Alternative approaches to budget creation, including incremental approaches, zero-based budgeting and activity-based budgets.
4 **discuss the principles that underlie the use of budgets for control.**	(a) discuss the concept of the budget as a control system and the use of responsibility accounting and its importance in the construction of functional budgets that support the overall master budget.	• The use of budgets in planning and control e.g. rolling budgets and flexed budgets. • The concepts of feedback and feed-forward control. • Responsibility accounting and the link to controllable and uncontrollable costs.
5 **analyse performance using budgets, recognising alternative approaches and sensitivity to variable factors.**	(a) analyse the consequences of 'what if' scenarios.	• 'What if' analysis based on alternate projections of volumes, prices and cost structures. • The evaluation of out-turn performance using variances based on 'fixed' and 'flexed' budgets.

P1 – C. SHORT-TERM DECISION MAKING (30%)

Learning outcomes On completion of their studies, students should be able to:		**Indicative syllabus content**
Lead	**Component**	
1 explain concepts of cost and revenue relevant to pricing and product decisions.	(a) explain the principles of decision making, including the identification and use of relevant cash flows and qualitative factors	• Relevant cash flows and their use in short-term decision making. • Consideration of the strategic implications of short-term decisions.
	(b) explain the conflicts between cost accounting for profit reporting and inventory valuation, and information required for decision making	• Relevant costs and revenues in decision making and their relation to accounting concepts.
	(c) explain the issues that arise in pricing decisions and the conflict between 'marginal cost' principles, and the need for full recovery of all costs incurred.	• Marginal and full cost recovery as bases for pricing decisions in the short and long-term.
2 analyse short-term pricing and product decisions.	(a) apply relevant cost analysis to various types of short-term decisions	• The application of relevant cost analysis to short-term decisions, including special selling price decisions, make or buy decisions, discontinuation decisions and further processing decisions.
	(b) apply break-even analysis in multiple product contexts	• Multi-product break-even analysis, including break-even and profit/volume charts, contribution/sales ratio, margin of safety etc.
	(c) analyse product mix decisions, including circumstances where linear programming methods are needed to identify 'optimal' solutions	• Simple product mix analysis in situations where there are limitations on product/service demand and one other production constraint. • Linear programming for situations involving multiple constraints. • Solution by graphical methods and simultaneous equations of two variable problems, and the meaning of 'optimal' solutions.
	(d) explain why joint costs must be allocated to final products for financial reporting purposes but why this is unhelpful when decisions concerning process and product viability have to be taken.	• The allocation of joint costs and decisions concerning process and product viability based on relevant costs and revenues.

P1 – D. DEALING WITH RISK AND UNCERTAINTY (15%)

Learning outcomes On completion of their studies, students should be able to:		**Indicative syllabus content**
Lead	**Component**	
1 analyse information to assess risk and its impact on short-term decisions.	(a) discuss the nature of risk and uncertainty and the attitudes to risk by decision makers	• The nature of risk and uncertainty. • The effect of risk attitudes of individuals on decisions.
	(b) analyse risk using sensitivity analysis, expected values, standard deviations and probability tables	• Sensitivity analysis in decision modelling and the use of 'what if' analysis to identify variables that might have significant impacts on project outcomes. • Assignment of probabilities to key variables in decision models. • Analysis of probability distributions of project outcomes. • Standard deviations. • Expected value tables and the value of perfect and imperfect information. • Decision trees for multi-stage decision problems.
	(c) apply decision models to deal with uncertainty in decision making.	• Maximin, maximax and minimax regret criteria. • Payoff tables.

chapter

1

Traditional costing

Chapter learning objectives

Lead	**Component**
A1. Discuss costing methods and their results.	(a) Apply marginal (or variable) and absorption accounting methods in respect of profit reporting and stock valuation, including the reconciliation of budget and actual profit using absorption and/or marginal costing principles.
C1. Explain concepts of cost and revenue relevant to pricing and product decisions.	(c) Explain the issues that arise in pricing decisions and the conflict between 'marginal cost' principles and the need for full recovery of all costs incurred.

1 Chapter overview diagram

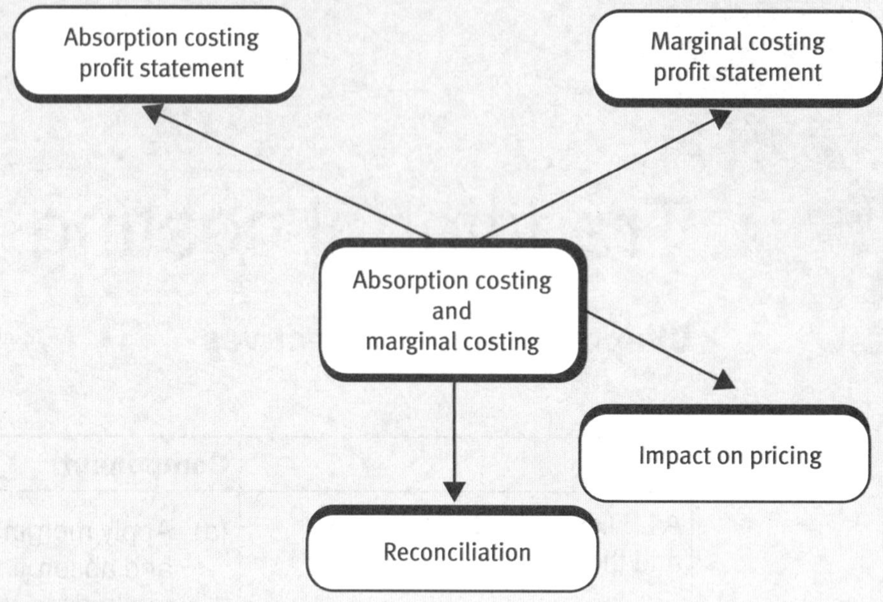

2 The purpose of costing

In the first few chapters of the syllabus we examine different techniques for determining the total costs of products and services. It's therefore useful to remind ourselves why we might need to know this cost.

- Inventory valuation – the cost per unit can be used to value inventory in the statement of financial position (balance sheet).
- To record costs – the costs associated with the product need to be recorded in the statement of profit or loss.
- To price products – the business may use the cost per unit to assist in pricing the product or service. For example, if the cost per unit is $0.30, the business may decide to price the product at $0.50 per unit in order to make the required profit of $0.20 per unit.
- Decision making – the business may use the cost information to make important decisions regarding which products or services should be made/offered and in what quantities.

How can we calculate the cost per unit?

So we know why it's so important for the business to determine the cost of its products or services. We now need to consider how we can calculate this cost.

Revision of cost behaviour

Many factors affect the level of costs incurred; for instance, inflation will cause costs to increase over a period of time. In management accounting, when we talk about cost behaviour we are referring to the way in which costs are affected by fluctuations in the level of activity. The level of activity can be measured in many different ways. For example, we can record the number of units produced, miles travelled, hours worked, percentage of capacity utilised and so on.

An understanding of cost behaviour patterns is essential for many management tasks, particularly in the areas of planning, decision-making and control. It would be impossible for managers to forecast and control costs without at least a basic knowledge of the way in which costs behave in relation to the level of activity.

In this section, we will look at the most common cost behaviour patterns and we will consider some examples of each.

Fixed cost

The CIMA Terminology defines a fixed cost as *'a cost which is incurred for an accounting period that, within certain output or turnover limits, tends to be unaffected by fluctuations in the levels of activity (output or turnover)'.*

Another term which can be used to refer to a fixed cost is 'period cost'. This highlights the fact that a fixed cost is incurred according to the time elapsed, rather than according to the level of activity.

Examples of fixed costs are rent, rates, insurance and executive salaries.

However, it is important to note that this is only true for the relevant range of activity. Consider, for example, the behaviour of the rent cost. Within the relevant range it is possible to expand activity without needing extra premises and therefore the rent cost remains constant. However, if activity is expanded to the critical point where further premises are needed, then the rent cost will increase to a new, higher level. This cost behaviour pattern can be described as a *stepped fixed cost*. The cost is constant within the relevant range for each activity level but when a critical level of activity is reached, the total cost incurred increases to the next step.

This warning does not only apply to fixed costs: it is never wise to attempt to predict costs for activity levels outside the range for which cost behaviour patterns have been established.

Also, whilst the fixed cost total may stay the same within a relevant activity range, the fixed cost per unit reduces as the activity level is increased. This is because the same amount of fixed cost is being spread over an increasing number of units.

Variable cost

The CIMA Terminology defines a variable cost as a '*cost that varies with a measure of activity*'.

Examples of variable costs are direct material, direct labour and variable overheads. In most examination situations, and very often in practice, variable costs are assumed to be linear.

Although many variable costs do approximate to a linear function, this assumption may not always be realistic. Non-linear variable costs are sometimes called curvilinear variable costs. There may be what are known as economies of scale whereby each successive unit of activity adds less to total variable cost than the previous unit. An example of a variable cost which follows this pattern could be the cost of direct material where quantity discounts are available.

On the other hand, there may be what are known as diseconomies of scale which indicates that each successive unit of activity is adding more to the total variable cost than the previous unit. An example of a variable cost which follows this pattern could be the cost of direct labour where employees are paid an accelerating bonus for achieving higher levels of output.

The important point is that managers should be aware of any assumptions that have been made in estimating cost behaviour patterns. They can then use the information which is based on these assumptions with a full awareness of its possible limitations.

Semi-variable cost

A semi-variable cost is also referred to as a semi-fixed, hybrid, or mixed cost. The CIMA Terminology defines it as '*a cost containing both fixed and variable components and thus partly affected by a change in the level of activity*'.

Examples of semi-variable costs are gas and electricity. Both of these expenditures consist of a fixed amount payable for the period, with a further variable amount which is related to the consumption of gas or electricity.

Alternatively, The cost might remain constant up to a certain level of activity and then increase as the variable cost element is incurred. An example of such a cost might be the rental cost of a photocopier where a fixed rental is paid and no extra charge is made for copies up to a certain number. Once this number of copies is exceeded, a constant charge is levied for each copy taken.

3 Absorption costing

The aim of traditional absorption costing is to determine the full production cost per unit.

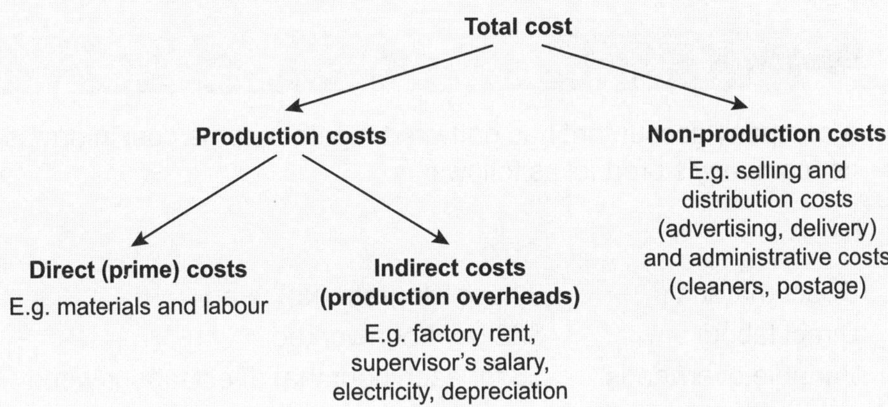

When we use absorption costing to determine the cost per unit, we focus on the production costs only. We can summarise these costs into a cost card:

	$
Direct materials per unit	X
Direct labour per unit	X
Production overhead per unit (Note 1)	X
	—
Full production cost per unit	X
	—

Note 1:

All production overheads must be absorbed into units of production, using a suitable basis, e.g. units produced, labour hours or machine hours. The assumption underlying this method of absorption is that overhead expenditure is connected to the volume produced.

If, for example, units produced are used as the basis, the absorption rate is calculated as:

$$\frac{\text{Total overhead cost (allocated and apportioned)}}{\text{Budgeted production volume}}$$

Example 1

A company accountant has gathered together some cost information for her company's product as follows:

	Cost
Direct materials	$4 per kilogram (kg) used
Direct labour	$22 per hour worked
Variable overheads	$6 for each hour that direct labour work

She has also determined that fixed production overheads will be $400,000 in total. Overheads are absorbed on a per unit basis.

Investigation has shown that each unit of the product uses 3 kilograms of material and needs 2 hours of direct labour work.

Sales and production were budgeted at 20,000 units, but only 16,000 were actually produced and 14,000 actually sold.

There was no opening inventory.

Required:

Produce a standard cost card using absorption costing and value the company's closing inventory on that basis.

More on calculating absorption rates

It is relatively easy to estimate the cost per unit for direct materials and labour. In doing so we can complete the first two lines of the cost card. However, it is much more difficult to estimate the production overhead per unit. This is an indirect cost and so, by its very nature, we do not know how much is contained in each unit. Therefore, we need a method of attributing the production overheads to each unit.

Review of overhead absorption procedure

Accounting for overhead costs in an absorption costing system can be quite complex, and production overhead costs are first allocated, then apportioned and finally absorbed into production costs (or service costs).

- **Overhead allocation**. Indirect production costs are initially allocated to cost centres or cost codes. Allocation is the process of charging a cost directly and in full to the source of the expenditure. For example, the salary of a maintenance engineer would be allocated to the engineering maintenance department.
- **Overhead apportionment**. The overhead costs that have been allocated to cost centres and cost codes other than direct production departments must next be apportioned to direct production departments. Apportionment is the process of sharing on a fair basis. For example, factory rental costs might be apportioned between the production departments on the basis of the floor area occupied by each department. Similarly, the costs of the engineering maintenance department might be apportioned between production departments on the basis of the operating machine hours in each department. At the end of the apportionment process, all the production overheads have been allocated or apportioned to the direct production departments.
- **Overhead absorption**. An absorption rate is calculated for each production department. This is the rate at which production overheads will be added to the cost of production going through the department.

When the department produces a single product, production volume can be measured as the number of units produced, and the absorption rate would be a rate per unit produced.

More usually, organisations produce different products or carry out non-standard jobs for customers, and production volume is commonly measured as one of the following:

- direct labour hours worked in the department, and the absorption rate is a rate per direct labour hour worked
- machine hours worked in the department, and the absorption rate is a rate per machine hour operated
- sometimes the cost of direct labour might be used as a measure of production volume, and the absorption rate is then calculated as a percentage of direct labour cost.

Predetermined absorption rates

Although it is possible to calculate absorption rates using actual overhead costs and actual production volume, this is not the usual practice. This is because:

- It is usually inconvenient to wait until the end of an accounting period to work out what the absorption rates should be. In absorption costing systems, overhead costs are added to the cost of production as it passes through each stage in the production process, and overhead costs are absorbed when the production happens.
- A predetermined rate is required to enable a price to be estimated.
- Overhead costs may vary throughout the year. The overhead absorption rate smoothes variations in overheads by applying an average overhead cost to each unit of product throughout the year.

The normal practice is therefore to absorb production overhead costs at a predetermined rate, based on budgeted overhead expenditure and budgeted production volume.

This however can lead to an over-or under-absorption of the overheads when compared to the actual overheads incurred.

This **over-or under-absorption** can be calculated as follows:

= (Budgeted overhead rate per unit × actual units) – Actual overheads incurred

Absorption advantages/disadvantages

Advantages of absorption costing

The arguments used in favour of absorption costing are as follows:

- Fixed production costs can be a large proportion of the total production costs incurred. Unless production overheads are absorbed into product costs, a large proportion of cost would be excluded from the measurement of product costs.
- Absorption costing follows the matching concept (accruals concept) by carrying forward a proportion of the production cost in the inventory valuation to be matched against the sales value when the items are sold.
- It is necessary to include fixed production overhead in inventory values for financial statements; absorption costing produces inventory values which include a share of fixed production overhead.
- Analysis of under-/over-absorbed overhead may be useful for identifying inefficient utilisation of production resources.
- There is an argument that in the longer term, all costs are variable, and it is appropriate to try to identify overhead costs with the products or services that cause them. This argument is used as a reason for activity-based costing (ABC). ABC is a form of absorption costing, and is described in a later chapter.

Disadvantages of absorption costing

There are serious disadvantages with using absorption costing to measure costs and profits.

- **The apportionment and absorption of overhead costs is arbitrary**

  The way in which overhead costs are apportioned between cost centres and absorbed into production costs is subjective and many methods of cost allocation may be deemed appropriate. Although the process attempts to be 'fair', it is arbitrary.

For example, suppose that a factory rental cost is apportioned between production departments on the basis of the floor area for each department. This might seem a fair way of sharing out the costs, but it is still subjective. Why not apportion the costs on the basis of the number of employees in each department? Or why not allow for the fact that some of the accommodation might be more pleasant to work in than others? In a manufacturing environment, production overheads might be absorbed on the basis of either direct labour hours or machine hours. However, choosing one instead of the other can have a significant effect on job costs or product costs, and yet it still relies on a subjective choice.

It may be easier in some departments than others. If a department is labour intensive then allocations can be made on the basis of labour hours worked. Or if the department is machine intensive then allocations can be made on the basis of machine hours. But not every department will have this clear distinction.

- **Profits vary with changes in production volume**

  A second criticism of absorption costing is that profits can be increased or reduced by changes in inventory levels. For example, by increasing output, more fixed overhead is absorbed into production costs, and if the extra output is not sold, the fixed overhead costs are carried forward in the closing inventory value. This can encourage managers to over-produce in order to inflate profits.

4 Marginal costing

Marginal costing is a costing method which charges products or services with variable costs alone. The fixed costs are treated as period costs and are written off in total against the contribution of the period.

Marginal cost

Marginal cost is the extra cost arising as a result of producing one more unit, or the cost saved as a result of producing one less unit. It comprises:

- Direct material
- Direct labour
- Variable overheads

Example 2

Use the same data as that provided in Example 1.

Required:

Produce a standard cost card using marginal costing and value the company's closing inventory on that basis.

Marginal costing advantages/disadvantages

Advantages of marginal costing

- It is a simpler costing system, because there is no requirement to apportion and absorb overhead costs.
- Marginal costing reflects the behaviour of costs in relation to activity. When sales increase, the cost of sales rise only by the additional variable costs. Since most decision-making problems involve changes to activity, marginal costing information is more relevant and appropriate for short-run decision-making than absorption costing.
- Marginal costing avoids the disadvantages of absorption costing, described above.

Disadvantages of marginal costing

- When fixed costs are high relative to variable costs, and when overheads are high relative to direct costs, the marginal cost of production and sales is only a small proportion of total costs. A costing system that focuses on marginal cost and contribution might therefore provide insufficient and inadequate information about costs and product profitability. Marginal costing is useful for short-term decision-making, but not for measuring product costs and profitability over the longer term.
- It could also be argued that the treatment of direct labour costs as a variable cost item is often unrealistic. When direct labour employees are paid a fixed wage or salary, their cost is fixed, not variable.

5 Absorption and marginal costing profit statements

Absorption costing format

	$	$
Sales		X
Less: Cost of sales		
Opening inventory	X	
+ Production costs	X	
	—	
	X	
Less: Closing inventory	(X)	
	—	(X)
		—
		X
(Under)/over absorption		±X
		—
Gross profit		X
Less: Selling, distribution and admin. costs,		
Variable	X	
Fixed	X	
	—	
		(X)
		—
Net profit/(loss)		X
		—

Marginal costing format

	$	$
Sales		X
*Less: **Variable** cost of sales*		
Opening inventory	X	
+ ***Variable*** production costs	X	
	—	
	X	
Less: Closing inventory	(X)	
	—	(X)
		—
		X
Less: **Variable** selling, distribution and admin. costs		(X)
		—
Contribution		X
Less: Fixed costs		
Production	X	
Selling, distribution and admin.	X	
	—	
		(X)
		—
Net profit/(loss)		X
		—

Example 3

Perry Ltd makes and sells a single product with the following information:

	$/unit
Selling price	50
Direct material	15
Direct labour	10
Variable overhead	5

Fixed overheads are $5,000. Budgeted and actual output and sales are 1,000 units.

(a) Using absorption costing:

(i) calculate the profit for the period

(ii) calculate the profit per unit.

(b) Using marginal costing:

(i) calculate the contribution per unit

(ii) calculate the total contribution

(iii) calculate the profit for the period.

6 Reconciling the profits

The differences between the two profits can be reconciled as follows:

	$
Absorption costing profit	X
(Increase)/decrease in inventory × fixed overheads per unit	(X)/X
Marginal costing profit	X

Justification

The profit differences are caused by the different valuations given to the closing inventories in each period. With absorption costing, an amount of fixed production overhead is carried forward in inventory to be charged against sales of later periods.

If inventories increase, then absorption costing profits will be higher than marginal costing profits. This is because some of the fixed overhead is carried forward in inventory instead of being written off against sales for the period.

If inventories reduce, then marginal costing profits will be higher than absorption costing profits. This is because the fixed overhead which had been carried forward in inventory with absorption costing is now being released to be charged against the sales for the period.

Marginal costing and absorption costing systems give the same profit when there is no change in inventories.

Profit differences in the long term

In the long term the total reported profit will be the same whichever method is used. This is because all of the costs incurred will eventually be charged against sales; it is merely the timing of the sales that causes the profit differences from period to period.

Example 4

The details are exactly the same as for Example 3, but output and sales are now 3,000 units instead of 1,000.

Calculate the profit for the period using both absorption and marginal costing? Answer the question in any way that you want.

Example 5

Z Limited manufactures a single product, the budgeted selling price and variable cost details of which are as follows:

	$
Selling price	15.00
Variable costs per unit:	
Direct materials	3.50
Direct labour	4.00
Variable overhead	2.00

Budgeted fixed overhead costs are $60,000 per annum charged at a constant rate each month.

Budgeted production is 30,000 units per annum.

In a month when actual production was 2,400 units and exceeded sales by 180 units, identify the profit reported under absorption costing:

A $6,660

B $7,570

C $7,770

D $8,200

Profits from one period to the next can be reconciled in a similar way. For example, the difference between periods can be explained as the change in unit sales multiplied by the contribution per unit if using marginal costing.

Further explanation on reconciling profits between periods

Just like reconciling profits between the two accounting systems can be achieved via a proforma, similar proformas can be used for reconciling profits between one period and the next using the same accounting system as follows:

Marginal costing reconciliation

	$
Profit for period 1	X
Increase/(decrease) in sales × contribution per unit	X/(X)
Profit for period 2	X

Absorption costing reconciliation

This is a little trickier as the reconciliation needs to be adjusted for any over/under-absorptions that may have occurred of fixed overheads.

	$
Profit for period 1	X
Increase/(decrease) in sales × profit per unit	X/(X)
(Over–)/under-absorption in period 1	(X)/X
Over– /(under)-absorption in period 2	X/(X)
Profit for period 2	X

Note:

You must be careful with the direction of the absorption. For example, an over-absorption in period 1 makes profit for that month higher, therefore it must be deducted to arrive at period 2's profit. On the other hand, an over-absorption in period 2 makes period 2's profit higher than period 1's, therefore it must be added in the reconciliation.

7 Pricing strategies based on cost

Some organisations set their selling price based on the cost of producing the product or providing the service. Often referred to as 'cost-plus pricing', this involves adding a mark-up to the total cost of the product or service in order to arrive at the selling price.

Choosing the mark up percentage

If an organisation does use cost as the basis for pricing it has to decide whether to employ a standard mark-up or whether to vary the mark-up according to the market conditions, type of customer, etc. A standard mark-up is used by some organisations, such as government contractors and some job costing companies, but the majority of companies vary the percentage to reflect differing market conditions for their products or services.

This mark up may be influenced by factors such as:

- The amount that customers are willing to pay. For example, the product may have a high perceived value (if, say, it is in short supply) which would therefore encourage the organisation to use a higher mark up.
- The level of competition that the product will experience. If the product has many close competitors and substitutes then the organisation may be forced to use a lower mark up.
- The organisation's objectives. For example, when first trying to break into a market and gain market awareness and market share an organisation might use a lower mark up percentage.
- Alternatively, the profit mark-up may be fixed so that the company makes a specific return on capital based on a particular capacity utilisation.

Under different circumstances there may be different interpretations of what gets included in the 'cost' element of cost plus pricing. In some circumstances full cost may be used (including absorbed overheads), in other circumstances it might be more appropriate to use marginal cost.

Full cost plus pricing

Using this method, the selling price for the product is determined as follows:

Selling price = Full cost per unit × (1 + mark up percentage)

So that, for example, if the full cost was $40 and the organisation was using a 15% mark up percentage then the selling price would be set at $46 (i.e. $40 × 1.15).

Full cost can be interpreted in different ways. It will always include the full production cost, including all absorbed overheads. But some organisations may also interpret it to include sales, distribution and administration costs.

(**Note:** typically, the more costs that are included in the full cost then the lower that the mark up percentage used is likely to be).

Illustration – Full cost-plus pricing

A company is replacing product A with an updated version, B, and must calculate a base cost, to which will be added a mark-up in order to arrive at a selling price. The following variable costs have been established by reference to the company's experience with product A, although they may be subject to an error margin of + or – 10 % under production conditions for B:

	$
Direct material	4
Direct labour (1/4 hr @ $16/hr)	4
Variable manufacturing overheads (1/4 hr of machine time @ $8/hr)	2
Total variable cost per unit	**10**

As the machine time for each B would be the same as for A, the company estimates that it will be able to produce the same total quantity of B as its current production of A, which is 20,000 units. 50,000 machine hours may be regarded as the relevant capacity for the purposes of absorbing fixed manufacturing overheads. Current fixed costs are $240,000 for the production facilities, $200,000 for selling and distribution, and $180,000 for administration. For costing purposes, the 20,000 units of B can be assumed to consume 10 per cent of the total selling, distribution and administration costs.

***Alternative 1**, using conventional absorption costing principles and building in the conservative error margin*

	$
Variable production costs (as above)	10
Add: allowance for underestimate 10%	1
Add: manufacturing cost 1/4 hour of machine time @ $4.80/hour ($240,000/50,000 hours)	1.2
Full cost	**12.2**

***Alternative 2**, as 1 but including administrative costs*

	$
Base cost as under 1 above	12.2
Add: fixed administrative costs ($180,000 × 10% = $18,000/20,000 units)	0.9
Full cost	**13.1**

Alternative 3, as 2 but including selling and distribution costs

	$
Base cost as under 2 above	13.1
Add: fixed selling and distribution costs ($200,000 × 10% = $20,000/20,000 units)	1.0
Full cost	**14.1**

Depending on the analysis adopted, the full cost varies from $12.2 to $14.1. The full cost rises with each alternative, as an increasing proportion of the total costs is recovered. The profit mark-up built into the pricing formula is therefore likely to fall with each alternative from 1 to 3.

Advantages and disadvantages of full cost plus pricing

A number of advantages are claimed for full cost-plus pricing:

(1) The required profit will be made if budgeted sales volumes are achieved.

(2) It is a particularly useful method in contract costing industries such as building, where a few large individual contracts can consume the majority of the annual fixed costs and the fixed costs are low in relation to the variable costs.

(3) Assuming the organisation knows its cost structures, full cost-plus is quick and cheap to employ. Its routine nature lends itself to delegation, thus saving management time.

(4) Full cost-plus pricing can be useful in justifying selling prices to customers; if costs can be shown to have increased, this strengthens the case for an increase in the selling price.

However, there are a number of **problems** with full cost-plus pricing:

(1) There will always be problems associated with the selection of a 'suitable' basis on which to charge fixed costs to individual products or services. Selling prices can show great variation, depending on the apportionment basis chosen. This can lead to over-or under-pricing relative to competitors causing the firm to either lose business or make sales at an unintentional loss.

(2) If prices are set on the basis of normal volume, and actual volume turns out to be considerably lower, overheads will not be fully recovered from sales and predicted profits may not be attainable.

(3) The mark up can be very arbitrary and may not properly account for factors such as competition levels, how much customers are willing to pay etc.

Marginal cost-plus pricing

Using this method, the selling price for the product is determined as follows:

Selling price = Marginal cost per unit × (1 + mark up percentage)

To the accountant, marginal cost is the same as variable cost. In setting the selling price using this method a larger mark-up percentage is added because both fixed costs and profit must be covered.

It is a particularly useful method when determining a minimum acceptable selling price (for example, for a one-off product order) and this is examined in more detail in a later chapter.

Benefits and problems when using marginal cost pricing

Some of the reasons for using marginal cost in preference to full cost are as follows:

(1) It is just as accurate as total cost-plus pricing. A larger mark-up percentage is added because both fixed costs and profit must be covered, but the uncertainty over the fixed costs per unit remains in both pricing methods.

(2) Knowledge of marginal cost gives management the option of pricing below total cost when times are bad, in order to fill capacity.

(3) It is particularly useful in pricing specific one-off contracts because it only accounts for costs which are likely to change because of the new contract. This pricing decision is covered in more detail in a later chapter.

(4) It also recognises the existence of scarce or limiting resources. Where these are used by competing products and services it must be reflected in the selling price if profit is to be maximised. If there is a scarce or bottleneck resource the aim must be to maximise the total contribution from the limiting factor. The contribution that each alternative product or service makes from each unit of the scarce resource must be calculated and a suitable profit margin added.

The main criticisms of marginal cost pricing are:

(1) Like any cost based pricing method, it ignores other factors such as levels of competition, customer attitudes etc.

(2) The mark-up becomes even more arbitrary than that used in full cost plus as now it must also include a subjective element which allows for the selling price to cover fixed costs. For this reason, many accountants argue that marginal cost plus pricing should only be used for marginal (short-term or one-off) decisions.

Target return on capital

As well as determining the selling price by adding a mark-up on cost, an organisation may also set the mark-up at a level that provides a target return on the investment that has been made in the product.

The mark-up is calculated as:

Profit mark-up = Targeted return on investment in the product/budgeted level of production

The targeted return on investment is calculated as:

Targeted return on investment in the product = Total investment in the product × targeted rate of return

Example 6

This method involves determining the amount of capital invested to support a product. For example, some fixed or non-current assets and certain elements of working capital such as inventory and trade receivables can be attributed to individual products.

The selling price is then set to achieve a specified return on the capital invested on behalf of the product. The following example will demonstrate how the method works.

LG Ltd manufactures product B. Data for product B are as follows:

Direct material cost per unit	$62
Direct labour cost per unit	$14
Direct labour hours per unit	4 hours
Production overhead absorption rate	$16 per direct machine hour
Mark-up for non-production overhead costs	8% of total production cost

LG Ltd sells 1,000 units of product B each year. Product B requires an investment of $400,000 and the target rate of return on investment is 12% per annum.

Calculate the selling price for one unit of product B, to the nearest cent.

Target return on sales

An organisation can use a similar technique to determine a selling price which provides a target return on sales. This pricing method involves determining the full cost of a cost unit and then adding a mark-up that represents a specified percentage of the final selling price.

WP Ltd manufactures product A. Data for product A are as follows:

Direct material cost per unit	$7
Direct labour cost per unit	$18
Direct labour hours per unit	2 hours
Production overhead absorption rate	$6 per direct labour hour
Mark-up for non-production overhead costs	5% of total production cost

WP Ltd requires a 15% return on sales revenue from all products.

Calculate the selling price for product A, to the nearest cent.

Solution

	$ per unit
Direct material cost	7.00
Direct labour cost	18.00
Total direct cost	25.00
Production overhead absorbed (2 hours × $6)	12.00
Total production cost	37.00
Mark-up for non-production costs (5% × $37.00)	1.85
Full cost	38.85
Profit mark-up (15/85* × $38.85)	6.86
Selling price	45.71

*Always read the question data carefully. The 15% required return is expressed as a percentage of the sales revenue, not as a percentage of the cost.

Profit margin

As an alternative calculation, the examiner may provide a profit margin rather than a mark-up on cost. The selling price using a profit margin can be calculated as follows:

Selling price = Total cost ÷ (1 – required margin)

The decision as to what gets included in the total cost (for example, whether that is the absorption or marginal cost) and the associated calculations required to get to the total cost will be the same as when using a mark-up on cost.

8 Chapter summary

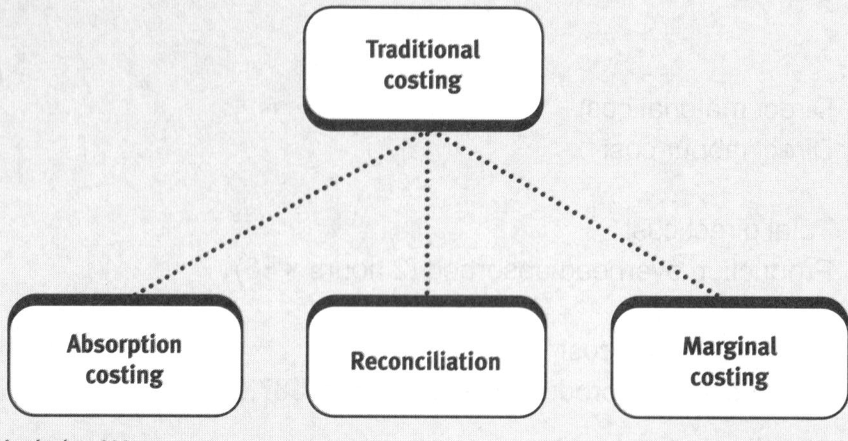

Absorption costing

- includes ALL production costs
- $\text{OAR} = \dfrac{\text{Total overheads}}{\text{Production volume}}$
- consistent with financial accounting
- better for long-term pricing
- selling price = Full cost per unit × (1 + mark up percentage)
- pricing may include sales and admin costs as well as production overheads

Reconciliation

	£
AC profit	X
(Increase)/Decrease in stock × fixed o/h per unit	(X)/X
MC profit	X

Marginal costing

- includes only VARIABLE production costs
- better for decision making
- easier
- but unsuited to capital intensive environments
- selling price = marginal cost per unit × (1 + mark up percentage)

9 Practice questions

Test your understanding 1

Scenario

Saturn, a chocolate manufacturer, produces three products:

- The Sky Bar, a bar of solid milk chocolate.
- The Moon Egg, a fondant filled milk chocolate egg.
- The Sun Bar, a biscuit and nougat based chocolate bar.

Information relating to each of the products is as follows:

	Sky Bar	**Moon Egg**	**Sun Bar**
Direct labour cost per unit ($)	0.07	0.14	0.12
Direct material cost per unit ($)	0.17	0.19	0.16
Actual production/sales (units)	500,000	150,000	250,000
Direct labour hours per unit	0.001	0.01	0.005
Direct machine hours per unit	0.01	0.04	0.02
Selling price per unit ($)	0.50	0.45	0.43
Annual production overhead = $80,000			

Tasks

Using traditional absorption costing, calculate the full production cost per unit and the profit per unit for each product. Explain the implications of the figures calculated.

(Time allowed: 20 minutes)

Test your understanding 2

E plc operates a marginal costing system. For the forthcoming year, variable costs are budgeted to be 60% of sales value and fixed costs are budgeted to be 10% of sales value.

If E plc increases its selling prices by 10%, but if fixed costs, variable costs per unit and sales volume remain unchanged, identify the effect on E plc's contribution:

A a decrease of 2%

B an increase of 5%

C an increase of 10%

D an increase of 25%

Test your understanding 3

When comparing the profits reported under marginal and absorption costing during a period when the level of inventories increased, identify which of the following statements would be true:

A absorption costing profits will be higher and closing inventory valuations lower than those under marginal costing

B absorption costing profits will be higher and closing inventory valuations higher than those under marginal costing

C marginal costing profits will be higher and closing inventory valuations lower than those under absorption costing

D marginal costing profits will be lower and closing inventory valuations higher than those under absorption costing

Test your understanding 4

Exe Limited makes a single product whose total cost per unit is budgeted to be $45. This includes fixed cost of $8 per unit based on a volume of 10,000 units per period. In a period, sales volume was 9,000 units, and production volume was 11,500 units. The actual profit for the same period, calculated using absorption costing, was $42,000.

If the profit statement were prepared using marginal costing, identify the profit for the period:

A $10,000

B $22,000

C $50,000

D $62,000

Test your understanding 5

Scenario

Keats plc commenced business on 1 March making one product only, the standard cost of which is as follows:

	$
Direct labour	5
Direct material	8
Variable production overhead	2
Fixed production overhead	5
	—
Standard production cost	20
	—

The fixed production overhead figure has been calculated on the basis of a budgeted normal output of 36,000 units per annum.

You are to assume that actual fixed overheads were as expected and that all the budgeted fixed expenses are incurred evenly over the year. March and April are to be taken as equal period months.

Selling, distribution and administration expenses are:

Fixed	$120,000 per annum
Variable	15% of the sales value

The selling price per unit is $35 and the number of units produced and sold were:

	March (units)	*April* (units)
Production	2,000	3,200
Sales	1,500	3,000

Tasks

(a) prepare profit statements for each of the months of March and April using:

(i) absorption costing, and

(ii) marginal costing

(b) prepare a reconciliation of the profit or loss figures given in your answers to (a)(i) and (a)(ii) accompanied by a brief explanation.

(Time allowed: 20 minutes)

Test your understanding 6

If inventory levels have increased during the period, the profit calculated using marginal costing would be _____ (*choose between 'higher' and 'lower'*) than the profit when compared with that calculated using absorption costing.

Test your understanding 7

Identify which of the following statements would be true: fixed production overheads will always be under-absorbed when:

A actual output is lower than budgeted output

B actual overheads incurred are lower than budgeted overheads

C overheads absorbed are lower than those budgeted

D overheads absorbed are lower than those incurred

Test your understanding 8

A company uses a standard absorption costing system. The fixed overhead absorption rate is based on labour hours.

Extracts from the company's records for last year were as follows:

	Budget	Actual
Fixed production overhead	$450,000	$475,000
Output	50,000 units	60,000 units
Labour hours	900,000	930,000

The ______ *(choose between 'over' and 'under')* -absorbed fixed production overheads for the year were $______ *(fill in the value).*

Test your understanding 9

GY Ltd budgets to produce and sell 3,800 units of product R in the forthcoming year. The amount of capital investment attributable to product R will be $600,000 and GY Ltd requires a rate of return of 15% on all capital invested.

Further details concerning product R are as follows:

Direct material cost per unit	$14
Direct labour cost per unit	$19
Variable overhead cost per unit	$3
Machine hours per unit	8

Fixed overhead is absorbed at a rate of $11 per machine hour.

Required:

Calculate all answers to the nearest cent.

(a) The variable cost of product R is $ ________ per unit.

(b) The total (full) cost of product R is $ ________ per unit.

(c) The selling price of product R which will achieve the specified return on investment is $ ________ per unit.

Test your understanding 10

A company manufactures a range of products one of which, product Y, incurs a total cost of $20 per unit. The company incurs a total cost of $600,000 each period and the directors wish to achieve a return of 18% on the total capital of $800,000 invested in the company.

Required:

Based on this information the cost-plus selling price of one unit of product Y should be $ _______.

Test your understanding 11

Scenario

ML is an engineering company that specialises in providing engineering facilities to businesses that cannot justify operating their own facilities in-house. ML employs a number of engineers who are skilled in different engineering techniques that enable ML to provide a full range of engineering facilities to its customers.

Most of the work undertaken by ML is unique to each of its customers, often requiring the manufacture of spare parts for its customers' equipment, or the building of new equipment from customer drawings. As a result most of ML's work is short-term, with some jobs being completed within hours while others may take a few days.

To date, ML has adopted a cost plus approach to setting its prices. This is based upon an absorption costing system that uses machine hours as the basis of absorbing overhead costs into individual job costs. The Managing Director is concerned that, over recent months, ML has been unsuccessful when quoting for work with the consequence that there has been an increase in the level of unused capacity. It has been suggested that ML should adopt an alternative approach to its pricing based on marginal costing since 'any price that exceeds variable costs is better than no work'.

Tasks

With reference to the above scenario:

(a) briefly explain absorption and marginal cost approaches to pricing

(b) discuss the validity of the comment 'any price that exceeds variable costs is better than no work'.

(Time allowed: 20 minutes)

Test your understanding answers

Example 1

Standard cost card

		$
Direct materials per unit	3 kgs × $4/kg	12
Direct labour per unit	2 hrs × $22/hr	44
Variable overheads	2 hrs × $6/hr	12
Production overhead per unit (note)		20
		—
Full/absorption cost per unit		88
		—

Note:

Production overhead per unit in the standard cost card should be based on *budgeted* production. Therefore in this example they will be ($400,000/20,000 units =) $20 per unit.

Inventory valuation

If 16,000 units were produced and 14,000 units sold then there will be 2,000 units in closing inventory.

Valuing that inventory at the absorption cost will give a value of

= 2,000 × $88

= $176,000

Example 2

Standard cost card

		$
Direct materials per unit	3 kgs × $4/kg	12
Direct labour per unit	2 hrs × $22/hr	44
Variable overheads	2 hrs × $6/hr	12
		—
Marginal cost per unit		68
		—

Note:

Fixed production overhead is not included in a marginal costing standard cost card.

Inventory valuation

Valuing that inventory at the marginal cost will give a value of

= 2,000 × $68

= $136,000

Example 3

(a) (i)

		$	$
Sales	1,000 units × $50		50,000
Direct materials	1,000 units × $15	15,000	
Direct labour	1,000 units × $10	10,000	
Variable overheads	1,000 units × $5	5,000	
Fixed overheads		5,000	
		———	
			35,000
			———
Profit			15,000
			———

(ii)

$$\text{Profit per unit} = \frac{\$15000}{1{,}000 \text{ units}} = 15/\text{unit}$$

(b) (i) Contribution per unit = $50 – ($15 + $10 + $5) = $20

(ii) Total contribution = $20/unit × 1,000 units = $20,000

(iii)

	$
Contribution	
$20/unit × 1,000 units	20,000
Fixed cost	5,000
Profit	15,000

The two systems give the same profit provided there is no change in inventory.

Example 4

Either marginal costing or absorption costing principles can be used. The two systems will give the same profit as there is no change in inventory (production = sales). Marginal costing will be simpler and is illustrated first.

	$
Contribution	
$20 per unit × 3,000 units	60,000
Fixed cost	5,000
Profit	55,000

Alternatively:

		$	$
Sales	3,000 units × $50		150,000
Direct materials	3,000 units × $15	45,000	
Direct labour	3,000 units × $10	30,000	
Variable overheads	3,000 units × $5	15,000	
Fixed overheads	3,000 units × $5	15,000	
			(105,000)
Over-absorption of fixed overheads	($15,000 – $5,000)		10,000
			55,000

Notice that we did not use the $15 per unit profit figure. Unlike contribution per unit, profit per unit is not constant.

Example 5

B

A common short-cut in multiple choice questions is to calculate the marginal costing profit and then use the reconciliation of profits to get to the absorption costing profit.

First of all – the profit under marginal costing:

Contribution per unit = $15 – (3.50 + 4.00 + 2.00) = $5.50

No of units sold = 2,400 – 180 = 2,220

	$
Contribution	
$5.50/unit × 2,220 units	12,210
Fixed cost	
$60,000 p.a./12 months	5,000
	7,210

As production is greater than sales, absorption costing will show the higher profit.

Difference in profit = change in inventory × fixed production overhead per unit.

Difference in profit = 180 units × $2/unit = $360.

Therefore, profit reported under absorption costing = $7,210 + 360 = $7,570.

The FOAR was worked out as $\dfrac{\text{Budgeted overheads}}{\text{Budgeted level of activity}} = \dfrac{\$60{,}000}{30{,}000 \text{ units}} = \$2$ per unit

Example 6

The selling price is calculated as follows:

	$ per unit
Direct material cost	62.00
Direct labour cost	14.00
Total direct cost	76.00
Production overhead absorbed (4 hours × $16)	64.00
Total production cost	140.00
Mark-up for non-production costs (8% × $140)	11.20
Full cost	151.20
Profit mark-up (see working)	48.00
Selling price	199.20

Working:

Target return on investment in product B = $400,000 × 12% = $48,000

Target return per unit of product B = $48,000/1,000 units = $48

Test your understanding 1

As mentioned, it is relatively easy to complete the first two lines of the cost card. The difficult part is calculating the production overhead per unit, so let's start by considering this. We need to absorb the overheads into units of production. To do this, we will first need to calculate an overhead absorption rate (OAR):

$$\text{OAR} = \frac{\text{Production overhead}}{\text{Activity level}} \quad \begin{matrix}\text{(this is \$80,000, as per the question)} \\ \text{(this must be chosen)}\end{matrix}$$

The activity level must be appropriate for the business. Saturn must choose between three activity levels:

- Units of production – This would not be appropriate since Saturn produces more than one type of product. It would not be fair to absorb the same amount of overhead into each product.
- Machine hours or labour hours – It is fair to absorb production overheads into the products based on the labour or machine hours taken to produce each unit. We must decide if the most appropriate activity level is machine or labour hours. To do this we can look at the nature of the process. Production appears to be more machine intensive than labour intensive because each unit takes more machine hours to produce than it does labour hours. Therefore, the most appropriate activity level is machine hours.

Working – OAR

$$\text{OAR} = \frac{\$80{,}000 \text{ production overhead}}{(0.01 \times 500\text{k}) + (0.04 \times 150\text{k}) + (0.02 \times 250\text{k}) \text{ hours}}$$

$$= \frac{\$80{,}000}{16{,}000 \text{ hours}}$$

= $5 per machine hour

We can now absorb these into the units of production:

	Sky Bar	Moon Egg	Sun Bar
Production overheads ($) = machine hours per unit × $5	0.05	0.20	0.10

This is the difficult part done. We can now quickly complete the cost card and answer the question:

	Sky Bar	Moon Egg	Sun Bar
	$	$	$
Direct labour cost per unit	0.07	0.14	0.12
Direct material cost per unit	0.17	0.19	0.16
Production overhead per unit	0.05	0.20	0.10
Full production cost per unit	**0.29**	**0.53**	**0.38**
Selling price per unit	0.50	0.45	0.43
Profit/(loss) per unit	**0.21**	**(0.08)**	**0.05**

Outcome of absorption costing

Based on absorption costing, the Sky Bar and the Sun Bar are both profitable. However, the Moon Egg is loss making. Managers would need to consider the future of the Moon Egg. They may look at the possibility of increasing the selling price and/or reducing costs. If this is not possible, they may make the decision to stop selling the product. However, this may prove to be the wrong decision because absorption costing does not always result in an accurate calculation of the full production cost per unit. ABC can be a more accurate method of calculating the full production cost per unit and as a result should lead to better decisions. ABC is explored in the next chapter.

Test your understanding 2

D

The easiest way to answer this question is to make up a number for sales, say $1,000, then the relationships will be much easier to visualise.

If sales = $1,000, then:

Variable cost = 60% × $1,000 = $600

Current situation

	$
Sales	1,000
Variable cost	600
Contribution	400

New situation

	$
Sales (10% higher)	1,100
Variable cost	600
Contribution	500

Contribution increases by $100, which is an increase of 25% on its original value.

Fixed cost should be ignored as it does not affect contribution.

Test your understanding 3

B

Test your understanding 4

B

Production is greater than sales, so absorption costing will have the higher profit.

Difference in profit = change in inventory × fixed production overhead per unit.

Difference in profit = 2,500 units × $8/unit = $20,000.

Therefore, profit reported under marginal costing = $42,000 – 20,000 = $22,000.

Test your understanding 5

(a) (i)

	March		April	
	$	$	$	$
Sales		52,500		105,000
Cost of sales				
Op. stock (W1)	0		10,000	
Production costs (@$20/unit)	40,000		64,000	
	40,000		74,000	
Less cl. inventory (@$20/unit) (W2)	10,000		14,000	
		30,000		60,000
		22,500		45,000
(Under)/over-absorption (W3)		(5,000)		1,000
Gross profit		17,500		46,000
Selling etc costs				
Fixed (W4)	10,000		10,000	
Variable	7,875		15,750	
		17,875		25,750
Net Profit/Loss		(375)		20,250

(ii)

		March		April
	$	$	$	$
Sales		52,500		105,000
Variable cost of sales				
Op. inventory (W1)	0		7,500	
Variable production costs (@$15/unit)	30,000		48,000	
	30,000		55,500	
Less cl. inventory (@$15/unit) (W2)	7,500		10,500	
		22,500		45,000
		30,000		60,000
Variable selling etc costs		7,875		15,750
Contribution		22,125		44,250
Fixed costs				
Production	15,000		15,000	
Selling etc	10,000		10,000	
		25,000		25,000
Profit/Loss		(2,875)		19,250

Workings

(W1) The closing inventory for March becomes the opening stock for April.

(W2)

	March	April
	Units	Units
Op. inventory	0	500
Production	2,000	3,200
	2,000	3,700
Less sales	1,500	3,000
Cl. inventory	500	700

(W3) Under-/over-absorption is the difference between overheads incurred and overheads absorbed.

"Overheads incurred" means actual overheads and we are told that the actual fixed overheads were as expected. Therefore the actual fixed overheads incurred are the same as the budgeted fixed overheads.

Budgeted fixed overhead = $5 per unit × 36,000 units	= $180,000 per annum
	÷ 12
	= 15,000 per month

March

Overheads incurred	15,000
Overheads absorbed	
$5/unit × 2,000 units	10,000
Under-absorption	(5,000)

April

Overheads incurred	15,000
Overheads absorbed	
$5/unit × 3,200 units	16,000
Over-absorption	1,000

(W4) Selling, etc fixed overhead = $120,000/12 = $10,000 per month.

(b) If there is no change in inventory, the 2 systems give the same profit. If production is greater than sales then absorption costing shows the higher profit.

Difference in profit = change in inventory × fixed production overhead cost per unit

In both March and April, production is greater than sales and thus absorption costing will show the higher profit (the smaller loss in March).

	March	April
Marginal costing profit/loss	(2,875)	19,250
Difference in profit		
(2,000 – 1,500) × $5 per unit	2,500	
(3,200 – 3,000) × $5 per unit		1,000
Absorption costing profit/loss	(375)	20,250

This difference occurs because marginal costing writes off the entire fixed overhead in the period incurred, whereas absorption costing carries forward some fixed production overhead into the next period in the valuation of closing inventory.

Test your understanding 6

Missing word: lower

Marginal costing values inventory at a lower amount because it does not include fixed overheads in the valuation. Therefore as inventory levels increase the value of closing inventory under marginal costing will be lower. This will give a higher cost of sales and a lower profit.

Test your understanding 7

D

Under-absorption occurs when the amount absorbed is less than the actual overheads incurred.

Test your understanding 8

The **over**-absorbed fixed production overheads for the year were **$65,000**.

Absorption rate	=	$\frac{\$450,000}{900,000}$	= $0.50/hour
Absorbed overheads		60,000 units × 18 hrs/unit × $0.50/hour	= $540,000
Actual overheads	=	$475,000	
Over-absorption	=	$65,000	

Test your understanding 9

(a) The variable cost per unit of product R is $36.00 per unit.

Direct material $14 + direct labour $19 + variable overhead $3 = **$36**.

(b) The total (full) cost of product R is $124.00 per unit.

Variable cost $36 + fixed overhead (8 hours × $11) = **$124**.

(c) The selling price of product R which will achieve the specified return on investment is $147.68 per unit.

Working:

Required return from investment in product R
= $600,000 × 15% = $90,000

Required return per unit sold = $90,000/3,800 units = $23.68

Required selling price = $124.00 full cost + $23.68 = **$147.68**

Test your understanding 10

The cost-plus selling price of one unit of product Y should be **$24.80**.

Required annual return = $800,000 × 18% = $144,000

Return as a percentage of total cost =144,000/$600,000 = 24%

Required cost-plus selling price = $20 + (24% + $20) = **$24.80**

Test your understanding 11

[Make sure that you focus your answer on absorption and marginal cost approaches to pricing (not costing). A main issue is therefore how the level of mark-up is determined. Your answer should take a balanced view of the comment in the short and long term. While it may be true in the short term, under certain circumstances a price which does not generate a profit in the long term could not be acceptable.]

(a) An absorption cost approach to pricing involves adding a profit margin to the full cost of the product. The full cost is calculated by taking prime cost and adding a share of overhead which, in ML's case, is absorbed using machine hours.

A marginal cost approach to pricing takes the variable cost of the product and adds a mark-up to cover fixed cost and profit. Fixed overheads are not absorbed to product but are treated as a period cost in the accounts.

The mark-up added using a marginal costing approach would have to be greater than that under an absorption costing approach to ensure that the same profit level is achieved. Mark-ups may be varied depending on the market conditions. ML's work is unique to each of its customers and it may therefore be difficult to estimate a suitable mark-up.

(b) The comment 'any price that exceeds variable costs is better than no work' may have some validity in the short term. In the case of a company like ML, which has unused capacity, fixed costs will be incurred in the short term irrespective of workload, i.e. the fixed costs will not change as no extra capacity is required (for example, premises will not have to be expanded in order to accommodate the extra production), and they can therefore be ignored for decision making purposes. Any price that exceeds variable cost will provide some contribution and will reduce losses.

Care must be taken that special prices based on variable cost do not become the normal expectation or upset existing customers who are paying a price which generates a profit.

In the long run fixed cost must be covered and a profit made in accordance with company objectives. An absorption costing approach may not provide an accurate total product costs and an activity-based approach may improve the accuracy of total costs and enable ML to identify those products or customers which generate most profit.

If resources are scarce (i.e. they cannot easily be obtained at the prices or rates contained in the standard cost card) then this statement is not true, even in the short term, as scarce resources typically cost a premium and the marginal cost will increase. This concept will be explored in the decision making chapter later in the text.

chapter

2

Activity-based costing

Chapter learning objectives

Lead	Component
A1. Discuss costing methods and their results.	(b) Compare and contrast activity-based costing with traditional marginal and absorption costing methods.

1 Chapter overview diagram

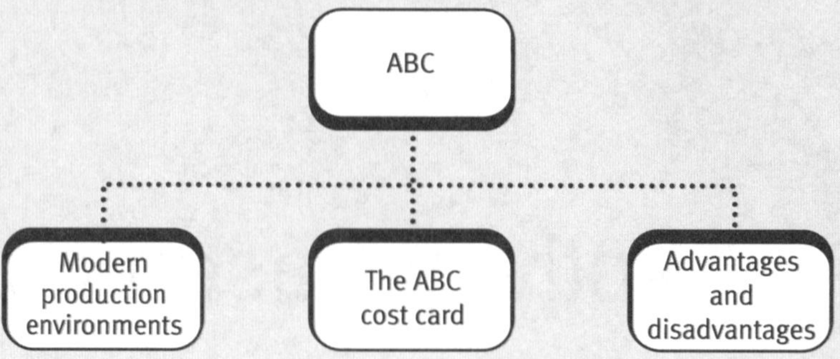

2 Modern production environments

Modern producers have changed the way that they produce so that they have:

- much more machinery and computerised manufacturing systems
- smaller batch sizes
- less use of 'direct' labour

This has had the following **impact on production costs:**

- more indirect overheads (for example, insurance and depreciation of the machines and computers)
- less direct labour costs

This means that the **traditional** methods of costing (marginal and absorption) produce **standard cost cards that are less useful** due to inaccurate product costs:

- the largest cost of production is indirect overheads but these are categorised together in one figure that lacks detail and is not useful to management
- because management does not know what the components are of the largest production cost (indirect overheads) they cannot implement proper cost control
- the costs are often allocated between products on the basis of direct labour hours – despite the fact that direct labour is becoming a smaller proportion of product costs and does not fairly reflect the relationship between the products and the indirect overheads

- because costs are inappropriately or inaccurately shared between products it means that the total production cost can be wrong which can lead to poor pricing and production decisions.

Activity based costing **(ABC) has been developed to solve the problems** that traditional costing methods create in these modern environments.

Traditional costing problems

Problems with traditional absorption costing

Traditional absorption costing charges overhead costs to products (or services) in an arbitrary way. In product costing, overheads are absorbed on the basis of the volume of production in each production department or centre. The basis for setting an absorption rate is volume-related, such as an overhead absorption rate per unit produced, a rate per direct labour hour or a rate per machine hour.

The assumption underlying this method of costing is that overhead expenditure is connected to the volume of production activity.

- This assumption was probably valid many years ago, when production systems were based on labour-intensive or machine-intensive mass production of fairly standard items. Overhead costs were also fairly small relative to direct materials and direct labour costs; therefore any inaccuracy in the charging of overheads to products costs was not significant.
- The assumption is not valid in a complex manufacturing environment, where production is based on smaller customised batches of products, indirect costs are high in relation to direct costs, and a high proportion of overhead activities – such as production scheduling, order handling and quality control – are not related to production volume.
- For similar reasons, traditional absorption costing is not well-suited to the costing of many services.

The criticism of absorption costing is that it cannot calculate a 'true' product cost that has any valid meaning. Overheads are charged to departments and products in an arbitrary way, and the assumption that overhead expenditure is related to direct labour hours or machine hours in the production departments is no longer realistic.

Problems with marginal costing

There are also major problems with marginal costing, but for different reasons. In marginal costing, products or services are valued at their marginal cost, and profitability is assessed by calculating the contribution earned from each product or service. Fixed costs are assumed to be time-related and are charged against profits as a cost for the period. This can be a useful costing method when variable costs are a large proportion of total costs.

The main criticisms of marginal costing as a method of measuring product costs and profitability are that:

- variable costs might be small in relation to fixed costs
- 'fixed' costs might be fixed in relation to production volume, but they might vary with other activities that are not volume-related or even production-related.

In many manufacturing and service environments, it is therefore inappropriate to treat overhead costs as fixed period costs, and they should be charged to products or services in a more meaningful way

3 Activity-based costing

Activity-based costing (ABC) is an alternative approach to product costing. It is a form of absorption costing, but , rather than absorbing overheads on a production volume basis it firstly allocates them to **cost pools** before absorbing them into units using **cost drivers**.

- A **cost pool** is an activity that consumes resources and for which overhead costs are identified and allocated. For each cost pool, there should be a cost driver.
- A **cost driver** is a unit of activity that consumes resources. An alternative definition of a cost driver is a factor influencing the level of cost.

Illustration 1

Imagine the machining department in a traditional absorption costing system. The OAR would be based on machine hours because many of the overheads in the machine department would relate to the machines, e.g. power, maintenance, machine depreciation, etc., so using a machine hour basis would seem fair. However, not only does the machine department have machine related costs, but also in an absorption costing system, it would also have picked up a share of rent and rates, heating, lighting, building depreciation, canteen costs, personnel cost, etc. These costs would also be absorbed on a machine hour basis, because everything in the machine department is absorbed on machine hours and whilst this is fair for power, maintenance and machine depreciation, it is inappropriate for the other costs.

ABC overcomes this problem by not using departments as gathering points for costs, but instead using activities, and there would, for example, be a machine-related activity to which power would be charged, machine depreciation would be charged, and machine maintenance would be charged. It would not pick up a share of personnel costs or rent or rates or indeed anything not machine related. ABC's flexibility thus reduces the incidence of arbitrary apportionments.

Identifying activities and drivers

If a business decides to adopt activity-based costing to measure the costs and profitability of its products or services, it must identify the key activities that consume resources and the cost driver for each of those activities.

- There might be a large number of different activities, but in an accounting system it is usually necessary to simplify the overhead cost analysis and select a fairly small number of activities. If a large number of activities are identified and used in ABC, the task of analysing costs becomes more complex and time-consuming, and the value of the additional accuracy might not justify the cost and effort.
- For any activity there might be just one cost driver or several different cost drivers. Where there are several cost drivers, it is necessary to select just one for the purpose of ABC analysis.

Identifying activities

The main activities that consume overhead resources differ from one type of business to another. A useful approach to identifying suitable activities within a business is to consider four different categories of activity or transaction:

- **Logistical transactions.** These are activities or transactions concerned with moving materials or people, and with tracking the progress of materials or work through the system.
- **Balancing transactions.** These are concerned with ensuring that the resources required for an operation are available. For example, the buying department has to make sure that raw materials are available to meet production requirements.
- **Quality transactions.** These are concerned with ensuring that output or service levels meet quality requirements and customer expectations. Inspections and handling customer complaints are both examples of quality transactions.
- **Change transactions.** These are activities required to respond to changes in customer demand, a change in design specifications, a scheduling change, a change in production or delivery methods, and so on.

For any business, there could be important resource-consuming activities in each of these categories.

Identifying cost drivers

For each selected activity, there should be a cost driver. The chosen cost driver must be:

- **Relevant.** In other words, there should be a connection between the cost driver and the consumption of resources for the activity.
- **Easy to measure.** Measuring the units of cost driver and identifying the products or services to which they relate needs to be a fairly easy and straightforward process.

Often, the cost driver is the number of transactions relating to the activity. For example:

- the cost of setting up machinery for a production run might be driven by the number of set-ups (jobs or batches produced)
- the cost of running machines might be driven by the number of machine hours for which the machines are running
- the cost of assembling the product may be based on the number of direct labour hours

- the cost of order processing might be related to the number of orders received
- the cost of dispatch might be related to the number of orders dispatched or to the weight of items dispatched
- the costs of purchasing might be related to the number of purchase orders made
- the costs of quality control might be related to the number of inspections carried out, or to the incidence of rejected items.

It is possible to identify three types of cost driver:

Transaction drivers

Here, the cost of an activity is affected by the number of times a particular action is undertaken. Examples would include number of set-ups, number of power drill operations, number of batches of material received, number of purchase orders, etc.

Duration drivers

In this case, the cost of the activity is not so much affected by the number of times the action is undertaken as by the length of time that it takes to perform the action, e.g. set-up costs may not be related to the number of set-ups so much as to the set-up time, because some products involve more complicated and time consuming set-ups than others.

Intensity drivers

In this case, efforts would be directed at determining what resources were used in the making of a product or service, e.g. rather than charging all purchase orders with the same cost per order, we might determine that overseas orders involve more work than home orders and apply a weighting to the overseas orders to reflect the extra work.

Calculating the full production cost per unit using ABC

There are five basic steps to calculating an activity based cost:

Step 1: Group production overheads into activities, according to how they are driven.

A cost pool is the grouping of costs relating to a particular activity which consumes resources and for which overhead costs are identified and allocated. For each cost pool, there should be a cost driver.

Step 2: Identify cost drivers for each activity, i.e. what causes these activity costs to be incurred.

A cost driver is a factor that influences (or drives) the level of cost.

Step 3: Calculate a cost driver rate for each activity.

The cost driver rate is calculated in the same way as the absorption costing OAR. However, a separate cost driver rate will be calculated for each activity, by taking the activity cost and dividing by the cost driver information.

Step 4: Absorb the activity costs into the product.

The activity costs should be absorbed by applying the cost driver rate into the individual products.

Step 5: Calculate the full production cost and/ or the profit or loss.

Some questions ask for the production cost per unit and/ or the profit or loss per unit.

Other questions ask for the total production cost and/or the total profit or loss.

Example 1

A manufacturing business makes a product in two models, model M1 and model M2. details of the two products are as follows.

	Model M1	**Model M2**
Annual sales	8,000 units	8,000 units
Number of sales orders	60	250
Sales price per unit	$54	$73
Direct material cost per unit	$11	$21
Direct labour hours per unit	2.0 hours	2.5 hours
Direct labour rate per hour	$8	$8
Special parts per unit	2	8
Production batch size	2,000 units	100 units
Setups per batch	1	3

	$	Cost driver
Setup costs	97,600	Number of setups
Material handling costs	42,000	Number of batches
Special part handling costs	50,000	Number of special parts
Invoicing	31,000	Number of sales orders
Other overheads	108,000	Direct labour hours
Total overheads	328,600	

A customer has indicated an interest in placing a large order for either model M1 or M2, and the sales manager wished to try to sell the higher-priced model M2.

Required:

(a) Calculate the profit per unit for each model, using ABC.

(b) Using the information above identify which product the sales manager should try to sell on the basis of the information provided by your ABC analysis.

ABC in service industries

Activity based costing was originally developed for manufacturing industries. But it has now gained widespread use in many service organisations such as hospitals, accountancy practices, banks and insurance companies. It is just as important for these businesses to control costs, maximise the use of resources and improve pricing as it is in a manufacturing business.

Illustration

Boomer Jones is a firm of business advisors. It offers two services to its clients – tax advisory services (TAS) and business advisory services (BAS). Revenue from service is expected to be $3m. The cost for each service is budgeted as follows:

	TAS $	BAS $
Direct labour	300,000	400,000
Overheads (W1)	3,000,000	2,000,000
Total costs	3,300,000	2,400,000
Revenue	3,000,000	3,000,000
Profit/(loss)	(300,000)	600,000

Workings

(W1) Overhead recovery out rate

Total budgeted overheads* = $5m
Total budgeted direct labour hours = 25,000 hours (15,000 hours in TAS, 10,000 hours in BAS)
Recovery rate per hour of service provided = $200 per hour
Budgeted overheads include material costs within the firm which are negligible.

Switch to ABC

As labour costs have become a lesser proportion of total costs and overheads have become more significant, Boomer Jones wants to examine a switch to activity based costing (ABC). The finance director has put together the following information on overheads:

			Drivers	
	Cost ($)	Cost Driver	TAS	BAS
Marketing	500,000	Number of client lunches	500	3,500
Client meetings	1,000,000	Number of clients	9,000	1,000
Data input	1,500,000	Computer hours	10,000	5,000
Analysis and research	1,500,000	Research hours	5,000	10,000
Training and development	500,000	Number of staff	1,000	1,000

This has allowed the finance director to re-allocate the overheads and create a new charge out rate for clients as follows:

	TAS	BAS
	$	$
Direct labour	300,000	400,000
Overheads		
Marketing	62,500	437,500
Client meetings	900,000	100,000
Data input	1,000,000	500,000
Analysis of research	500,000	1,000,000
Training and development	250,000	250,000
Total costs	3,012,500	2,687,500
Revenue	3,000,000	3,000,000
Profit/(loss)	(12,500)	312,500

Boomer Jones now has a better understanding of its costs. TAS continues to make a loss but Boomer Jones now better understands the reasons behind it. It could, for example, seek out ways to reduce the amount of computer hours needed for client work by either training staff to use the computers more efficiently or seeking out more efficient software.

From this illustration it can be seen how service organisations can get great benefit from a switch to activity based costing.

4 When is ABC relevant?

ABC is a more expensive system to operate than traditional costing, so it should only be introduced when it is appropriate to do so. Activity-based costing could provide much more meaningful information about product costs and profits when:

- indirect costs are high relative to direct costs
- products or services are complex
- products or services are tailored to customer specifications
- some products or services are sold in large numbers but others are sold in small numbers.

In these situations, ABC will often result in significantly different product or service overhead costs, compared with traditional absorption costing.

The difference between traditional costing and ABC costing will also be dependent on the make up of the overhead cost. Overhead costs can be divided into 4 different types of activities

(i) *Unit-level activities* – where the consumption of resources is very strongly correlated with the number of units produced.

(ii) *Batch-level activities* – where the consumption of resources is very strongly correlated with the number of batches produced.

(iii) *Product-level activities* – where consumption of resources may be related to the existence of particular products.

(iv) *Facility-level activities* – where the cost cannot be related in any way to the production of any particular product line.

Comparison to traditional costing

Any unit cost, no matter how it is derived, can be misinterpreted. There is temptation to adopt a simplistic approach, which would say, for example, that if it cost $1,000 to produce ten units, it will cost $10,000 to produce 100 units. As we know, this in incorrect in the short term, owing to the existence of short-term fixed costs. The ABC approach does not eliminate this problem anymore than the traditional approach. The alternative to presenting full absorption costing information in a traditional costing system has been to provide the user with a marginal costing statement which distinguishes clearly between the variable cost of production and the fixed cost of production. This carries an implication for the decision-maker that if the variable cost of production is $50 for 10 units, the additional cost of producing a further 40 units will be 40 × $5 = $200.

Activity-based costing, on the other hand, can provide the user with a more sophisticated breakdown of cost. This breakdown relates cost to the level of activities undertaken. The structure of reporting will vary from company to company, but Cooper (1992) has suggested that four levels of activity, which he terms a hierarchy of cost, will commonly be found in practice.

These are shown below:

(i) *Unit-level activities.* These are activities where the consumption of resources is very strongly correlated with the number of units produced. Costs traditionally defined as direct costs would fall into this category, for example direct material and direct labour.

(ii) *Batch-level activities.* Some activities – for example, machine set-up, materials handling and batch inspection – consume resources in proportion to the number of batches produced, rather than in proportion to the number of units produced. By identifying the consumption of resources at a batch rather than a unit level, it is easier than in a traditional costing system for a user to visualise the changing cost that will come about in the long term by changing a product mix or production schedule.

(iii) *Product-level activities.* Consumption of resources by, for example, administration, product specification or purchasing may be related to the existence of particular products. If the activity is performed to sustain the existence of a particular product line, it is a product-level activity.

(iv) *Facility-level activities.* Even within an ABC system, it is accepted that there are some costs that relate simply to being in business and that therefore cannot be related in any way to the production of any particular product line. Grounds maintenance, plant security and property taxes would be examples of this type of cost.

Consideration of (i)–(iv) shows that the difference between traditional costing and ABC costing will be dependent on the proportion of overhead cost that falls into each of the four categories. If this overhead is made up primarily of (i) and (iv), it is obvious that the traditional approach and the ABC approach will lead to very similar product costs. However, if the bulk of overhead cost falls into category (ii) and/or category (iii), there will be a very significant difference between the two.

The debate as to whether ABC is actually a new technique, or whether it simply encourages a more accurate tracing of costs to products in a manner that is perfectly consistent with the traditional approach, is interesting but sterile – and misses the point of ABC, as is demonstrated in the rest of this chapter. Nevertheless, it is worth pointing out that ABC product costs are full absorption costs and, as such, suffer from the same type of deficiencies in a decision-making context as do traditional full absorption costs – they are historical, based on current methods of organisation and operation and, at the level of the product, contain allocations of joint/common costs, etc.

However, it can be strongly argued that ABC has an important 'attention-directing' role to play in both cost management and decision-making. ABC is defined in the CIMA Official Terminology as:

> *an approach to the costing and monitoring of activities which involves tracing resource consumption and costing final outputs. Resources are assigned to activities, and activities to cost objects based on consumption estimates. The latter utilise cost drivers to attach activity costs to outputs.*

In decision-making, it is arguable that activity-based costs are much more helpful than traditional costs in determining the costs relevant for decision-making and, more particularly, in drawing attention to the likely impact on long-run variable costs of short-term decisions.

Advantages and disadvantages of ABC

Advantages	Disadvantages
• more accuracy	• not always relevant
• better cost understanding	• still need arbitrary cost allocations
• fairer allocation of costs	• need to choose appropriate drivers and activities
• better cost control	• complex
• can be used in complex situations	• expensive to operate
• can be applied beyond production	
• can be used in service industries	

Advantages and disadvantages of ABC

ABC has a number of advantages:

- It provides a more accurate cost per unit. As a result, pricing, sales strategy, performance management and decision making should be improved (see next section for detail).
- It provides much better insight into what drives overhead costs.
- ABC recognises that overhead costs are not all related to production and sales volume.
- In many businesses, overhead costs are a significant proportion of total costs, and management needs to understand the drivers of overhead costs in order to manage the business properly. Overhead costs can be controlled by managing cost drivers.
- It can be applied to derive realistic costs in a complex business environment.
- ABC can be applied to all overhead costs, not just production overheads.
- ABC can be used just as easily in service costing as in product costing.

Disadvantages of ABC:

- ABC will be of limited benefit if the overhead costs are primarily volume related or if the overhead is a small proportion of the overall cost.
- It is impossible to allocate all overhead costs to specific activities.
- The choice of both activities and cost drivers might be inappropriate.
- ABC can be more complex to explain to the stakeholders of the costing exercise.
- The benefits obtained from ABC might not justify the costs.

The implications of switching to ABC

The use of ABC has potentially significant commercial implications:

- Pricing can be based on more realistic cost data.
  - Pricing decisions will be improved because the price will be based on more accurate cost data
- Sales strategy can be more soundly based.
  - More realistic product costs as a result of the use of ABC may enable sales staff to:
    - target customers that appeared unprofitable using absorption costing but may be profitable under ABC
    - stop targeting customers or market segments that are now shown to offer low or negative sales margins.
- Decision making can be improved.
  - Research, production and sales effort can be directed towards those products and services which ABC has identified as offering the highest sales margins.
- Performance management can be improved.
  - Performance management should be enhanced due to the focus on selling the most profitable products and through the control of cost drivers.
  - ABC can be used as the basis of budgeting and longer term forward planning of overhead costs. The more realistic budgeted overhead cost should improve the system of performance management.

5 Chapter summary

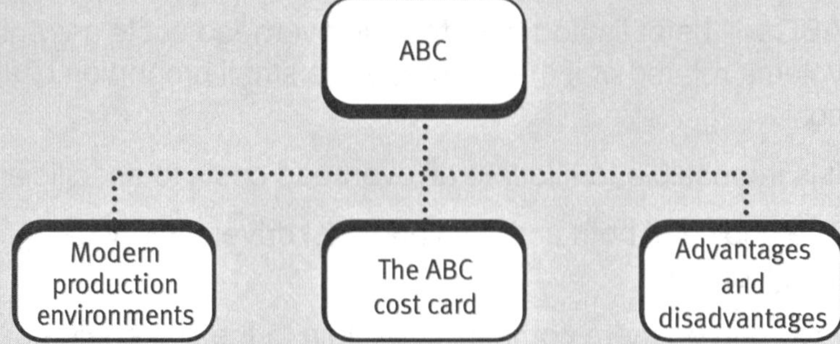

- Less use of direct labour
- Overheads becoming more important
- More detail needed on overheads
- Need fairer ways to share overheads

- Allocates costs to pools rather than departments
- Costs in pools are charged to products using cost drivers
- Cost drivers are more representative of the cause of the cost

- More detail is provided on overheads
- Overheads are shared better between products
- Impacts on pricing
- But it is complex
- Some arbitrary allocations remain

6 Practice questions

Test your understanding 1

An organisation has a single production process with expected material receipt and inspection costs of $35,000 for the next period. The following budgeted information has been obtained for the period:

	Product A	Product B	Product C
Production quantity (units)	2,000	1,500	800
Batches of material	20	10	5

The organisation uses an activity based costing system.

The amount of material and inspection costs attributed to Product B in the period will be:

A $6.67

B $6.98

C $10.89

D $19.97

Test your understanding 2

PB manufactures and sells three products, E, G and F. Budgeted costs for machine running time for the next year are $4,560,000.

The following information is given on budgeted plans for each product:

	Product E	Product G	Product F
Production quantity (units)	5,000	4,000	6,000
Machine hours per unit	2	4	2
Labour hours per unit	1	2	4
Machine set ups	10	6	8

To the nearest $, the machine running cost per unit for Product F using activity based costing will be $_____

Test your understanding 3

A bank regularly samples business customer accounts and reviews these for risks to the bank. These review costs totalled $1,050,280 in the last period. The following budgeted information has been obtained for the period:

	Sole traders	Partnerships	Companies
Number of customers	250,000	10,000	90,000
Number of reviews	100,00	3,000	18,000

The bank uses an activity based costing system.

To the nearest $, the total amount of review costs attributed to sole trader customers is $_____

Test your understanding 4

A company manufacturers three products with total production overheads of $2,600,000. The company uses an ABC system and has identified associated cost drivers:

Activity cost pool	Cost driver	Cost associated with activity cost pool
Receiving/inspecting quality assurance	Purchase requisitions	$1,400,000
Production scheduling/machine set-ups	Number of batches	$1,200,000

Details on the three products are as follows:

	P	R	S
Production (units)	10,000	20,000	30,000
Number of purchase requisitions	1,200	1,800	2,000
Number of set ups	240	260	300

The receiving/inspecting quality assurance cost per unit attributed to product P is:

A $25.20

B $33.60

C $36.00

D $280.00

Test your understanding 5

A company manufacturers three products with total production overheads of $2,600,000. The company uses an ABC system and has identified associated cost drivers:

Activity cost pool	Cost driver	Cost associated with activity cost pool
Receiving/inspecting quality assurance	Purchase requisitions	$1,400,000
Production scheduling/machine set-ups	Number of batches	$1,200,000

Details on the three products are as follows:

	P	R	S
Production (units)	10,000	20,000	30,000
Number of purchase requisitions	1,200	1,800	2,000
Number of set ups	240	260	300

The charge out rate for production scheduling/machine set-ups used to attribute the cost to product S is $_____

Test your understanding 6

An organisation has a single production process with expected material handling costs of $13,650 for the next period.

The following budgeted information has been obtained for the period:

	Product X	Product Y	Product Z
Production quantity (units)	2,000	1,500	800
Batches of material	10	5	16
Data per product unit			
Direct material (sq. metres)	4	6	3
Direct material ($)	5	3	6

The organisation uses an activity based costing system and the cost driver for material handling is the quantity of material (sq. metres) handled.

The amount of material handling costs attributed to Product X in the period will be:

A $2.81

B $2.83

C $14.05

D $14.15

Test your understanding 7

A small accountancy firm provides three services as follows:

	Statutory audit	Tax services	Other services
Budgeted services	5,000	10,000	40,000
Budgeted labour hours per service	18	2	4
Average number of reviews per service	3	0.5	2

Other services includes services such as pension planning, business consultancy and business valuations.

The budgeted activity cost for reviews was $55,000.

To the nearest cent, if an ABC system is used by the accountancy firm, how much review cost is attached to each statutory audit service?

A $0.55

B $1.65

C $3.00

D $3.67

Test your understanding 8

Machine set up costs are likely to be classed as which type of activity in the hierarchy of costs?

A Unit level activity

B Batch level activity

C Product level activity

D Facility level activity

Test your understanding 9

Scenario

Fixed overhead absorption rates are often calculated using a single measure of activity. It is suggested that fixed overhead costs should be attributed to cost units using multiple measures of activity (Activity Based Costing).

Task

Explain Activity Based Costing and how it may provide useful information to managers.

(Your answer should refer to both the setting of cost driver rates and subsequent overhead cost control).

(Time allowed: 10 minutes)

Test your understanding 10

Explain the benefits of using multiple activity bases for variable overhead absorption.

(Time allowed: 10 minutes)

Test your understanding 11

Explain the factors that should be considered when selecting cost drivers for an activity based costing system.

(Time allowed: 10 minutes)

Test your understanding 12

Scenario

An organisation manufactures three products in a single process. It has used absorption costing in the past and absorbed overheads on the basis of direct labour hours. It has prepared the following standard cost card for each product on that basis:

	Product X	Product Y	Product Z
Direct material	5.00	3.00	6.00
Direct labour	3.60	6.00	9.00
Production overhead	7.50	12.50	18.75
	$16.10	$21.50	$33.75

The accountant has proposed a switch to activity based costing and has prepared revised standard cost cards on that basis as follows:

	Product X	Product Y	Product Z
Direct material	5.00	3.00	6.00
Direct labour	3.60	6.00	9.00
Production overhead			
Material receipt/inspection	2.52	1.68	10.06
Process power	6.46	3.23	2.15
Material handling	2.81	4.22	2.11
Cost per unit	$20.39	$18.13	$29.32

Process power has been charged to products on the basis of the number of drill operations carried out on each product. A cost driver for drill operations of $1.0773 has been determined.

Task:

Using the power drill costs as an illustration, explain the relevance of cost drivers in activity based costing.

(Time allowed: 10 minutes)

Test your understanding 13

Scenario

Cabal makes and sells two products, Plus and Doubleplus. The direct costs of production are $12 for one unit of Plus and $24 per unit of Doubleplus.

Information relating to annual production and sales is as follows:

	Plus	**Doubleplus**
Annual production and sales	24,000 units	24,000 units
Direct labour hours per unit	1.0	1.5
Number of orders	10	140
Number of batches	12	240
Number of setups per batch	1	3
Special parts per unit	1	4

Information relating to production overhead costs is as follows:

	Cost driver	**Annual cost**
		$
Setup costs	Number of setups	73,200
Special parts handling	Number of special parts	60,000
Other materials handling	Number of batches	63,000
Order handling	Number of orders	19,800
Other overheads	–	216,000
		432,000

Other overhead costs do not have an identifiable cost driver, and in an ABC system, these overheads would be recovered on a direct labour hours basis.

The following cost cards were created for the products using a traditional absorption costing system:

	Plus	Double plus
	$	$
Direct costs	12.00	24.00
Production overhead	7.20	10.80
Full production cost	19.20	34.80

The accountant has also prepared the following standard cost card to support a suggestion that the company switch to an ABC costing system:

	Plus	Double plus
	$	$
Direct cost	12.00	24.00
Overhead cost per unit	4.33	13.67
Full cost	16.33	37.67

Tasks:

(a) Explain the reasons for the differences in the production cost per unit between the two methods.

(Time allowed: 10 minutes)

(b) Explain the implications for management of using an ABC system instead of an absorption costing system.

(Time allowed: 10 minutes)

Note:

	Plus	Double plus
Assume the selling prices are	$25.00	$40.00
Using absorption costing sales margins are	23.2%	13.0%
ABC sales margins are	34.7%	5.8%

Test your understanding answers

Example 1

Solution

(a)

Workings	**M1**	**M2**	**Total**
Number of batches	4	80	84
Number of setups	4	240	244
Special parts	16,000	64,000	80,000
Direct labour hours	16,000	20,000	36,000

Activity	**Cost**		**M1**	**M2**
	$		$	$
Setups	97,600	Cost per setup $400	1,600	96,000
Materials handling	42,000	Cost per batch $500	2,000	40,000
Special parts handling	50,000	Cost per part $0.625	10,000	40,000
Invoicing	31,000	Cost per order $100	6,000	25,000
Other overheads	108,000	Cost per hour $3	48,000	60,000
	328,600		67,600	261,000

	M1		**M2**	
	$	$	$	$
Sales		$432,000		584,000
Direct materials	88,000		168,000	
Direct labour	128,000		160,000	
Overheads	67,600		261,000	
Total costs		283,600		589,000
Profit/(loss)		148,400		(5,000)
Profit/loss per unit		18.55		(0.625)

(b) The figures suggest that model M2 is less profitable than M1. The sales manager should try to persuade the customer to buy model M1. Note that the apparent loss on M2 does not necessarily mean that production should be ceased. To assess this management should consider the incremental relevant cash flows involved – e.g. is the product making positive contribution, how many overheads are avoidable? They could also consider ways to reduce the cost drivers for the product to reduce its share of the overheads and convert the product loss into a profit.

Test your understanding 1

Firstly a cost driver must be determined. For material receipts and inspections this is likely to be based on the number of batches produced:

Material receipt and inspection $= \frac{\$35,000}{20 + 10 + 5} = \$1,000$ per batch

These should then be charged to each product. For product B, the cost per unit will be:

Product Y $1,000/batch × 10 batches/1,500 units = $6.67/unit

Option **A** is the correct answer.

Test your understanding 2

Machine running time cost is likely to be driven by the machine hours. Total number of machine hours:

	Product E	**Product G**	**Product F**
Machine hours (Production units × hours per unit)	10,000	16,000	12,000

Charge out rate = $4,560,000/38,000 machine hours = $120 per machine hour

Cost per unit for Product F = $120 per machine hour × 2 hour per unit = $**240**

Test your understanding 3

Firstly a cost driver must be determined for the review costs:

$$\text{Review costs driver rate} = \frac{\$1,050,280}{100,000 + 3,000 + 18,000} = \$8.68 \text{ per review}$$

The total amount charged to sole trader accounts will be:

Product Y $8.68 per review × 100,000 reviews = **$868,000**

Test your understanding 4

Cost driver rate:

$$\text{Receiving/inspecting quality assurance (based on purchase requisitions)} = \frac{\$1,400,000}{5,000} = \$280$$

Charge to product P = $280 × 1,200/10,000 = $33.60

Option **B** is the correct answer.

Test your understanding 5

Cost driver rate:

$$\text{Production scheduling/machine set-ups (based on number of set-ups)} = \frac{\$1,200,000}{800} = \mathbf{\$1,500}$$

Test your understanding 6

Firstly a cost driver must be determined:

$$\text{Material handling} = \frac{\$13,650}{(2,000 \times 4) + (1,500 \times 6) + (800 \times 3)}$$

$$= \$0.70361 \text{ per sq. metre handled}$$

These should then be charged to each product. For product X, the cost per unit will be:

Product X $0.70361/$m^2$ of material × 4m^2 = $2.81

Option **A** is the correct answer.

Test your understanding 7

The most appropriate cost driver for reviews would be the number of reviews per service.

Total number of reviews = (5,000 × 3) + (10,000 × 0.5) + (40,000 × 2) = 100,000

Cost per review = $55,000/100,000 = $0.55

The review cost for statutory audit services = $0.55 × 3 = $1.65

The correct answer is option **B.**

Test your understanding 8

Machines are likely to be set-up for production of a batch of units. The associated costs would therefore be classed as a batch level activity.

Option **B** is the correct answer.

Test your understanding 9

Activity Based Costing (ABC) is a system of full costing which recognises that the more traditional method of absorption costing using cost centre absorption rates may not provide accurate product costs.

ABC identifies the activities of a production process and the extent to which individual products make use of those activities. Costs are then estimated for each of these activities which are referred to as cost pools. The number of times which the activity is expected to be carried out is also estimated and a cost driver rate calculated:

$$\frac{\text{Estimated cost of pool}}{\text{Estimated number of times activity is to be performed}}$$

An individual product will probably make use of a number of different activities, and a proportion of the cost of each activity will be attributed to the product using these predetermined cost driver rates.

The actual costs of each cost pool together with the number of times the activity is performed will be collected and a comparison made with the corresponding estimated values. This is similar to the comparison of actual and budgeted costs and volumes using the traditional absorption costing approach except that there are likely to be a greater number of cost driver rates using ABC than the one per cost centre absorption rate found in traditional absorption costing.

Test your understanding 10

Such an approach is beneficial because it identifies overhead costs with their cause, rather than assuming that they are all driven by a single cause.

This should enable management to control such costs more easily, the variances reported will be more meaningful and this will help management to control costs.

Test your understanding 11

The cost driver for a particular activity is the factor that causes a change in the cost of the activity. For the cost driver to be useful there must be an identifiable relationship between the cost and the cost driver, i.e. changes in the number of cost drivers must cause corresponding changes in the total cost incurred on the activity.

Another major consideration is the ease of accurately recording the number of cost drivers incurred. If the process of recording the cost drivers is very complex and time-consuming then the cost of the recording system might outweigh the benefits derived from the information obtained.

Test your understanding 12

A cost driver is that factor which is most closely related to the way in which the costs of an activity are incurred. It could be said to cause the costs. Under ABC an organisation does not need to restrict itself to just one overall overhead absorption rate. An organisation can choose whatever basis it considers suitable to charge overheads to the product.

Examining process power in this organisation, under traditional absorption costing Product Z was the dearest for process power merely because it used the most labour hours per unit – a fact completely and utterly unconnected with the way in which process power costs are incurred. Under ABC the accountant has likely investigated the business and actually taken the time to find out what factor is most closely related to the cost and use that factor to charge overheads. The outcome is that Product X should be the dearest because it uses the most power drill operations.

ABC supporters would argue that this cost/power drill operation is useful information. The costs of power drill operations for product X is not insignificant and in fact is nearly as much as the direct material cost and direct labour cost combined. It would be inconceivable that the direct material costs and direct labour costs would not be very carefully controlled and yet under traditional absorption costing the process power costs would be included within the general overheads and would not be subject to such severe scrutiny.

Under ABC, once we realise that power drill operations cost $1.0773 each then when designing new products, the organisation would have better cost information and thus would be able to make better informed decisions.

Test your understanding 13

(a) **The reasons for the difference in the production cost per unit between the two methods**

- The allocation of overheads under absorption costing was unfair. This method assumed that all of the overheads were driven by labour hours and, as a result, the Double Plus received 1.5 times the production overhead of the Plus.
- However, this method of absorption is not appropriate. The overheads are in fact driven by a number of different factors. There are five activity costs, each one has its own cost driver. By taking this into account we end up with a much more accurate production overhead cost per unit.
- Using ABC, the cost per unit of a Double Plus is significantly higher. This is because the Double Plus is a much more complex product than the Plus. For example, there are 140 orders for the Double Plus but only 10 for the Plus and there are 4 special parts for the Double Plus compared to only one for the Plus. As a result of this complexity, the Double Plus has received more than three times the overhead of the Plus.
- This accurate allocation is important because the production overhead is a large proportion of the overall cost.

(b) **The implications of using ABC**

- Pricing – pricing decisions will be improved because the price will be based on more accurate cost data.
- Decision making – this should also be improved. For example, research, production and sales effort can be directed towards the most profitable products.
- Performance management – should be improved. ABC can be used as the basis of budgeting and forward planning. The more realistic overhead should result in more accurate budgets and should improve the process of performance management. In addition, an improved understanding of what drives the overhead costs should result in steps being taken to reduce the overhead costs and hence an improvement in performance.
- Sales strategy – this should be more soundly based. For example, target customers with products that appeared unprofitable under absorption costing but are actually profitable, and vice versa.

chapter

3

Other costing techniques

Chapter learning objectives

Lead	**Component**
A1. Discuss costing methods and their results.	(a) Apply marginal (or variable) throughput and absorption accounting methods in respect of profit reporting and stock valuation.
A3. Explain the role of environmental costing.	(a) Explain the role of environmental costing as part of an environmental management system.
C2. Analyse short-term pricing and product decisions.	(d) Explain why joint costs must be allocated to final products.

1 Chapter overview diagram

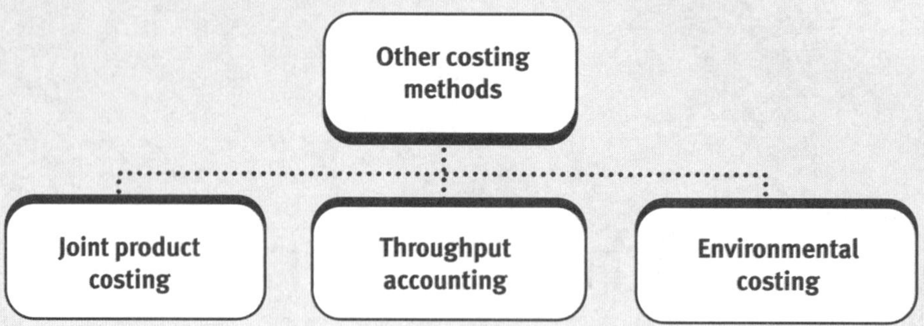

Previous chapters have looked at the most common costing methods used by organisations. However, there are other costing methods which may be used by organisations, either because it suits the way that the organisation operates or because the organisation wants to more fully understand its costs. Better costing methods may lead to better decision making.

The three costing methods that we will examine in this chapter are:

- joint product costing
- throughput accounting, and
- environmental costing.

2 Joint product costing

Some products may be produced at the same time in the same process before being separated for sale or further individual processing. These products are known as joint products and the separation point is known as the split-off point.

For example, different types of carbonated drinks might use a common starting process where syrup, sweeteners and malt are added before they are split up and individual flavourings added.

Joint costs are the total of the raw material, labour, and overhead costs incurred up to the initial split-off point.

Joint costs and common costs

A joint cost is the cost of a process that results in more than one main product. A common cost is a cost relating to more than one product or service.

The term 'joint cost' refers to the cost of some common process before a split-off point after which various joint products and by-products can be identified. 'Common costs' is a wider term that need not relate to a process. For example, the absorption of fixed production overheads in total absorption costing described in an earlier chapter is an example of assigning common costs to cost units.

The joint costs can not normally be directly attributable to individual joint products or by-products. Therefore, arbitrary allocations may have to be used instead.

Joint products and by-products

The nature of process costing is that the process incurs joint costs and often produces more than one product. These additional products may be described as either joint products or by-products. Essentially joint products are all the main products, whereas by-products are incidental to the main products.

- *Joint products* are two or more products produced by the same process and separated in processing, each having a sufficiently high saleable value to merit recognition as a main product.
- A *by-product* is output of some value produced incidentally in manufacturing something else (main product).

These definitions still leave scope for subjective judgement, but they provide a basis for such judgement. The distinction is important because the accounting treatment of joint and by-products differs. Costs incurred in processing prior to the separation of the products are known as **joint costs**.

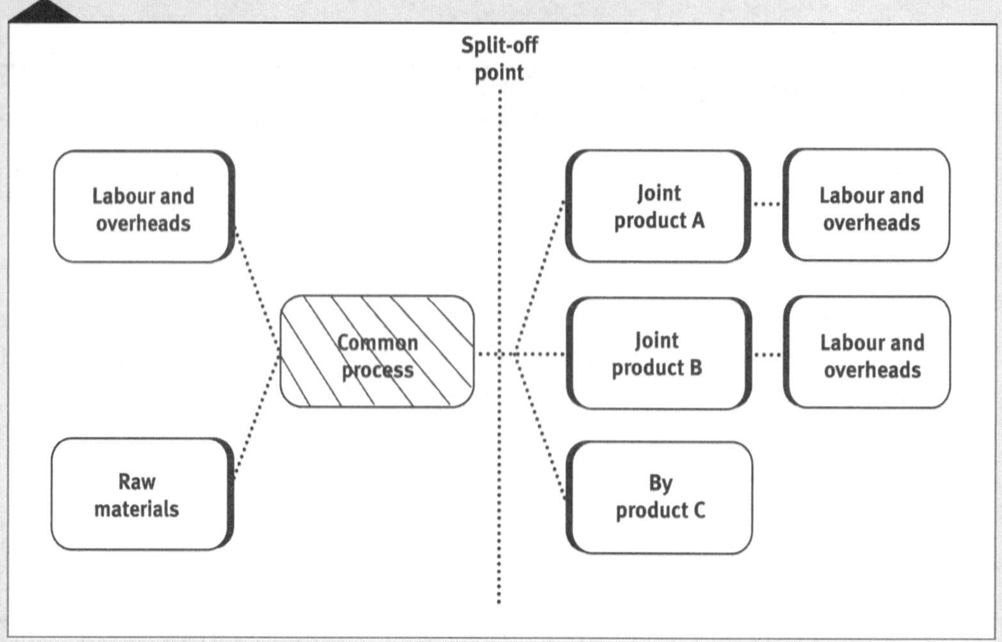

Methods of joint cost apportionment

There are many ways in which joint costs can be apportioned to products such as:

- physical measurement
- market value at point of separation
- net realisable value/net relative sales value

In turn, the methods will result in different inventory valuations and, therefore, different recorded profits.

Further details and explanation

Accounting for joint products

Joint products are, by definition, subject to individual accounting procedures.

Joint costs will require apportionment between products for inventory valuation purposes. The main bases for appointment are as follows:

- *Physical measurement of joint products:* Joint costs can be apportioned to the units of output of each joint product. When the unit of measurement is different, e.g. litres and kilos, some method should be found of expressing them in a common unit. Some joint costs are not incurred equally for all joint products: such costs can be separated and apportioned by introducing weighting factors. Alternatively, a *technical estimate of relative usage* by each product may be made by the organisation.

- *Market value:* Joint costs can be apportioned on the basis of the market value of each joint product at the point of separation. The effect is to make each product appear to be equally profitable.
- *Net realisable value:* Where certain products are processed after the point of separation, further processing costs may be deducted from the market values before joint costs are apportioned.

It is essential to realise that apportionment is, of necessity, an arbitrary calculation and product costs that include such an apportionment can be misleading if used as a basis for decision-making.

Accounting for by-products

Either of the following methods may be adopted: the proceeds from the sale of the by-product may be treated as pure profit, or the proceeds from the sale, less any handling and selling expenses, may be used to reduce the cost of the main products.

If a by-product needs further processing to improve its marketability, the cost will be deducted in arriving at net revenue. Note that recorded profits will be affected by the method adopted if inventories of the main product are maintained.

Example 1

An organisation produces two joint products Product A and Product B. The total joint costs are $750 and the following information is provided on each product:

	Kgs produced	*Kgs sold*	*Selling price per kg*	*Joint cost*
Product A	100	80	$5	
				$750
Product B	200	150	$2	

Apportion the joint costs between the products using the following apportionment methods:

- physical measurement
- market value at point of separation
- net realisable value/net relative sales value

Joint costs in decision making

Even if careful technical estimates are made of relative benefits, any apportionment of common costs or joint costs will inevitably be an arbitrary calculation. When providing information to assist decision-making, therefore, the cost accountant will emphasise cost and revenue differences arising from the decision.

The main decisions involving joint products are:

- To carry out the whole process or not. This decision is made by considering the total revenues and costs of the process. A decision cannot be taken to just process some of the products as all products are produced simultaneously. The basis of common cost apportionment is irrelevant but the common costs in total are relevant.
- Whether or not to further process products. This decision is based on the incremental costs and incremental revenues of further processing. Revenue and cost at the split-off point are irrelevant to the decision as they will not change.

Decision making on joint products is explored in more detail in a later chapter.

3 Throughput accounting

Throughput accounting is very similar to marginal costing, but it can be used to make longer-term decisions about capacity/production equipment.

Throughput accounting is based on three concepts: throughput, inventory (or investment) and operating expenses. The basic premise is that managers should aim to increase throughput while simultaneously reducing inventory and operational expense.

Throughput

In throughput accounting, the only cost that is deemed to relate to volume of output is the direct material cost. All other costs (including all labour costs) are deemed to be fixed. These fixed costs may be called Total Factory Costs (TFC).

Throughput contribution = Revenue – Totally variable costs

The aim of throughput accounting is to maximise this measure of throughput contribution.

Since totally variable costs are normally just raw materials and bought-in components, it is often convenient to define throughput contribution as:

Throughput contribution = Revenue – direct material costs

Conversion costs

A distinction can be made between material and other manufacturing costs. These other manufacturing costs are sometimes collectively referred to as conversion costs. Therefore, costs such as direct labour, factory rent, equipment depreciation, inspection costs etc. will come together under the heading of conversion costs. This is a term that you may encounter in questions on this topic.

Investment

This is defined as all the money the business invests to buy the things that it intends to sell and all the money tied up in assets so that the business can make the throughput. Investment therefore includes unused raw materials, work-in-progress and unsold finished goods. It can also include non-current assets if these are used for buying or creating materials (such as equipment and buildings used to produce materials or research and development costs that can be attributed to its creation) .

Operating expenses

Operating expenses are defined as all the money a business spends to produce the throughput (i.e. to turn the inventory into throughput). It is not correct to think of operating expenses as fixed costs. They are costs that are not totally variable.

Profit reporting

Since a business makes its money from throughput, management accounting systems should focus on the value of throughput created. Profit should therefore be reported as follows (illustrative figures are included):

		$
Revenue		750,000
Raw material cost	(totally variable cost)	200,000
Throughput contribution		550,000
Operating expenses		400,000
Net profit		150,000

Super variable costing

Throughput accounting has been described as a form of 'super-variable costing' because the concept of throughput has similarities to the concept of contribution. It could therefore be seen as an alternative to marginal costing as a costing method. However, this is not an accurate description. This is because in throughput accounting, the concept of product cost is rejected. The throughput earned by individual products is calculated, but no attempt is made to charge operating expenses to products. This makes throughput accounting radically different from both traditional cost accounting systems such as absorption costing and marginal costing and also from activity based costing.

Inventory valuation

Inventory should be valued at the purchase cost of its raw materials and bought-in parts.

It should not include any other costs, not even labour costs. No value is added by the production process, not even by labour, until the item is sold.

Example 2

A company makes 1,000 units of an item during a period and sells 800 units for $8,000. Costs of production were as follows:

	$
Materials	3,000
Direct labour	2,000
Fixed production overhead	1,000
Other overhead	1,000

Actual production volume and production overhead expenditure were both the same as budgeted.

Required:

Calculate the profit for the period using:

(a) absorption costing

(b) marginal costing

(c) throughput accounting.

4 Multi-product decision making in throughput accounting

The usual requirement in questions is to maximise contribution (given that fixed costs are unaffected by the production decision in the short run) per unit of the limiting factor. In throughput accounting the approach should be to maximise the *throughput* contribution earned.

Maximising throughput

Using throughput accounting, the aim should be to maximise throughput, on the assumption that operating expenses are a fixed amount in each period.

- If the business has more capacity than there is customer demand, it should produce to meet the demand in full.
- If the business has a constraint that prevents it from meeting customer demand in full, it should make the most profitable use that it can of the constraining resource. **This means giving priority to those products earning the highest throughput for each unit of the constraining resource that it requires**.

This goal is achieved by determining what factors prevent the throughput being higher. This constraint is called a *bottleneck*. A bottleneck may be a machine whose capacity limits the output of the whole production process. The aim is to identify the bottlenecks and remove them, or, if this is not possible, ensure that they are fully utilised at all times. Non-bottleneck resources should be scheduled and operated based on the constraints within the system, and should not be used to produce more than the bottlenecks can absorb.

The following provides a step-by-step technique for resolving the problem

Step 1: identify the bottleneck constraint.

Step 2: calculate the throughput contribution per unit for each product.

Step 3: calculate the throughput contribution per unit of the bottleneck resource for each product.

Step 4: rank the products in order of the throughout contribution per unit of the bottleneck resource.

Step 5: allocate resources using this ranking and answer the question.

Example 3

The following data relates to two products manufactured by DJ Ltd

	Product X	**Product Y**
Selling price per unit	$15	$20
Direct material cost per unit	$10	$11
Maximum demand (units)	25,000	30,000
Time required on the bottleneck (hours per unit)	2	6

The firm has 80,000 bottleneck hours available each period.

Total factory costs amount to $128,000 in the period.

Required:

Calculate the optimum product mix and the maximum profit.

Contrasting TA with the limiting factor approach

Illustration

A company produces two products, A and B, the production costs of which are shown below:

	A	**B**
	$	$
Direct materials	10	10
Direct labour	5	9
Variable overhead	5	9
Fixed overhead	5	9
	25	37

Fixed overhead is absorbed on the basis of direct labour cost.

The products pass through two processes, Y and Z, with associated labour cost of $10 per direct labour hour in each. The direct labour time taken associated with the two products for these processes is shown below:

Process	Product A	Product B
Y	10 mins	39 mins
Z	20 mins	15 mins

Selling prices are set by the market. The current market price for A is $65 and that for B, $52. At these prices, the market will absorb as many units of A and B as the company can produce. The ability of the company to produce A and B is limited by the capacity to process the products through Y and Z. The company operates a two-shift system, giving 16 working hours per day. Process Z is a single-process line and 2 hours in each shift will be downtime. Process Y can process two units simultaneously, although this doubles the requirement for direct labour. Process Y can operate for the full 16 working hours each day.

Required:

What production plan should the company follow in order to maximise profits?

Solution

In order to find the profit maximising solution in any problem, the constraints which prevent the profit from being infinite must be identified; the greater the number of constraints, the more difficult the problem is to solve. In the simplest case, where there is only one binding constraint, the profit maximising solution is found by maximising the contribution per unit of the scarce resource, that is binding constraint. Linear programming (covered in a later chapter) may be used to solve the problem where more than one constraint is binding for some, but not all, feasible solutions.

Where the number of products is limited to two, and such constraints are relatively few in number, the problem can easily be expressed graphically to reveal the profit maximising solution, and/or the problem can be expressed in the form of a set of simultaneous equations. As the number of potentially binding constraints increases, the use of a computer becomes the only feasible way to solve the necessary number of simultaneous equations.

In this question, the only constraint is the company's ability to process the product. The total daily processing time for processes Y and Z are:

- Maximum process time Y = 2 × 16 hours × 60 minutes = 1,920 minutes
- Maximum process time Z = 12 hours × 60 minutes = 720 minutes

So the maximum number that could be produced of each of the two products is:

	Product A *Maximum units*		Product B *Maximum units*	
Y	$\frac{1,920}{10}$	= 192	$\frac{1,920}{39}$	= 49.23
Z	$\frac{720}{20}$	= 36	$\frac{720}{15}$	= 48

In the case of both products, the maximum number of units which can be produced in Process Y exceeds the number that can be produced in Process Z, and thus the capacity of Process Y is not a binding constraint. The problem therefore becomes one of deciding how to allocate the scarce production capacity of Process Z in such a way as to maximise profit.

Traditional approach – maximising the contribution per minute in Process Z

Contribution of A = $65 (selling price) – $20 (variable cost) = $45
Contribution of B = $52 (selling price) – $28 (variable cost) = $24

Contribution of A per minute in process Z = $45/20 = $2.25
Contribution of B per minute in process Z = $24/15 = $1.60

The profit maximising solution is therefore to produce the maximum possible number of units of A, 36, giving a contribution of $45 × 36 = $1,620.

Throughput approach – maximising throughput per minute in bottleneck resource Z

Throughput of A = $65 (selling price) – $10 (material cost) = $55
Throughput of B = $52 (selling price) – $10 (material cost) = $42

Throughput contribution of A per minute in process Z = $55/20 = $2.75
Throughput contribution of B per minute in process Z = $42/15 = $2.80

The profit maximising solution is therefore to produce the maximum number of units of B, 48, giving a throughput contribution of $42 × 48 = $2,016.

It is clear that, given the different solutions, the two approaches cannot both lead to profit maximisation. Which technique is correct depends on the variability or otherwise of labour and variable overheads, which in turn depends on the time horizon of the decision. This type of profit maximisation technique is a short-term one and in today's world labour is likely to be fixed in the short term and so it can be argued that TA provides the more correct solution. Variable overheads would need to be analysed to assess their variability.

Marginal costing rose to popularity in the 1930s when labour costs were usually variable as the workforce was usually paid on a piece-rate basis. Since then textbooks, at least, have always assumed that labour is a variable cost in the short term. All that has happened with TA is that it tends to recognise the present reality, which is that most cost excluding materials are now fixed in the short term.

The marginal costing approach should of course be modified to accommodate this, as it requires only variable costs to be used to calculate contribution. If only material costs are variable, then only those costs should be used in the calculation of contribution. Thus there should be no difference between the two systems in this respect.

Throughput accounting measures

Various performance measures have been devised to help measure throughput:

$$\text{Return per factory hour} = \frac{\text{Throughput contribution}}{\text{Product' s time on the bottleneck resource}}$$

$$\text{Cost per factory hour} = \frac{\text{Total factory cost}}{\text{Total time on the bottleneck resource}}$$

$$\text{Throughput accounting ratio} = \frac{\text{Return per factory hour}}{\text{Cost per factory hour}}$$

Explanation of the ratios

The return per factory hour shows the value added by the organisation and managers are encouraged to maximise this (for example, by increasing throughput or reducing the time taken in the process).

The cost per factory hour shows the cost of operating the factory in terms of overheads, labour costs etc.

The throughput accounting ratio measures the return from a product against the cost of running the factory. Some people would argue that only products with a throughput accounting ratio greater than 1 are worthwhile. This is because the ratio is telling us that the return that is made at this point is less than the cost of producing that return. For example, if the return was \$2 per hour but it was costing \$4 per hour to operate the factory, then the throughput accounting ration would be 0.5. This could easily be benchmarked against the target of 1 to tell us that production is not worthwhile.

But notice that the return per factory hour and the throughput accounting ratios are for each individual product, whereas the cost per factory hour is for the company as a whole. So it could be argued that a throughput accounting ratio of less than 1 does not reveal the full story.

Example 4

Calculate the throughput accounting ratio for each product in the previous example.

Criticism of throughput accounting

A criticism of throughput accounting is that it concentrates on the short term, when a business has a fixed supply of resources and operating expenses are largely fixed.

It is more difficult to apply throughput accounting concepts to the longer term, when all costs are variable, and vary with the volume of production and sales or another cost driver.

This criticism suggests that although throughput accounting could be a suitable method of measuring profit and performance in the short term, an alternative management accounting method, such as activity based costing, might be more appropriate for measuring and controlling performance from a longer-term perspective.

5 Environmental management accounting

Organisations are beginning to recognise that environmental awareness and management are not optional, but are important for long-term survival and profitability.

The importance of environmental management

All organisations:

- are faced with increasing legal and regulatory requirements relating to environmental management
- need to meet customers' needs and concerns relating to the environment
- need to demonstrate effective environmental management to maintain a good public image
- need to manage the risk and potential impact of environmental disasters

- can make cost savings by improved use of resources such as water and fuel
- are recognising the importance of sustainable development, which is the meeting of current needs without compromising the ability of future generations to meet their needs.

Illustration – Manchester United Football Club

Manchester United are one of the largest sporting organisations in the world. However, the club recognises that success as a company will not just be judged via sporting and financial success. Their environmental policy statement is updated annually but has included statements such as:

> *We know that our performance as an internationally recognised institution will be measured not only by our success on the field of play or our profitability as a business but also by our impact on the quality of life in our communities and on the environment we share.*
>
> *We will continue to develop plans to improve the environmental performance of our suppliers and contractors where appropriate. We will look for opportunities to promote environmental best practice initiatives with our commercial partners.*

Some of the environmental policies that the football club have introduced in recent years are:

- the club created a nature reserve at its training ground to provide a pond and grassland for wildlife which has become a haven for many species which may otherwise have been disturbed by the club's ongoing building improvements
- the club signed an agreement with Cheshire Wildlife Trust to enable the Trust to manage the land at the training ground for nature conservation purposes
- the training centre also features a lagoon with reed bed technology, where dirty water is cleaned and recycled in order to provide water for the training pitches
- a wide range of products are sent for re-use or are recycled including glass, plastics, cans, green waste from the pitches, wood, surplus event materials like carpets and signage boards, office stationery and marketing materials
- printed publications are now produced from sustainable sources
- old IT equipment and printer cartridges are also recycled or re-used and donated for charitable purposes

- stadium short distance vehicles (which used to run on carbon fuel) have been replaced with 'green' vehicles which are battery operated
- all incandescent light bulbs and strip lighting at the clubs stadium and training facilities have been replaced with energy efficient light bulbs
- the club promotes sustainability to suppliers and supporters – with senior players often becoming spokespeople for the cause.

These are just some of the many policies that the club have introduced. They have won many awards through these schemes and, since 2012, the Manchester United stadium has achieved ISO 14001 certification, becoming the first major stadium in the UK to achieve this international Environmental Management System standard.

Depletion of natural resources

One of the key elements is that natural resources such as carbon, energy and water may run out in the future. For example, it is predicted that by 2030, the global demand for fresh water will exceed supply by 40 percent. Also, fossil fuel consumption contributes to around 90% of all of the world's energy consumption, but estimates suggest that current oil reserves, for example, will run out within the next 50 years. On top of this, since the beginning of the Industrial Revolution, the burning of fossil fuels has contributed to the increase in carbon dioxide in the atmosphere which is attributed to global warming and climate change which are creating more frequent natural disasters. This is forcing companies to consider

- reducing existing usage of carbon, energy and water
- finding future alternative sources of these resources
- reducing unnecessary detrimental impacts on these resources.

Where organisations have avoided making these decisions voluntarily, governments are stepping in to enforce environmental standards in order to force organisations to do so. For example, 192 national states have signed up to what is known as the Kyoto accord which is an international agreement and plan to reduce worldwide carbon emissions and energy usage. Governments have created targets for the reduction of carbon in their environments and are using controls, limits and grants in order to encourage businesses and individuals help the country meet its targets set out in the Kyoto accord.

Organisations are also finding that stakeholders such as employees and customers are becoming increasingly aware of and concerned about environmental policies. Companies with a poor record on abusing natural resources might find that they lose customers and staff to rivals who are more environmentally 'friendly'.

The contribution of environmental management accounting (EMA)

EMA is concerned with the accounting information needs of managers in relation to corporate activities that affect the environment as well as environment-related impacts on the corporation. This includes:

- identifying and estimating the costs of environment-related activities
- identifying and separately monitoring the usage and cost of resources such as water, electricity and fuel and to enable costs to be reduced
- ensuring environmental considerations form a part of capital investment decisions
- assessing the likelihood and impact of environmental risks
- including environment-related indicators as part of routine performance monitoring
- benchmarking activities against environmental best practice.

EMA and effect on financial performance

There are a number of ways in which environmental issues can have an impact on the financial performance of organisations.

Improving revenue

Producing new products or services which meet the environmental needs or concerns of customers can lead to increased sales.

It may also be possible to sell such products for a premium price. RecycleMatch is an online business-to-business (B2B) marketplace that allows companies to buy, sell or give away large volumes of waste including plastics, textiles, paper, chemicals, food, metals and building materials.

Improved sales may also be a consequence of improving the reputation of the business.

It is possible that in the future, rather than good environmental management resulting in improved sales, poor management will lead to losses. All businesses will be expected to meet a minimum standard related to environmental issues.

Cost reductions

Paying close attention to the use of resources can lead to reductions in cost. Often simple improvements in processes can lead to significant costs savings. For example, Manchester United have estimated that they have saved around US$790,000 since introducing its environmental policies (explained earlier).

Increases in costs

There may be increases in some costs, for example the cost of complying with legal and regulatory requirements, and additional costs to improve the environmental image of the organisation. A recent study of the Syrian olive oil industry suggested that compliance costs could run to as much as 2% of total revenue.

However some of these costs may be offset by government grants and this expenditure may save money in the long-term as measures taken may prevent future losses.

For example, in countries such as the United Kingdom, Germany and Australia grants are available for companies who install solar panels as alternative energy supply systems. There is a high initial cost for the company but typically around two thirds of this is funded by government grants. Users also report that the balance of the cost is recovered over around four or five years through savings in energy bills.

Costs of failure

Even if short-term increases in costs through compliance or environmental policies cannot be recovered via increased revenue or other cost savings, it may still be considered to be financially acceptable if it avoids potential longer-term failure costs.

Poor environmental management can result in significant costs, for example the cost of clean-up and fines following an environmental disaster.

In April 2010, oil company British Petroleum was responsible for an oil spill off the Gulf of Mexico. By 2012 the company had spent US$21bn on the clean up operation and for compensation payments, and it had also reserved $40bn for expected future costs concerned with this environmental issue.

6 Identifying and accounting for environmental costs

Classification of environmental costs

Management are often unaware of the extent of environmental costs and cannot identify opportunities for cost savings. In order to determine the potential for costs savings it will be important to understand the nature of environmental costs that can be experienced by a firm.

Environmental costs can be categorised as quality related costs (quality costs are explored again in a later chapter). This results in four cost categories:

- Environmental **prevention costs** – those costs associated with preventing adverse environmental impacts
- Environmental **appraisal costs** – the cost of activities executed to determine whether products, service and activities are in compliance with environmental standards and policies
- Environmental **internal failure costs** – costs incurred to eliminate environmental impacts that have been created by the firm
- Environmental **external failure costs** – costs incurred after environmental damage has been caused outside the organisation.

Further details

Environmental prevention costs

The aim here is to prevent adverse environmental impacts occurring in the first place. Examples include:

- evaluating and selecting pollution control equipment
- selecting and evaluating suppliers
- training staff
- designing processes and products
- creating environmental policies
- environmentally driven research and development
- site and feasibility studies
- investment in protective equipment
- community relations and outreach programmes.

Environmental appraisal costs

The aim in incurring these costs is to determine whether adverse impacts are being created and whether environmental standards and internal policies are being complied with. Examples include:

- monitoring, testing and inspection costs
- site survey costs
- reporting costs
- improved systems and checks in order to prevent fines/penalties
- permit costs
- certification costs
- developing performance measures
- monitoring supplier performance.

Environmental internal failure costs

These costs are borne exclusively by the organisation. Examples include:

- the cost of recycling or disposing of waste or harmful materials
- product take back costs (i.e. in the EU, for example, companies must provide facilities for customers to return items such as batteries, printer cartridges etc. for recycling. The seller of such items must bear the cost of these "take backs")
- clean up costs (as in the case of British Petroleum discussed earlier)
- legal costs, insurance and fines
- site decontamination
- back-end costs such as decommissioning costs on project completion
- compensation payments to employees and customers
- off-set costs (for example, many paper manufacturers also plant trees in order to off-set the damage they may be creating to existing forestry).

Environmental external failure costs

These are the most significant costs: they are incurred after the hazardous materials have been introduced into the environment. Examples of such costs are:

- adverse impact on the organisation's reputation. This may lead to bans on or boycotts of the company's products.
- adverse impact on natural resources such as rivers, forests and rock formations
- carbon emissions and the adverse impact these have on the global climate
- medical costs for employees and local communities.

Some external failure costs might be caused by the company but the 'cost' will be borne by society at large. However, governments are becoming increasingly aware of these external costs and are using taxes and regulations to convert them to internal costs. For example, companies might have to have a tree replacement programme if they cause forest degradation, or they receive lower tax allowances on vehicles that cause a high degree of harm to the environment. On top of this, some companies are voluntarily converting external costs to internal costs.

A study by accountants KPMG in 2012 estimated that if a company were to internalise all environmental external failure costs then, on average, this would reduce profits by around 41% per annum. This highlights the need for further investment in prevention and appraisal costs. There is often a trade-off here: investment in prevention and appraisal can often reduce the occurrence of failure costs.

Example 5

Environmental costs can be classified into one of four different categories:

- prevention costs
- appraisal costs
- internal failure costs
- external failure costs.

Classify the following costs into these categories:

(i) environmental insurance costs

(ii) site survey costs

(iii) compensation payments to employees

(iv) staff training costs

(v) medical costs of local communities.

Accounting for environmental costs

Conventional management accounting practices do not provide adequate information for managing the environment in a world where environmental concerns, as well as environment-related costs, revenues, and benefits, are on the rise. Environmental costs are not traced to particular processes or activities and are instead "lumped in" with general business overheads or other activity costs.

Environmental activity-based accounting

In ABC, environmental costs are removed from general overheads and traced to products and services. This means that cost drivers are determined for these costs and products are charged for the use for these environmental costs based on the amount of cost drivers that they contribute to the activity. This should give a good attribution of environmental costs to individual products.

Illustration

A consumer electronics manufacturing company has established the following cost driver rates for internal environmental costs:

Category	Cost	Total cost	Cost driver	Cost driver rate
Prevention cost	Staff environmental training costs	$8m	40,000 training hours	$200 per training hour
Appraisal cost	Power usage inspection costs	$5m	150m kw hours consumed in final output	$0.033 per kw hour consumption
Internal failure cost	Product take back costs	$25m	15m batteries used in products	$1.67 per battery used

By including these costs in standard cost cards the company hope to encourage managers to focus on reducing total costs as well as the associated drivers. So, for example, managers may try to reduce the amount of batteries used in the product in order to be able to reduce that cost and also the selling price of the product.

The company now also wants to incorporate external environmental failure costs into its standard costing system. It has estimated the total external failure costs to be $15m. This is made up of pollution and clean up costs associated with the company's CO2 emissions. It has therefore determined that the cost driver will be based on the number of tons of resources to be consumed. In total 600,000 tonnes of resources were consumed last year and this gives a cost driver rate of $25 per tonne of resources consumed. Again, the company is hoping that this will encourage more awareness and control by managers.

Advantages of environmental costing	**Disadvantages**
• better/fairer product costs	• time consuming
• improved pricing – so that products that have the biggest environmental impact reflect this by having higher selling prices	• expensive to implement
• better environmental cost control	• determining accurate costs and appropriate cost drivers is difficult
• facilitates the quantification of cost savings from "environmentally-friendly" measures	• external costs not experienced by the company (e.g. carbon footprint) may still be ignored/unmeasured
• should integrate environmental costing into the strategic management process	• some internal environmental costs are intangible (e.g. impact on employee health) and these are still ignored
• reduces the potential for cross-subsidisation of environmentally damaging products	• a company that incorporates external costs voluntarily may be at a competitive disadvantage to rivals who do not do this

Input/output analysis

An alternative technique which can be used to identify and allocate environmental costs is Input/output analysis.

This technique records material flows with the idea that 'what comes in must go out – or be stored' (Jasch, 2003).

The purchased input is regarded as 100% and is balanced against the outputs – which are the produced, sold and stored goods and the residual (regarded as waste). Materials are measured in physical units and include energy and water. At the end of the process, the material flows can be expressed in monetary units. Process flow charts can help to trace inputs and outputs, in particular waste. They demonstrate the details of the processes so that the relevant information can be allocated to main activities.

The United Nations Centre for Sustainable Development (UNCSD) provides the following example:

Input	**Output**	
	Product	60%
	Scrap for recycling	20%
	Disposed of as waste	15%
	Not accounted for	5%
100%		100%

Flow management involves not only material flows, but also the organisational structure. Classic material flows are recorded as well as material losses incurred at various stages of production.

EMA can benefit from flow cost accounting because it aims to reduce the quantities of materials, which leads to increased ecological efficiency.

7 Chapter summary

Other costing methods

Joint product costing

- Allocate costs using
  - Net realisable value
  - Physical output
  - Market value
- By-product revenue can be deducted from joint costs

Throughput accounting

- Throughput contribution = Revenue – direct material costs
- Rank products in order of the contribution per unit of the bottleneck resource
- TAR = Return per factory hour divided by cost per factory hour

Environmental costing

- There are 4 cost categories
- Accounting for these costs can be difficult and expensive
- But it should lead to better understanding and better pricing of products

8 Practice questions

Test your understanding 1

The total production cost of joint products can be apportioned between products using which of the following methods? *(Tick all that apply)*

(1) Weight

(2) Sales revenue

(3) Selling prices

(4) Net realisable value

Test your understanding 2

Products A and B are manufactured in a joint process. The following data is available for a period:

Joint process costs		$30,000
Output:	Product A	2,000 kg
	Product B	4,000 kg
Selling price:	Product A	$12 per kg
	Product B	$18 per kg

What is Product B's share of the joint process costs if the sales value method of cost apportionment is used?

A $7,500

B $18,000

C $20,000

D $22,500

Test your understanding 3

Charleville operates a continuous process producing three products and one by-product. Output from the process for a month was as follows:

Product	Selling price per unit	Units of output from process
1	$18	10,000
2	$25	20,000
3	$20	20,000
4 (by product)	$2	3,500

Total output costs were $277,000.

The unit valuation for Product 3 (using the sales revenue basis for allocating joint costs) was $_____ *(Fill in the missing number)*

Test your understanding 4

Scenario

A business makes four products, W, X, Y and Z. Information relating to these products is as follows:

	W	**X**	**Y**	**Z**
Sales price/unit	$20	$25	$18	$40
Materials required/unit	$10	$15	$11	$22
Labour hours/unit	4	5	2	6
Monthly sales demand (units)	500	800	1,000	400

There is a limit to the availability of labour, and only 8,000 hours are available each month.

Task:

Identify which products the business should produce using a throughput accounting approach.

Test your understanding 5

A company manufactures a product that requires machine time of 1.5 hours per unit. Machine time is a bottleneck resource, due to the limited number of machines available. There are 10 machines available and each machine can be used for up to 40 hours each week. The product is sold for $85 per unit and the material cost per unit is $42.50. Total operating expenses are $8,000 each week.

Required:

Calculate the throughput accounting ratio.

Test your understanding 6

Scenario

Justin Thyme manufactures four products, A, B, C and D. Details of sales prices, costs and resource requirements for each of the products are as follows.

	Product A	**Product B**	**Product C**	**Product D**
	$	$	$	$
Sales price	1.40	0.80	1.20	2.80
Materials cost	0.60	0.30	0.60	1.00
Direct labour cost	0.40	0.20	0.40	1.00
	Minutes	Minutes	Minutes	Minutes
Machine time per unit	5	2	3	6
Labour time per unit	2	1	2	5
	Units	Units	Units	Units
Weekly sales demand	2,000	2,000	2,500	1,500

Machine time is a bottleneck resource and the maximum capacity is 400 machine hours each week. Operating costs, including direct labour costs, are $5,440 each week. Direct labour costs are $12 per hour, and direct labour workers are paid for a 38-hour week, with no overtime.

Tasks:

(a) Identify the quantities of each product that should be manufactured and sold each week to maximise profit using a throughput accounting approach and calculate the weekly profit.

(b) Calculate the throughput accounting ratio at this profit-maximising level of output and sales.

(Time allowed: 15 minutes)

Test your understanding 7

The following data relate to the single product made by Squirrel Ltd:

Selling price per unit	$16
Direct material cost per unit	$10
Maximum demand (units) per period	40,000
Time required (hours) in Process X, per unit	1
Time required (hours) in Process Y, per unit	1.5

The capacities are 35,000 hours in Process X and 42,000 hours in Process Y.

The total factory costs are $105,000 in the period.

Tasks:

(a) Identify the process bottleneck.

(b) Calculate the throughput accounting ratio.

(**Note:** This would be two separate questions in an examination)

Test your understanding 8

Explain why throughput accounting has been described as a form of 'super variable costing' and how the concept of contribution in throughput accounting differs from that in marginal costing.

(Time allowed: 10 minutes)

Test your understanding 9

A company manufactures three products: W, X and Y. The products use a series of different machines, but there is a common machine that is a bottleneck. The standard selling price and standard cost per unit for each product for the next period are as follows:

	W	X	Y
	$	$	$
Selling price	180	150	150
Cost:			
Direct material	41	20	30
Direct labour	30	20	50
Variable production overheads	24	16	20
Fixed production overheads	36	24	30
	—	—	—
Profit	49	70	20
	—	—	—
Time (minutes) on bottleneck machine	7	10	7

The company is trying to plan the best use of its resources.

(a) **Using a traditional limiting factor approach, the rank order (best first) of the products would be:**

A W, X, Y

B W, Y, X

C X, W, Y

D Y, X, W

(b) **Using a throughput accounting approach, the rank order (best first) of the products would be:**

A W, X, Y

B W, Y, X

C X, W, Y

D Y, X, W

(**Note:** This would be two separate questions in an examination)

Test your understanding 10

A supermarket chain is considering building a new shop. There are two possible locations. Explain the environmental factors that the management accountant should consider when providing information to support the decision making.

(Time allowed: 10 minutes)

Test your understanding 11

Scenario

A table manufacturing company is considering introducing a new environmental policy and specialist control team as a reaction to some concerns that buyers are having over the company's potential adverse impact on natural resources. The company is concerned about how following an environmental policy might impact on its costs.

Tasks:

State what types of environmental costs the company might incur and explain how these might change in the future with the introduction of an environmental policy.

(Time allowed: 10 minutes)

Test your understanding answers

Example 1

Apportionment by physical measurement

$$\frac{\text{Joint cost}}{\text{Kgs produced}} = \frac{\$750}{300} = \$2.50 \text{ per kg for A+B}$$

Trading results

	Product A		*Product B*		*Total*
		$		$	$
Sales	80 × $5.00	400	150 × $2.00	300	700
Cost of sales	80 × $2.50	200	150 × $2.50	375	575
Profit/(Loss)		200		(75)	125
Value of closing inventory	20 × $2.50	50	50 × $2.50	125	

The main point to emphasise about joint products is the production mix. In this case the production ratio is 100 : 200 which means that, in order to obtain 1 kg of A, it is necessary also to produce 2 kg of B. Although in the longer term it may be possible through research and development work to change the mix, in many processes this is not possible and for exam purposes you should assume that the ratio of output is fixed.

In attempting to assess the profitability of the common process it is necessary to assess the overall position as follows:

		$
Sales value of product A	100 × $5	500
Sales value of product B	200 × $2	400
		900
Joint cost		750
Profit		150

This total profit figure should be used to evaluate the viability of the common process.

Referring back to the trading results, it is important to appreciate that the 'loss' on B has been created by the joint cost apportionment, i.e.:

	$
Selling price	2.00
Share of joint cost	2.50
Loss	0.50

A decision not to produce and sell product B is not possible because, if product B were not produced, then neither could product A be produced. A further point to note is that inventory of B could not be valued in the financial statements at $2.50 bearing in mind that inventory should be valued at the lower of cost and net realisable value.

Apportionment by market value at point of separation

	Sales value of production	*Proportion*	*Joint cost apportionment*	*Per kg*
	$		$	$
A 100 × $5	500	5/9	417	4.17
B 200 × $2	400	4/9	333	1.67
			750	

Trading results:

	A	*B*	*Total*
Sales	400	300	700
Cost of sales	333.6	250.5	584.1
Profit	66.4	49.5	115.9
Profit/sales	16.6%	16.5%	
Closing inventory	(20 × 4.17)	(50 × 1.67)	
	83	83	

Notes:

(1) Apportionment is on the basis of proportionate sales value of production.

(2) Profit per unit is the same (with a small rounding difference).

(3) This approach provides a more realistic estimate of cost to use for valuing inventory of B, i.e. $1.67.

Apportionment by net realisable value

This approach should be used in situations where the sales value at the split-off point is not known – either because the product is not saleable, or if the examiner does not tell you – or if specifically asked for by the examiner.

Further information needed:

Further processing costs	*Selling price after further processing*
$280 + $2.00 per kg	$8.40
$160 + $1.40 per kg	$4.50

Apportionment of joint costs:

	Product A	*Product B*
	$	$
Final sales value of production (100 × $8.40; 200 × $4.50)	840	900
Further processing cost (280 + 100 × $2; 160 + 200 × $1.40)	480	440
	360	460
Joint cost apportionment (360 : 460)	329	421
Joint cost per kg	$3.29	$2.10

Trading result (for common process only):

	$	$	$
Sales			700
Joint cost		750	
Less: Closing inventory			
A 20 × $3.29	66		
B 50 × $2.10	105		
		171	
Cost of sales			579
Profit			121

Notes:

(1) As we know sales value of product B at the point of separation is \$2, we can see that this method results in an unrealistic inventory value of \$2.10. Bear in mind that this approach should only be used where the sales value at the split-off point is not known, or if instructed to use it by the examiner.

Example 2

The valuation of closing inventory is:

- \$1,200 (\$6,000 × 200/1,000) in absorption costing
- \$1,000 (\$5,000 × 200/1,000) in marginal costing
- \$600 (\$3,000 × 200/1,000) in throughput accounting.

Profit statements

(a) **Absorption costing**

Value of closing inventory = \$1,200

	\$	\$
Sales		8,000
Cost of production	6,000	
Less: Closing inventory	1,200	
Cost of sales		4,800
Gross profit		3,200
Non-production overhead		1,000
Profit		2,200

(b) **Marginal costing**

Value of closing inventory = $1,000

	$	$
Sales		8,000
Cost of production	5,000	
Less: Closing inventory	1,000	
Cost of sales		4,000
Contribution		4,000
Fixed overhead		1,000
Non-production overhead		1,000
Profit		2,000

(c) **Throughput accounting**

Value of closing inventory = $600

	$	$
Sales		8,000
Material costs	3,000	
Less: Closing inventory	600	
Cost of sales		2,400
Throughput		5,600
Operating expenses		4,000
Profit		1,600

Example 3

	Product X	Product Y
	$	$
Selling price	15	20
Direct material	10	11
Throughput	5	9
No. of bottleneck hours per unit	2	6
Return per factory hour	2.50	1.50
	1st	2nd

	Units	Bottleneck hrs per unit	Bottleneck hrs	Throughput $
Product X	25,000	2	50,000	125,000
Product Y	5,000[Bal]	6	30,000[Bal]	45,000
			80,000	170,000
Total factory cost				128,000
Gross profit				42,000

Example 4

				Product A	Product B
Return per factory hour	=	Throughput per unit / Bottleneck hrs per unit	=	(15 – 10) / 2 hrs	(20 – 11) / 6 hrs
				= $2.50	= $1.50
Cost per factory hour	=	Total factory cost / Total bottleneck hrs	=	$128,000 / 80,000 hrs	
				= $1.60	
Throughput accounting ratio	=	Return per factory hour / Cost per factory hour	=	$2.50 / $1.60	$1.50 / $1.60
				= 1.56	= 0.94

Product X has the higher throughput accounting ratio and thus should be given priority over Product Y.

Example 5

The costs are classified as follows:

(i) environmental insurance costs – internal failure cost

(ii) site survey costs – appraisal costs

(iii) compensation payments to employees – internal failure cost

(iv) staff training costs – prevention cost

(v) medical costs of local communities – external failure cost.

Test your understanding 1

1, 2 and 4 are all recognised ways of splitting joint costs. Selling prices (i.e. per unit) are not an acceptable basis as this does not take into account the relative volumes of each joint product.

Test your understanding 2

The correct answer is answer **D**.

	Output (kg)	Sales value ($)	Apportionment	Joint costs ($)
Product A	2,000	24,000	(24/96)	7,500
Product B	4,000	72,000	(72/96)	22,500
		96,000		30,000

Test your understanding 3

The unit valuation for Product 3 (using the sales revenue basis for allocating joint costs) was $**5**

Total sales revenue	= ($18 × 10,000) + ($25 × 20,000) + ($20 × 20,000)
	= $1,080,000
Joint costs to be allocated	= $277,000 – ($2 × 3,500)
	= $270,000
Allocation rate	= (270,000/1,080,000)
	= 0.25 of sales revenue
Joint costs allocated to Product 3	= 0.25 × ($20 × 20,000)
	= $100,000
Per unit	= $100,000/20,000 units
	= $**5** per unit

Test your understanding 4

The business should seek to maximise the total throughput.

	W	X	Y	Z
	$	$	$	$
Sales price/unit	20	25	18	40
Materials required/unit	10	15	11	22
Throughput/unit	10	10	7	18
Labour hours/unit	4	5	2	6
Throughput/labour hour	$2.50	$2.00	$3.50	$3.00
Priority	3rd	4th	1st	2nd

The production volumes that will maximise throughput and net profit are:

Product	Units	Labour hours	Throughput $
Y	1,000	2,000	7,000
Z	400	2,400	7,200
W	500	2,000	5,000
		6,400	
X (balance)	320	1,600	3,200
		8,000	22,400

Test your understanding 5

Throughput per bottleneck machine hour = (\$85 – \$42.50)/1.5 hours = \$28.33

Operating expenses per bottleneck machine hour = \$8,000/(10 × 40) = \$20

Throughput accounting ratio = \$28.33/\$20 = 1.42

Test your understanding 6

(a) **Step 1:** Determine the bottleneck constraint

The bottleneck resource is machine time. 400 machine hours available each week = 24,000 machine minutes.

Step 2: Calculate the throughput per unit for each product

	A	**B**	**C**	**D**
	$	$	$	$
Sales price	1.40	0.80	1.20	2.80
Materials cost	0.60	0.30	0.60	1.00
Throughput/unit	0.80	0.50	0.60	1.80

Step 3: Calculate the throughput per machine minute

Machine time per unit	5 minutes	2 minutes	3 minutes	6 minutes
Throughput per minute	$0.16	$0.25	$0.20	$0.30

Step 4: Rank

Rank	4th	2nd	3rd	1st

Step 5: Allocate resources using this ranking and answer the question.

The profit-maximising weekly output and sales volumes are as follows.

Product	**Units**	**Machine minutes**	**Throughput per unit**	**Total throughout**
			$	$
D	1,500	9,000	1.80	2,700
B	2,000	4,000	0.50	1,000
C	2,500	7,500	0.60	1,500
		20,500		
A (balance)	700	3,500	0.80	560
		24,000		5,760
Operating expenses				5,440
Profit				320

(b) Throughput per machine hour: $5,760/400 hours = $14.40

Cost (operating expenses) per machine hour: $5,440/400 hours = $13.60.

TPAR: $14.40/$13.60 = 1.059.

Test your understanding 7

(a) **Process bottleneck**

$$\text{Capacity in Process X} = \frac{35,000}{1} = 35,000 \text{ units per period}$$

$$\text{Capacity in Process Y} = \frac{42,000}{1.5} = 28,000 \text{ units per period}$$

Process Y has the lower capacity and therefore this is the bottleneck.

(b) **Throughput accounting ratio**

$$\text{Throughput per unit} = \$16 - \$10 = \$6$$

$$\text{Return per factory hour} = \frac{\$6}{1.5} = \$4$$

$$\text{Cost per factory hour} = \frac{\$105,000}{42,000 \text{ hours}} = \$2.50$$

$$\text{Throughput accounting ratio} = \frac{\$4}{\$2.50} = 1.60$$

As the throughput accounting ratio is greater than 1 it provides a satisfactory result.

Test your understanding 8

Throughput accounting has been described as a form of 'super variable costing' because the concept of throughput has similarities to the concept of contribution. However there is a major difference in the definition of contribution in the two systems or, more specifically, in what is described as a variable cost.

The traditional marginal costing approach assumes that direct labour is a variable cost. Although this may have been true in the past when labour was typically paid a piece rate, this is no longer the case. In the short term, throughput accounting treats labour as a fixed cost.

Marginal costing also tends to emphasise cost behaviour, especially overheads, and usually attempts to separate these into fixed and variable components. As with labour costs, throughput accounting treats all production overhead as fixed in the short term and aggregates these with labour into what is referred to as 'total factory cost'. Consequently, in throughput accounting the only cost that is treated as variable is the direct material cost.

Furthermore, throughput accounting uses the total of direct materials purchased in the period in the calculation of throughput, rather than the cost of material actually used, as is the case with marginal costing.

Test your understanding 9

(a) **A**

	W	**X**	**Y**
	$	$	$
Contribution	85	94	50
Time at bottle neck	7	10	7
Contribution per minute	12	9	7
Rank	1	2	3

(b) **B**

	W	**X**	**Y**
	$	$	$
Throughput*	139	130	120
Time at bottle neck	7	10	7
Throughput per minute	20	13	17
Rank	1	3	2

* throughput = sales less material costs

Test your understanding 10

Suggestions for issues to consider

- The design of the shop and its usage of utilities such as water and electricity.
- The costs of ensuring that the building and the operation comply with any local environmental regulations and requirements such as those of planning authorities.
- The environmental impact on the local area and the cost of any measures needed to minimise it – for example the potential increase in traffic and the provision of a free bus service as an alternative for customers.
- The locations and their position relative to the chain's distribution network and the fuel costs of supplying goods.
- The views and influence of local environmental pressure groups and the likely cost of public relations activities and modifications to plans to address their concerns.
- The product range to be offered and the market locally for higher-priced environmentally-friendly products such as organic fruit and vegetables.

Test your understanding 11

There are four main types of environmental costs:

- prevention costs – such as improvements in staff training and awareness
- appraisal costs – such as measuring the adverse impact on natural resources
- internal failure costs – such as fines that might be incurred for breaches of environmental standards, and
- external failure costs – such as a loss of sale from a damaged reputation and customer boycotts.

If the company was to focus more on its environmental policies and have a specialist team to do so then they are likely to experience changes in all of these costs. It is likely, for example, that prevention and appraisal costs will increase. Creating the specialist team and performing more monitoring are likely to increase the company's overall costs.

But these might be offset by savings in other environmental costs. Better staff awareness and preventative measures should reduce the occurrence of internal failures. For example, the company may be less likely to breach environmental standards and incur fines. They might also see less product boycotts and increased sales so that external failure costs also fall.

Many organisations have found that the savings in failure costs can often outweigh the investment in prevention and appraisal costs.

chapter

4

The modern manufacturing environment and the importance of quality

Chapter learning objectives

Lead	**Component**
A1. Discuss costing methods and their results.	(f) Explain the impact of just-in-time (JIT) manufacturing methods on cost accounting methods.
A2. Discuss the role of quality costing.	(a) Discuss the role of quality costing as part of a total quality management (TQM) system.

1 Chapter overview diagram

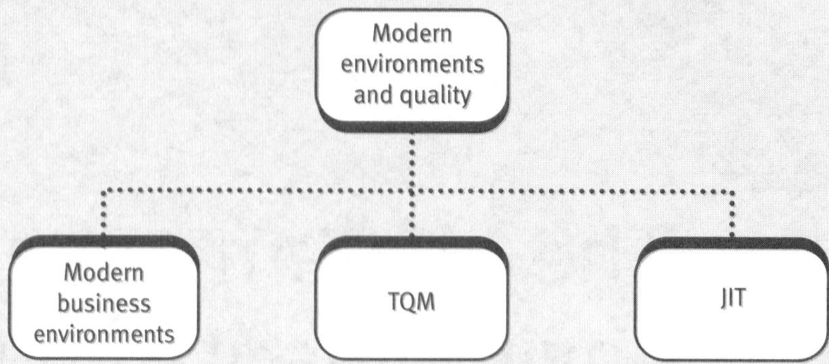

2 Modern business environment for manufacturers

The business environments in which organisations operate today are very different from the ones experienced when traditional costing methods where created. Environments change more quickly and more unpredictably. Rivals create products much more quickly and the ability to react to this as well as changes in buyer needs have become critical success factors.

Manufacturers have therefore had to constantly review and redesign existing products, and to shorten the time to market of each new line in order to ensure satisfactory returns from it. They are also **making customer satisfaction an overriding priority** – and this often requires a greater focus on quality of the product rather than the cost of production.

Many organisations that have successfully developed the ability to adapt to changing business environments are known as world class manufacturers.

The growth of world class manufacturers

'To compete successfully in today's highly competitive global environment companies are making customer satisfaction an overriding priority, adopting new management approaches, changing their manufacturing systems and investing in new technologies. These changes are having a significant influence on management accounting systems.

'Colin Drury in 'Management and Cost Accounting'.

Cost is an important competitive weapon. Low-cost producers will have an advantage in the marketplace over those whose cost base is higher. However, cost is only one competitive weapon and it is one that has become of declining importance in recent years. Other dimensions of competition have become increasingly important: product reliability, product innovation, shortened time to market, and flexibility of response to customer demands – these last three being features of time-based competition.

It is obvious that a manufacturer would gain competitive advantage if it were able to produce the diversity of output seen in a jobbing system (where each product is almost unique) at a cost associated with mass production (so that economies of scale make the cost per unit much smaller). In recent years, some manufacturers, most notably the Japanese, have been successful in moving towards this. Furthermore, the products of these manufacturers have an enviable reputation for reliability. These suppliers have clearly gained competitive advantage in the marketplace, forcing competitors to follow or exit the market. Consumers, given the opportunity to enjoy diversity and reliability at a mass-produced cost, have reacted not unexpectedly by requiring all manufacturers to offer these features. Further, a corollary of the requirement for greater diversity has been a shortening of product life cycles.

This fundamental shift in demand patterns dictates a need for companies to constantly review and redesign existing products, and to shorten the time to market of each new line in order to ensure satisfactory returns from it. Against this new background, companies will find it increasingly difficult to gain economic returns from an expensive, dedicated mass-production line operated in traditional way. Means must be found whereby manufacturing facilities cannot only accommodate the production of existing lines and their inevitable redesigned successors, but also facilitate the rapid introduction of new products at minimum cost. The challenge of the modern, globally competitive market is to offer an increased and increasing choice of high-quality products at a cost traditionally associated with mass production; to enjoy economies of scale, along with the economies of scope that result from the increased manufacturing flexibility. This challenge can be met by investment in new technology, and the adoption of alternative production management strategies. Those who successfully meet this challenge are the 'world-class manufacturers' that provide the benchmark against which other manufacturers are measured.

'World class' organisations make products using the latest manufacturing technologies and techniques. Those products are typically sold around the world and are generally viewed as being first rate in terms of quality, design, performance and reliability. Companies such as Toyota, BMW and Boeing have been described at various times as being world-class manufacturers. The world-class manufacturer will probably invest heavily in research, product design, CAD/CAM technology. It will also make extensive use of modern management concepts such as Total quality management (TQM), flexible manufacturing systems and customer relationship management. These concepts variously known as advanced manufacturing technologies (AMTs) or the new manufacturing are discussed in detail below.

Characteristics of the modern manufacturing environment

For manufacturers to be successful in a modern business environment they often have to change in areas such as:

- greater use of Advanced Manufacturing Technology (**AMT**)
- a much more **global environment**
- a greater focus on **cost reduction**
- better **customer focus**
- a need for more **flexible** production systems
- more **employee participation**
- **shorter product life cycles**
- a greater emphasis on **quality**.

More details

Advanced manufacturing technology (AMT)

AMT is a collective term for a wide variety of modern practices and techniques based on computer systems. For example, computers are used to improve product design, test products, as well as being used in the manufacturing process itself. You do not need to know these in detail for the P1 syllabus, just the effect they have on manufacturers today – for instance, the vast reduction in labour costs.

AMT includes systems such as Just In Time (JIT) for controlling inventories and other resources which is explored in more detail in this chapter.

Global environment

- Companies operate in a world economy
- Customers and competitors come from all over the world
- Products are made from components from around the world
- Firms have to be world class to compete.

Cost reduction

Clearly an important factor to the customer, a key part of World Class Manufacturing can be to be the lowest cost supplier. This means that during a price war the business has the opportunity to quote lower than its competitors, but also more importantly, in less severe circumstances similar pricing to competitors will lead to greater profitability.

Customer focus

In the past the linking of product to consumer was relatively hazy in many instances. A product would be produced within a large production run and then a customer would be 'sold' that unit. As competition increases, customers are demanding ever-improving levels of service in cost, quality, reliability, delivery and the choice of innovative new products. Companies need to be able to react quickly to changes in the environment to survive these days. They must be able to meet these customer requirements.

Flexibility

The move away from standardised units of production towards individual customised units means that mass production techniques are redundant, instead, it is of greatest importance to take an order from placement to completion in the shortest time possible. This means that production processes will be designed differently to accommodate flexibility of production rather than just throughput.

Employee participation

To ensure this flexibility, managers need to empower their employees to make decisions quickly, without reference to more senior managers. By empowering employees and giving them relevant information they will be able to respond faster to customers, increase process flexibility, reduce cycle times and improve morale.

The changes required in the way that the workforce is managed are frequently the most difficult aspects of World Class Manufacturing to implement. The changes often require a considerable amount of time and education so that trust, mutual respect and a common purpose can be established between the company's managers and production personnel. The employees are given a great deal more responsibility for production quality and scheduling. The operators are cross-trained so that they can perform a wide variety of tasks and therefore provide more production flexibility. A team approach is established which is designed to encourage all company employees to work co-operatively, eradicating the traditional job demarcation and incentive pay plans

Management Accounting Systems are moving from **providing information to managers** to monitor employees to **providing information to employees** to empower them to focus on continuous improvement.

Shorter product life cycles

Companies need to be continually developing new products in order to survive.

Quality

The World Class Manufacturing approach to quality is quite different from the traditional approach because the primary emphasis is placed on the resolution of the problems that cause poor quality, rather than merely detecting it. These systems are more proactive and try to prevent problems from occurring in the first place rather than waiting for them to occur and then fixing them.

The system might be developed formally under Total Quality Management.

As a consequence of these changes:

- many companies now have very diverse product ranges, with a high level of tailormade products and services
- product life cycles have dramatically reduced, often from several years to just a few months
- standard costing techniques are becoming less relevant to businesses and new techniques such as throughput accounting are becoming more widespread.

It has also resulted in a much greater emphasis on the management of quality.

Example 1

Choose from the following list the features that would typically distinguish a modern manufacturing environment from traditional production environments:

- short product development times
- high labour costs
- high levels of indirect overheads
- long product life cycles
- small batch production
- reduced focus on quality.

3 Total quality management (TQM)

Total quality management (TQM) is a philosophy of quality management that has a number of important features.

- Total – means that everyone in the value chain is involved in the process, including employees, customers and suppliers.
- Quality – products and services must meet the customers' requirements.
- Management – quality is actively managed rather than controlled so that problems are prevented from occurring.

There are three basic principles of TQM:

(1) 'Get it right, first time'.

(2) Continuous improvement.

(3) Customer focus.

The key impacts of TQM are often that problems are avoided rather than solved, and inventory levels can be greatly reduced.

Further details

There are three basic principles of TQM:

(1) **'Get it right, first time'**

TQM considers that the costs of prevention are less than the costs of correction. One of the main aims of TQM is to achieve *zero* rejects or defects and to ensure that all customer needs or expectations are satisfied.

TQM will often involve the use of Just-In-Time inventory control in order to eliminate any waste in stock. JIT is explored later in this chapter.

(2) **Continuous improvement**

The second basic principle of TQM is dissatisfaction with the status-quo. Realistically a zero-defect goal may not be obtainable. It does however provide a target to ensure that a company should never be satisfied with its present level of rejects. The management and staff should believe that it is always possible to improve and to be able to get it more right next time!

The system is based on a 'kaizen' approach which is a costing technique to reflect continuous efforts to reduce product costs, improve product quality, and/or improve the production process after manufacturing activities have begun.

(3) **Customer focus**

Quality is examined from a customer perspective and the system is aimed at meeting customer needs and expectations.

Commitment to quality

For TQM to bring about improved business efficiency and effectiveness it must be applied throughout the whole organisation. It begins at the top with the managing director, the most senior directors and managers who must demonstrate that they are totally committed to achieving the highest quality standards. The role of middle management is also crucial. They have to understand the importance of TQM and communicate this and their own commitment to quality to the people for whom they are responsible. It is essential that TQM is adopted by all parts of the organisation. Middle management must ensure that the efforts and achievements of their subordinates receive appropriate recognition, attention and reward. This helps secure everyone's full involvement – which is crucial to the successful introduction of TQM.

Quality chains

Throughout and beyond all organisations, whether they are manufacturing concerns, retail stores, universities or hotels, there is a series of quality chains. The ability to meet the customers' requirements is vital, not only between two separate organisations, but within the same organisation. These quality chains may be broken at any point by one person or by one piece of equipment not meeting the requirements of the customer, internal or external.

Quality circles

A quality circle is a team of four to 12 people usually coming from the same area who voluntarily meet on a regular basis to identify, investigate, analyse and solve work-related problems. The team presents its solutions to management and is then involved in implementing and monitoring the effectiveness of the solutions. The voluntary approach and the process by which the team selects and solves its own problems are key features which give the quality circle a special character: a character which is very different to other problem-solving teams. The problems that circles tackle may not be restricted to quality of product or service topics, but may include anything associated with work or its environment. Items such as pay and conditions and other negotiated items are, however, normally excluded.

A contrast to Business Process Re-Engineering

The continuous improvement philosophy contrasts sharply with the concept underlying business process re-engineering (BPR). BPR is concerned with making far-reaching **one-off changes** to improve operations or processes.

A business process consists of a collection of activities that are linked together in a co-ordinated manner to achieve a specific objective. Business process re-engineering involves examining business processes and radically redesigning these processes to achieve cost reduction, improved quality and customer satisfaction. BPR is all about major changes to how business processes operate.

Material handling is an example of a business process and may consist of the following separate activities; material requisitioning, purchase requisitioning, processing purchase orders, inspecting materials, storing materials and paying suppliers. This process could be re-engineered by sending the material requisitions directly to an approved supplier and entering into an agreement which entails delivering high quality material in accordance with the production requirements. This change in business process could result in cost reduction by the elimination of; the administration involved in placing orders, the need for material inspection and storage. By re-engineering the material handling business process the company will reduce costs without compromising the quality of the products delivered to customers.

The costs of quality

A quality-related cost is the 'cost of ensuring and assuring quality, as well as the cost incurred when quality is not achieved. Quality costs are classified as prevention costs, appraisal cost, internal failure cost and external failure cost' (BS6143).

Organisations have realised that **there is a high cost of poor quality**. Studies have shown that failing to satisfy customers' needs and expectations, or failing to get it right first time, costs the average company between 15 and 30 per cent of sales revenue.

Conformance and non-conformance costs

Quality costs are divided into compliance costs (or 'conformance costs') and costs of failure to comply ('non-conformance costs').

Conformance costs are further divided into prevention costs (incurred in preventing mistakes from happening) and appraisal costs (incurred in looking for mistakes before a product is manufactured).

Non-conformance costs are divided into 'internal failure' costs, that occur when the units produced fail to reach the set standard; and 'external failure' costs – these arise when the faulty product is not detected until after it reaches the customer.

Quality related costs

(1) **Prevention cost**

Prevention costs represent the cost of any action taken to prevent or reduce defects and failures. It includes the design and development of quality control equipment and the maintenance of the equipment.

(2) **Appraisal costs**

Appraisal costs are the costs incurred, such as inspection and testing, in initially ascertaining the conformance of the product to quality requirements. They include the costs of goods inwards inspection, and the monitoring of the production output.

(3) **Internal failure cost**

Internal failure costs are the costs arising from inadequate quality where the problem is discovered before the transfer of ownership from supplier to purchaser. They include the cost of reworking or rectifying the product, the net cost of scrap, downtime of machinery due to quality problems, etc.

(4) **External failure cost**

The cost arising from inadequate quality discovered after the transfer of ownership from supplier to purchaser such as complaints, warranty claims, recall cost, costs of repairing or replacing returned faulty goods, etc.

It is generally accepted that an increased investment in prevention and appraisal is likely to result in a significant reduction in failure costs. As a result of the trade-off, there may be an optimum operating level in which the combined costs are at a minimum. In short, an investment in "prevention" inevitably results in a saving on total quality costs.

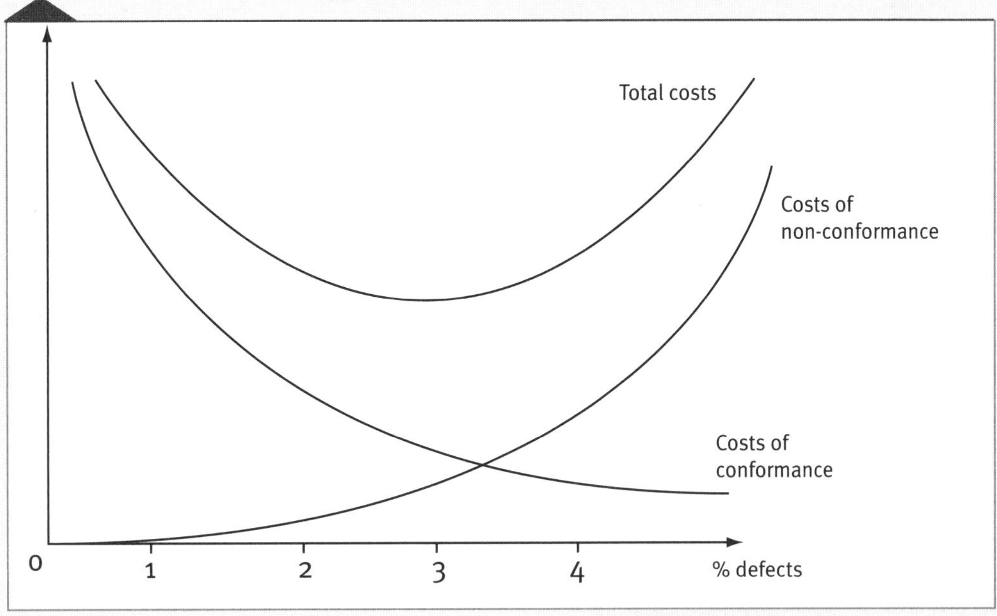

Quality costs

Examples of quality costs:

Prevention costs	**Internal failure costs**
(1) Routine preventive repairs and maintenance to equipment (2) Quality training for operatives to improve skills and efficiency. Training employees works, provided the employee also understand and accept the benefits of such training. Training can occur both inside and outside the workplace. Internal training may include the ideas of team working and quality discussion groups, which are known as quality circles	(1) Costs of scrap (2) Reworking costs (3) Manufacturing and process engineering required to correct the failed process (4) Machine and labour downtime. **Note:** It is the aim of total quality management (TQM) programmes to completely eliminate these internal failure costs by working towards a goal of zero defects. It is contended that, in many companies, the costs of internal failure are so great that a total quality programme can be financed entirely from the savings that are made from it – hence we sometimes see the expression 'quality is free'.

(3) Building of quality into the design and manufacturing processes. When a product is designed, its specification should consider factors that will minimise future rectification costs. Production methods should be as simple as possible and use the skills and resources existing within the sphere of knowledge of the organisation and its employees (4) Determining whether quality factors have been correctly engineered into the design of products may only be apparent when costs are reported on a 'life cycle' basis. Effective performance management involves monitoring costs and results over the whole life cycle of a product. Just considering production costs over a one-month period (in the form of traditional standard costing and variance analysis which we will look at later) may be of marginal relevance.	
Appraisal costs	**External failure costs**
(1) Cost of incoming inspections (note that if suppliers adopt a total quality approach, the cost of incoming inspections can be eliminated) (2) Cost of set-up inspections (3) Cost of acquiring and operating the process control and measuring equipment.	(1) Marketing costs associated with failed products and loss of customer goodwill (2) Manufacturing or process engineering costs relating to failed products (3) Compensation/replacement for units returned by customers (4) Repair costs (5) Travel costs to visit sites with faulty products (6) Liability claims.

TQM and EMA

Organisations should be striving to achieve an integrated environmental strategy underpinned by the same type of culture that is required for the successful operation of a programme of total quality management (TQM).

It is arguable that the two are inextricably linked insofar as good environmental management is increasingly recognised as an essential component of TQM. The focus is upon 'continuous improvement' and the pursuit of excellence. Such organisations pursue objectives that may include zero complaints, zero spills, zero pollution, zero waste and zero accidents. Information systems need to be able to support such environmental objectives via the provision of feedback – on the success or otherwise – of the organisational efforts in achieving such objectives. In this respect, the organisation becomes self-regulating and the undertaking of environmental audits on a regular basis provides the platform for organisations to adopt a self-critical and analytical posture as part of their routine organisational management processes.

This approach to environmental quality management requires the development of environmental performance measures and indicators that will enable a comprehensive review of environmental performance to be undertaken. Many – if not all – total quality management accounting techniques can be modified and used in environmental management accounting (EMA).

TQM and standard costing

TQM is often seen as being at odds with traditional standard costing methods for the following reasons:

- TQM expects continuous improvement rather than standard performance.
- TQM expects everyone to take responsibility for failures in the system.
- TQM systems do not accept waste as being acceptable.
- TQM is concerned with quality related costs rather than production costs.
- TQM often incorporates JIT inventory control (explained later) so that material variances are less likely.

More details

TQM is often seen as being at odds with traditional standard costing methods for the following reasons:

- In the pursuit of continuous improvement, standard costs become out of date and irrelevant. In TQM environments managers are expected to find better ways to perform tasks, eliminate waste etc. The business itself is likely to be operating in a changing environment and therefore the idea of a 'standard' or repetitive cost is unlikely.
- Standard costing techniques attempt to allocate responsibility for each cost to an individual manager. With TQM There is an expectation that everyone takes responsibility for failures in the system.
- Traditional standard costing techniques allow for elements of waste and scrap in product costs. The cost of materials in the standard cost card, for example, will be altered if some materials experience 'normal' wastage levels. TQM systems accept no waste as being acceptable.
- TQM is concerned with quality related costs rather than financial costs solely concerned with cost control and efficiency. For example, traditional costing might be concerned with how quickly a product is produced (e.g. the labour efficiency variance, whereas TQM would be most interested in how well it has been produced (e.g. whether there has been a significant number of returns from customers – known as external failure costs).
- TQM often incorporates JIT inventory control (explained later) so that material variances are less likely and less significant. Close relationships with suppliers mean that material price variances are unlikely and a focus on quality means that adverse materials usage variances become less likely.

As a result, in TQM environments, benchmarking is preferred to standard costing as a performance measurement technique because TQM emphasises continuous improvement and reference to a predetermined internal standard gives no incentive to improve. Benchmarking involves making comparisons to best practices (either internally or externally) rather than comparing to pre-set standards.

Benchmarking is explored in more detail in CIMA Paper P2.

Successful implementation of TQM

An organisation should undertake to achieve each of the following to ensure TQM is successful:

- Total commitment throughout the organisation.
- Get close to their customers to fully understand their needs and expectations.
- Plan to do all jobs right first time.
- Agree expected performance standards with each employee and customer.
- Implement a company-wide improvement process.
- Continually measure performance levels achieved.
- Measure the cost of quality mismanagement and the level of firefighting.
- Demand continuous improvement in everything you and your employees do.
- Recognise achievements.
- Make quality a way of life.

Impact on the organisation's management information

Management accounting systems can help organisations achieve their quality goals by providing a variety of reports and measures that motivate and evaluate managerial efforts to improve quality – including financial and non-financial measures.

Traditionally, the management accounting systems focused on output, not quality. The management information focused on information such as how much extra was paid for materials or how many units were produced when compared to the budget.

Under TQM financial measures focus more on quality and will include reports such as the:

- cost of downtimes
- cost of job reworks
- lost revenue from customer returns
- training costs as a percentage of revenue.

Non-financial measures

Under TQM non-financial measures are also generated by the management information system in order to further assess the impact of quality improvement programmes and the impact on quality costs. These include reports on areas such as:

- Number of defects at inspection expressed as a percentage of the number of units completed.
- Number of reworked units expressed as a percentage of total sales value.
- Number of defective units delivered to customers as a percentage of total units delivered.
- Number of customer complaints.
- Number of defectives supplied by suppliers.
- Time taken to respond to customer requests.

Quality reports

These measures will be reported regularly (often weekly or monthly). The key focus will be on keeping track of incurred quality costs and matching these up to cost of quality reductions.

Example 2

E plc provides a computer upgrading, servicing and repair facility to a variety of business and personal computer users.

An issue which concerns the management of E plc is the quality of the service provided for clients. The Operations Manager has suggested that the company should introduce Total Quality Management (TQM) but the management team is unsure how to do this and of the likely costs and benefits of its introduction.

Required:

(a) Explain Total Quality Management in the context of E plc.

(b) Describe the likely costs and benefits that would arise if E plc introduced a TQM policy.

4 Just In Time

Just-in-time (JIT) is a method of inventory control based on two principles

- goods and services should be **produced only when they are needed**.
- products (or services) must be **delivered to the customer at the time the customer wants them** ('just in time').

This in turn requires that suppliers deliver raw materials to production just as they are needed so that **purchasing happens just-in-time for production**.

JIT is often a crucial element of TQM. JIT sees inventory as waste and a cost burden, and, in its extreme form, a JIT system seeks to have **zero inventories**.

Further details

Just-in-time (JIT) is an approach to operations management based on the idea that goods and services should be **produced only when they are needed**.

At the same time, products (or services) must be **delivered to the customer at the time the customer wants them** ('just in time'). To be able to do this with no inventory, the production cycle must be short, and there can be no hold-ups in production due to defective items, bottlenecks or inefficiency.

JIT sees inventory as a cost burden and in its extreme form, a JIT system seeks to have **zero inventories**. When there are no inventories of raw materials, part-finished work-in-progress or finished goods, a break-down or disruption in one stage of the production chain will have an immediate impact on all the other stages of the chain. In practice, it might be impossible to have no inventory at all, but management should be trying continually to reduce and minimise inventory levels.

This is expanded to the **purchasing system** to ensure that receipt and usage of materials, to the maximum extent possible, coincide.

- JIT can be described as a 'pull through' system. This is a system that responds to customer demand: components are drawn through the system as required, so that items are manufactured only when ordered by a customer. Similarly, raw materials are obtained from suppliers only when they are needed for production.
- This contrasts with a 'push' system, in which items are produced, and if there is no immediate demand, inventories build up.

Another aspect of the JIT philosophy is **high quality**, and JIT is consistent with Total Quality Management.

The JIT philosophy is based on:

- continuous improvement ('kaizen') – doing things well and gradually doing them better, and
- the elimination of waste.

Examples of waste

Waste is defined as any activity that does not add value. Examples of waste are:

- **Overproduction**. Producing more than is needed immediately creates unnecessary inventory.
- **Waiting time**. Waiting time is evidence of a hold-up in the flow of production through the system. Set-up time is also non-productive time. ('Set-up' is the work needed at the end of one job or batch of work to get the production process ready for the next job or batch.) The aim is to achieve quick set-up times and low-cost set-up.
- **Unnecessary movement** of materials or people. Moving items around a production area does not add value.
- **Waste in the process**, caused by design defects in the product, or poor maintenance work. Work flow is an important element in JIT. Work needs to flow without interruption in order to avoid a build-up of inventory or unnecessary waiting times. The movement of materials and part-finished work is wasteful, and this waste can be reduced by laying out the work floor and designing the work flow so as to minimise movements. JIT production is associated with the use of work cells: a work cell is a small area on the factory floor that is given responsibility for the production of an entire product or part. The employees in the work cell do all the work on the product from the beginning to the end of the process, and so the work cell manager or supervisor is entirely responsible for the work flow and the product quality.
- **Inventory** is wasteful. The target should be to eliminate all inventory by removing the reasons why it builds up.

- **Complexity in work processes**. Simplification of work gets rid of waste in the system (the 'waste of motion') by eliminating unnecessary actions.
- **Defective goods** are a significant cause of waste in many operations.
- **Inspection time** is wasteful because it adds nothing to value. Inspection time can be eliminated by making the process free from errors and defects.

Pre-requisites for JIT

The operational requirements for the successful implementation of JIT production are as follows:

- **High quality.** Without high quality there will be disruptions in production, reducing throughput. Production must be reliable and not subject to hold-ups.
- **Speed.** Throughput in the operation must be fast, so that customer orders can be met by production. Without fast throughput, it will be necessary to hold some inventory to meet customer orders.
- **Flexibility.** The production system must be able to respond immediately to customer orders. Production must therefore be flexible, and in small batch sizes. The ideal batch size is 1.
- **Lower costs.** Fewer errors, less waste, greater reliability and flexibility and faster throughput should all help to reduce costs.

The most suitable conditions for applying JIT management are where:

- there are short set-up times and low set-up costs
- there are short lead times and low ordering costs for buying raw materials from suppliers
- work flow is fairly constant over time, and customer demand is not uneven and unpredictable
- production throughput time is very short
- there are no downtimes due to poor quality or stock-outs.

Just In Time in practice

Organisations in the West have traditionally used a 'push' production flow system. This system has the following stages:

(1) Buy raw materials and put them into inventory.

(2) Produce a production schedule based on sales forecasts.

(3) Withdraw goods from inventory and make products according to the production schedule.

(4) Put completed units into finished goods store.

(5) Sell from finished goods store when customers request products.

Work in progress (WIP) is an unavoidable feature of such a system.

Toyota developed a different system known as JIT. This system is not a 'push' system but a 'pull' system. A product is not 'made' until the customer requests it, and components are not made until they are required by the next production stage. In a full JIT system virtually no inventory is held, that is no raw material inventory and no finished goods inventory is held, but there will be a small amount of WIP, say one-tenth of a day's production. The system works by the customer triggering the final stage of production, the assembly. As the product is assembled, components are used and this in turn triggers the component stage of production and a small amount of WIP is made ready for the next product. So the cycle goes on until the final trigger requests more raw material from the supplier.

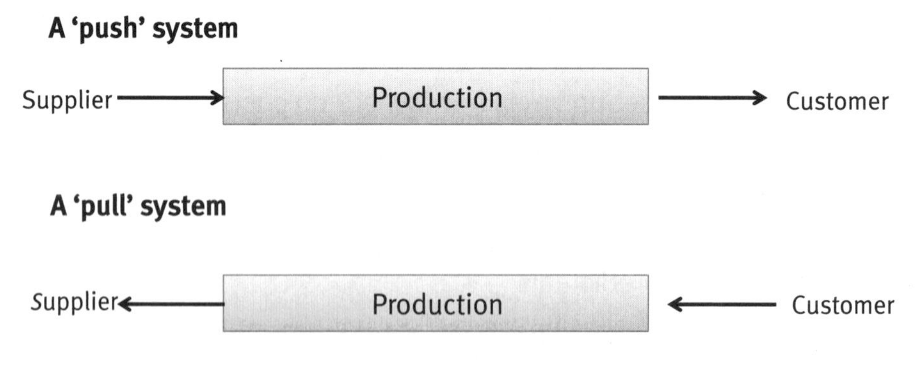

If a JIT system is to work satisfactorily, suppliers must deliver several times a day and so when the raw material arrives it may go straight into the factory and be used immediately. This means that the production lead time (i.e. the time from raw materials entering production to the finished goods emerging) should equal the processing time. In many Western organisations in the past it took several months to make a product from start to finish, despite the fact that if worked on continuously it could be made in, say, two days. The difference in time is largely due to WIP waiting to be used in the next process. It will be apparent that value is only added to the product during the actual processing stages. These have been estimated to represent as little as 10 per cent of the total manufacturing lead time in many companies, and thus up to 90 per cent of production time adds costs but no value.

JIT requires the following:

(1) The **labour force must be versatile** so that they can perform any job within reason to keep production flowing as required. Workers in a JIT cell are trained to operate all the machines within it, and perform routine preventive maintenance on them.

(2) Production processes must be **grouped by product line** rather than by function in order to eliminate inventory movements between workstations and to speed flow.

(3) A simple, **infallible information system**. Originally the Japanese used a system based on cards which were called *kanbans*. There would be a small container of components (WIP) between each workstation with a kanban resting on top. When the container was taken for use by the following workstation the card would be taken off and left behind. This would act as a trigger for the previous workstation to produce another container of that component. Nowadays computer systems are likely to be used instead of cards but the basic simplicity of the system should not change.

(4) A **'get it right first time'** approach and an aim of **'zero defects'**. Defects cause breakdowns in the value chain: they stop the flow of production, create expensive rework and lead to late deliveries to customers.

(5) **Strong supplier relationships**. Suppliers must take responsibility for the quality of their goods; the onus is on the supplier to inspect the parts or materials before delivery and guarantee their quality. The not inconsiderable savings in inspection costs go happily with the benefits of increased quality to achieve cost reduction – another facet of continuous improvement. This enhanced level of service is obtained by reducing the number of suppliers and increasing the business given to each of them. Longer-term commitments are entered into, assuring the supplier of continuity of demand, and enabling the supplier to plan to meet customers' production schedules. In essence the supplier becomes a key part of the value chain.

An important consequence of the 'pull' system, is that problems in any part of the system will immediately halt the production line, as earlier workstations will not receive the 'pull' signal and later stations will not have their own 'pull' signals answered. This has the powerful effect of concentrating all minds on finding a long-term solution to the problem. JIT exposes problems within a plant, and forces management to address problems and rectify them, rather than simply burying them by holding excess inventory.

The aims of JIT are to produce the required items, at the required quality and in the required quantities, at the precise time they are required.

The impact of JIT on the accounting system

Implementing JIT will impact on the accountant in terms of what information is gathered, the nature of that information, the use of that information and how new information will be reported. Examples of the changes that are likely to be experienced in the accounting system are:

- simplified inventory records
- a change in the nature of costs
- a change in the asset base
- absorption and marginal costing will have fewer differences
- some disadvantages of absorption costing will disappear
- new information will have to be gathered
- recording more frequent supplier deliveries
- recording the cost of increased preventative maintenance
- performance will be measured in new ways.

Further details

The implementation of JIT will have a number of impacts on the accounting and performance management systems of an organisation:

- Inventory record keeping will be simplified. There will be no need for inventory counts and the accounting entries for recording inventory movements will be much less complex.
- JIT promotes quality and therefore quality costs will be impacted. For example, there should be lower internal failure costs from wastage or obsoletion. Though there is likely to be an increase in prevention costs. The overhead structure is likely to change with a greater focus on quality and improvements and a lower emphasis on inventory management. In an ABC system this might see further improvements in cost control and pricing.

- As inventory levels are virtually non-existent, there will be lower current assets held. This could adversely affect some commonly used measures of liquidity but the inventory should have been turned into cash and therefore overall liquidity should not be affected.
- Marginal and absorption costing profits will be the same. It has been illustrated earlier that absorption costing profit differs from marginal costing profit due to the fixed overheads carried forward in inventories. If there are no inventories then this issue does not arise and the marginal profits will not need to be reconciled to absorption costing profits.
- This in turn can remove some of the disadvantages associated with absorption costing. In an earlier chapter it was explained that absorption costing can encourage managers to over-produce as this is a way of boosting profits and the associated measures of performance. This will no longer be possible and over-production will not be accepted within a JIT system.
- New productivity measures may be required to reflect the change in the nature of production. For example, there may be a greater focus on measuring scrap reduction or number of reworks. Quality measures will become more important.
- Suppliers will deliver in smaller quantities and deliver more often. Not only will more administration and costs be incurred in checking and monitoring these deliveries, but the accounting system will have to be adjusted in order to achieve the efficiency required in recording these deliveries in the accounting system. Many organisations will aim to use information technology systems such as automated purchase order checking systems in order to ease the burden on the accounting system.
- There will also be a requirement to record and monitor the cost of preventative maintenance. The accountant will need to track outstanding and completed work type, description, times and costs. These will need to be compared to budgets and targets (which are likely to aim for a continuous reduction in time and costs over time). Again, many organisations will turn to computerised maintenance management systems (CMMS) to track and record their maintenance activities.
- Many performance and control measures will have to be adjusted. Purchase costs will change, manufacturing costs will change, and sales may become more variable. This is likely to affect budgets for purchasing, production and sales. Managers who are appraised against these budgets are likely to require different performance measures and possibly even a new rewards system to be implemented.

Other performance measures will be impacted by the change in the nature of the operations. For example, there will be less storage space required for inventory so measures of capita l employed will alter. The measures themselves may continue to be useful, but targets for these measures will be very different.

There will also be a greater focus on non-financial performance measures. Areas such as the average production time, the set-up time for machines, changes in the percentage of reworks, average delivery times etc. will also become more important and require closer monitoring. For example, the purchasing department (which may have previously been assessed solely on the basis of its control of purchasing costs) might now need to be assessed in terms of whether deliveries are on time and whether materials are of the requisite quality.

Benefits and problems of JIT

Benefits	Problems
• less cash tied up in inventory • less storage space needed • better quality • more flexible production • fewer bottlenecks • better co-ordination • more reliable and supportive suppliers	• relies on predictable demand, flexible supplier and a flexible workforce • there will be initial set-up costs • for businesses with a wide geographical spread • there is no fallback position if disruptions occur in the supply chain • it may be harder to switch suppliers

More details

Successful adopters of JIT production have enjoyed tremendous savings. The most obvious saving arises from the much lower investment required to hold inventory. When inventory levels are reduced from three months to one month of sales (increasing the inventory turnover from 4 times to 12 times) financing costs are reduced by two thirds. In fact, inventory turnover can be increased to 30 or 60 once production problems, made visible by inventory reductions are solved.

Beyond these obvious financing savings, companies also discovered large space savings. They found that up to 50% of factory space had previously been used to store in process inventory. Having eliminated WIP, companies found another factory inside their old factory. Such savings permitted planned expansions to be curtailed, and previously dispersed operations could be consolidated inside a single location.

But even the carrying cost and floor space savings were smaller than the savings from improved JIT operations as companies attempted to reduce inventories, many problems emerged in the factory that had formerly been hidden by inventory buffers: quality problems, bottlenecks, coordination problems, inadequate documentation, and supplier unreliability, among others. Without the discipline to achieve JIT operations, these problems would remain unsolved. The rationalisation of production processes, the elimination of waste, and the more visible display of production problems that were achieved under successful JIT operations led to great reductions in material losses and great improvement in overall factory productivity.

Example 3

The adoption of **JIT** normally requires which one of the following factors to increase?

A Inventory levels

B Work-in-progress levels

C Batch sizes

D Quality standards

5 Chapter summary

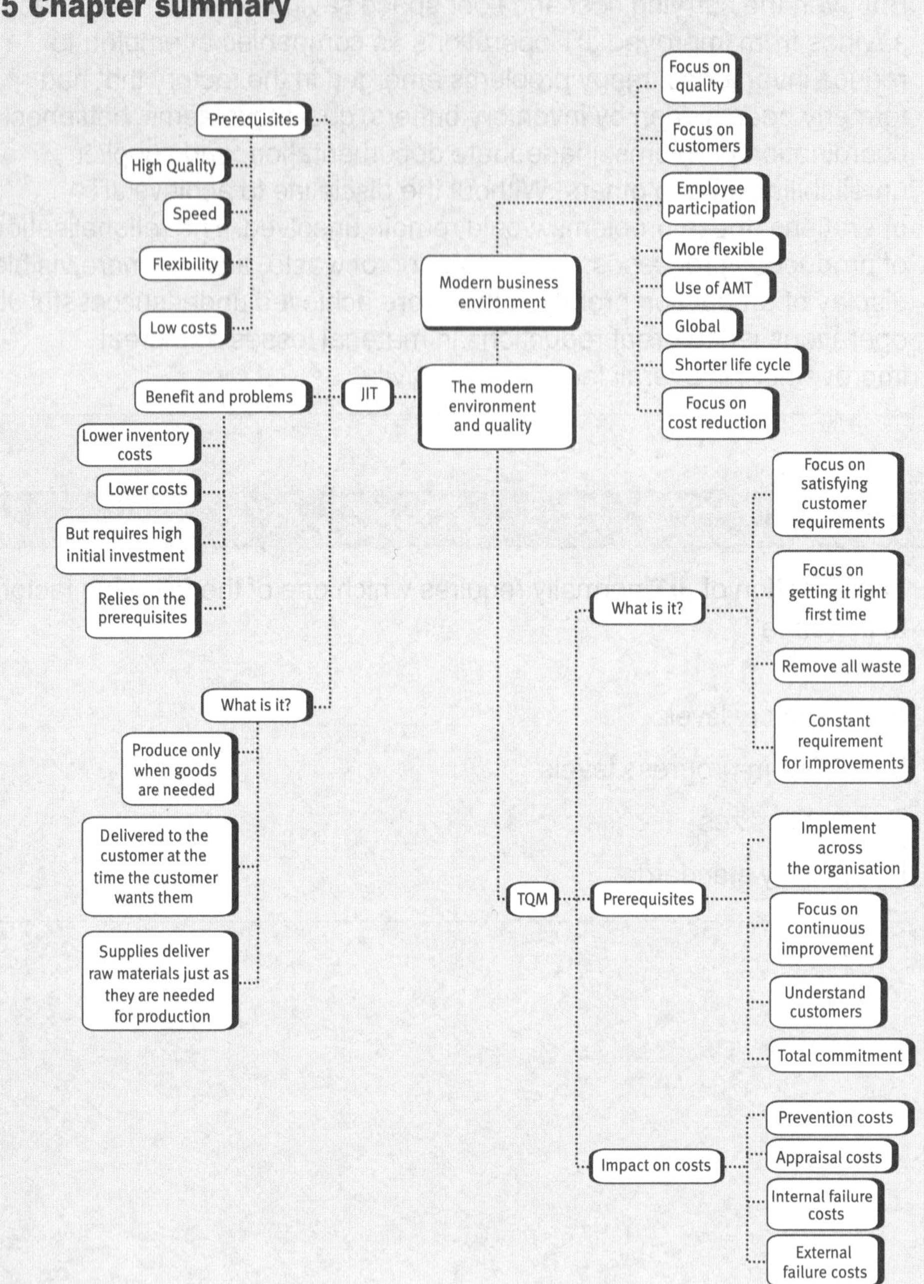

6 Practice Questions

Test your understanding 1

In a TQM environment, external benchmarking is preferred to standard costing as a performance measurement technique because:

A Standard costs quickly become obsolete

B TQM emphasises continuous improvement and reference to a pre-determined internal standard gives no incentive to improve

C TQM places an emphasis on employee empowerment, and the concept of a standard cost is alien to this

D The use of standard costs is only possible in a traditional mass-production industry

Test your understanding 2

Match the cost to the correct cost category:

Costs

(a) Reliability Studies

(b) Returned Material processing and repair

(c) Quality audits

(d) Quality Control investigations of failures

Cost categories

- Prevention costs
- Appraisal costs
- Internal failure costs
- External failure costs

Test your understanding 3

Scenario

A company experiences changing levels of demand, but produces a constant number of units during each quarter. The company allows inventory levels to rise and fall to satisfy the differing quarterly demand levels for its product.

Tasks:

(a) Identify and explain the reasons for three cost changes that would result if the company changed to a Just-In-Time production method. Assume there will be no inventory at the start and end of the year.

(b) Briefly discuss the importance of Total Quality Management to a company that operates a Just-In-Time production method.

(Time allowed: 20 minutes)

Test your understanding 4

Scenario

X manufactures and distributes three types of car (the C1, C2 and C3). Each type of car has its own production line. The company is worried by extremely difficult market conditions and forecasts losses for the forthcoming year.

Current operations

The budgeted details for next year are as follows:

	C1	**C2**	**C3**
	$	$	$
Direct materials	2,520	2,924	3,960
Direct labour	1,120	1,292	1,980
Total direct cost per car	3,640	4,216	5,940
Budgeted production (cars)	75,000	75,000	75,000
Number of production runs	1,000	1,000	1,500
Number of orders executed	4,000	5,000	5,600
Machine hours	1,080,000	1,800,000	1,680,000

Annual overheads

	Fixed	Variable
	$000	$
Set-ups	42,660	13,000 per production run
Materials handling	52,890	4,000 per order executed
Inspection	59,880	18,000 per production run
Machining	144,540	40 per machine hour
Distribution and warehousing	42,900	3,000 per order executed

Proposed JIT system

Management has hired a consultant to advise them on how to reduce costs. The consultant has suggested that the company adopts a just-in-time (JIT) manufacturing system. The introduction of the JIT system would have the following impact on costs (fixed and variable):

Direct labour	Increase by 20%
Set-ups	Decrease by 30%
Materials handling	Decrease by 30%
Inspection	Decrease by 30%
Machining	Decrease by 15%
Distribution and warehousing	Eliminated

Tasks:

(a) Based on the budgeted production levels, calculate the total annual savings that would be achieved by introducing the JIT system.

(b) Write a report to the management of X which explains the conditions that are necessary for the successful implementation of a JIT manufacturing system.

(Time allowed: 30 minutes)

Test your understanding 5

Scenario

SG is a long-established food manufacturer which produces semi-processed foods for fast food outlets. While for a number of years it has recognised the need to produce good quality products for its customers, it does not have a formalised quality management programme.

A director of the company has recently returned from a conference, where one of the speakers introduced the concept of Total Quality Management (TQM) and the need to recognise and classify quality costs.

Tasks:

(a) Explain what is meant by TQM and use examples to show how it may be introduced into different areas of SG's food production business.

(Time allowed: 10 minutes))

(b) Explain why the adoption of TQM is particularly important within a Just-in-Time (JIT) production environment.

(Time allowed: 5 minutes))

(c) Explain four quality cost classifications, using examples relevant to the business of SG.

(Time allowed: 15 minutes)

Test your understanding 6

Explain how quality cost can be measured in a programme of Total Quality Management (TQM).

(Time allowed: 10 minutes)

Test your understanding answers

Example 1

Typical characteristics of a modern manufacturing environment are:

- short product development times – in order to react quicker to changing market needs
- high levels of indirect overheads – for example, in terms of running costs for AMT
- small batch production – in order to provide better flexibility.

A traditional manufacturing environment would typically have:

- higher labour costs – as fewer computerised systems were used
- longer product life cycles – as markets were more static and predictable.

Quality is important in both the modern and the traditional environments, although it could be argued that there is a greater focus in modern environments.

Example 2

(a) Total quality management (TQM) has two main concepts:

(1) **Get it right first time**

TQM considers that the costs of prevention are less than the costs of correction. One of the main aims of TQM is to achieve *zero* rejects or defects and to ensure that all customer needs or expectations are satisfied.

(2) **Continuous improvement**

The second basic principle of TQM is dissatisfaction with the status quo. Realistically a zero-defect goal may not be obtainable. It does however provide a target to ensure that a company should never be satisfied with its present level of rejects. The management and staff should believe that it is always possible to improve and to be able to get it more right next time!

There must be a focus on the customer and what they require and there must be a constant review of costs and performance to ensure that the aims of the TQM programme are being met.

The aim is to build good quality in rather than inspect poor quality out. The aim in the end is to design such good products and processes and obtain such good materials that inspection is no longer necessary.

E plc should focus on the whole of its operation from start to finish if it wishes the TQM programme to be a success.

It must ensure that the input to its processes is defect-free. It must choose first-class suppliers who will guarantee the quality of their components. It must communicate with the suppliers to let them know what is expected of them. E plc is likely to have to pay a premium price to obtain these premium quality components.

It must also examine its own processes to ensure that there are as few quality problems as possible. Where there are known quality problems efforts should be directed at improving the processes by whatever means are appropriate, e.g. training, preventative maintenance, newer more reliable machines, etc.

The output process must also be controlled, i.e. the relationship with the customer. Efforts must be made to ensure that no defective products reach the customer, perhaps by means of final inspection before the goods leave the business and that where problems do occur, they are corrected as soon as possible. Communication with the customer is very important to ensure that the customer's needs are being met.

It is not enough to decide that a TQM system should be introduced. The programme should be carefully considered and communication to the staff should be clear. They should be educated as to the ideas behind TQM and given the necessary training to accomplish its aims. TQM should permeate the whole of the organisation and must be continually assessed to ensure that its goals are still being achieved.

(b) The likely costs that would arise include:

(1) **Extra prevention cost**

These are any costs incurred in order to prevent quality problems from occurring. Examples would include training, preventative maintenance, the purchase or hire of new, more reliable machines, the sourcing of better quality components, etc.

(2) **Extra appraisal costs**

Appraisal costs are the costs incurred in checking the raw materials and the product against the quality standard. These would include the wages and salaries of the quality control staff and any capital expenditure on testing equipment.

We would expect appraisal costs to increase at first when a TQM programme is introduced but then decline as quality is 'built in' rather than inspected out.

The likely benefits for E plc would be:

(1) A reduction in internal failure costs. Internal failure costs are the costs incurred as a result of quality problems where the problem is discovered before the product leaves the business, e.g. less mistakes when upgrading, servicing or repairing which then have to be corrected involving more labour and possibly more components.

(2) A reduction in external failure costs. External failure costs are the costs incurred as a result of quality problems where the problem is only discovered after the product leaves the business, e.g. loss of customer through delivering poor quality work, the material cost and labour cost of repairing poor quality which has been returned by the customer.

(3) An improvement in the company's reputation as a result of its good quality work.

Example 3

Answer D. An increase in quality standards is one of the key factors that allows the other items listed to be reduced.

Test your understanding 1

B

External benchmarking is preferred to standard costing as a performance measurement technique because TQM emphasises continuous improvement and reference to a pre-determined internal standard gives no incentive to improve.

Test your understanding 2

(a) Prevention costs

(b) External failure costs

(c) Appraisal costs

(d) Internal failure costs

Test your understanding 3

(a) The introduction of Just-In-Time production methods would output items as and when needed, and not build up inventories in period of low demand. Because of the absence of inventories, the company can expect the following changes:

(i) A decrease in inventory-related costs such as warehousing costs and holding costs.

(ii) An increase in ordering costs; smaller orders will be placed more frequently to match production requirements exactly and avoid the build-up of inventory.

(iii) However, because of the need to work overtime to meet fluctuating levels of demand, the company can expect an increase in labour and overhead costs.

(b) In a company operating on JIT principles, the absence of inventories deprives production of a safety net or 'buffer stock'. This exposes the business to production problems or delays and, ultimately, to lost sales and damaged customer goodwill.

In this context, the adoption of a TQM philosophy is key. In this, quality is a feature rooted in the production process and every individual is responsible for the quality of his/her output.

This will encourage good quality at all times and therefore minimise production problems that would otherwise occur due to poor quality.

Test your understanding 4

(a) **Original budget**

	Calculations	Costs for existing system	Impact of JIT	Costs in JIT system
	$000	$000		$000
Set-ups	42,660			
£13,000 × 3,500	45,500	88,160	–30%	61,712
Materials handling	52,890			
£4,000 × 14,600	58,400	111,290	–30%	77,903
Inspection	59,880			
£18,000 × 3,500	63,000	122,880	–30%	86,016
Machining	144,540			
£40 × 4,560,000	182,400	326,940	–15%	277,899
Distribution & warehousing	42,900			
£3,000 × 14,600	43,800	86,700		–
		735,970		503,530

Direct material			
($2,520 × 75,000) + ($2,924 × 75,000) ($3,960 × 75,000) + [189,000 + 219,300 + 297,000]	705,300		705,300
Direct labour			
($1,120 × 75,000) + ($1,292 × 75,000) ($1,980 × 75,000) + [84,000 + 96,900 + 148,500]	329,400	+20%	395,280
Total costs	$1,770,670		$1,604,110
Savings made in a JIT system		$166,560	

(b)

To: Management of X

From: Management Accountant

Date: Today

Subject: Successful implementation of JIT

Introduction

The following report explains some of the conditions that are necessary for the successful implementation of a JIT manufacturing system within X.

These conditions will include:

Supplier relationships

JIT systems require a huge reduction in inventory levels. In order to facilitate this, inventory order sizes must be small. Hence suppliers must be capable of AND willing to deliver small quantities on a regular basis. X will need to have a good relationship with its accredited suppliers.

JIT systems aim to eliminate raw material inventories. In order to do this suppliers must be capable of achieving all aspects of quality – delivering the correct quantity to the correct location at the correct time. Ideally suppliers should also deliver defect-free items.

Quality issues

For JIT to be effective achieving the highest possible levels of quality is essential. Production scheduling becomes demand-based and in order to meet customers' requirements quality problems need to be eliminated. It is often necessary to implement a quality programme such as Total Quality Management. The aim is to prevent the problems in the first place.

Quality should be considered from several angles:

- From suppliers – as mentioned above.
- In machinery – equipment should be well-maintained to avoid breakdown and the manufacture of sub-standard output.
- In staff – all staff should be appropriately trained and skilled to carry out the task required of them.

Education and training

JIT will only be successful if our employees are willing to make it so. All levels of staff throughout the organisation should be appropriately trained and educated as to the objectives of the new system and the benefits that it will bring to X.

Work scheduling

Cellular manufacturing or group technology brings great benefits for JIT companies. This is where whole products are made within each manufacturing cell. X appears to have this system already as each car has its own production line.

Information systems

The new management systems that will be put in place will require new information systems. There will be major changes in the communication line with suppliers and the work scheduling system may need redeveloping in order to cope with the new pull-system.

Financing

Appropriate funds must be available to finance the development and implementation of JIT. Without sufficient funding JIT will fail.

Conclusion

In order to move forward with the JIT proposal we should investigate which of the conditions can be met.

Should you require any further advice, then please do not hesitate to contact me.

Signed: Management Accountant

Test your understanding 5

(a) Total Quality Management (TQM) has two main concepts:

(1) **Get it right first time**

TQM considers that the costs of prevention are less than the costs of correction. One of the main aims of TQM is to achieve zero rejects and 100% quality.

(2) **Continuous improvement**

The second basic principle of TQM is dissatisfaction with the status quo. Realistically a zero-defect goal may not be obtainable. It does, however, provide a target to ensure that a company should never be satisfied with its present level of rejects. The management and staff should believe that it is always possible to improve and to be able to get it more right next time!

There must be a focus on the customer and what they require and there must be a constant review of costs and performance to ensure that the aims of the TQM programme are being met.

The aim is to build good quality in rather than inspect poor quality out. The aim in the end is to design such good products and processes and obtain such good materials that inspection is no longer necessary.

SG should focus on the whole of its operation from start to finish if it wishes the TQM programme to be a success.

It must ensure that the input to its processes is defect-free. It must choose first-class suppliers who will guarantee the quality of their ingredients. It must communicate with the suppliers to let them know what is expected of them. SG is likely to have to pay a premium price to obtain these premium quality ingredients.

It must also examine its own processes to ensure that there are as few quality problems as possible. Where there are known quality problems, efforts should be directed at improving the processes by whatever means are appropriate, e.g. training, preventative maintenance, newer more reliable machines, etc.

The output process must also be controlled, i.e. the relationship with the customer. Efforts must be made to ensure that no defective products reach the customer, perhaps by means of final inspection before the goods leave the business and that where problems do occur, they are corrected as soon as possible. Communication with the customer is very important to ensure that the customer's needs are being met.

It is not enough to decide that a TQM system should be introduced. The programme should be carefully considered and communication to the staff should be clear. They should be educated as to the ideas behind TQM and given the necessary training to accomplish its aims. TQM should permeate the whole of the organisation and must be continually assessed to ensure that its goals are still being achieved.

(b) With a Just-In-Time (JIT) situation there are negligible inventories. There is no buffer stock. If there is a problem in production there is nothing to fall back on. The company does not keep inventory of raw materials or finished goods just-in-case. Thus, in a JIT system any problems can be catastrophic and therefore the idea is not to have any problems, i.e. perfect quality with zero defects. A TQM system is therefore necessary. In a JIT system quality is the responsibility of each employee.

(c) **Prevention costs**

These are the costs of preventing quality problems from occurring. They would include training, preventative maintenance, the purchase or hire of new more reliable machines, the sourcing of better quality ingredients, etc.

Appraisal costs

Appraisal costs are the costs incurred in checking the raw materials and products against the quality standard expected. They would include inspecting the ingredients and the semi-processed food destined for SG's customers, etc.

Internal failure costs

There are the costs incurred as a result of quality problems, where the problem is discovered before the product leaves the business, e.g. the cost of any out-of-date food which has to be disposed of, the material cost and labour cost of replacing a batch of defective product, etc.

External failure cost

These are the costs incurred as a result of quality problems, where the problem is discovered after the product leaves the business, e.g. loss of customer through delivering poor quality products, the material cost and labour cost of replacing a defective batch, the cost of being sued because of food poisoning, etc.

Test your understanding 6

There are different philosophies about the cost of quality. Many businesses engineer quality into their processes while others set up systems to provide quality assurance.

The typical characteristics of quality cost are sometimes cited as follows:

Prevention cost

This would consist perhaps of the cost of the salaries of a quality control unit that carries out the sampling process to detect quality failures and prevents them from getting to the customer.

Inspection/appraisal cost

This would include the cost of investigation into quality failures as well as the cost of consumable items used to carry out routine examinations.

Internal failure cost

This would cover the cost of scrapped items, reworking any defective output or undertaking any re-engineering process to improve quality.

External failure cost

This would cover the cost of warranties, free replacements, repairs and other efforts to repair the loss of customer goodwill.

chapter

5

Break-even analysis

Chapter learning objectives

Lead	Component
C2. Analyse short term pricing and product decisions	(b) Apply break even analysis in multiple product contexts.

1 Session Content Diagram

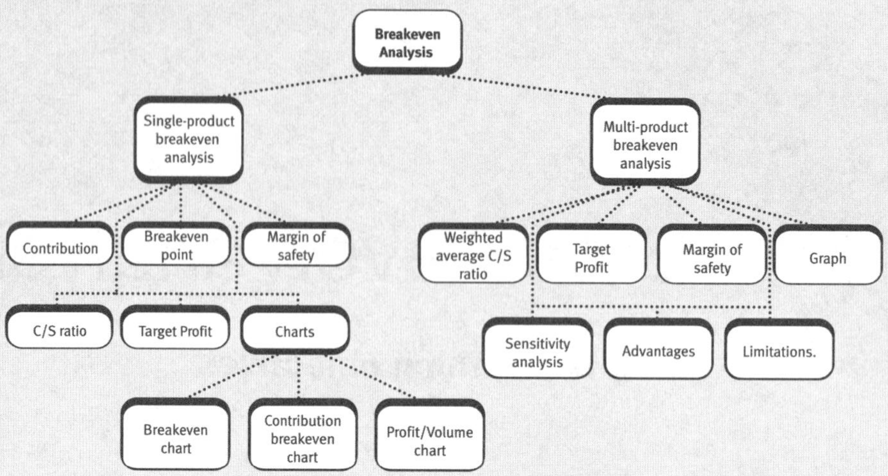

2 Introduction

One of the most important decisions that needs to be made before any business even starts, or a new product or service is launched, is 'how much do we need to sell in order to break even?' By 'break-even' we mean simply covering all our costs without making a profit. This type of analysis is more formally known as Cost-Volume-Profit Analysis (CVP Analysis).

CVP definition

Cost –Volume – Profit analysis is defined in CIMA's *Official Terminology* as 'the study of the effects on future profit of changes in fixed cost, variable cost, sales price, quantity and mix.'

CVP analysis is a particular example of *'what if?'* analysis. A business sets a budget based upon various assumptions about revenues, costs, product mixes and overall volumes. CVP analysis considers the impact on the budgeted profit of changes in these various factors.

Cost-Volume-Profit (CVP) analysis

CVP analysis makes use of the contribution concept in order to assess the following measures for a single product:

- contribution to sales (C/S) ratio
- breakeven point
- margin of safety.

The contribution concept

We have previously determined that variable costs are those that vary with the level of activity. If we can identify the variable costs associated with producing and selling a product or service we can highlight a very important measure: ***contribution.***

Contribution = sales value LESS variable cost

Variable costs are sometimes referred to as **marginal costs**. The two terms are often used interchangeably.

Contribution is so called because it 'contributes' towards fixed costs and profit. Once the fixed costs have been fully covered, then any extra contribution contributes towards the profit of the organisation.

Illustration

Consider a product with a variable cost per unit of $26 and selling price of $42. Fixed costs for the period are $12,000.

(a) What is the contribution per unit for the product?

(b) If 1,000 units are sold, what is the total contribution?

(c) What is the total profit and the profit per unit at this level of sales?

(d) Calculate the total profit for the following levels of sales:
- 500
- 1,000
- 1,200

(e) Calculate the contribution per unit and profit per unit for each level of sales.

Solution:

(a) Contribution per unit = sales – variable cost
$42 – $26 = $16

(b) Total contribution = contribution per unit × number of units
$16 × 1,000 = $16,000

(c) Total profit = total contribution – fixed costs
$16,000 – $12,000 = $4,000

Profit per unit = total profit/number of units
$4,000/1,000 = $4

(d) It is easier to use a table for these calculations:

Units	500	1,000	1,200
	$	$	$
Sales	21,000	42,000	50,400
Variable cost	13,000	26,000	31,200
	———	———	———
Total contribution	8,000	16,000	19,200
Fixed costs	12,000	12,000	12,000
	———	———	———
Total Profit/(Loss)	(4,000)	4,000	7,200
	———	———	———
(e) Contribution per unit	$16	$16	$16
Profit per unit	($8)	$4.00	$6

You can see from this that the contribution per unit does not change, but that the profit per unit can change significantly as the volume changes.

This makes contribution much more useful than profit in many decisions.

In the above example, it would have been quicker to start with contribution when working out the profit, as shown below. This saves some unnecessary calculations:

	$	$	$
Contribution per unit	16	16	16
× units	500	1,000	1,200
Total contribution	8,000	16,000	19,200
Fixed costs	12,000	12,000	12,000
Total Profit/(Loss)	(4,000)	4,000	7,200

C/S ratio

The contribution to sales ratio is a useful calculation in CVP analysis. It is usually expressed as a percentage. It can be calculated as follows.

$$\text{C/S ratio} = \frac{\text{Contribution per unit}}{\text{Selling price per unit}} \quad \text{or} \quad \frac{\text{Total contribution}}{\text{Total sales revenue}}$$

The C/S ratio is sometimes referred to as the P/V (Profit/Volume) ratio.

Explanation of the contribution sales ratio

The C/S ratio of a product is the proportion of the selling price that contributes to fixed overheads and profits. It is comparable to the gross profit margin.

A higher contribution to sales ratio means that contribution grows more quickly as sales levels increase. Once the breakeven point has been passed, profits will accumulate more quickly than for a product with a lower contribution to sales ratio.

Breakeven point

The breakeven point is the point at which neither a profit nor a loss is made.

- At the breakeven point the following situations occur.

  Total sales revenue = Total costs, i.e. Profit = 0
  or
  Total contribution = Fixed costs, i.e. Profit = 0

- It can be calculated in terms of numbers of units sold.

  $$\textbf{Breakeven point (in terms of numbers of units sold)} = \frac{\textbf{Fixed costs}}{\textbf{Contribution per unit}}$$

- It is also possible to calculated in terms of sales revenue using the C/S ratio.

  $$\textbf{Breakeven point (in terms of sales revenue)} = \frac{\textbf{Fixed costs}}{\textbf{C/S ratio}}$$

Margin of safety

The margin of safety is the amount by which anticipated sales (in units) can fall below budget before a business makes a loss. It can be calculated in terms of numbers of units or as a percentage of budgeted sales.

The following formulae are used to calculate the margin of safety:

Margin of safety calculation:

in units = **Budgeted sales – Breakeven point sales**

$$\text{as a \% of budgeted sales} = \frac{\textbf{Budgeted sales – Breakeven sales}}{\textbf{Budgeted sales}} \times 100\%$$

Example 1

A company manufactures and sells a single product that has the following cost and selling price structure:

	$/unit
Selling price	120
Direct material	(22)
Direct labour	(36)
Variable overhead	(14)
Fixed overhead	(12)
Profit per unit	36

The fixed overhead absorption rate is based on the normal capacity of 2,000 units per month.

Assume that the same amount is spent each month on fixed overheads.

Budgeted sales for next month are 2,200 units.

Required:

(i) the breakeven point, in sales units per month

(ii) the margin of safety for next month

(iii) the budgeted profit for next month

(iv) the sales required to achieve a profit of $96,000 in a month.

Using the margin of safety to calculate the expected profit

As a short cut to determining the expected profit for an organisation, the margin of safety can be used as follows:

Expected profit = Margin of safety (in units) × contribution per unit

This can be best explained through the use of an illustration.

Illustration

RT organisation manufactures one product. The product sells for $250, and has variable costs per unit of $120. Fixed costs for the month were $780,000. The monthly projected sales for the product were 8,000. The margin of safety can be calculated as:

First calculate the breakeven sales: 780,000/(250 –120) = 6,000

Margin of safety in units = projected sales – breakeven sales

= 8,000 – 6,000 = 2,000

Margin of safety % = (projected sales – breakeven sales)/projected sales

= (8,000 – 6,000)/8,000 = 25%

The margin of safety can also be used as one route to a profit calculation. We have seen that the contribution goes towards fixed costs and profit. Once breakeven point is reached the fixed costs have been covered. After the breakeven point there are no more fixed costs to be covered and all of the contribution goes towards making profits grow.

In this illustration, the monthly profit from projected sales of 8,000 would be $260,000.

This can be calculated the normal way:

Contribution	$130
Total contribution ($130 × 8,000)	$1,040,000
Fixed costs	$ 780,000
Profit	$ 260,000

Or using margin of safety:

Margin of safety = 2,000 units per month
Monthly profit = 2,000 × contribution per unit
= 2,000 × $130
= $260,000

3 Break even charts

The information from CVP analysis can be represented diagramatically using a break even chart.

For example, if we were using the following data in our calculations

Selling price	$50 per unit
Variable cost	$30 per unit
Fixed costs	$20,000 per month
Forecast sales	1,700 units per month

the results of our analysis could be illustrated on a diagram as follows:

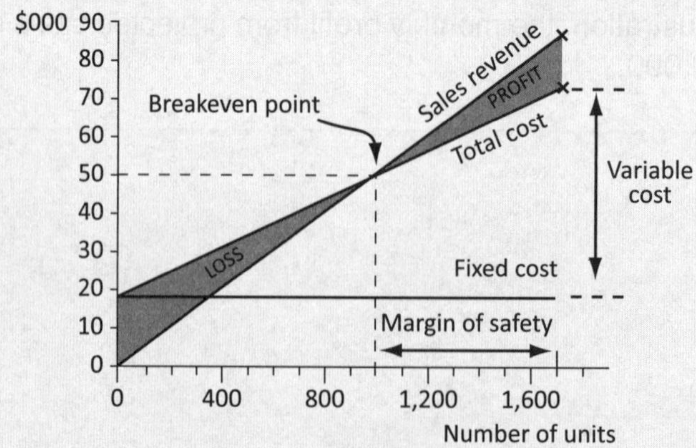

Interpretation of a break even chart

An interpretation of the diagram would tell us many things:

- Fixed costs are $20,000 – this is the point at which the total cost line cuts the vertical axis.
- The break even point occurs at 1,000 units – this is the point at which the line for total revenue crosses the line for total costs.
- At the break even point, costs and revenues total $50,000 each – this can be found by reading across to the vertical axis at this point.
- We can see by reading along the horizontal axis that the margin of safety is 700 units.
- Budgeted sales are 1,700 units – this is determined by adding the margin of safety to the break even point.

Example 2

Choose from the following list all the information than can be easily determined from a break even chart (choose all that apply):

- the break even point (in units)
- the break even point (in terms of total revenue)
- selling price per unit
- total fixed costs
- total costs
- variable cost per unit
- margin of safety

Drawing a break even chart

Learning to draw a chart to scale will provide a firm foundation for your understanding of breakeven charts. To give yourself some practice, it would be a good idea to follow the step-by-step guide which follows to produce your own chart on a piece of graph paper.

A basic breakeven chart records costs and revenues on the vertical axis (y) and the level of activity on the horizontal axis (x). Lines are drawn on the chart to represent costs and sales revenue. The breakeven point can be read off where the sales revenue line cuts the total cost line.

Let's look at constructing the diagram that has just been illustrated.

- *Step 1. Select appropriate scales for the axes and draw and label them.* Your graph should fill as much of the page as possible. This will make it clearer and easier to read. You can make sure that you do this by putting the extremes of the axes right at the end of the available space.

  The furthest point on the vertical axis will be the monthly sales revenue, that is

  1,700 units × $50 = $ 85,000

  The furthest point on the horizontal axis will be monthly sales volume of 1,700 units.

  Make sure that you do not need to read data for volumes higher than 1,700 units before you set these extremes for your scales.

- *Step 2. Draw the fixed cost line and label it.* This will be a straight line parallel to the horizontal axis at the $20,000 level.

  The $20,000 fixed costs are incurred in the short term even with zero activity.

- *Step 3. Draw the total cost line and label it.* The best way to do this is to calculate the total costs for the maximum sales level, which is 1,700 units in our example. Mark this point on the graph and join it to the cost incurred at zero activity, that is, $20,000.

	$
Variable costs for 1,700 units (1,700 × $30)	51,000
Fixed costs	20,000
Total cost for 1,700 units	71,000

- *Step 4. Draw the revenue line and label it.* Once again, the best way is to plot the extreme points. The revenue at maximum activity in our example is 1,700 × $50 = $85,000. This point can be joined to the origin, since at zero activity there will be no sales revenue.
- *Step 5. Mark any required information on the chart and read off solutions as required.* You can check that your chart is accurate by reading off the breakeven point and then check this against the calculation for breakeven:

$$\text{Breakeven point in units} = \frac{\text{Fixed costs}}{\text{Contribution per unit}}$$

= 20,000/(50 – 30) = **1,000 units.**

The margin of safety can be seen as the area to the right of the breakeven point up to the forecast sales level of 1,700.

The contribution breakeven chart

One of the problems with the conventional or basic breakeven chart is that it is not possible to read contribution directly from the chart. A contribution breakeven chart is based on the same principles but it shows the variable cost line instead of the fixed cost line. The same lines for total cost and sales revenue are shown so the breakeven point and profit can be read off in the same way as with a conventional chart. However, it is also possible also to read the contribution for any level of activity.

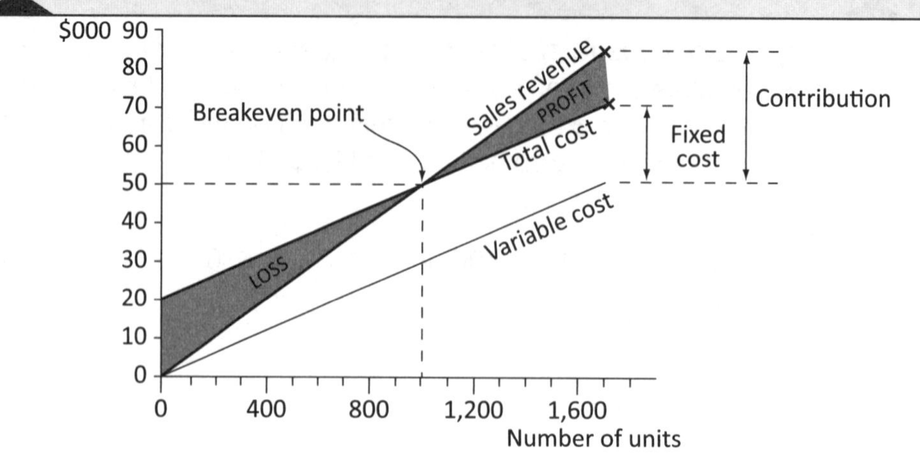

Using the same basic example as for the conventional chart, the total variable cost for an output of 1,700 units is 1,700 × $30 = $51,000. This point can be joined to the origin since the variable cost is nil at zero activity.

The contribution can be read as the difference between the sales revenue line and the variable cost line.

This form of presentation might be used when it is desirable to highlight the importance of contribution and to focus attention on the variable costs.

Ensure you are familiar with these charts and that you are able to identify all the component parts.

However, it can be difficult in this diagram to see how much profit (or loss) is made at each level of activity. For this we would need a profit-volume chart.

4 The profit–volume chart

The profit volume chart

Another form of breakeven chart is the profit–volume chart. This chart plots a single line depicting the profit or loss at each level of activity.

A profit–volume graph for our example is shown below.

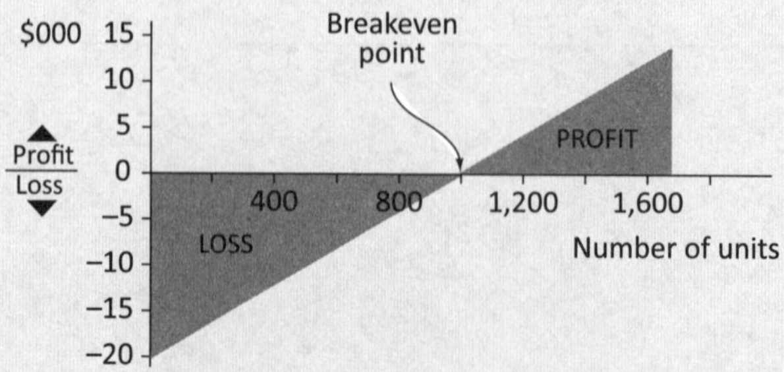

Drawing and interpreting a profit-volume chart

Drawing a profit-volume chart

The vertical axis shows profits and losses and the horizontal axis is drawn at zero profit or loss.

In order to plot the profit line only two points are required and a line is plotted through these:

- Firstly, at zero activity the loss is equal to $20,000, that is, the amount of fixed costs.
- Secondly, the line needs to cross the horizontal axis at the calculated breakeven point (1,000 units).

Note: the profit–volume chart may also be called a profit graph or a contribution–volume graph.

Interpretation

An analysis of this profit volume chart would highlight the following:

- The break even point occurs where the line crosses the horizontal axis.
- This would appear to be at 1,000 units.
- A user of the chart could quickly see the expected profit or loss for any expected level of activity. For example, if sales were to be 1,400 units then a profit of around $8,000 would be expected.

The main advantage of the profit–volume chart is that it is capable of depicting clearly the effect on profit and breakeven point of any changes in the variables.

Example 3

An organisation is considering launching a new product, but it has yet to determine final production design. This decision will affect the costs and quality of the product, as well as its ultimate selling price.

Two situations are being considered:

- In situation (a), a lower product specification will be used, resulting in a lower selling price and production cost per unit.
- In situation (b), a higher product specification will be used, resulting in a higher selling price and a higher production cost per unit.

A profit volume chart has been prepared illustrating the impact of each situation as follows:

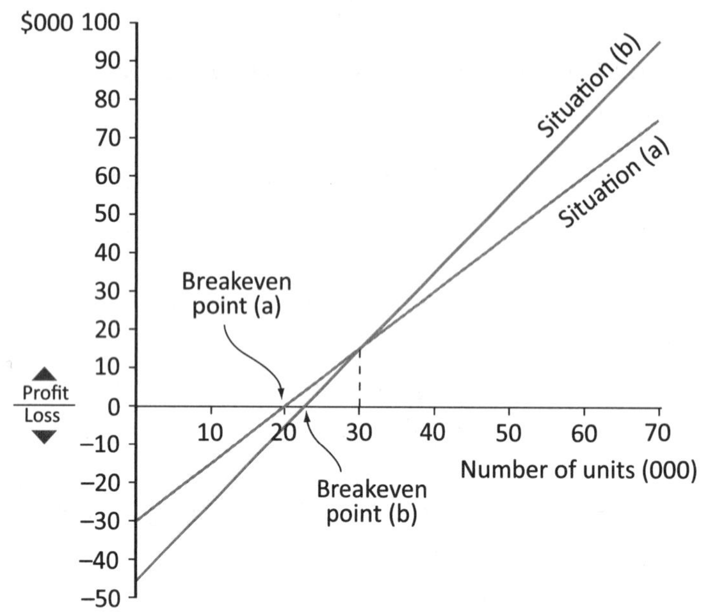

Answer the following questions based on this profit-volume chart:

The situation which results in the higher contribution per unit is situation __ ?

This is because....

A Situation (a) has a lower production cost per unit

B Situation (b) has a higher selling price

C Situation (a) has a lower break even point

D The graph for situation (b) has a steeper slope

At what level of sales would the organisation be indifferent between the two options?

A 20,000 units

B 22,500 units

C 30,000 units

D 70,000 units

The impact of cost structures on the break even point

Different organisations will have different cost structures. This will often be heavily influenced by the industry in which they operate. For example, a service company, such as a firm of accountants, will find that most of their costs are fixed costs such as salaries and rent. On the other hand, a retailer is likely to find that most of its costs are variable (such as the purchasing costs of the items it is selling). Other factors such as the level of computerisation and mechanisation will also impact on the cost structure.

The proportion of costs which are fixed is refered to as operating gearing. An organisation with a high operating gearing, such as a firm of accountants, will have a high proportion of costs which are fixed. An organisation with a low operating gearing will have a small proportion of fixed costs relative to variable costs.

Organisations with a high operating gearing will have a higher break even point than organisations with a low operating gearing. These organisations will also have a higher contribution margin meaning that small changes in revenue will have a large impact on profit. Therefore, as sales increase beyond the break even point profits and margins will increase greatly.

The opposite will be true for organisations with a low operating gearing. However, organisations with low operating gearing will perform better as sales fall (for example, in a recession) as they will be able to cut back on costs. For example, in a recession a supermarket can reduce its purchasing cost but an accountancy practice must still pay its salaries and rent.

5 Multi-product break-even analysis

Where an organisation produces and sells more than one product, a weighted average C/S ratio is calculated by using the formula:

$$\textbf{Weighted average C/S ratio} = \frac{\textbf{Total contribution}}{\textbf{Total revenue}}$$

The breakeven point in sales revenue is then calculated as:

$$\textbf{Breakeven revenue} = \frac{\textbf{Fixed costs}}{\textbf{Weighted average C/S ratio}}$$

Explanation of the weighted average calculation

The basic breakeven model can be used satisfactorily for a business that produces and sells only one product. However, most companies sell a range of different products, and the model has to be adapted when one is considering a business operation with several products.

If a company sells multiple products, break even analysis is somewhat more complex. The reason is that the different products will have different selling prices, different costs, and different contribution margins. Consequently, the break even point will depend on the mix in which the various products are sold.

In order to cope with this, CVP analysis assumes that a **pre-determined sales mix will remain constant** for all volumes of activity. For example, if product A makes up 20% of production and sales and product B makes up 80%, CVP analysis assumes that these proportions will continue into the future.

This allows for the calculation of a **weighted average contribution margin** or a **weighted average contribution sales ratio** which can be used in the break even calculations. The weightings used in the calculations are those from the predetermined sales mix.

The calculation of the weighted averages is explained in the following example.

Example 4

Company A produces Product X and Product Y. Fixed overhead costs amount to $200,000 every year. The following budgeted information is available for both products for next year:

	Product X	*Product Y*
Sales price	$50	$60
Variable cost	$30	$45
Contribution per unit	$20	$15
Budgeted sales (in units)	20,000	10,000

To the nearest $000, what is the break even sales revenue?

A $500,000

B $582,000

C $628,000

D $800,000

Margin of safety calculations

The basic breakeven model for calculating the margin of safety can be adapted to multi-product environments. Three alternative approaches are considered in the example below.

A business operation produces three products, the X, the Y and the Z. Relevant details are:

	Product X	*Product Y*	*Product Z*
Normal sales mix (units)	2	2	1
Selling price per unit	$9	$7	$5
Variable cost per unit	$6	$5	$1
Contribution per unit	$3	$2	$4
Forecast unit sales	400	400	200

Fixed costs are $2,000 per period, not attributable to individual products. A budget for the forecast is as follows:

	Product X	*Product Y*	*Product Z*	*Total*
Sales revenue	$3,600	$2,800	$1,000	$7,400
Variable cost	$2,400	$2,000	$200	$4,600
Contribution	$1,200	$800	$800	$2,800
Fixed costs				$2,000
Profit				$800

The margin of safety

The contribution ratio is 37.84% (i.e. $2,800/$7,400). The break even point, in terms of sales revenue, can be determined by dividing the total fixed costs ($2,000) by this contribution ratio = $2,000/37.84% = $5,285

The margin of safety is the difference between forecast sales and this break even sales revenue = $7,400 forecast sales – $5,285 = $2,115. It may also be expressed as a percentage of forecast sales = $2,115/ $7,400 = 28.58%.

6 Establishing a target profit for multiple products

The approach is the same as in single product situations, but the weighted average contribution to sales ratio is now used so that:

$$\text{Revenue required to generate a target profit} = \frac{\text{Fixed costs + required profit}}{\text{Weighted average C/S ratio}}$$

Example 5

Referring to the previous example, what is the target revenue required (to the nearest $000) to achieve a profit of $300,000?

A $873,000

B $882,000

C $1,384,000

D $1,455,000

7 The multi-product profit-volume graph

In a multi-product environment, two lines must be shown on the profit-volume graph: one straight line, where a constant mix between the products is assumed; and one bow shaped line, where it is assumed that the company sells its most profitable product first and then its next most profitable product and so on.

Example:

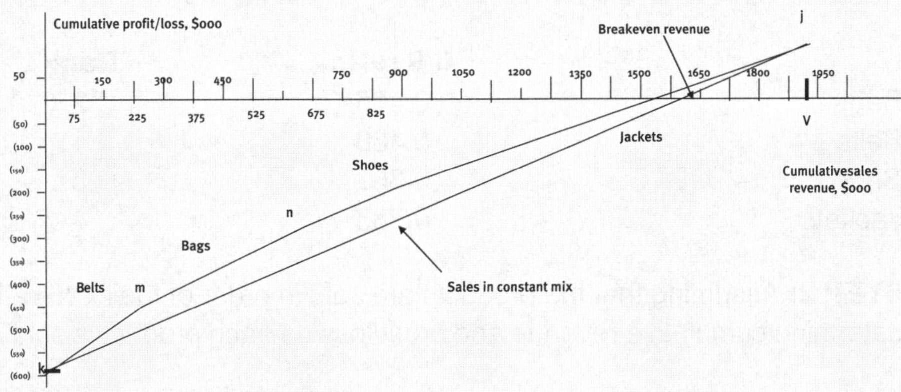

In this example, a ranking of the c/s ratio of each product would put belts first, bags next, shoes thirds and jackets last. This can be seen from the diagram as it is the order in which the products appear on the upper of the two lines.

The diagram illustrates two potential break even points:

- the lower line indicates the breakeven point if the products are sold in the standard product mix.
- the upper line indicates the break even point if the products are sold in order of the c/s ratio ranking.

Drawing and interpreting a multi-product PV graph

We will use the following example to illustrate a step-by-step approach:

	Sales units	Selling price per unit	Variable cost per unit
Bags	1,000	$400	$210
Belts	2,000	$125	$65
Shoes	1,500	$150	$95
Jackets	3,500	$300	$215

Fixed costs amount to $580,000.

STEP 1: Calculate the contribution to sales (C/S) ratio of each product being sold, and rank the products in order of profitability.

	C/S ratio	Rank
Bags	0.475	2
Belts	0.480	1
Shoes	0.367	3
Jackets	0.283	4

STEP 2: Assuming that the products are sold in order of their C/S ratio, determine cumulative revenue and profit/loss as each product is sold..

In our example:

Sales	Cumulative revenue	Individual product contribution	Cumulative profit or loss
None	$0	$0	$(580,000)
Belts	$250,000	$120,000	$(460,000)
Bags	$650,000	$190,000	$(270,000)
Shoes	$875,000	$82,500	$(187,500)
Jackets	$1,925,000	$297,500	$110,000

STEP 3: Draw a graph, showing cumulative sales revenue on the x-axis and the initial cumulative profit or loss on the vertical axis.

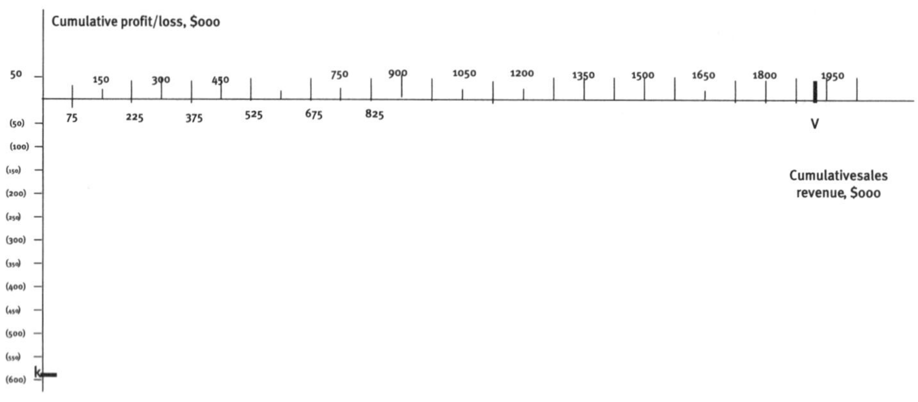

Point K on the graph (on the vertical axis) represents the profit or loss when revenue is zero. This will always be the total of the fixed costs.

Point V on the graph represents the total cumulative revenue (in this case, $1,925,000).

STEP 4: Starting from point k, plot the first point of cumulative revenue.

This represents the revenue from the product with the highest C/S ratio (in this case, belts). The slope of the line is determined by the C/S ratio achieved on sales of that product. We can see that it goes to the point of $250,000 on the revenue axis and –$460,000 on the profit/loss axis. These points can be read from the table created in Step 2.

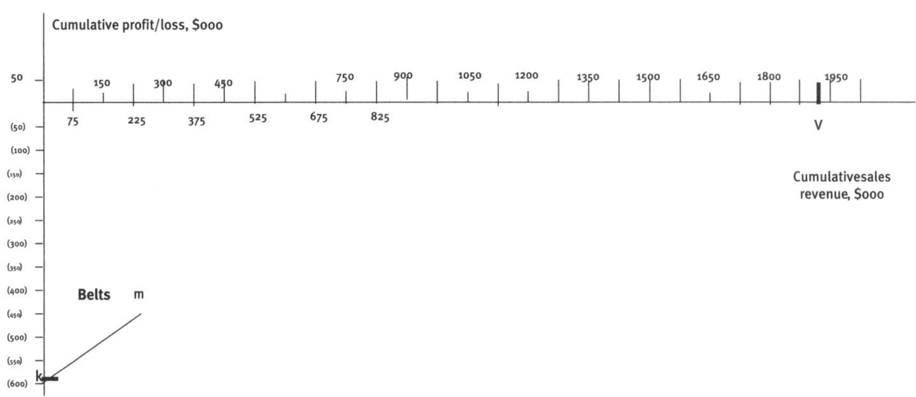

STEP 5: Plot each subsequent point from the table in Step 2 and join the points together with a line.

In our example, 'Bags' is ranked at 2nd and 'Shoes' at 3rd. The lines could be drawn as follows:

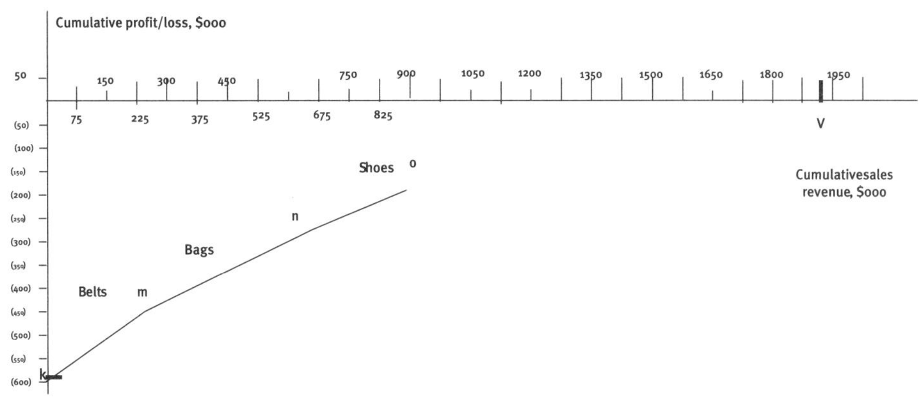

Note how the lines become flatter (or less steep) as they are drawn in turn. This reflects the lower C/S ratio of each product.

STEP 6: Draw a final line between the starting point (k) and the finishing point.

The final point will be the final figure from the table in Step 2, where cumulative revenue is $1,925,000 (the co-ordinates for the horizontal axis) and cumulative profit or loss of $110,000 (the co-ordinates for the vertical axis).

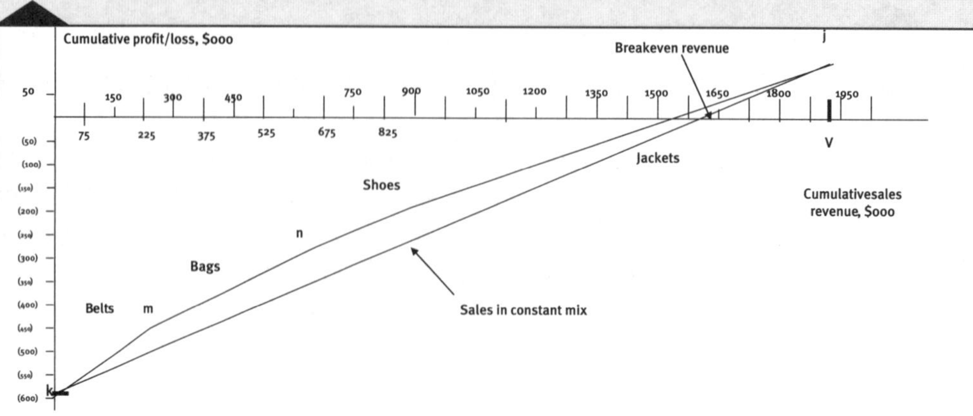

It can be seen that the resulting diagram provides two potential break even points (i.e. the horizontal axis is crossed twice – indicating that there are two points at which profits will be zero).

The first point that is crossed (the lower value of revenue) represents the break even point if products are sold in the order of highest to lowest C/S ratio.

The higher break even point would be achieved if products are sold in a constant standard mix.

Example 6

BJS Ltd produces and sells the following three products:

Product	*X*	*Y*	*Z*
Selling price per unit	$16	$20	$10
Variable cost per unit	$5	$15	$7
Contribution per unit	$11	$5	$3
Budgeted sales volume	50,000 units	10,000 units	100,000 units

The company expects the fixed costs to be $300,000 for the coming year. Assume that sales arise throughout the year in a constant mix.

Required:

(a) Calculate the weighted average C/S ratio for the products.

(b) Calculate the break-even sales revenue required.

(c) Calculate the amount of sales revenue required to generate a profit of $600,000.

(d) A multi-product profit-volume chart (assuming the budget is achieved) for the products is provided as follows.

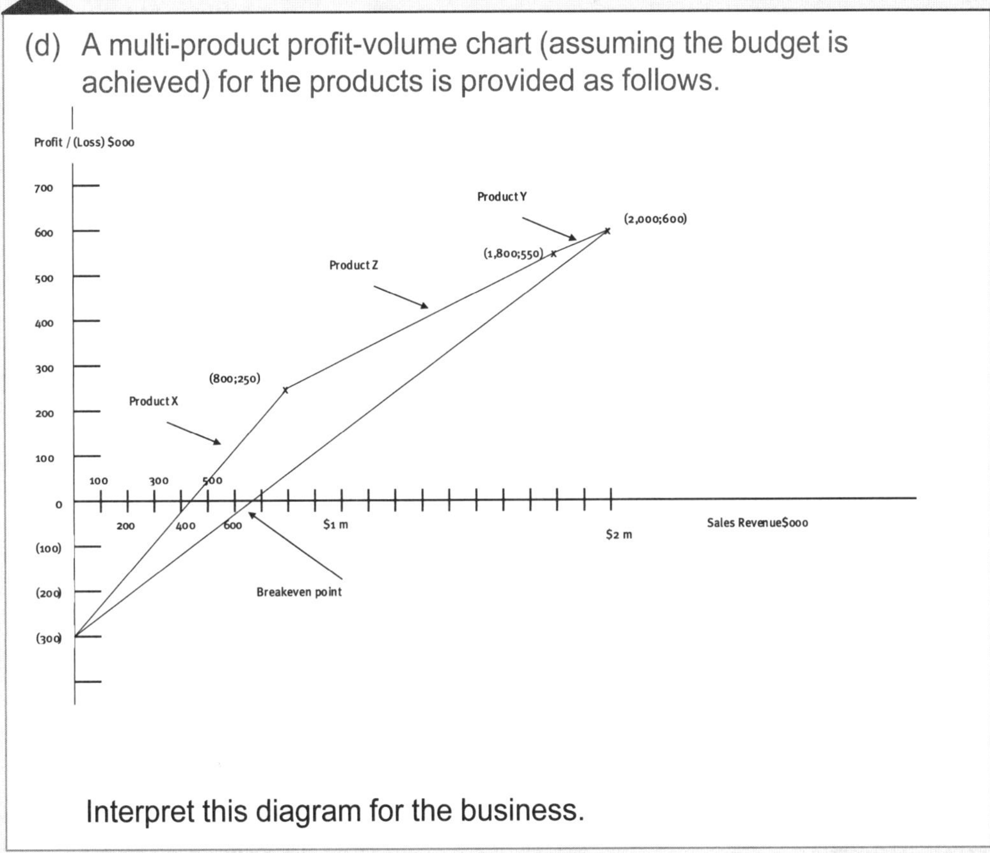

Interpret this diagram for the business.

8 Sensitivity analysis

Sensitivity (or 'What-if?') analysis involves determining the effects of various types of changes in the CVP model. These effects can be determined by simply changing the constants in the CVP model, i.e., prices, variable cost per unit, sales mix ratios etc. For example, it answers questions such as '*What will be the impact on our revenue if variable cost per unit increases by 30%?'*

The sensitivity of revenue to various possible outcomes broadens the perspective of management regarding what might actually occur before making cost commitments. This would be fairly easy with spreadsheets, or other software developed to handle these calculations.

Example 7

Vivaldi Ltd manufactures and sells four types of products under the brand name Summer, Autumn , Winter and Spring. The Sales Mix in value comprises the following:

Brand name	*Percentage*
Summer	33.33%
Autumn	41.67%
Winter	16.67%
Spring	8.33%
	100%

Total Budgeted sales are set to reach 600,000 units per month.

Variable costs are as follows:

Brand name	
Summer	60% of selling price
Autumn	68% of selling price
Winter	80% of selling price
Spring	40% of selling price

Fixed costs amount to $159,000 per month.

Required:

(a) Calculate the breakeven point for the products on an overall basis.

(b) It has been proposed to change the sales mix as follows, with the sales per month remaining at 600,000 units:

Brand name	*Percentage*
Summer	25%
Autumn	40%
Winter	30%
Spring	5%
	100%

Assuming that the above proposal is implemented, calculate the new breakeven point.

9 Advantages and disadvantages of CVP analysis

Advantages	**Disadvantages**
Provides a target volume	Profits can be affected by other factors besides volume
Helps the understanding of costs and revenues and the relationship between them	A small change in the assumptions could have a large change in the outcome

More details

Advantages of CVP analysis

The major benefit of using breakeven analysis is that it indicates the lowest amount of activity necessary to prevent losses.

Breakeven analysis aids Decision Making as it explains the relationship between cost, production volume and returns. It can be extended to show how changes in fixed costs – variable costs relationships or in revenues will affect profit levels and breakeven points.

CVP disadvantages

Any CVP analysis is based on assumptions about the behaviour of revenue, costs and volume. A change in expected behaviour will alter the break-even point; in other words, profits are affected by changes in other factors besides volume. Other factors include unit prices of input, efficiency, changes in production technology, wars, strikes, legislation, and so forth.

A CVP chart must be interpreted in the light of the limitations imposed by its underlying assumptions. The following underlying assumptions will limit the precision and reliability of a given cost-volume-profit analysis.

(1) The behaviour of total cost and total revenue has been reliably determined and is linear over the relevant range.

(2) All costs can be divided into fixed and variable elements.

(3) Total fixed costs remain constant over the relevant volume range of the CVP analysis.

(4) Total variable costs are directly proportional to volume over the relevant range.

(5) Selling prices are to be unchanged.

(6) Prices of the factors of production are to be unchanged (for example, material, prices, wage rates).

(7) Efficiency and productivity are to be unchanged.

(8) The analysis either covers a single product or assumes that a given sales mix will be maintained as total volume changes.

(9) Revenue and costs are being compared on a single activity basis (for example, units produced and sold or sales value of production).

(10) Perhaps the most basic assumption of all is that volume is the only relevant factor affecting cost. Of course, other factors also affect costs and sales. Ordinary cost-volume-profit analysis is a crude oversimplification when these factors are unjustifiably ignored.

(11) The volume of production equals the volume of sales, or changes in beginning and ending inventory levels are insignificant in amount.

In multi-product situations, CVP analysis is further hampered by the assumption that the sales mix will remain constant. This is unlikely and it also ignores the situation in some organisations where products may be inter-related – an increase in sales for one product might result in a decrease in sales for another. For example, a theatre might find that as adult ticket sales rise (for example, if stage shows are more attractive to this age group) then there is a corresponding fall in sales to children. A multi-product CVP analysis would ignore this and assume that the ratio of adult to child tickets remains constant.

Also, in multi-product situations, the presence of two potential break even points is both confusing and misleading. It confuses because it is difficult for managers to understand (and it is based on a very unlikely assumption). But it is also misleading in that as more of each product is introduced into the mix (i.e. rather than selling each product in turn in order of its C/S ratio) then the break even point will start to increase and there will in fact be multiple break even points.

10 Chapter summary

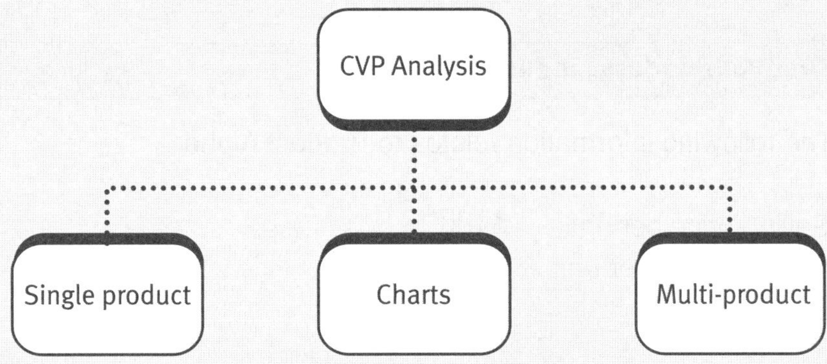

Single product

- Break-even point $= \dfrac{\text{Fixed costs}}{\text{Contribution per unit}}$
- Margin of safety = Budgeted sales – break even sales

Charts

- A profit-volume chart plots a single line depicting the profit or loss at each level of activity
- In multi-product situations products are plotted in order of their c/s ratio
- Multi-product charts provide two possible break even points

Multi-product

- Similar to single product situations but uses a weighed average contribution per uni
- Weighted Average C/S ratio $= \dfrac{\text{Total contribution}}{\text{Total Revenue}}$

11 Practice Questions

Test your understanding 1

The following information relates to Product Alpha.

Selling price per unit	$100
Variable cost per unit	$56
Fixed costs	$220,000

Budgeted sales are 7,500 units.

Required:

(a) Calculate the breakeven point in terms of units sold and overall sales revenue.

(b) Calculate the margin of safety (expressed as a percentage of budgeted sales).

Test your understanding 2

A company manufactures and sells a single product which has the following cost and selling price structure.

	$/unit	*$/unit*
Selling price		120
Direct material	22	
Direct labour	36	
Variable overhead	14	
Fixed overhead	12	
	—	
		84
		—
Profit per unit		36
		—

The fixed overhead absorption rate is based on the normal capacity of 2,000 units per month. Assume that the same amount is spent each month on fixed overheads.

Budgeted sales for next month are 2,200 units.

You are required to calculate:

(i) the breakeven point, in sales units per month

(ii) the margin of safety for next month

(iii) the budgeted profit for next month

(iv) the sales required to achieve a profit of $96,000 in a month

(v) the contribution to sales ratio

(vi) the breakeven revenue that must be generated in order to break even.

Test your understanding 3

A break down of KP's profit in the last accounting period showed the following:

	$000
Sales	450
Variable costs	(220)
Fixed costs	(160)
Profit	70

Due to a downturn in market conditions the company is worried that next year may result in losses and would like to know the change in sales that would make this happen.

Required:

The percentage fall in sales that would be necessary before the company would begin to incur losses is ____% (work to two decimal places).

Test your understanding 4

OT Ltd plans to produce and sell 4,000 units of product C each month, at a selling price of $18 per unit. The unit cost of product C is as follows:

	$ per unit
Variable cost	8
Fixed cost	4
	12

To the nearest whole number, the monthly margin of safety, as a percentage of planned sales is _________ %.

Test your understanding 5

A company's summary budgeted operating statement is as follows:

	$000
Revenue	400
Variable costs	240
Fixed costs	100
Profit	60

Assuming that the sales mix does not change, identify the percentage increase in sales volume that would be needed to increase the profit to $100,000:

A 10%

B 15%

C 25%

D 40%

Test your understanding 6

Scenario

A company manufactures five products in one factory. The company's budgeted fixed costs for the next year are $300,000. The table below summarises the budgeted sales and contribution details for the five products for the next year.

Product	A	B	C	D	E
Unit selling price	$40	$15	$40	$30	$20
Total sales ($000)	400	180	1,400	900	200
Contribution to sales ratio	45%	30%	25%	20%	(10%)

The following diagram has been prepared to summarise the above budget figures:

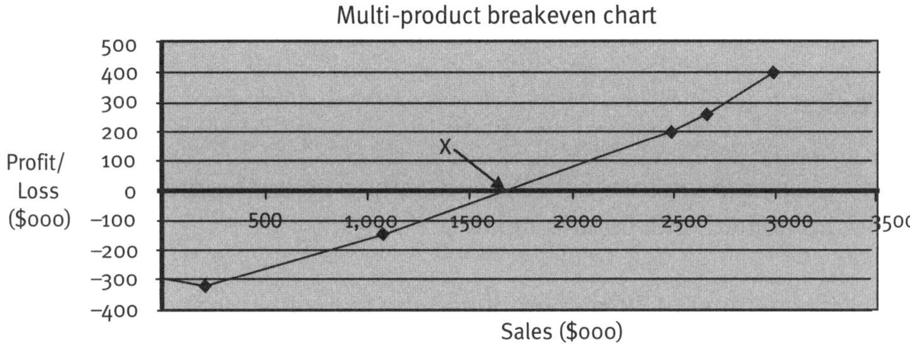

Tasks:

(a) Explain the meaning of point X on the chart.

(b) Calculate the breakeven revenue for the next year using the budgeted sales mix.

(Time allowed: 10 minutes)

Test your understanding 7

Scenario

JK has prepared a budget for the next 12 months when it intends to make and sell four products, details of which are shown below:

Product	*Sales in units (thousands)*	*Selling price per unit $*	*Variable cost per unit $*
J	10	20	14.00
K	10	40	8.00
L	50	4	4.20
M	20	10	7.00

Budgeted fixed costs are $240,000 per annum and total assets employed are $570,000.

Tasks:

(a) Calculate the total contribution earned by each product and their combined total contributions.

The accountant at JK has produced the following profit-revenue graph for the products:

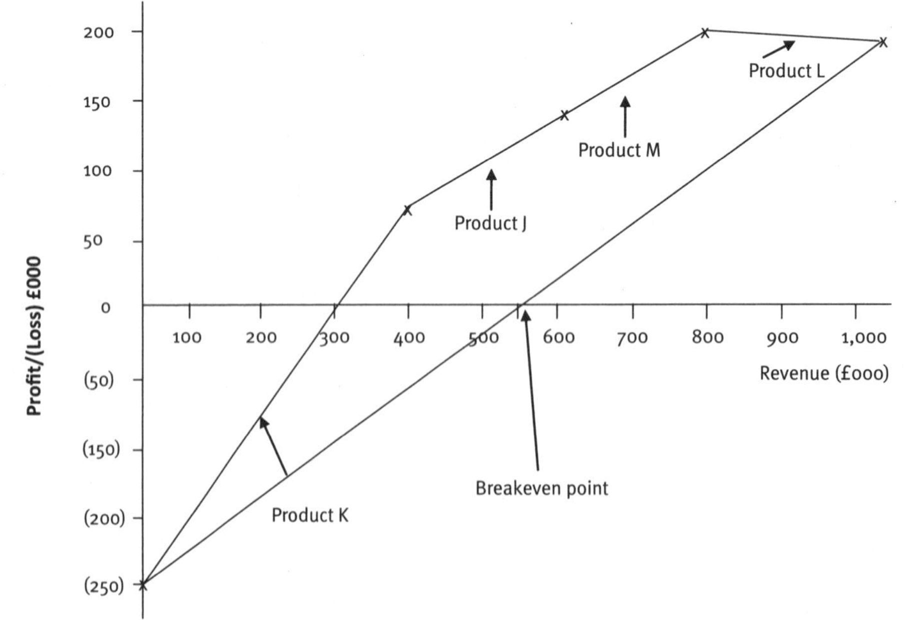

(b) Explain this graph to management, comment on the results shown and state the break-even point.

(c) Describe briefly three ways in which the overall contribution to sales ratio could be improved.

(Time allowed: 30 minutes)

Test your understanding 8

Scenario

A summary of a manufacturing company's budgeted profit statement for its next financial year, when it expects to be operating at 75% capacity, is given below.

	$	$
Sales 9,000 units at $32		288,000
Less:		
direct materials	54,000	
direct wages	72,000	
production overhead – fixed	42,000	
– variable	18,000	
		186,000
Gross profit		102,000
Less: admin., selling and dist'n costs:		
– fixed	36,000	
– varying with sales volume	27,000	
		63,000
Net profit		39,000

It has been estimated that:

(i) if the selling price per unit were reduced to $28, the increased demand would utilise 90 per cent of the company's capacity without any additional advertising expenditure

(ii) to attract sufficient demand to utilise full capacity would require a 15 per cent reduction in the current selling price and a $5,000 special advertising campaign.

Tasks:

(a) Calculate the breakeven point in units, based on the original budget.

(b) Calculate the profits and breakeven points which would result from each of the two alternatives and compare them with the original budget.

(c) The manufacturing company decided to proceed with the original budget and has asked you to calculate how many units must be sold to achieve a profit of $45,500.

(Time allowed: 30 minutes)

Test your understanding 9

A company makes and sells three products, R, S and T. Extracts from the weekly profit statements are as follows:

	R	*S*	*T*	*Total*
	$	$	$	$
Sales revenue	10,000	15,000	20,000	45,000
Variable cost of sales	4,000	9,000	10,000	23,000
Fixed costs (*)	3,000	3,000	3,000	9,000
Profit	3,000	3,000	7,000	13,000

(*) General fixed costs absorbed using a unit absorption rate.

If the sales revenue mix of products produced and sold were to be changed to : R 20%, S 50% and T 30%, the new average contribution to sales ratio would be ______ (*choose from higher, lower, or remain unchanged*)?

Test your understanding 10

MC manufactures one product only, and for the last accounting period has produced the simplified profit and loss statement below:

	$	$
Sales		300,000
Costs		
Direct materials	60,000	
Direct wages	40,000	
Prime cost	100,000	
Variable production overhead	10,000	
Fixed production overhead	40,000	
Fixed administration overhead	60,000	
Variable selling overhead	40,000	
Fixed selling overhead	20,000	
		270,000
Net profit		**30,000**

The organisation has created the following profit–volume graph from this information as follows:

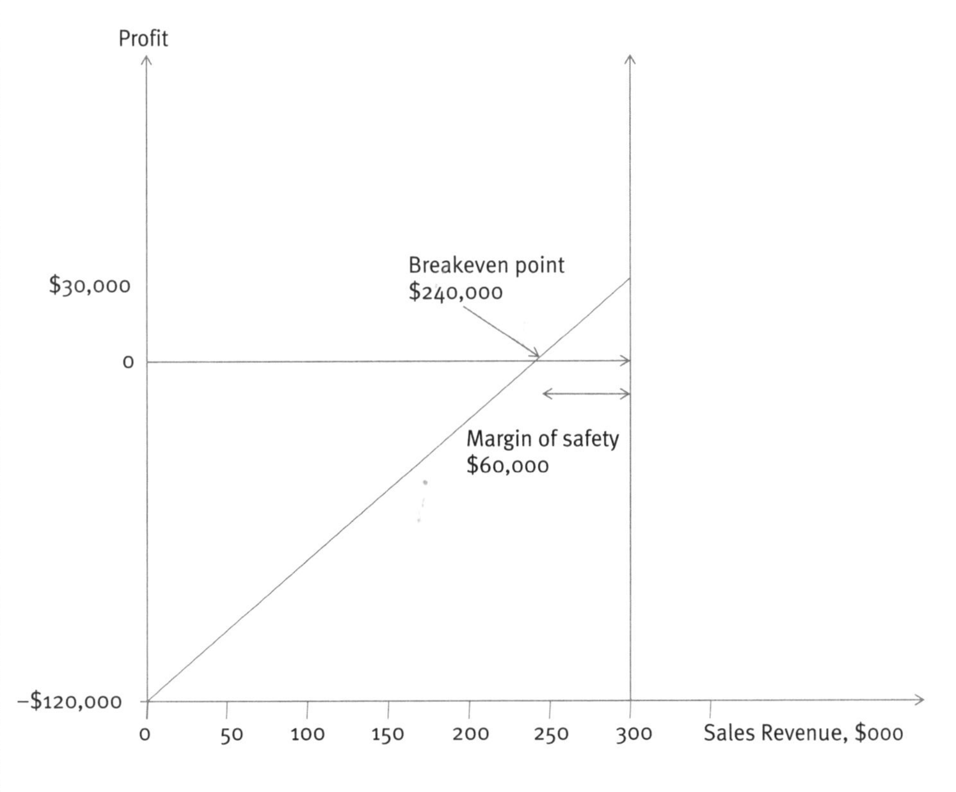

Examine the following diagrams:

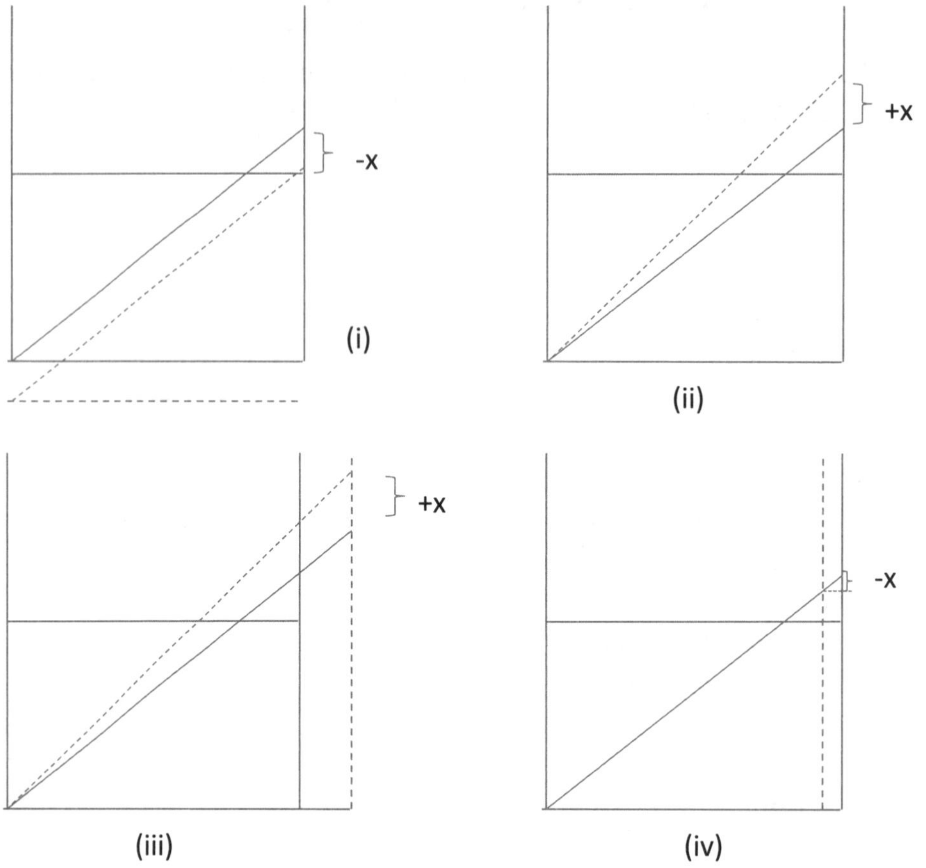

These graphs show increase or decrease in profit by +x or –x.

Match each diagram to each of the following potential changes to the business' assumptions:

- a decrease in variable cost
- a decrease in sales volume
- an increase in fixed cost
- an increase in sales price

Test your understanding 11

A company provides three different holiday packages to a popular destination. Details on the profits made from the packages are as follows:

	Standard	Premium	Superior
	$	$	$
Retail price	450	600	800
Variable costs	70	90	120
Fixed costs	180	200	240
Profit per package	200	310	440

The total annual fixed costs are budgeted to be $200,000 and, whilst none of these costs are specific to any particular package, they are charged to packages on the basis of average numbers of service staff per package.

The company expects to sell the packages in the following proportion:

- Standard 50%
- Premium 30%
- Superior 20%

The annual revenue that needs to be generated in order to break even is closest to:

A $200,000

B $236,000

C $237,000

D $402,000

Test your understanding 12

A provider of language courses has three courses with the following information:

Product	Introductory	Intermediate	Advanced
Contribution to sales ratio	40%	80%	60%
Expected sales mix	60%	30%	10%

Total fixed costs are budgeted to be $120,000.

To the nearest $, the total break-even revenue is $_______

Test your understanding answers

Example 1

(i) **Break even point**

The key to calculating the breakeven point is to determine the contribution per unit.

Contribution per unit = 120 – 22 – 36 – 14 = $48

Breakeven point (in terms of number of units sold) = $\frac{\text{Fixed costs}}{\text{Contribution per unit}}$

Breakeven point = $\frac{\$12 \times 2{,}000 \text{ units}}{\$48}$

Breakeven point = 500 units

(ii) **Margin of safety**

Margin of safety = Budgeted sales – Breakeven point sales
Margin of safety = 2,200 – 500
Margin of safety = 1,700 units (or 77% of budgeted sales)

(iii) **Budgeted profit**

Once breakeven point has been reached, all of the contribution goes towards profits because all of the fixed costs have been covered.

Budgeted profit = 1,700 units (margin of safety) × $48
Budgeted profit = $81,600

(iv) **Target profit**

To achieve the desired level of profit, sufficient units must be sold to earn a contribution that covers the fixed costs and leaves the desired profit for the month.

$$\text{Unit sales required} = \frac{\text{Fixed overhead + desired profit}}{\text{Contribution per unit}}$$

$$\text{Unit sales required} = \frac{\$24{,}000 + \$96{,}000}{\$48}$$

Unit sales required = 2,500 units

Example 2

It would be possible to determine the following information:

- the break even point (in units) – this can be seen from reading down from where total revenue cuts the total cost line and reading along the horizontal axis
- the break even point (in terms of total revenue) – this can be seen from reading along from where total revenue cuts the total cost line and reading up the vertical axis
- total fixed costs – this is the point at which the total costs line cuts the vertical axis
- total costs – this is a line used in the construction of the chart
- margin of safety – this is usually indicated on the chart.

However, it would not be possible to easily determine the following:

- selling price per unit
- variable cost per unit.

The chart deals in total revenue and total costs and individual revenue and cost per unit values are difficult to determine.

Example 3

Note: the profit–volume graph is the clearest way of presenting information like the one presented in this scenario. If we were to attempt to draw two conventional breakeven charts on one set of axes the result would be a jumble, which is very difficult to interpret.

The profit-volume chart is easier for analysts to interpret. The graph depicts clearly the larger profits available from option (b). It also shows that the breakeven point increases from 20,000 units to 22,500 units but that this is not a large increase when viewed in the context of the projected sales volume. It is also possible to see that for sales volumes above 30,000 units the profit achieved will be higher with option (b). For sales volumes below 30,000 units option (a) will yield higher profits (or lower losses).

In answer to the specific questions:

- Scenario (b) has the higher contribution.
- This cannot be deduced from the difference in selling price or costs. For example, having a higher selling price would normally lead to a higher contribution, but only if the costs remain the same. If selling price and costs change then it is difficult to determine what will happen to contribution. This rules out options A and B in the next question.
- It also cannot be deduced from the different break even points as this is influenced by the level of fixed costs for each option.
- But the fact that situation (b) has a steeper slope indicates that as volume increases profit is increasing at a higher rate. This would indicate that situation (b) has a higher contribution per unit (answer D).
- For the final question, the point of indifference between the two situations would occur when the profit from each situation is the same. This occurs where their profit lines cross, at 30,000 units (answer C).

Example 4

The breakeven revenue can be calculated as:

$$\text{Breakeven revenue} = \frac{\text{Fixed costs}}{\text{Weighted average C/S ratio}}$$

We know that the fixed costs are $200,000. We need the weighted average C/S ratio as follows:

$$\text{Weighted average C/S ratio} = \frac{\text{Total contribution}}{\text{Total revenue}}$$

$$\text{Weighted average C/S ratio} = \frac{(20{,}000 \times \$20) + (10{,}000 \times \$15)}{(20{,}000 \times \$50) + (10{,}000 \times \$60)}$$

$$\text{Weighted average C/S ratio} = 34.375\%$$

This indicates that for every $1 of revenue generated, the company will earn $0.34 in contribution.

The breakeven revenue can now be calculated this way for company A:

$$\text{Breakeven revenue} = \frac{\text{Fixed costs}}{\text{Weighted average C/S ratio}}$$

$$\text{Breakeven revenue} = \frac{\$200{,}000}{0.34375}$$

$$\text{Breakeven revenue} = \$581{,}819$$

Answer B is therefore the correct answer.

Calculations in the illustration above provide only estimated information because they assume that products X and Y are sold in a constant mix of 2x to 1y. In reality, this constant mix is unlikely to exist and, at times, more Y may be sold than X. Such changes in the mix throughout a period, even if the overall mix for the period is 2:1, will lead to the actual breakeven point being different than anticipated.

Alternative solution

An alternative (though potentially more complex solution) to this question would be to use the weighted average contribution per unit in the calculations (rather than the c/s ratio). In an exam, you would only use this method if there is not enough information available to calculate the weighted average contribution sales ratio.

The weighted average contribution per unit can be calculated as follows:

$$\text{Weighted average contribution per unit} = \frac{(20{,}000 \times \$20) + (10{,}000 \times \$15)}{(20{,}000 + 10{,}000)}$$

Weighted average contribution per unit = $18.33 per unit

The break even point can then be calculated as follows:

$$\text{Breakeven units} = \frac{\text{Fixed costs}}{\text{Weighted average contribution per unit}}$$

$$\text{Breakeven units} = \frac{\$200{,}000}{\$18.33}$$

Breakeven units = 10,911 units

This represents the total number of units that must be sold in order to break even. If we assume that the pre-determined sales mix still applies (i.e. that the company plans to sell twice as many Product X and Product Y) then this can be split between the products so that Product X needs to sell two thirds of 10,911 units (i.e. 7,274 units) and Product X needs to sell one third of 10,911 (i.e. 3,637 units).

This would give a target revenue of:

	Product X	*Product Y*
Sales price	$50	$60
Break even sales (in units)	7,274	3,637
Break even revenue	$363,700	$218,220

The total break even revenue would then be ($363,700 + $218,220) $581,920.

There is a little bit of a rounding difference but we could still conclude that Answer B is the correct answer.

Example 5

To achieve a target profit of $300,000 in Company A:

$$\text{Sales revenue required for profit of \$300,000} = \frac{\text{(Fixed costs + required profit)}}{\text{W.A. C/S ratio}}$$

$$\text{Sales revenue required for profit of \$300,000} = \frac{\$200,000 + \$300,000}{0.34375}$$

Sales revenue required for profit of $300,000 = $1,454,545

The correct answer is Answer D.

Example 6

(a)

Product	*Contribution* $000	*Sales revenue* $000	*C/S ratio*
X	550	800	0.6875
Y	50	200	0.25
Z	300	1,000	0.30
Total	900	2,000	

Weighted average contribution to sales ratio $= \frac{\text{Total contribution}}{\text{Total sales}}$

$= \frac{\$900,000}{\$2,000,000}$

$=$ 0.45 or 45%

(b)

Breakeven sales revenue required $= \frac{\text{Fixed costs}}{\text{C/S ratio}}$

$= \frac{\$300,000}{45\%}$

$=$ $666,667

(c)

Sales revenue required $= \frac{\text{Fixed costs + required profit}}{\text{C/S ratio}}$

$= \frac{\$300,000+ \$600,000}{0.45}$

$=$ $2,000,000

(d)

The chart is, essentially, a profit/volume chart. Cumulative profit is plotted against cumulative sales revenue.

Like P/V charts for single products the line drawn starts at the fixed costs below the line. It can therefore be determined that the fixed costs for the business are $300,000.

The product lines are then drawn in order of the ranking of their contribution/sales ratio. From the diagram we can therefore determine that the c/s ratio of product X must be the highest of the three products and that product Y must be the lowest of the three products.

The highest point on the diagram represents the highest potential revenue ($2m) and profits for the business ($600,000).

Assuming that the products are sold in the standard sales mix then the break even point is the point at which the lower line crosses the horizontal axis. This is at around 650,000 units of production.

If, however, the products were sold in order of their c/s ratios, then the higher line shows a potentially lower break even point. The higher line indicates that this would be achieved at around 440,000 units.

Note: the table below provides the workings which enabled the chart to be drawn.

Product	*Contribution* $000	*Cumulative Profit/ (Loss)* $000	*Revenue* $000	*Cumulative revenue* $000
		(300)		0
X	550	250	800	800
Z	300	550	1,000	1,800
Y	50	600	200	2,000

Example 7

(a) To calculate the overall breakeven point (expressed in sales value terms), we need to calculate a weighted average contribution to sales ratio. To this end, we will need a total sales revenue, as well as a total contribution in $:

	Summer	*Autumn*	*Winter*	*Spring*	***Total***
Sales mix	33.33%	41.67%	16.67%	8.33%	100%
Sales in $	200,000	250,000	100,000	50,000	600,000
Less: Variable costs in $	120,000	170,000	80,000	20,000	390,000
Contribution	80,000	80,000	20,000	30,000	210,000

Weighted average C/S ratio = ($210,000/$600,000)

Weighted average C/S ratio = $35%

Breakeven point (sales value) = $\frac{\text{Fixed costs}}{\text{WA C/S ratio}}$

Breakeven point (sales value) = **$454,286**

(b) After the change in sales mix, contribution can be calculated as follows:

	Summer	*Autumn*	*Winter*	*Spring*	*Total*
Sales mix	25%	40%	30%	5%	100%
Sales in $	150,000	240,000	180,000	30,000	600,000
Less: Variable costs in $	90,000	163,200	144,000	12,000	409,200
Contribution	60,000	76,800	36,000	18,000	190,800

Weighted average C/S ratio = ($190,800/$600,000)

Weighted average C/S ratio = $31.8%

Breakeven point (sales value) = $\frac{\text{Fixed costs}}{\text{WA C/S ratio}}$

Breakeven point (sales value) = **$500,000.**

Test your understanding 1

(a) **Break even point**

Contribution per unit = $(100 – 56) = $44

$$\text{C/S ratio} = \frac{\text{Contribution per unit}}{\text{Selling price per unit}} = \frac{\$44}{\$100} = 0.44$$

Breakeven point in terms numbers of units sold

$$= \frac{\text{Fixed costs}}{\text{Contribution per unit}}$$

$$= \frac{\$220{,}000}{\$44} = 5{,}000 \text{ units}$$

Breakeven point in terms of sales revenue

$$= \frac{\text{Fixed costs}}{\text{C/S ratio}}$$

$$= \frac{\$220{,}000}{0.44} = \$500{,}000 \text{ units}$$

(Proof: breakeven units × selling price per unit = 5,000 × $100 = $500,000)

(b) **Margin of safety**

(as a % of Budgeted sales)

$$= \frac{\text{Budgeted sales – Break-even sales}}{\text{Budgeted sales}} \times 100\%$$

$$= \frac{7{,}500 - 5{,}000}{7{,}500} \times 100\%$$

= 33.33%

Test your understanding 2

(i) The key to calculating the breakeven point is to determine the contribution per unit.

Contribution point = $120 – ($22 + $36 + $14) = $48

$$\text{Breakeven point} = \frac{\text{Fixed overhead}}{\text{Contribution per unit}}$$

$$= \frac{\$12 \times 2{,}000}{\$48} = \textbf{500 units}$$

(ii) Margin of safety = budgeted sales – breakeven point
= 2,200 – 500
= **1,700 units** (or 1,700/2,200 × 100 %)
= **77 %**

(iii) Once breakeven point has been reached, all of the contribution goes towards profits because all of the fixed costs have been covered.

Budgeted profit = 1,700 units margin of safety × $48 contribution per unit
= **$81,600**

(iv) To achieve the desired level of profit, sufficient units must be sold to earn a contribution which covers the fixed costs and leaves the desired profit for the month.

$$\text{Number of sales units required} = \frac{\text{Fixed overhead + desired profit}}{\text{Contribution per unit}}$$

$$= \frac{(\$12 \times 2{,}000) + \$96{,}000}{\$48}$$

= **2,500 units**

(v) Contribution per unit is calculated as $120 – $72 sum of variable costs = $48.

$$\text{Contribution to sales ratio} = \frac{\text{Contribution per unit}}{\text{Sales revenue per unit}}$$

$$= \frac{\$48}{\$120}$$

$$= \mathbf{40\%}$$

(iv) Breakeven revenue can be calculated in two ways .

$$\text{B.E.R} = \frac{\text{Monthly fixed costs}}{\text{Contribution to sales ratio}}$$

$$= \frac{\$12 \times 2{,}000 \text{ units}}{40\%}$$

$$= \mathbf{\$60{,}000}$$

This could also have been calculated as Breakeven Point 500 units × Selling price $120

= **$60,000**

Test your understanding 3

Firstly we need to calculate the breakeven sales revenue.

Because we haven't been given any information on units, we must have to use the contribution sales revenue technique:

$$\text{C/S ratio} = \frac{\text{Total contribution}}{\text{Total sales revenue}} = \frac{(450 - 220)}{450}$$

= 0.511 (or 51.1%)

$$\text{Breakeven point (in terms of sales revenue)} = \frac{\text{Fixed costs}}{\text{C/S ratio}}$$

$$\text{Breakeven point (in terms of sales revenue)} = \frac{\$160{,}000}{0.511}$$

Breakeven point (in terms of sales revenue) = $313,000

Now that we know the break-even position we can calculate the margin of safety (this is what is required in the second element of the question).

$$\text{Margin of safety (as a \% of budgeted sales)} = \frac{\text{Budgeted sales} - \text{Breakeven sales}}{\text{Budgeted sales}} \times 100\%$$

$$\text{Margin of safety (as a \% of budgeted sales)} = \frac{450 - 313}{450} \times 100\%$$

= 0.3044 (or 30.44%)

This tells us that for the company to fall into a loss making position its sales next year would have to fall by over 30.44% from their current position.

Test your understanding 4

Monthly fixed costs = 4,000 units × \$4 = \$16,000.

First calculate the breakeven sales: 16,000/(18 – 8) = 1,600

Margin of safety % = (projected sales – breakeven sales)/projected sales

= (4,000 – 1,600)/4,000 = 60%

Test your understanding 5

C

$$\text{Contribution margin} = \frac{160}{400} = 40\%$$

$$\text{Target revenue} = \frac{100 + 100}{40\%} = 500$$

$$\text{\% Increase in revenue} = \frac{500}{400} = 25\%$$

Test your understanding 6

(a) Point X on the chart shows the highest value of sales at which break-even will occur, assuming that the budgeted sales value is the maximum achievable for each of the products. It looks like that breakeven point is achieved when all of E, all of D and some of Cs are sold.

Note that it is not meaningful here, because it is unlikely that in reality, all of D and Es products will be sold whilst none of As or Bs will.

(b)

Working 1 – Weighted average contribution to sales ratio:

$$\text{Breakeven revenue} = \frac{\text{Fixed costs}}{\text{Weighted average contribution to sales ratio}}$$

$$\text{Breakeven revenue} = \frac{\$300{,}000}{24.16\% \text{ (working 1)}}$$

$$= \mathbf{\$1{,}241{,}935}$$

Product	*A*	*B*	*C*	*D*	*E*	*Total*
Unit selling price	$40	$15	$40	$30	$20	
Total sales ($000)	400	180	1,400	900	200	3,080
Contribution to sales ratio	45%	30%	25%	20%	(10%)	
Contribution ($000)	180	54	350	180	(20)	744

$$\text{Weighted average C/S ratio} = \frac{\text{Total contribution } \$744{,}000}{\text{Total sales } \$3{,}080{,}000}$$

$$= \mathbf{0.2416 \text{ or } 24.16\%}$$

Test your understanding 7

(a)

Product	*Revenue* $000	*Variable costs* $000	*Contribution* $000	*C/S ratio*
J	200	140	60	0.30
K	400	80	320	0.80
L	200	210	(10)	(0.05)
M	200	140	60	0.30
	1,000	**570**	**430**	

(b) The products are plotted in the order of their C/S ratios. The fixed costs of the company are $240,000. The chart reveals that if only product K is produced, the company will generate a profit of $80,000. The profit of the company is maximised at $200,000. This is achieved by producing Products K, J and M only.

If all four products are produced then JK Ltd can expect a profit of $190,000 from sales revenue of $1,000,000. If all four products are sold in the budget sales mix then the company will break even when revenue reaches $558,140. This point has been indicated on the graph. This point can also be calculated. Thus:

Average contribution/sales ratio = 430/1,000 = 43%

$$\text{Break-even point} = \frac{\text{Fixed costs}}{\text{Average C/S ratio}}$$

$$= \frac{\$240,000}{0.43} = \$558,140$$

Note: the diagram was constructed using the following product information:

Product	*Contribution* $000	*Cumulative Profit/(Loss)*	*Revenue* $000	*Cumulative revenue*
		(240)		0
K	320	80	400	400
J	60	140	200	600
M	60	200	200	800
L	(10)	190	200	1,000

(c) The overall C/S ratio could be improved by:

- Changing the product mix in favour of products with above-average C/S ratios. In this example that would mean increasing production of Product K.
- Increasing sales prices or cutting production costs.
- Deleting product L.

Test your understanding 8

(a) First calculate the current contribution per unit.

	$000	$000
Sales revenue		288
Direct materials	54	
Direct wages	72	
Variable production overhead	18	
Variable administration etc.	27	
		171
Contribution		117
Contribution per unit ($117,000/9,000 units)		$13

Now you can use the formula to calculate the breakeven point.

Breakeven point =

$$\frac{\text{Fixed costs}}{\text{Contribution per unit}} = \frac{\$42{,}000 + \$\ 36{,}000}{\$13} = 6{,}000 \text{ units}$$

(b) *Alternative (i)*

Budgeted contribution per unit	$13
Reduction in selling price ($32 – $28)	$4
Revised contribution per unit	$9
Revised breakeven point = $78,000/$9	8,667 units
Revised sales volume = 9,000 × (90/75)	10,800 units
Revised contribution = 10,800 × $9	$97,200
Less fixed costs	$78,000
Revised profit	$19,200

Alternative (ii)

Budgeted contribution per unit	$13.00
Reduction in selling price (15% × $32)	$4.80
Revised contribution per unit	$8.20
Revised breakeven point = $\frac{\$78,000 + \$5,000}{\$8.20}$	10,122 Units
Revised sales volume = 9,000 units × (100/75)	12,000 Units
Revised contribution = 12,000 × $8.20	$98,400
Less fixed costs	$83,000
Revised profit	$15,400

Neither of the two alternative proposals is worthwhile. They both result in lower forecast profits. In addition, they will both increase the breakeven point and will therefore increase the risk associated with the company's operations.

(c) This exercise has shown you how an understanding of cost behaviour patterns and the manipulation of contribution can enable the rapid evaluation of the financial effects of a proposal. We can now expand it to demonstrate another aspect of the application of CVP analysis to short-term decision-making.

Once again, the key is the required contribution. This time the contribution must be sufficient to cover both the fixed costs and the required profit. If we then divide this amount by the contribution earned from each unit, we can determine the required sales volume.

$$\text{Required sales} = \frac{\text{Fixed costs + required profit}}{\text{Contribution per unit}}$$

$$= \frac{(\$42{,}000 + \$36{,}000 + \$45{,}500)}{\$13} = \underline{\textbf{9,500 units}}$$

Test your understanding 9

Answer: lower

	R	*S*	*T*	*Total*
	$	$	$	$
Sales revenue	10,000	15,000	20,000	45,000
Contribution	6,000	6,000	10,000	22,000
C/S ratio	0.6	0.4	0.5	0.489
New weightings	20%	50%	30%	13,000
New C/S ratio	0.12	0.2	0.15	0.47

So the new C/S ratio is lower.

Test your understanding 10

(i) An increase in fixed costs

(ii) A decrease in variable costs

(iii) An increase in sales price

(iv) A decrease in sales volume

Test your understanding 11

The correct answer is option **B.**

Package	Volume	Contribution per package	Total contribution	Selling price per package	Total revenue
		$	$	$	$
Standard	50	380	19,000	450	22,500
Premium	30	510	15,300	600	18,000
Superior	20	680	13,600	800	16,000
			47,900		56,500

Average C/S ratio = 47,900/56,500 = 0.8478

Breakeven point = $200,000/0.8478 = $235,908

Test your understanding 12

To the nearest $, the total break-even revenue is $**222,222**

The weighted average contribution margin is:

= [(40% × 60%) + (80% × 30%) + (60% × 10%)] = [24% + 24% + 6%] = 54%

The break even point = $120,000/54% = $222,222.

chapter

6

Relevant costs and decision making

Chapter learning objectives

Lead	**Component**
C1. Explain concepts of cost and revenue relevant to pricing and product decisions.	(a) Explain the principles of decision making including the identification and use of relevant cash flows and qualitative factors. (b) Explain the conflicts between cost accounting for profit reporting and stock valuation and information required for decision making.
C2. Analyse short term pricing and product decisions.	(a) Apply relevant cost analysis to various types of short-term decisions. (d) Explain the impact of joint costs on decisions concerning process and product viability.

1 Session Content Diagram

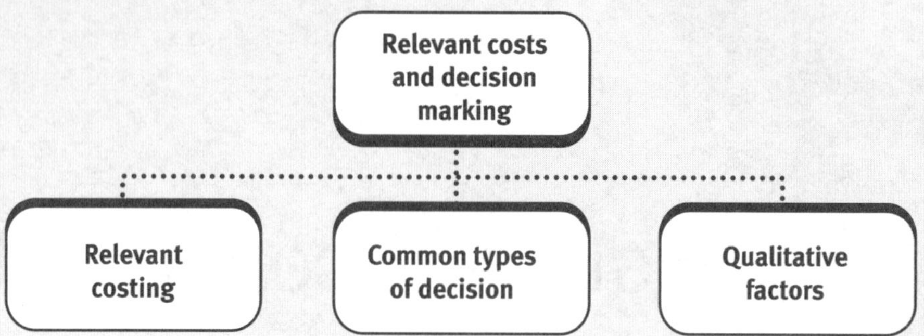

2 Introduction to relevant costs and revenues

Organisations face many decisions, and they usually must choose between two or more alternatives. Decisions will generally be based on taking the decision that maximises shareholder value, so all decisions will be taken using relevant costs and revenues. **Relevant costs and revenues are those costs and revenues that *change* as a direct result of a decision taken.**

Characteristics of relevant costs

In its *Official Terminology,* CIMA defines **'relevant costs'** and 'relevant revenues' as the 'costs and revenues appropriate to a specific management decision; they are represented by future cash flows whose magnitude will vary depending upon the outcome of the management decision made(...)'.

Relevant costs and revenues have the following features:

(1) **They are future costs and revenues** – as it is not possible to change what has happened in the past, then relevant costs and revenues must be future costs and revenues.

(2) **They are incremental** or **differential** – relevant costs are incremental costs and it is the increase in costs and revenues that occurs as a direct result of a decision taken that is relevant. Common costs can be ignored for the purposes of decision making. Look out for costs detailed as *differential, specific or avoidable.*

CIMA defines 'avoidable costs' as 'the specific costs of an activity or sector of a business which would be avoided if that activity or sector did not exist.'

For example, if a company is considering shutting down a department, then the avoidable costs are those that would be saved as a result of the shutdown. Such costs might include the labour costs of those employed in the department and the rental cost of the space occupied by the department. The latter is an example of an **attributable** or **specific** fixed cost. Costs such as apportioned head office costs that would not be saved as a result of the shutdown are unavoidable costs. They are not relevant to the decision.

(3) **They are cash flows** – in addition, future costs and revenues must be cash flows arising as a direct consequence of the decision taken. Relevant costs do not include items which do not involve cash flows (depreciation and notional costs for example).

In an examination, unless told otherwise, assume that variable costs are relevant costs.

Non-relevant costs

A distinction must be made between **relevant** and **non-relevant** costs for the purposes of management decision-making.

This has many implications:

Sunk costs

A sunk cost has already been incurred and therefore will not be relevant to the investment decision.

Committed costs

Expenditure that will be incurred in the future, but as a result of decisions taken in the past that cannot now be changed. These are known as **committed costs** and are not treated as relevant costs for decision making.

Fixed costs

Should be treated as a whole, and only where relevant. This means that fixed overheads that are "absorbed"/"charged"/"allocated"/"apportioned" to a project should be ignored. Only extra/incremental changes in fixed overheads should be included in decisions.

Depreciation

Depreciation is not a cash flow, and so should **never** be included in decisions.

Further details

Relevant costs are those which will be affected by the decision being taken. All relevant costs should be considered in management decision-making. If a cost will remain unaltered regardless of the decision being taken, then it is called a non-relevant cost or irrelevant cost.

Costs that are not usually relevant in management decisions include the following:

(a) Sunk or past costs. This is a 'cost that has been irreversibly incurred or committed and cannot therefore be considered relevant to a decision. Sunk costs may also be termed irrecoverable costs' *(CIMA Official Terminology).* An example of a sunk cost is expenditure that has been incurred in developing a new product. The money cannot be recovered even if a decision is taken to abandon further development of the new product. The cost is therefore not relevant to future decisions concerning the product.

(b) Expenditure that will be incurred in the future, but as a result of decisions taken in the past that cannot now be changed. These are known as committed costs. They can sometimes cause confusion because they are future costs. However, a committed cost will be incurred regardless of the decision being taken and therefore it is not relevant. An example of this type of cost could be expenditure on special packaging for a new product, where the packaging has been ordered and delivered but not yet paid for. The company is obliged to pay for the packaging even if they decide not to proceed with the product; therefore it is not a relevant cost.

(c) Absorbed fixed overheads that will not increase or decrease as a result of the decision being taken. The amount of overhead to be absorbed by a particular cost unit might alter because of the decision; however, this is a result of the company's cost accounting procedures for overheads. If the actual amount of overhead incurred by the company will not alter, then the overhead is not a relevant cost.

(d) Historical cost depreciation. Depreciation is an accounting adjustment but does not result in any future cash flows. They are merely the book entries that are designed to spread the original cost of an asset over its useful life.

(e) Notional costs such as notional rent and notional interest. These are only relevant if they represent an identified lost opportunity to use the premises or the finance for some alternative purpose.

In these circumstances, the notional costs would be opportunity costs. This explanation will become clearer when you learn more about opportunity costs later in this chapter.

Conclusion

It is essential to look to the future when deciding which costs are relevant to a decision. Costs that have already been incurred or that will not be altered in the future as a result of the decision being taken are not relevant costs.

Example 1

As part of a new product development a company has employed a building consultant to perform an initial survey. This initial survey has cost $40,000. But there will be an ongoing need for her services if the company decides to proceed with the project. This work will be charged at a fixed rate of $20,000 per annum.

What relevant cost should be included for the building consultants services in the first year when considering whether the project should proceed?

A $0

B $20,000

C $40,000

D $60,000

Opportunity cost

'Opportunity cost' is an important concept in decision making. It represents **the best alternative that is forgone in taking the decision.** The opportunity cost emphasises that decision making is concerned with alternatives and that a cost of taking one decision is the profit or contribution forgone by not taking the next best alternative.

If resources to be used on projects are scarce (e.g. labour, materials, machines), then consideration must be given to profits or contribution which could have been earned from alternative uses of the resources.

For example, the skilled labour which may be needed on a new project might have to be withdrawn from normal production. This withdrawal would cause a loss in contribution which is obviously relevant to the project appraisal.

The cash flows of a single department or division cannot be looked at in isolation. It is always the effects on cash flows of the whole organisation which must be considered.

Further details on opportunity costs

An opportunity cost is a special type of relevant cost. It is defined in the *CIMA Terminology* as 'the value of the benefit sacrificed when one course of action is chosen, in preference to an alternative. The opportunity cost is represented by the forgone potential benefit from the best rejected course of action.'

With opportunity costs we are concerned with identifying the value of any benefit forgone as the result of choosing one course of action in preference to another.

Examples of opportunity costs

The best way to demonstrate opportunity costs is to consider some examples.

(a) A company has some obsolete material in inventory that it is considering to use for a special contract. If the material is not used on the contract it can either be sold back to the supplier for $2 per tonne or it can be used on another contract in place of a different material that would usually cost $2.20 per tonne.

The opportunity cost of using the material on the special contract is $2.20 per tonne. This is the value of the next best alternative use for the material, or the benefit forgone by not using it for the other contract.

(b) Chris is deciding whether or not to take a skiing holiday this year. The travel agent is quoting an all-inclusive holiday cost of $675 for a week. Chris will lose the chance to earn $200 for a part-time job during the week that the holiday would be taken.

The relevant cost of taking the holiday is $875. This is made up of the out-of-pocket cost of $675, plus the $200 opportunity cost, that is the part-time wages forgone.

Notional costs and opportunity costs

Notional costs and opportunity costs are often similar. This is particularly noticeable in the case of notional rent. The notional rent could be the rental that the company is forgoing by occupying the premises itself, that is it could be an opportunity cost. However, it is only a true opportunity cost if the company can actually identify a forgone opportunity to rent the premises. If nobody is willing to pay the rent, then it is not an opportunity cost.

Avoidable, differential and incremental costs

There are two other types of relevant cost that you will need to know about: avoidable costs and differential/incremental costs.

Avoidable costs

CIMA defines avoidable costs as 'the specific costs of an activity or sector of a business which would be avoided if that activity or sector did not exist'.

For example, if a company is considering shutting down a department, then the avoidable costs are those that would be saved as a result of the shutdown. Such costs might include the labour costs of those employed in the department and the rental cost of the space occupied by the department. The latter is an example of an attributable or specific fixed cost. Costs such as apportioned head office costs that would not be saved as a result of the shutdown are unavoidable costs. They are not relevant to the decision.

Differential/incremental costs

CIMA defines a differential/incremental cost as 'the difference in total cost between alternatives. This is calculated to assist decision making'.

For example, if the relevant cost of contract X is $5,700 and the relevant cost of contract Y is $6,200, we would say that the differential or incremental cost is $500, that is the extra cost of contract Y is $500.

Using incremental costs

Incremental costs can be useful if the cost accountant wishes to highlight the consequences of taking sequential steps in a decision. For example, the accountant might be providing cost information for a decision about whether to increase the number of employees in a department.

Instead of quoting several different total-cost figures, it might be more useful to say 'the incremental cost per five employees will be $5,800 per month'.

Remember that only relevant costs should be used in the calculations.

Example 2

A company which manufactures and sells one single product is currently operating at 85% of full capacity, producing 102,000 units per month. The current total monthly costs of production amount to $330,000, of which $75,000 are fixed and are expected to remain unchanged for all levels of activity up to full capacity.

A new potential customer has expressed interest in taking regular monthly delivery of 12,000 units at a price of $2.80 per unit.

All existing production is sold each month at a price of $3.25 per unit. If the new business is accepted, existing sales are expected to fall by 2 units for every 15 units sold to the new customer.

What is the overall increase in monthly profit which would result from accepting the new business?

Incremental revenue

Just as incremental costs are the differences in cost between alternatives, so incremental revenues are the differences in revenues between the alternatives. Matching the incremental costs against the incremental revenues will produce a figure for the incremental gain or loss between the alternatives.

3 The relevant cost of variable costs and overheads

When we put the principles of relevant and non-relevant costs together, and then combine these with the complications brought in by opportunity costs, we have many things to consider in determining the relevant costs of areas such as materials, labour and overheads. This section looks at some of these costs in more detail in order to develop some criteria for determining the relevant cost.

The relevant cost of materials

The following flow chart should provide a useful reminder of the points that must be considered when ascertaining the relevant cost of materials:

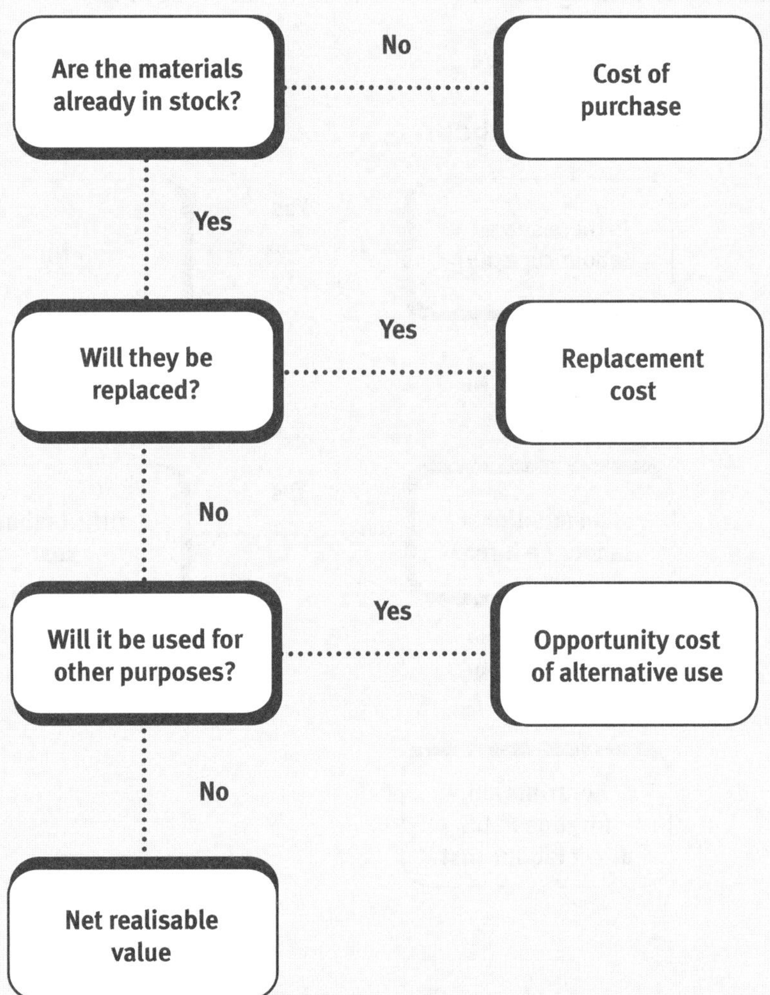

Example 3

A company is considering a short-term pricing decision for a contract that would utilise some material P that it has held in inventory for some time. The company does not foresee any other use for the material. The work would require 1,000 kgs of Material P.

There are 800 kgs of Material P in inventory, which were bought some time ago at a cost of $3 per kg. The material held in inventory could currently be sold for $3.50 per kg. The current purchase price of Material P is $4.50 per kg.

What is the relevant cost of Material P for the company to use when making its pricing decision for the contract closest to?

The relevant cost of labour

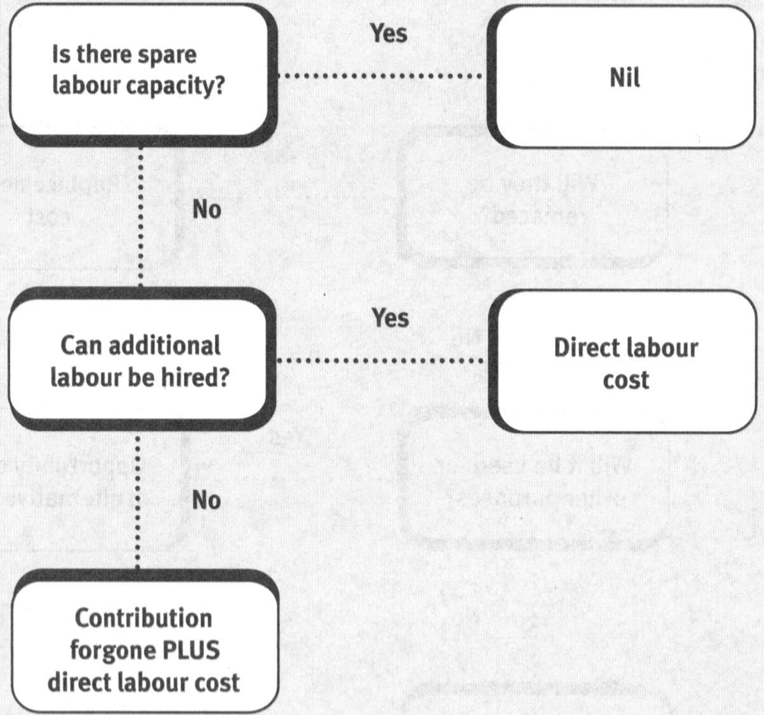

Example 4

100 hours of skilled labour are needed for a special contract. The staff are working at full capacity at the moment and the workers would have to be taken off production of a different product in order to work on the special contract. The details of the other product are shown below:

	$/unit
Selling price	60
Direct material	10
Direct labour 1 hour @ $10/hour	10
Variable overheads	15
Fixed overheads	15

The skilled workers' pay rate would not change, regardless of which product they worked on. What would be the relevant cost?

The relevant cost of overheads

In addition to calculating the relevant cost of materials and labour, you may also be required to calculate the relevant cost of overheads.

Relevant cost of overheads

Only those overheads that vary as a direct result of a decision taken are relevant overheads

Example 5

JB Ltd absorbs overheads on a machine hour rate, currently $20/hour, of which $7 is for variable overheads and $13 for fixed overheads. The company is deciding whether to undertake a contract in the coming year. If the contract is undertaken, it is estimated that fixed costs will increase for the duration of the contract by $3,200. The contract would require 800 hours of machine time.

What is the relevant cost of overheads for the contract?

A $3,200

B $5,600

C $8,800

D $16,000

The relevant cost of non-current assets

The relevant costs associated with non-current assets, such as plant and machinery, are determined in a similar way to the relevant costs of materials.

- If plant and machinery is to be replaced at the end of its useful life, then the relevant cost is the current replacement cost.
- If plant and machinery is not to be replaced, then the relevant cost is the higher of the sale proceeds (if sold) and the net cash inflows arising from the use of the asset (if not sold).

Example 6

Equipment owned by a company has a net book value of $1,800 and has been idle for some months. It could now be used on a six months contract that is being considered. If not used on this contract, the equipment would be sold now for a net amount of $2,000. After use on the contract, the equipment would have no resale value and would be dismantled.

What is the total relevant cost of the equipment to the contract?

A $0

B $1,800

C $2,000

D $3,800

Example 7

The CS group is planning its annual marketing conference for its sales executives and has approached the VBJ Holiday company (VBJ) to obtain a quotation. VBJ has been trying to win the business of the CS group for some time and is keen to provide a quotation which the CS group will find acceptable in the hope that this will lead to future contracts.

The manager of VBJ has produced the following cost estimate for the conference:

Coach running costs	$2,000
Driver costs	$3,000
Hotel costs	$5,000
General overheads	$2,000
Sub total	**$12,000**
Profit 30%	$3,600
Total	**$15,600**

You have considered this cost estimate but you believe that it would be more appropriate to base the quotation on relevant costs. You have therefore obtained the following further information:

Coach running costs represent the fuel costs of $1,500 plus an apportionment of the annual fixed costs of operating the coach. No specific fixed costs would be incurred if the coach is used on this contract. If the contract did not go ahead, the coach would not be in use for eight out of the ten days of the conference. For the other two days a contract has already been accepted which contains a significant financial penalty clause. This contract earns a contribution of $250 per day. A replacement coach could be hired for $180 per day.

Driver costs represent the salary and related employment costs of one driver for 10 days. If the driver is used on this contract the company will need to replace the driver so that VBJ can complete its existing work. The replacement driver would be hired from a recruitment agency that charges $400 per day for a suitably qualified driver. Hotel costs are the expected costs of hiring the hotel for the conference.

General overheads are based upon the overhead absorption rate of VBJ and are set annually when the company prepares its budgets. The only general overhead cost that can be specifically identified with the conference is the time that has been spent in considering the costs of the conference and preparing the quotation. This amounted to $250.

Required:

Prepare a statement showing the total relevant cost of the contract. Explain clearly the reasons for each of the values in your quotation and for excluding any of the costs (if appropriate).

4 Decision making based on relevant costing principles

There are many decisions that an organisation might have to make which will either be to solve short term problems (such as a short term scarcity of resources) or that may only be one-off in nature (such as whether to close a particular division).

The types of decisions that you may be asked to deal with include and which are explored in the following sections are:

- Limiting factor decisions
- Make or buy decisions
- Shutdown decisions, including deleting a segment or temporary closure
- Accept or reject an order decisions
- Minimum pricing decisions
- Joint product and further processing decisions.

In all of these decisions it will be important to remember that only **relevant costs** should be used in the calculations.

Limiting factor decisions

A limiting factor refers to a resource which prevents a company from achieving the output and sales that it would like to achieve. Businesses often operate under short term restrictions on resources (for example, staff time may be limited during a strike). They therefore may not be able to produce all products that make a positive contribution and need to prioritise products and choose between them.

Single limiting factor

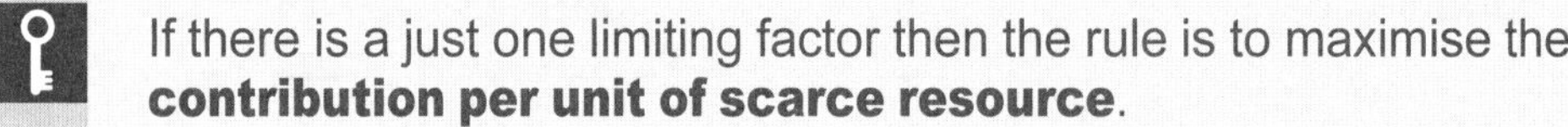

If there is a just one limiting factor then the rule is to maximise the **contribution per unit of scarce resource**.

The contribution per unit of each product is calculated and divided by the amount of scarce resource each product uses. The higher the contribution per unit of scarce resource the greater the priority that should be given to the product.

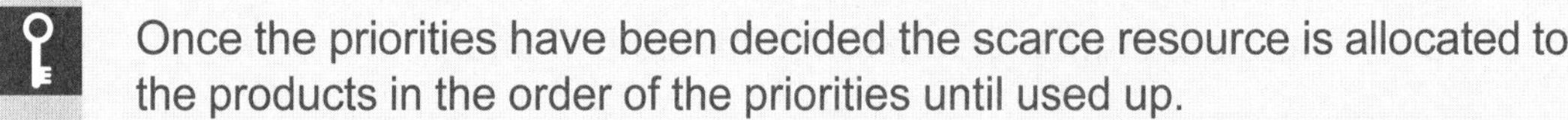

Once the priorities have been decided the scarce resource is allocated to the products in the order of the priorities until used up.

Limiting factor analysis step-by-step technique

The usual objective in questions is to maximise profit. Given that fixed costs are unaffected by the production decision in the short run, the approach should be to maximise the contribution earned.

If there is one limiting factor, then the problem is best solved as follows:

Step 1: identify the bottleneck constraint (also known as the limiting factor, key budget factor or principal budget factor).
Step 2: calculate the contribution per unit for each product.
Step 3: calculate the contribution per unit of the bottleneck resource for each product.
Step 4: rank the products in order of the contribution per unit of the bottleneck resource.
Step 5: allocate resources using this ranking and answer the question.

Example 8

A company produces three products, and is reviewing the production and sales budgets for the next accounting period. The following information is available for the three products:

	Product P		**Product Q**		**Product R**	
	$	$	$	$	$	$
Selling price		600		300		100
Labour ($20 per hour)	300		160		40	
Other variable costs	90		68		14	
		(390)		(228)		(54)
Contribution/unit		210		72		46
Maximum demand (units)		200		600		1,000

Labour hours are strictly limited to 7,800 hours in total.

Required:

(a) Calculate the optimum product mix and the maximum contribution.

(b) A special contract requires 3,000 labour hours. What is the relevant cost of obtaining these hours?

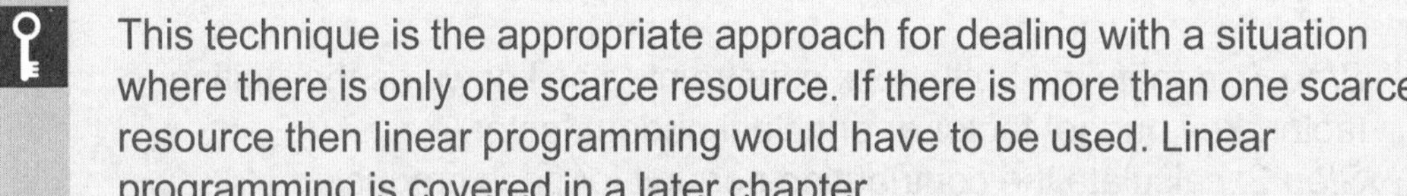

This technique is the appropriate approach for dealing with a situation where there is only one scarce resource. If there is more than one scarce resource then linear programming would have to be used. Linear programming is covered in a later chapter.

Make or buy decisions

This is an extension of the limiting factor problem. If it is possible to buy-in the product and therefore avoid the use of the limiting factor then the products need to be ranked differently:

Products should be ranked (from highest to lowest) based on the **saving made** (the difference between the buy-in cost and the incremental cost of internal production) **per usage of the scarce resource**.

Further details

Businesses may be faced with the decision whether to make components for their own products themselves or to concentrate their resources on assembling the products, obtaining the components from outside suppliers instead of making them 'in house'.

If the resources are bought in, their purchase cost is wholly marginal (i.e. direct). However, if it is decided to manufacture the components internally, the comparative costs of doing so will be the direct materials and wages costs, plus the variable factory overhead. If the total variable costs of internally manufactured components is seen to be greater than the cost of obtaining similar components elsewhere, it is obviously uneconomic to produce these items internally.

Business therefore need to compare these two costs (the buy-in cost and the internal production cost). The techniques to determine the production plan is then based on the same techniques used in any other limiting factor decision.

Example 9

A company manufactures four components (L, M, N and P) which are incorporated into different products. All the components are manufactured using the same general purpose machinery. The following production cost and machine hour data are available, together with the purchase prices from an outside supplier.

	L	*M*	*N*	*P*
Production cost:	$	$	$	$
Direct material	12	18	15	8
Direct labour	25	15	10	8
Variable overhead	8	7	5	4
Fixed overhead	10	6	4	3
Total	**55**	**46**	**34**	**23**
Purchase price from outside supplier	$57	$55	$54	$50
	Hours	Hours	Hours	Hours
Machine hours per unit	3	5	4	6

Manufacturing requirements show a need for 1,500 units of each component per week. The maximum number of general purpose machinery hours available per week is 24,000.

Required:

Calculate the number of units which should be purchased from the outside supplier.

Accept or reject decisions

This might occur where a customer has placed a one-off order for a product or a service.

The selling price will already be known and if it is greater than the relevant costs the order should be accepted.

Example 10

A company manufactures two models of a pocket calculator: The basic model sells for $5.50, has a direct material cost of $1.25 and requires 0.25 hours of labour time to produce. The other model, the Scientist, sells for $7.50, has a direct material cost of $1.63 and takes 0.375 hours to produce.

Labour, which is paid at the rate of $6 per hour, is currently very scarce, while demand for the company's calculators is heavy. The company is currently producing 8,000 of the basic model and 4,000 of the Scientist model per month, while fixed costs are $24,000 per month.

An overseas customer has offered the company a contract, worth $35,000, for a number of calculators made to its requirements. The estimating department has ascertained the following facts in respect of the work:

- The labour time for the contract would be 1,200 hours.
- The material cost would be $9,000 plus the cost of a particular component not normally used in the company's models.
- These components could be purchased from a supplier for $2,500 or alternatively, they could be made internally for a material cost of $1,000 and an additional labour time of 150 hours.

Required:

Advise the management as to the action they should take.

Shutdown decisions

This type of decision may involve deleting (or shutting down) a segment of the business, a product line, a service, etc. In the normal everyday reporting system of the business, it is likely that absorption costing will be used. It may appear under this system that one or more of the business segments appears unprofitable. Closure decisions taken on the basis of full absorption costs statements may fail to consider the fact that certain fixed costs allotted to the segment to be discontinued are fixed and may continue if the segment is dropped. The focus for shutdown decisions should be whether the costs and revenues are avoidable.

Businesses need to therefore determine the difference between forgone revenue from the closure and the incremental cost savings from closure.

Example 11

Wye plc makes and sells four products. The profit and loss statement for April is as follows:

	W	*X*	*Y*	*Z*	*Total*
	$	*$*	*$*	*$*	*$*
Sales	30,000	20,000	35,000	15,000	100,000
Cost of sales	16,000	8,000	22,000	10,000	56,000
Gross profit	14,000	12,000	13,000	5,000	44,000
Overhead cost:					
Selling	8,000	7,000	8,500	6,500	30,000
Administration	2,000	2,000	2,000	2,000	8,000
Net profit	4,000	3,000	2,500	(3,500)	6,000

The management team is concerned about the results, particularly those of product Z, and it has been suggested that Wye plc would be better off if it ceased production of product Z. The production manager has said that if product Z were discontinued the resources which would become available could be used to increase production of product Y by 40 per cent. You have analysed the cost structures of each of the products and discovered the following:

	W	*X*	*Y*	*Z*	*Total*
	$	*$*	*$*	*$*	*$*
Variable costs	4,800	1,600	13,200	5,000	24,600
Fixed costs	11,200	6,400	8,800	5,000	31,400
Gross profit	16,000	8,000	22,000	10,000	56,000

The total fixed costs figure includes $20,000 which is not specific to any one product, and which has been apportioned to each product on the basis of sales values. If the quantity of any product increases by more than 25 per cent, then the specific fixed production costs of the product will increase by 30 per cent.

The selling overhead comprises a fixed cost of $5,000 per product plus a variable cost which varies in proportion to sales value. The fixed cost is not specific to any product but the sales director believes that it should be shared equally by the four products.

The administration cost is a fixed central overhead cost; it is not affected by the products made.

Required:

(a) Prepare a statement which shows clearly the results of continuing to produce products W, X, Y and Z at the same volumes as were achieved in April. Present your statement in a format suitable for management decision-making.

(b) (i) Prepare a statement showing clearly the results if product Z is discontinued, and the number of units of Y is increased in accordance with the production manager's statement. (Assume that no change in selling price per unit is necessary to sell the additional units.)

(ii) Reconcile the profit calculated in (a) and (b) (i) above; advise the management team as to whether product Z should be discontinued.

(c) Explain briefly any non-financial factors which should be considered before discontinuing a product.

Minimum pricing decisions

The minimum pricing approach is a useful method in situations where there is a lot of intense competition, surplus production capacity, clearance of old inventories, getting special orders and/or improving market share of the product.

The minimum price should be set at the incremental costs of manufacturing, plus opportunity costs (if any).

For this type of pricing, the selling price is the lowest price that a company may sell its product at – usually the price will be the total relevant costs of manufacturing.

Illustration 1

ABC Company has prepared a summary of its relevant costs for a special order:

(i)	Material P	$120
	Material Q	$(280)
(ii)	Labour	–
(iii)	Variable overhead	$600
(iv)	Rent forgone	$210
	Total relevant cost	**$650**

This cost of $650 represents the minimum price that the company should charge for the order if they wish to make neither a profit nor a loss. As long as the customer pays $650 for the order, the company profits will not be affected.

Obviously, this represents the absolute minimum price that could be charged. It is unlikely that ABC Ltd would actually charge this amount. They would probably wish to add a profit margin to improve the company's profits. However, this absolute minimum value does give managers a starting point for their pricing decision. They know that the company will be worse off if the price is less than $650. If perhaps ABC Ltd is tendering for the order in competition with other suppliers, they may try to obtain some information on the likely prices to be tendered by their competitors. If these prices are less than or close to $650, then ABC knows that they will not be able to offer a competitive price.

On the other hand, if competitors are likely to tender a much higher price, then the managers know that they are able to price competitively.

Joint products and further processing decisions

Joint products were examined in a previous chapter where costs up until the split-off point were allocated to the products.

With many joint products it is possible to sell the product at the split-off point or to send it through a further process which will enhance its value. There are two rules to follow when ascertaining whether the further processing is worthwhile:

(1) Only the incremental costs and revenues of the further process are relevant.

(2) The joint process costs are irrelevant – they are already 'sunk' at the point of separation.

Further details

The main decisions involving joint products are:

- To carry out the whole process or not. This decision is made by considering the total revenues and costs of the process. A decision cannot be taken to just process some of the products as all products are produced simultaneously. The basis of common cost apportionment is irrelevant but the common costs in total are relevant.
- Whether or not to further process products. This decision is based on the incremental costs and incremental revenues of further processing. Revenue and cost at the split-off point are irrelevant to the decision as they will not change.

Example 12

A processing company operates a common process from which three different products emerge. Each of the three products can then either be sold in a market that has many buyers and sellers or further processed independently of each other in three other processes. After further processing, each of the products can be sold in the same market for a higher unit selling price.

Which of the following is required to determine whether or not any of the products should be further processed? *(choose all that apply)*

(i) Total cost of the common process

(ii) The basis of sharing the common process cost between the three products

(iii) The cost of each of the three additional processes

(iv) The unit selling price of each product after further processing

(v) The unit selling price of each product before further processing

(vi) The percentage normal loss of each further process

(vii) The actual units of output of each product from the common process

Qualitative factors in decision making

In some decision-making situations, qualitative aspects are more important than immediate financial benefit from a decision. They will vary with different business circumstances and are those factors relevant to a decision that are difficult or impossible to measure in terms of money.

CIMA's *Official Terminology* defines 'Qualitative factors' as '*factors that are relevant to a decision but are not expressed numerically*'.

For an organisation faced with a decision, qualitative factors may include:

(1) The state of the economy, and its levels of inflation

(2) The availability of cash

(3) Effect of a decision on employee morale, schedules and other internal elements

(4) Effect of a decision on relationships with and commitments to different stakeholders, such as:
   - Shareholders
   - Managers
   - Environment
   - Local Community
   - Suppliers

(5) Effect of a decision on long-term future profitability

(6) Effect of a decision on a company's public image and the reaction of customers

(7) The likely reaction of competitors.

5 Chapter summary

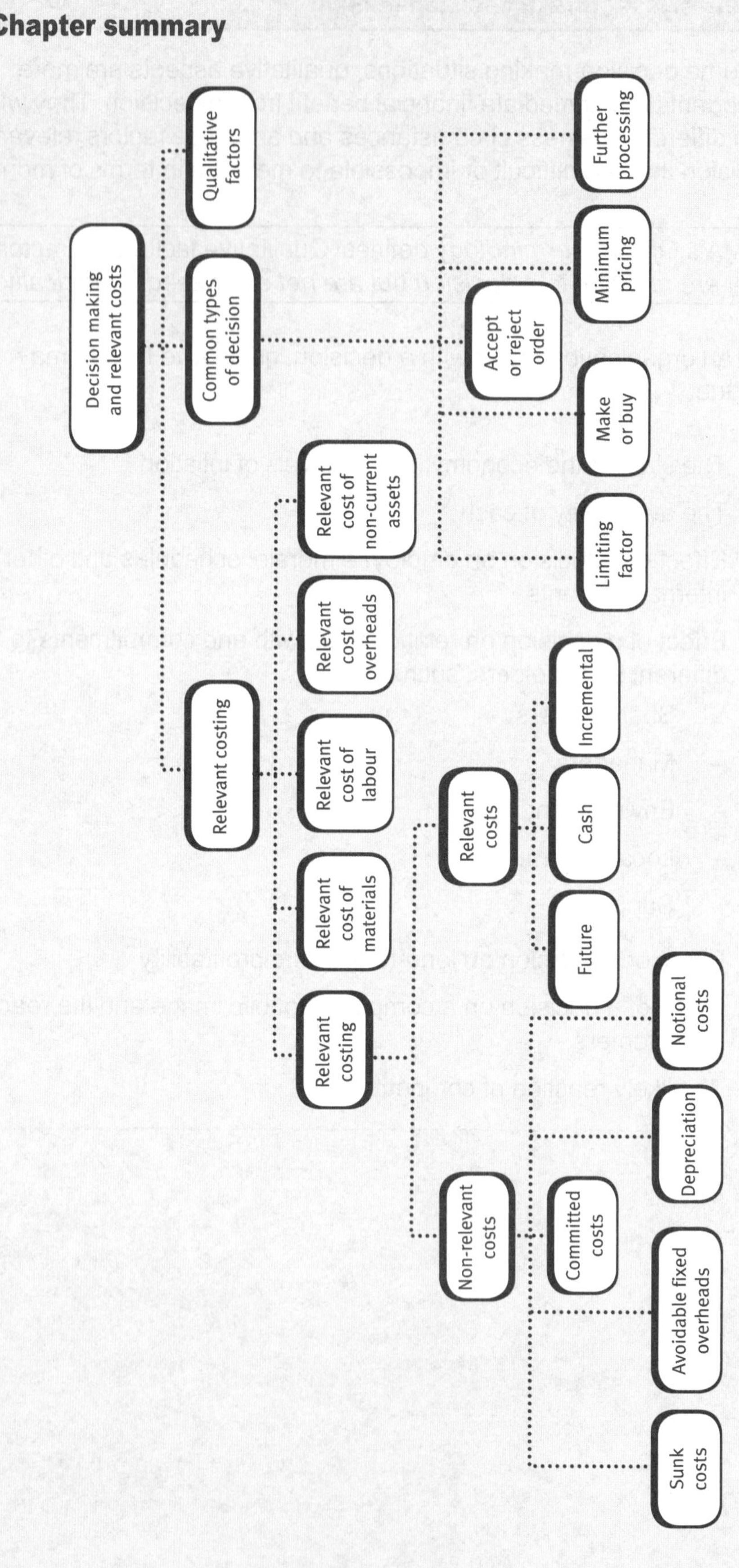

6 Practice Questions

Test your understanding 1

Which of the following costs for a proposed project are relevant?

(i) The salary to be paid to a market researcher who will oversee the development of a new product. This is a new post to be created especially for the new product but the $12,000 salary will be a fixed cost. Is this cost relevant to the decision to proceed with the development of the product?

(ii) The $2,500 additional monthly running costs of a new machine to be purchased to manufacture an established product. Since the new machine will save on labour time, the fixed overhead to be absorbed by the product will reduce by $100 per month. Are these costs relevant to the decision to purchase the new machine?

(iii) Office cleaning expenses of $125 for next month. The office is cleaned by contractors and the contract can be cancelled by giving 1 month's notice. Is this cost relevant to a decision to close the office?

(iv) Expenses of $75 paid to the marketing manager. This was to reimburse the manager for the cost of travelling to meet a client with whom the company is currently negotiating a major contract. Is this cost relevant to the decision to continue negotiations?

(select all costs that are relevant)

Test your understanding 2

A company is considering a short-term pricing decision to utilise some spare capacity. The item to be manufactured and sold would use 1,500 kgs of raw material Q.

Material Q is in regular use by the company. It currently has 1,000 kgs in inventory, which was purchased last month at a cost of $4 per kg. The current replacement cost of material Q is $4.80 per kg and the current inventory could be sold for $4.30 per kg.

Calculate the relevant cost of material Q for the purposes of this decision.

Test your understanding 3

A mining operation uses skilled labour costing $4 per hour, which generates a contribution, after deducting these labour costs, of $3 per hour.

A new project is now being considered that requires 5,000 hours of skilled labour. There is a shortage of the required labour. Any used on the new project must be transferred from normal working. Calculate the relevant cost of using the skilled labour on the project. Calculate the contribution cash flow that is lost if the labour is transferred from normal working.

Activity 2

Suppose the facts about labour are as above, but there is a surplus of skilled labour already employed (and paid) by the business which is sufficient to cope with the new project. The presently idle men are being paid full wages.

Calculate the contribution cash flow that is lost if the labour is transferred to the project from doing nothing.

Test your understanding 4

P Limited is considering whether to continue making a component or buy it from an outside supplier. It uses 12,000 of the components each year.

The internal manufacturing cost comprises:

	$/unit
Direct materials	3.00
Direct labour	4.00
Variable overhead	1.00
Specific fixed cost	2.50
Other fixed costs	2.00
	12.50

If the direct labour were not used to manufacture the component, it would be used to increase the production of another item for which there is unlimited demand. This other item has a contribution of $10.00 per unit but requires $8.00 of labour per unit.

The maximum price per component at which buying is preferable to internal manufacture is:

A $8.00

B $10.50

C $12.50

D $15.50

Test your understanding 5

Budgeted data relating to a single-product firm that is working to full capacity are as follows:

Production and sales for the year	20,000 units
Machine capacity available and fully utilised	40,000 hours

	$
Variable cost	8.20
Fixed cost	1.30
Total cost	9.50
Selling price	12.50
Net profit per unit	3.00

An order is received for 3,000 modified units which will use 6,600 hours of machine time and cost $1.00 per unit for additional materials.

At what price should the firm be indifferent between taking on, and rejecting, the order?

A $41,790

B $40,500

C $27,600

D $17,190

Test your understanding 6

Lauda operates a joint process from which four products arise. The products may be sold at the separation point of the process or can be refined further and be sold at a premium. Information regarding the products and the refining process can be found below:

Products	*E*	*F*	*G*	*H*
Selling prices per litre ($)				
At separation point	12	16	15	18
After refining	20	23	25	22
Costs ($)				
Joint process (per litre):	8	8	8	8
Refining process:				
Variable (per litre)	5	5	5	5
Specific fixed (in total)	1,000	2,000	3,000	4,000
Budgeted litres	2,000	500	5,000	6,000

The general fixed overheads in the refining process amount to $30,000.

Which products should be further processed?

A E, F and G only

B E and G only

C G only

D None of them

Test your understanding 7

Company A manufactures four products in two different locations. It operates under strict Just-In-Time principles and does not hold any inventory of either finished goods or raw materials.

Company A has a long-standing agreement to supply its main customer with 100 units of each of its products Product 1, Product 2, Product 3 and Product 4. No negotiation is possible and the contract must be fulfilled.

Details of the company's additional, non-contract related production on Site 1 are as follows:

	Product 1	Product 2	Product 3	Product 4
Selling price	$60	$70	$80	$90
Direct labour, at $8 per hour	$16	$8	$12	$16
Direct Material A, at $3 per litre	$4.50	$3.00	$0	$3.00
Direct Material B, at $5 per kg	$5.00	$-	$15	$10
Variable overhead, labour related (*)	$1.25	$0.63	$0.94	$1.25
Variable overhead, machine related (*)	$1.25	$2.00	$0.75	$1.00
Total variable cost	$28.00	$13.63	$28.69	$31.25
Machine hours per unit	5	8	3	4
Maximum demand per week	900 units	950 units	950 units	900 units

(*) An analysis of the variable overhead shows that some of it is caused by the number of labour hours and the remainder is caused by the number of machine hours.

All the above products use the same resources (materials A and B). Currently, the company also purchases a component, Component Alpha, from an external supplier in the US for $50. A single unit of this component is used in producing Product 5, the company's only other product, on Site 2. Product 5 yields a positive contribution and does not use any materials used by the other products.

Company A could manufacture Component Alpha on Site 1, but to do so would require 2 hours of direct labour, half an hour of machine time as well as 1.5 kilograms of Material B.

The purchasing director has recently advised you that the availability of Direct Materials A and B is to be restricted to 5,000 litres and 6,000 kilograms every week. This restriction is unlikely to change in the near future, but no restrictions are expected on any other materials.

Required:

(a) Calculate whether Company A should continue to purchase Component Alpha or whether it should manufacture it internally.

(b) Prepare a statement to show the optimum weekly usage of Site 1's available resources.

(c) Assuming no other changes, calculate the purchase price of Component Alpha at which your advice in (a) would change.

Test your understanding 8

Scenario

Z is one of a number of companies that produce three products for an external market. The three products, R, S and T may be bought or sold in this market. The common process account of Z for March 20X7 is shown below:

	Kg	*$*		*Kg*	*$*
Inputs:					
Material A	1,000	3,500	Normal loss	500	0
Material B	2,000	2,000	Outputs:		
Material C	1,500	3,000	Product R	800	3,500
Direct labour		6,000	Product S	2,000	8,750
Variable overhead		2,000	Product T	1,200	5,250
Fixed cost		1,000			
Totals	**4,500**	**17,500**		**4,500**	**17,500**

Z can sell products R, S or T after this common process or they can be individually further processed and sold as RZ, SZ and TZ respectively. The market prices for the products at the intermediate stage and after further processing are (Market prices per kg):

	$
R	3.00
S	5.00
T	3.50
RZ	6.00
SZ	5.75
TZ	6.75

The specific costs of the three individual further processes are:

Process R to RZ – variable cost of $1.40 per kg, no fixed costs

Process S to SZ – variable cost of $0.90 per kg, no fixed costs

Process T to TZ – variable cost of $1.00 per kg, fixed cost of $600 per month

Tasks:

(a) Produce calculations to determine whether any of the intermediate products should be further processed before being sold. Clearly state your recommendations together with any relevant assumptions that you have made.

(b) Produce calculations to assess the viability of the common process:

(i) assuming that there is an external market for products R, S and T; and

(ii) assuming that there is not an external market for products R, S and T.

State clearly your recommendations.

Test your understanding answers

Example 1

The correct answer is **B**.

The initial $40,000 fee will be deemed to be a sunk cost – it has already been committed and won't be affected by any decision to proceed from this point.

The $20,000 is a future cost. Despite the fact that it is called a fixed cost it will only be incurred if the project proceeds. It is therefore and extra or incremental cost of the project and should be included in any future decision making.

Example 2

100% capacity	= 102,000 ÷ 0.85	=	120,000 units

Spare capacity amounts to 18,000 units. So there is sufficient slack to meet the new order.

Variable costs	= $330,000 less $75,000	=	$255,000
Variable cost per unit	= $255,000 ÷ 102,000	=	$2.50
Contribution per unit from existing product		=	$3.25 – $2.50 = $0.75
Contribution per unit from new product		=	$2.80 – $2.50 = $0.30

	$
Increase in contribution from new product:	
$0.30 × 12,000 units	3,600
Fall in contribution from existing product:	
$0.75 × (12,000 ÷ 15) × 2	
$0.75 × 1,600	(1,200)
Net gain in contribution	**2,400**

Example 3

1,000 kgs of P:

Purchase 200 kgs; Current replacement price $4.50/Kg	= $900
Use 800 kgs from inventory 800 × $3.50	= $2,800
Total	**= $3,700**

Example 4

Existing product earns a contribution per hour of $60 – $10 – $10 – $15 = $25

Relevant cost	= Contribution forgone PLUS direct labour cost		
	= $25 + $10	=	$35 per hour
Total cost	= $35 × 100 hours	=	$3,500

Example 5

- The variable cost per hour of overhead is relevant since this cost would be avoidable if the contract were not undertaken. The relevant cost of variable overheads is therefore $7 per machine hour.
- The fixed cost per hour is an absorption rate. Actual fixed costs would not increase by $13 per hour, but by $3,200 in total. The incremental relevant cost of fixed overheads is therefore $3,200.
- This would make the total cost = (800 hours of machine time for variable overheads @ $7 per hour) + $3,200 or fixed overheads = $8,800.
- The correct answer is therefore Answer C.

Example 6

Opportunity cost now = **$2,000** (Answer C)

Example 7

	Note	$
Relevant costs:		
Fuel costs	1	1,500
Replacement coach	2	360
Replacement driver	3	800
Hotel costs	4	5,000
Total		7,660

Notes:

(1) The fuel cost is directly traceable to the contract and is therefore relevant. The apportionment of annual fixed costs for operating the coach are not relevant. The total fixed cost would remain the same whether the contract were accepted or not.

(2) The company should hire a replacement coach for two days @ $180 per day. This will ensure that the contribution of $250 per day continues to be earned from the other contract.

(3) The company's employed driver will be paid whether VBJ wins the contract or not. As a consequence of winning the contract, it would become necessary to hire a replacement driver for two days @ $400 per day to cover the existing work. This incremental cost is relevant.

(4) The hotel cost is directly attributable to the contract and is therefore relevant.

(5) The general overhead that has been traced to the contract ($250) should be ignored as this cost is sunk.

(6) The profit is not a relevant cost.

Example 8

(a)

	Product		
	P	*Q*	*R*
Contribution per unit	$210	$72	$46
Hours per unit	15	8	2
Contribution per hour	$14	$9	$23
Rank	2nd	3rd	1st

Product	*Units*	*Hrs/per unit*	*Total hours*	*Contribution per hour*	*Total contribution*
R	1,000	2	2,000	$23	$46,000
P	200	15	3,000	$14	$42,000
Q	350	8	2,800	$9	$25,200
			7,800		$113,200

(b) The special contract requires 3,000 SCARCE labour hours.

Relevant cost = Direct cost + Opportunity cost

Direct cost	3,000 hrs × $20	$60,000
Opportunity cost	2,800 hrs × $9	$25,200
	200 hrs × $14	$2,800
Relevant cost		$**88,000**

Example 9

Technique

The following method could be adopted in this example :

(1) The saving per unit of each product is calculated. Saving = Purchases price – VC to make.

(2) Divide this by the amount of scarce resource (a.k.a. limiting factor) each product uses. This gives the saving per unit of limiting factor (LF).

(3) Rank. The higher the saving per unit of LF the greater the priority to make that should be given to the product.

(4) Once the priorities have been decided, the scarce resource is allocated to the products in the order of the priorities until it is fully used up.

(5) Any products with unsatisfied demand can be satisfied by buying from the external source.

This can be applied as follows:

(1) Calculate saving = Purchases price – VC to make:

	L	*M*	*N*	*P*
External purchase price	$57	$55	$54	$50
Variable costs to make	$45	$40	$30	$20
Saving	$12	$15	$24	$30

(2) Calculate the saving per unit of limiting factor/scarce resource:

	L	*M*	*N*	*P*
Saving	$12	$15	$24	$30
Scarce resource (machine hours) per unit	3 hours	5 hours	4 hours	6 hours
Saving per unit of the scarce resource	$4	$3	$6	$5

(3) Rank

	L	*M*	*N*	*P*
Saving per unit of the scarce resource	$4	$3	$6	$5
Ran : product to make in priority	3	4	1	2

(4) Allocate scarce resource of 24,000 machine hours to production

Make all Ns (1,500 units). This will use up 1,500 × 4 hours = 6,000 hours.

Then, make all Ps (1,500 units). This will use up 1,500 × 6 hours = 9,000 hours. The cumulative total is 6,000 + 9,000 = 15,000 hours.

Then, make all Ls (1,500 units). This will use up 1,500 × 3 hours = 4,500 hours. The cumulative total is 15,000 + 4,500 = 19,500 hours.

This leaves (24,000 – 19,500) = 4,500 hours, in which to make

$$\frac{4{,}500}{5} = 900 \text{ units of Product M}$$

(5) Unsatisfied demand = 1,500 Ms – 900 Ms = 600 Ms. These will have to be bought externally.

	L	M	N	P
Variable production cost	$45	$40	$30	$20
External cost	$57	$55	$54	$50
Incremental cost	**$12**	**$15**	**$24**	**$30**
Hours per unit	÷ 3	÷ 5	÷ 4	÷ 6
Incremental cost per hour	**$4**	**$3**	**$6**	**$5**
Cheapest per hour	2nd	1st	4th	3rd

The analysis shows that it is actually cheaper to try and make ALL the components within the factory.

Hours required to make 1,500 units of each component:

(1,500 × 3) + (1,500 × 5) + (1,500 × 4) + (1,500 × 6) = 27,000 hours

The company only has 24,000 hours available. So, 3,000 hours of work must be sub-contracted. The CHEAPEST component per hour must be bought externally. This is component M.

3,000 hours of time on M equates to 3,000 ÷ 5 = **600 units of M.**

Example 10

In view of its scarcity, labour is taken as the limiting factor.

The decision on whether to make or buy the component has to be made before it can be decided whether or not to accept the contract. In order to do this the contribution per labour hour for normal production must first be calculated, as the contract will replace some normal production.

Normal products		*Basic*		*Scientist*
	$	$	$	$
Selling price		5.50		7.50
Materials	1.25		1.63	
Labour	1.50		2.25	
		2.75		3.88
Contribution		2.75		3.62
Contribution per direct labour hour (@0.25/0.375 hours per unit)		11.00		9.65

Therefore, if the company is to make the component it would be better to reduce production of the 'Scientist' model, in order to accommodate the special order.

The company should now compare the costs of making or buying the component.

An opportunity cost arises due to the lost contribution on the scientist model:

Special contract	*Manufacture of component*
	$
Materials	1,000
Labour ($6 × 150 hours)	900
Opportunity cost (150 hours × $9.6533)	1,448
	3,348

Since this is higher than the bought-in price of $2,500 the company would be advised to buy the component from the supplier if they accept the contract.

The contract can now be evaluated:

		Contract contribution
	$	$
Sales revenue		35,000
Material cost	9,000	
Component	2,500	
Labour ($6 × 1,200)	7,200	
		18,700
Contribution		16,300
Contribution per direct labour hour (for 1,200 labour hours)		$13.58

Since the contribution is higher than either of the existing products, the company should accept the contract assuming this would not prejudice the market for existing products.

Because the contribution is higher for the 'Basic' model, it would be wise to reduce production of the Scientist model. However, the hours spent on producing the Scientist model per month are (4,000 units × 0.375 hours =) 1,500, and so the contract would displace 80% of the production time of the scientist model. The recommendation assumes that this can be done without harming long-term sales of the scientist model (the scenario suggests that the demand for the product is high and therefore there would be no lost sales of the product in the long term).

As the customer is overseas, this seems a reasonable assumption. However, if this were not the case then the opportunity cost from the lost sales of scientific calculators should be deducted from the contribution calculated above

Before finalising the decision there are many other factors that should be considered such as:

- whether all costs have been considered (for example, extra delivery costs for the overseas customer)
- the potential impact of any foreign exchange rate movements
- whether this will be a one-off contract or whether it will open the door for more profitable work with this customer
- the value of the experience and impact on overseas reputation of beginning to export the product
- the level of competition for the contract

- the extra administration involved in dealing with a foreign customer (such as dealing in a foreign language and performing reasonable credit checks etc.
- the potential impact on existing customers who buy packages of basic and scientific models

Example 11

(a) The profit statement needs to be restated in a marginal costing format if it is to be useful for decision-making.

	W	*X*	*Y*	*Z*	*Total*
	$	$	$	$	$
Sales	30,000	20,000	35,000	15,000	
Variable cost of sales	4,800	1,600	13,200	5,000	
Variable selling overhead (*)	3,000	2,000	3,500	1,500	
Contribution	22,200	16,400	18,300	8,500	
Specific fixed costs (W1)	5,200	2,400	1,800	2,000	
Net benefit	17,000	14,000	16,500	6,500	54,000
Non-specific fixed cost of sales					20,000
Fixed selling overhead (W2)					(20,000)
Administration costs					(8,000)
Net profit					6,000

(*) Total overhead less $5,000 fixed cost.

Workings

(1)

	W	X	Y	Z	Total
	$	$	$	$	$
Fixed costs	11,200	6,400	8,800	5,000	31,400
Non-specific fixed costs (*)	6,000	4,000	7,000	3,000	20,000
Specific fixed costs	5,200	2,400	1,800	2,000	11,400

(*) Given as $20,000 apportioned on the basis of sales value (3:2:3.5:1.5)

(2) $5,000 per product × 4 = $20,000

(b) (i) **Z discontinued**

	$
Contribution from 40% additional sales of Y ($18,300 × 0.4)	7,320
Additional specific fixed costs	(540)
Loss of net benefit from Z	(6,500)
Net gain	280

(ii) **Profit reconciliation**

	$
Existing profit	6,000
Discontinuation of Z	(6,500)
Additional contribution from Y	7,320
Additional specific fixed costs	(540)
Profit if Z is discontinued and sales of Y substituted	6,280

(c) Non-financial factors to consider include:

(1) Possible redundancies among the workforce

(2) Signals which it may give to competitors, who may perceive the company as being unwilling to support its products

(3) The reaction of customers, particularly those who may recently have purchased the product.

Sometimes, even when management has made the decision to discontinue a product or activity, there is still a further decision to be made: when to discontinue it. The following exercise shows how such a decision could be made.

Example 12

The following costs are relevant:

(iii) The total cost of each of the three additional processes – this represents the incremental total cost

(iv) The unit selling price of each product after further processing – this is required to calculate incremental revenue

(v) The unit selling price of each product before further processing – this is required to calculate incremental revenue

(vi) The percentage normal loss of each further process – this will be required to calculate total output per product after further processing

(vii) The actual units of output of each product from the common process – this will be required to calculate total output per product after further processing

The following costs are not relevant:

(i) Total cost of the common process – this is related to the common cost

(ii) The basis of sharing the common process cost between the three products – this is related to the common cost

Test your understanding 1

(i) The salary is a relevant cost of $12,000. Do not be fooled by the fact that it is a fixed cost. The cost may be fixed in total but it is definitely a cost that is relevant to the decision to proceed with the future development of the new product. This is an example of a directly attributable fixed cost. A directly attributable fixed cost may also be called product-specific fixed cost.

(ii) The $2,500 additional running costs are relevant to the decision to purchase the new machine. The saving in overhead absorption is not relevant since we are not told that the total overhead expenditure will be altered. The saving in labour cost would be relevant but we shall assume that this has been accounted for in determining the additional monthly running costs.

(iii) This is not a relevant cost for next month since it will be incurred even if the contract is cancelled today. If a decision is being made to close the office, this cost cannot be included as a saving to be made next month. However, it will be saved in the months after that so it will become a relevant cost saving from month 2 onwards.

(iv) This is not a relevant cost of the decision to continue with the contract. The $75 is sunk and cannot be recovered even if the company does not proceed with the negotiations.

Test your understanding 2

In regular use, so relevant cost = replacement cost

Replacement cost for Q = 1,500 kgs × $4.80
= $7,200

Test your understanding 3

	$
Contribution per hour lost from normal working	3
Add back: labour cost per hour that is not saved	4
	7

The contract should be charged with 5,000 × $7 = $35,000

Activity 2

Nothing. The relevant cost is zero.

Test your understanding 4

D

The relevant cost of making the product is the variable cost of $3, $4 and $1 AND the specific fixed cost of $2.50. In addition there is another cost – an opportunity cost – every unit of the component that we make uses $4 of labour. If $8 of labour were used on the other product contribution would increase by $10. So therefore there is an extra opportunity cost of $5 per $4 of labour.

Test your understanding 5

A

The 6,600 hours of machine time for the special order would have produced 3,300 units (2 hours each).

Existing contribution	=	3,300 × $4.30
	=	$14,190

The firm will be indifferent to the new order if the 3,000 modified units also give $14,190 contribution.

Variable cost per unit of special order	= $9.20
Total variable costs	= 3,000 × $9.20
	= $27,600
Therefore required selling price	= $27,600 + $14,190
	= $41,790

Test your understanding 6

D

	E	*F*	*G*	*H*
Incremental revenue per litre	8	7	10	4
Variable cost of refining	(5)	(5)	(5)	(5)
Additional contribution from refining	3	2	5	(1) Sell at split-off
Units	2,000	500	5,000	
Additional total contribution($)	6,000	1,000	25,000	
Specific fixed costs	(1,000)	(2,000)	(3,000)	
Additional profit from refining	5,000	(1,000)	22,000	
	Refine	Sell at split-off	Refine	

Total relevant profit from refining is	$27,000
General fixed costs of refining are	30,000
Total loss from refining	$–3,000

None of the products should be further processed.

Test your understanding 7

(a) The Internal Manufacturing cost of Component Alpha is as follows:

	Component Alpha
2 hours of direct labour, at $8 per hour	$16.00
1.5 kg direct Material B, at $5 per kg	$7.50
Variable overhead, labour related 2 hours	$1.25
Variable overhead, machine related, 0.5 hours	$0.125
Total variable cost	**$24.875**

The buying price of the component is **$50** per unit. So, if resources are readily available, the company should manufacture the component, because it is cheaper than buying it. However, due to the scarcity of resources in the near future, the contribution earned from the component needs to be compared with the contribution that can be earned from the other products.

Using Product 1 (though any product could be used) the variable overhead rates per hour can be calculated:

Labour related variable overhead per unit = $1.25

Direct labour hours per unit = $16/$8 = 2 hours

Labour related variable overhead per hour = $1.25/2 hours = $0.625 per hour

Machine related variable overhead per unit = $1.25

Machine related variable overhead per hour = $1.25/5 hours = $0.25 per hour

Both material A and material B are limited in supply, but calculations are required to determine whether this scarcity affects our production plans. The resources required for the maximum demand must be compared with the resources available to determine whether either of the materials is a binding constraint.

	Product 1	Product 2	Product 3	Product 4	Total
Existing Contract	100 units	100 units	100 units	100 units	
Direct Material A	150 litres	100 litres	0 litres	100 litres	**350 litres**
Direct Material B	100 kgs	0 kgs	300 kgs	200 kgs	**600 kgs**

We can now determine whether Material A or Material B is a limiting factor:

	Maximum Availability	Post-contract availability	Needed for total production
Direct Mat. A	5,000 litres	4,650 litres	3,200 litres
Direct Mat. B	6,000 kgs	5,400 kgs	5,500 kgs

The scarcity of **material B** is a binding constraint and therefore the contributions of each product and the component per kg of material B must be compared. (At this point, Product 2 can be ignored because it does not use material B):

	Product 1	Product 3	Product 4	Component Alpha
Contribution	$32	$51.325	$58.75	
Direct Material B	1 kg	3 kgs	2 kgs	
Contribution per kg of Material B	$32.00	$17.10	$29.38	$16.75 **(W1)**
Rank	1	3	2	4

Since Component Alpha is the lowest ranked usage of material B, **the company should continue to purchase the component** so that the available resources can be used to manufacture Product 1, Product 4 and Product 3.

We can now determine whether Material A or Material B is a limiting factor:

W1 – Component Alpha – Contribution per kg of B

Buying cost of component Alpha	$50.00
2 hours of direct labour, at $8 per hour	($16.00)
1.5 kg direct Material B, at $5 per kg	($7.50)
Variable overhead, labour related 2 hours	($1.250)
Variable overhead, machine related, 0.5 hours	($0.125)
Contribution per component	**$25.125**

Contribution per kg of Material B = $25.125/1.5 kgs of B = **$16.75**

(b) Direct material B at $5/kg available: 5,400 kgs

First, we make **Product 1** : 900 units @ 1 kgs per unit = 900 kgs.

This leaves 4,500 kgs available for the next best-ranking product, **Product 4**. That is enough for (4,500 kgs/2 kgs per unit) = 2,250 units of Product 4. We only need 900 units of Product 4 though i.e. 1,800 kgs, which leaves (4,500 – 1,800 kgs = 2,700 kgs) available for the next product, **Product 3.**

Each unit of Product 3 uses 3 kgs of Material B, we can therefore make 900 units of Product 3.

Summary

	Product 1	**Product 2**	**Product 3**	**Product 4**
Contractual units	100 units	100 units	100 units	100 units
Non-contractual units	900 units	950 units	900 units	900 units
Total	1,000 units	1,050 units	1,000 units	1,000 units

(c) The decision concerning the purchase of the component would change if the contribution from its manufacture were equal to the least best contribution from the products using material B. Apart from the minimum demand constraint the least best usage is derived from product 3 which has a contribution per kg of $17.10 which is $0.35 per kg higher than that from component Alpha.

Since each unit of Alpha requires 1.5 kgs of B then the buying price would have to be 1.5 × $0.35 = $0.525 per component higher than at present before it would have the same rank as product 3. Thus the buying price at which the decision would change = $50 + $0.525 = $50.525.

Test your understanding 8

[**Tutorial note:** This an example of a question for which obtaining maximum marks depends not just on carrying out the calculations correctly but on demonstrating that you are aware of the other factors which affect the decision, such as marketing.]

(a) On financial grounds, further processing is worthwhile if the further processing cost is less than the incremental revenue.

Evaluation of further processing, based on March 20X7 output and assuming no losses in the further process:

Product	*Incremental revenue* $	*Incremental cost* $	*Increase/ (decrease) in profit*
RZ	800 × (6.00 – 3.00) = 2,400	800 × $1.40 = $1,120	1,280
SZ	2,000 × (5.75 – 5.00) = 1,500	2,000 × 0.90 = 1,800	(300)
TZ	1,200 × (6.75 – 3.50) = 3,900	1,200 × 1.00 + 600 = 1,800	2,100

Taking each product individually, it can be seen that products R and T should be converted as the incremental revenue exceeds the incremental cost of further processing. In the case of T, this assumes that the March 20X7 output is representative of other months and that the quantity produced is sufficient to ensure that the incremental revenue covers both the fixed and variable costs. However, as TZ can be sold for a relatively high price, volumes would have to drop considerably for this to become an issue.

This is not true of S. Considered in isolation product S should not be converted. However there may be other reasons for producing all three products, in particular marketing considerations such as whether the company needs to supply all three products in order to sell the two profitable products, RZ and TZ.

(b) (i) If there is a market for R, S and T, and assuming that all March 20X7 output can be sold at the prices given:

Product	*Selling price per kg in $*	*Output in kgs*	*Sales value in $*
R	$3.00	800	$2,400
S	$5.00	2,000	$10,000
T	$3.50	1,200	$4,200
			$16,600

Total cost of common process in March 20X7 = $17,500

Loss in March 20X7 = $900 and therefore the common process is not financially viable.

(ii) If there is not an external market for R, S and T:

Revenue from selling RZ, SZ, TZ:				$	
RZ	800 × $6.00			4,800	
SZ	2000 × $5.75			11,500	
TZ	1,200 × $6.75			8,100	24,400
				17,500	
Common costs					
Further costs:					
R –> RZ	800 × $1.40		1,120		
S–>SZ	2,000 × $0.90		1,800		
T–>TZ	1,200 × $1.00	1,200			
	Fixed	600	1,800	4,720	22,220
					2,180

Based on this analysis the common process is financially viable.

chapter

7

Linear programming

Chapter learning objectives

Lead	Component
C2. Analyse short term pricing and product decisions.	(c) Analyse product mix decisions, including circumstances where linear programming methods are needed to identify 'optimal' solutions.

1 Session Content Diagram

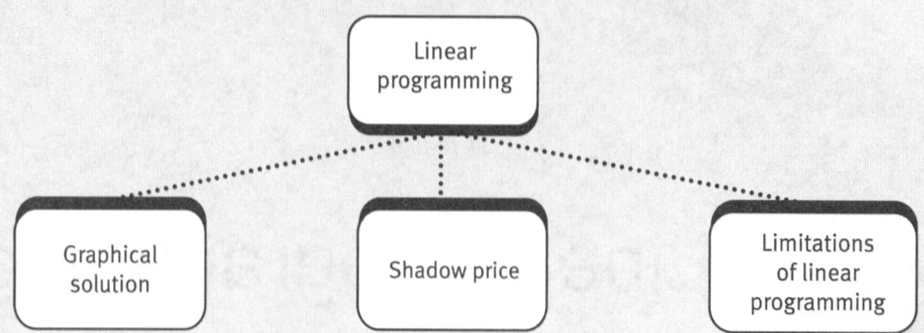

2 Introduction

In decision making when faced with one limiting factor, we calculate the contribution per unit of the limiting factor and rank the products, allocating the scarce resource to the best product and then the next best product and so on until the resource is fully utilised.

If faced with two or more limiting factors, then the situation is more complicated and linear programming techniques must be used (and the limiting factors are now called **constraints**).

Further details

In the previous chapter, you saw how to use basic limiting factor analysis to determine the profit-maximising sales mix for a company with a single resource constraint. The decision rule was to allocate the resource to products according to the **contribution earned per unit of scarce resource**, subject to any other constraints such as maximum or minimum demands for the individual products.

This technique cannot be applied when there is more than one limiting factor. In this situation a **linear programming** technique is used.

Linear programming is the name given to a collection of tools that are among the most widely used in management science. It is essentially a technique that encompasses the problem of allocating scarce resources between competing activities so as to maximise or minimise some numerical quantity, such as contribution or cost. In business it can be applied to areas such as planning production to maximise profit, mixing ingredients to minimise costs, selecting a portfolio of investments to maximise worth, transporting goods to minimise distance, assigning people to maximise efficiency and scheduling jobs to minimise time.

Linear programming involves the construction of a mathematical model to represent the decision problem. The model is then solved by an appropriate method or by the use of a computer package to obtain the optimal values for the activities.

The technique employed will require a basic level of mathematics that you should have obtained from previous studies.

Algebra revision

In this chapter you will need to be familiar with some algebraic mathematical techniques. This part of the text provides a revision of the ones that are most commonly used in linear programming.

Understanding inequalities

Inequalities are treated in almost exactly the same way as equations. In fact an inequality says much the same thing as an equation, except that one side will be

- less than the other (<)
- greater than the other, (>)
- less than or equal to the other, (≤), or
- greater than or equal to the other.(≥)

Inequalities can be manipulated in the same way as equations, except that when multiplying or dividing by a negative number it is necessary to **reverse** the inequality sign.

For example,

$5 - 2x < 25$

$-2x < 20$ (deduct 5 from each side)

$-x < 10$ (divide each side by 2)

$x > -10$ (divide each side by –1, so reverse direction of inequality)

Using simultaneous equations

Simultaneous equations are where you have two equations that must both be satisfied at the same time, of the type:

$3X + 4Y = 18$ (i)
$5X + 2Y = 16$ (ii)

which must both be satisfied by the solutions X and Y.

Provided you multiply both sides of an equation by the same amount, it continues to be true. In the solution of these equations, one or both of the equations are multiplied by numbers chosen so that either the X or the Y terms in the two equations become numerically identical.

We have labelled the equations (i) and (ii) for clarity. Suppose we were to multiply (i) by 5 and (ii) by 3. Both equations would contain a $15X$-term that we could eliminate by subtraction, it being the case that you can add or subtract two equations and the result remains true.

In this case, however, the simplest method is to multiply equation (ii) by 2, so that both equations will contain $4Y$ and we can subtract to eliminate Y. The full solution is shown below.

$3X + 4Y = 18$ (i)
$5X + 2Y = 16$ (ii)

Multiply (ii) by 2:

$10X + 4Y = 32$ (iii)

Subtract (iii) – (i):

$7X + 0 = 14$
$X = 14 \div 7 = 2$

Substitute X = 2 into (i)

$6 + 4Y = 18$
$4Y = 18 - 6 = 12$
$Y = 12 \div 4 = 3$

Check the results in (ii):

$5 \times 2 + 2 \times 3 = 16$

The solution is X = 2, Y = 3.

Had we chosen to substitute X = 2 into equation (ii) it would not have affected the result but we would then have checked in the other equation (i).

Solving simultaneous linear equations using graphs

Each equation represents a straight line and solving simultaneous equations is the same as identifying the point at which the two lines cross.

This is the graphical interpretation of the solution of simultaneous linear equations, and a graphical method could be used instead of an algebraic method (provided that the scale was big enough to give the required accuracy).

3 Step-by-step technique

The technique requires the translation of a decision problem into a system of variables, equations and inequalities.

For examination purposes a five-step procedure is used to construct the mathematical model. Any of these steps might be examined.

Product X and Product Y

A company produces two products in three departments. Details are shown below regarding the time per unit required in each department, the available hours in each department and the contribution per unit of each product:

	Product X Hours per unit	Product Y Hours per unit	Available hours
Department A	8	10	11,000
Department B	4	10	9,000
Department C	12	6	12,000
Contribution per unit ($)	4	8	

Required:

Following the procedure for the graphical solution, define the optimum production plan.

Step 1 – Define the variables

The first step is to simplify the equations by using abbreviations for the products or variables.

Step 1 – Product X and Product Y

Let x = number of units of Product X produced.

Let y = number of units of Product Y produced.

Step 2 – State the objective function

The objective function expresses the **total contribution** that will be made from the production of the two products.

Step 2 – Product X and Product Y

The objective of the business is usually to maximise profit, and as fixed costs are fixed this would mean the objective function is to **maximise contribution.**

The objective function is stated in terms of the defined variables.

Note however that in some questions the objective function might be to minimise costs. If that was the case then we would create an equation for the total cost line.

In our illustration the objective function is to maximise contribution (we should always make this assumption unless told specifically otherwise). The contribution on each unit of X is $4 and on each unit of Y, $8. The objective function 'Z' is to be maximised is as follows:

Contribution (Z) = 4x + 8y

It is important that the **contribution** per unit of each product is used in the construction of this formula, rather than, say, the selling price per unit.

Step 3 – State the constraints

Each constraint under which the organisation operates should be expressed as an equation. This involves illustrating that the total for that resource must be less than or equal to the total of that resource that is available.

Step 3 – Product X and Product Y

In our illustration, we can see that available hours are limited in Departments A, B and C and we therefore can illustrate that the total hours in each department must be less than or equal to the total hours available.

There are limited hours in Department A (11,000). Within that department each unit X takes 8 hours and each unit Y takes 10 hours. So the total hours in department A will be 8 hours for every Product X (i.e. 8x when expressed in our formula), and 10 hours for every Product Y (i.e. 10y when expressed in our formula). Because of the limitation on hours in Department A we know that these total hours must be less than or equal to 11,000 hours, and this then allows us to express a formula for the total hours equation in Department A as follows:

$$8x + 10y \leq 11,000$$

A similar equation can be created for Department B as follows:

$$4x + 10y \leq 9,000$$

Likewise, there are limited hours in Department C and its equation would be as follows:

$$12x + 6y \leq 12,000$$

Finally, we have to remember that we cannot make negative numbers of products, and, therefore, for completeness we should state that the values for x and y cannot be negative (this is known as the non-negativity constraint) as follows:

$$x,y \geq 0$$

Step 4 – Draw the graph

The constraints lines can then be plotted on a graph.

Each constraint is plotted at its maximum possible point. This should allow for the identification of the **feasible region** of production values.

The feasible region

The **feasible region** represents all the possible production combinations that the company may undertake.

> CIMA's *Official Terminology* defines a feasible area as *'an area contained within all of the constraint lines shown on a graphical depiction of a linear programming problem. All feasible combinations of output are contained within, or located on, the boundaries of the feasible region'*

If such an area does not exist, then the model has no solution.

You will not be asked to construct a graph in the examination. But you may be given a graph and asked to choose which line represents a particular constraint.

Step 4 – Product X and Product Y

The graph of the constraints in our illustration would appear as follows:

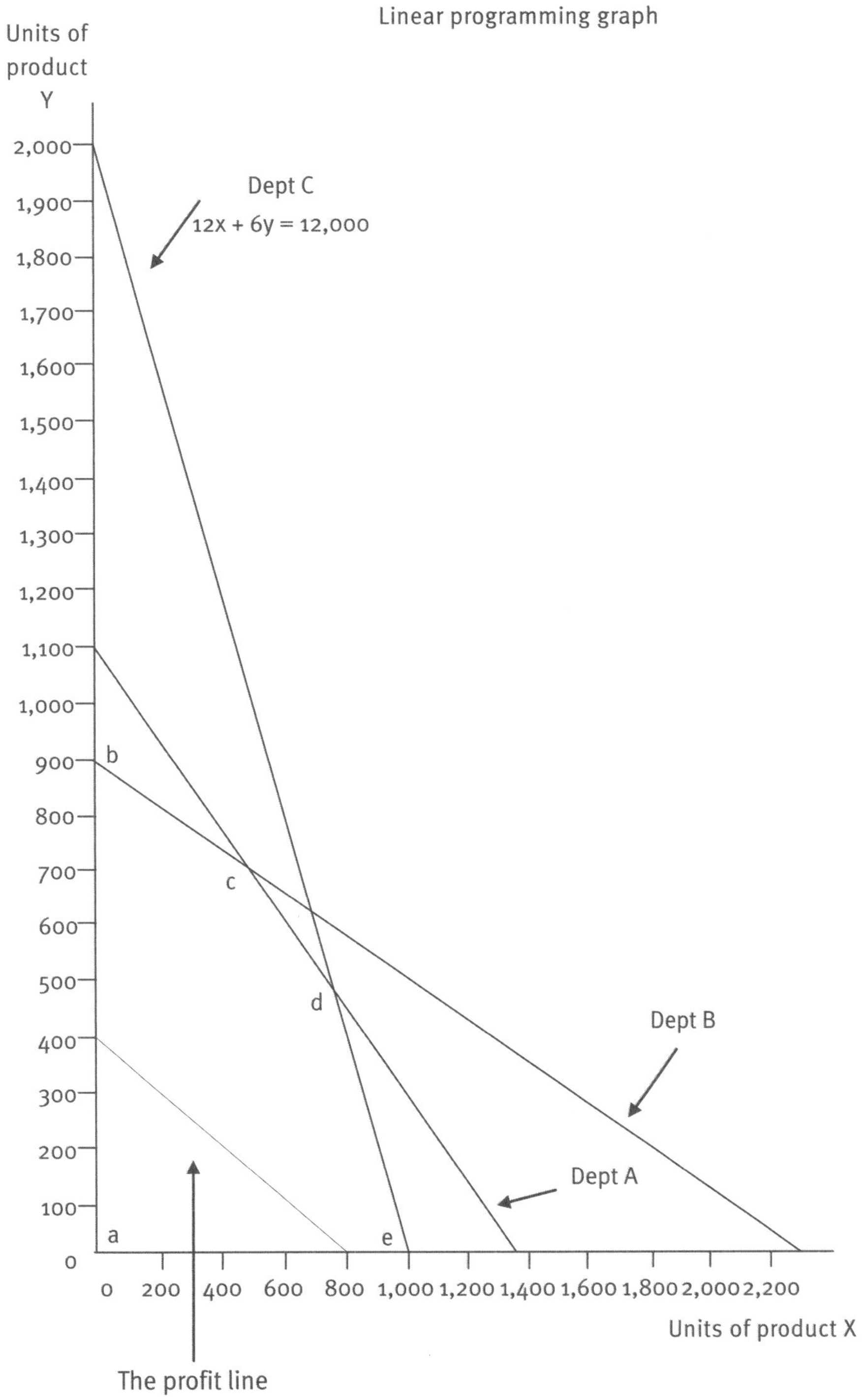

Linear programming graph

The feasible region for production is the area formed by the points a, b, c, d and e.

Step 5 – Find the optimum solution

A **profit line** can then be used to determine the outer most point of the feasible region. This will be the optimal point of production.

The profit line

In this step, consider how the objective can be achieved. The graph is used to determine the optimum production plan. There are two methods that may be used to determine the optimum point on the graph:

Method 1: Using simultaneous equations

In this method we calculate the coordinates of each vertex (furthest points) on the feasible region. Then calculate the contribution (objective function) at each vertex.

Method 2: Using an iso-contribution line

We do not know the maximum value of the objective function; however, we can draw an iso-contribution (or 'profit') line that shows all the combinations of x and y that provide the **same total value for the objective function**.

- If, for example, we need to maximise contribution \$4x + \$8y, we can draw a line on a graph that shows combination of values for x and y that give the same total contribution, when x has a contribution of \$4 and y has a contribution of \$8. Any total contribution figure can be picked, but a multiple of \$4 and \$8 is easiest.
- For example, assume 4x + 8y = 4,000. This contribution line could be found by joining the points on the graph x = 0, y = 500 and x= 1,000 and y = 0.
- Instead, we might select a total contribution value of 4x + 8y = \$8,000. This contribution line could be found by joining the points on the graph x = 0, y = 1,000 and x = 2,000 and y = 0.
- When drawing both of these contribution lines on a graph, we find that the two lines are parallel and the line with the higher total contribution value for values x and y (\$8,000) is further away from the origin of the graph (point 0).
- This can be used to identify the solution to a linear programming problem. We draw the iso-contribution line showing combinations of values for x and y that give the same total value for the objective function.

- Look at the slope of the contribution line and, using a ruler, identify which combination of values of x and y within the feasible area for the constraints is furthest away from the origin of the graph. This is the combination of values for x and y where an iso contribution line can be drawn as far to the right as possible that just touches one corner of the feasible area. This is the combination of values of x and y that provides the solution to the linear programming problem.

Given the difficulty in applying Method 2 in a computer-based exam, it is more likely that you would have to apply Method 1 in an exam. However, you may not be asked to check all points on the feasible region – the examiner may tell you which constraints form the optimal point so that you only have one point of intersection to calculate.

Step 5 – Product X and Product Y

Method 1

In our example, the co-ordinates of some of the points can easily be determined from the diagram and we can quickly calculate the level of contribution made at each of these points:

Potential optimal point	Production of X (units)	Production of Y (units)	Total contribution $
a	0	0	0
b	0	900	7,200
e	1,000	0	4,000

But for the remaining points (c and d) we must use simultaneous equations to determine their coordinates.

Point c occurs where the constraints for Dept A and Dept B intersect. Because the point is at the furthest point of each of the lines we know that all of the constraint is being used and the less than or equal to sign in the equations can be converted to an equal sign:

Dept A: $8x + 10y = 11,000$

Dept B: $4x + 10y = 9,000$

Using simultaneous equations to solve this problem provides the coordinates:

$x = 500$, $y = 700$.

Point d occurs where the constraints for Dept A and Dept C intersect. Because the point is at the furthest point of each of the lines we know that all of the constraint is being used and the less than or equal to sign in the equations can be converted to an equal sign:

Dept A: $8x + 10y = 11,000$

Dept C: $12x + 6y = 12,000$

Using simultaneous equations to solve this problem provides the coordinates:

$x = 750$, $y = 500$.

We have now got the coordinates for all 5 points at the vertex of the feasible region and can determine the total contribution at each point:

Potential optimal point	Production of X (units)	Production of Y (units)	Total contribution $
a	0	0	0
b	0	900	7,200
c	500	700	7,600
d	750	500	7,000
e	1,000	0	4,000

The optimal production plan occurs at the point at which contribution is maximised (as that was our objective in Step 2). This occurs at point c, where 500 units of Product X are produced, 700 units of Product Y are produced and the total contribution is $7,600.

Method 2

The line plotted from point 400 on the y axis to point 800 on the x axis is the profit line. If you were to put a ruler along this line and move it outwards in parallel to that line, the last point that you would meet in the feasible region would be point C. This tells us that the optimal point in the feasible region in our illustration is at point C.

We would then use simultaneous equations as in Method 1 to determine that the co-ordinates for this point are $x = 500$ and $y = 700$.

The optimum production plan is therefore to produce 500 units of Product X and 700 units of Product Y.

Contribution at this point = (500 × \$4) + (700 × \$8) = \$7,600.

Ensure that you answer the question that has been asked by the examiner. If asked for the optimal production plan then you need to state how much of each product should be manufactured (i.e. the co-ordinates for the optimal point on the diagram).

If instead you are asked for the optimal contribution then you must go further and calculate the contribution at the optimal point.

Illustration – Linear programming in practice

The airline industry uses **linear programming** to optimise profits and minimise expenses in their business.

The products

Initially, airlines charged the same price for any seat on the aircraft. In order to make money, they decided to charge different fares for different seats and promoted different prices depending on how early you bought your ticket.

This required some linear programming. Airlines needed to consider how many people would be willing to pay a higher price for a ticket if they were able to book their flight at the last minute and have substantial flexibility in their schedule and flight times. The airline also needed to know how many people would only purchase a low price ticket, without an in-flight meal.

Different prices brought different levels of contribution. These therefore became the airlines 'products' for the linear programming calculations. Through linear programming, airlines were able to find the optimal breakdown of how many tickets to sell at which price, including various prices in between.

The constraints

Airlines also need to consider plane routes, pilot schedules, direct and in-direct flights, and layovers. There are certain standards that require pilots to sleep for so many hours and to have so many days rest before flying (so available flying time became a constraint). Airlines want to maximise the amount of time that their pilots are in the air, as well. Pilots have certain specialisations, as not all pilots are able to fly the same planes, so the number of pilots available becomes a constraint. The most controllable factor an airline has is its pilot's salary, so it is important that airlines use their optimisation teams to keep this expense as low as possible. Because all of these constraints must be considered when making economic decisions about the airline, linear programming becomes a crucial job.

Because there is more than one scarce resource, computers were used to create solutions to the problem for airlines.

4 Minimisation problems

Linear programming enables organisations to find optimal solutions to economic decisions. Generally, this means maximising but it could aim to minimise costs instead; so, rather than finding a contribution line touching the feasible polygon at a tangent as far away from the origin as possible, the aim is to find a total cost line touching the feasible polygon at a tangent **as close to the origin as possible**.

5 The slack

At the optimal production point it is unlikely that all of the scarce resources will have been used up. If one of the constraints has remaining resources at this point this is known as slack.

Slack and surplus

Slack

This is the amount of a resource that is under-utilised when the optimum plan is implemented. The actual utilisation is below a maximum specification. In other terms, slack will occur when the optimum does not fall on a given resource line.

Slack is important, because unused resources can be put to another use, e.g. hired out to another manufacturer. A constraint that has a slack of zero is known as a **scarce resource**. Scarce resources are fully utilised resources.

CIMA's Official Terminology defines slack variables as 'the amount of each resource which will be unused if a specific linear programming solution is implemented.'

Surplus

This is utilisation of a resource over and above a minimum. Surpluses tend to arise in minimisation of cost problems. For example, a constraint may state that it is necessary to produce a minimum of 400 widgets. If the optimum plan then recommends producing 450 widgets, the surplus in this case would be 50 widgets.

At the optimal production point, there will be no slack in the constraints lines that make up the optimal point. These are known as **binding constraints**.

The only slack in the system will come from the other constraint lines on the graph. These are **non-binding constraints**.

Slack – Product X and Product Y

Slack in Department A, Department B and Department C can be calculated based on the optimum solution where x = 500 and y = 700, and production plan slacks are:

Department A = (500 units of Product X × 8 hours) + (700 units of Product Y × 10 hours) = 11,000 hours.

This uses all available hours in Department A. **No slack in A => The constraint is binding**.

Department B = (500 units of Product X × 4 hours) + (700 units of Product Y × 10 hours) = 9,000 hours.

This uses all available hours in Department B. **No slack in B => The constraint is binding**.

Department C = (500 units of Product X × 12 hours) + (700 units of Product Y × 6 hours) = 10,200 hours.

There are 12,000 hours available in Department C. Therefore, the slack is 12,000 – 10,200 hours = 1,800 hours. There is **slack in C => The constraint is non-binding**.

6 The shadow price

It may be that the problem of the scarce resources can be alleviated by, say, buying in the scarce resource at a premium price. The extra resource would allow the organisation to make more products and create more contribution.

The maximum premium on price that the organisation would pay for the extra resource is known as the shadow price.

More details on the shadow price

After finding an optimum solution to a graphical linear programming problem, it should be possible to provide further information by interpreting the graph more fully, to see what would happen if certain values in the scenario were to change.

It is **the premium (over and above the normal price) it would be worth paying to obtain one more unit of the scarce resource.**

CIMA's Official Terminology defines a shadow price as 'the increase in value which would be created by having available one additional unit of a limiting resource at its original cost. This represents the opportunity cost of not having the use of the one extra unit. This information is routinely produced when mathematical programming (especially linear programming) is used to model activity.'

The shadow price of a scarce resource is the extra contribution that would arise if one more unit of that scarce resource became available, or it is the drop in contribution that would result from having one fewer unit of that scarce resource.

Non-binding constraints have no shadow price.

Shadow prices – Product X and Product Y

Shadow prices in Department A:

We need to calculate the impact if one extra hour of Department A time was made available, so that 11,001 hours were available. The new optimum product mix would be at the intersection of the two constraint lines:

(i) $8x + 10y = 11{,}001$ hours
(ii) $4x + 10y = 9{,}000$ hours

With (i) – (ii), $4x = 2{,}001$ and therefore $x = 500.25$ units.

When substituting x with '500.25' in (i) or (ii) we get $y = 699.9$ and new total contribution is calculated as follows:

	Units	Contribution per unit	Total contribution
X	500.25	$4	$2,001
Y	699.9	$8	$5,599.2
			$7,600.20

The original contribution was equal to (500 units of X × $4) + (700 units of Y × $8) = **$7,600.**

Therefore, the increase in contribution from one extra hour in Department A is $0.20. In other words, the shadow price of an extra hour in Department A is $0.20. The company should be prepared to pay up to $0.20 extra per hour.

Shadow prices in Department B:

We need to calculate the impact if one extra hour of Department B time was made available, so that 9,001 hours were available. The new optimum product mix would be at the intersection of the two constraint lines:

(i) $8x + 10y = 11{,}000$ hours
(ii) $4x + 10y = 9{,}001$ hours

With (i) – (ii), $4x = 1{,}999$ and therefore $x = 499.75$ units.

When substituting x with '499.75' in (i) or (ii) we get y = 7,002 and new total contribution is calculated as follows:

	Units	Contribution per unit	Total contribution
X	499.75	$4	$1,999
Y	7,002	$8	$5,601.6
			$7,600.60

The original contribution was equal to (500 units of X × $4) + (700 units of Y × $8) = **$7,600.**

Therefore, the increase in contribution from one extra hour in Department B is $0.60. In other words, the shadow price of an extra hour in Department B is $0.60. The company should be prepared to pay up to $0.60 extra per hour.

Shadow prices in Department C:

The shadow price of an extra hour in Department C is 0, as there is slack in Department C (1,800 hours are still available.)

7 LP and Decision Making: minimum contractual requirements

When, in the question, information is given regarding a customer order the business has to meet, it is necessary to take this order into account **before** formulating the Linear Programming problem.

Example 1

ND Ltd produces two products, the Alpha and the Beta. For the next quarter, the following information is relevant:

Material A: 1,200 kgs are available.

Per unit of Alpha: 2 kgs

Per unit of Beta: 3 kgs

Material B: 1,500 kgs are available.

Per unit of Alpha: 5 kgs

Per unit of Beta: 2 kgs

Labour: 2,000 hours are available.

Per unit of Alpha: 7 hours

Per unit of Beta: 5 hours.

Each unit of Alpha and Beta make a contribution of $8 each.

ND Ltd has already agreed a contract to supply 20 Alphas and 20 Betas with a key customer. This order, if cancelled, would incur a significant financial penalty.

Required:

Formulate the Linear Programming problem.

8 Limitations to Linear Programming

There are a number of assumptions and limitations to this technique.

- Linear relationships must exist.
- Only suitable when there is one clearly defined objective function.
- When there are a number of variables, it becomes too complex to solve manually and a computer is required.
- It is assumed that the variables are completely divisible.
- Single value estimates are used for the uncertain variables.
- It is assumed that the situation remains static in all other respects.

9 Chapter summary

Linear Programming

Graphical method

- Step 1: Define the variables
- Step 2: State the objective function
- Step 3: State the constraints
- Step 4: Draw the graph
- Step 5: Find the optimum solution

Shadow prices

- The shadow price is maximum premium on price for one extra unit of a scarce resource
- Non-binding constraints have no shadow price

10 Practice questions

Test Your Understanding 1

Solve the equations:

$2X + 3Y = 190$ (i)
$7X + 4Y = 340$ (ii)

Test Your Understanding 2

A company is using linear programming to decide how many units of each of its two products to make each week. Weekly production will be x units of Product X and y units of Product Y. At least 50 units of X must be produced each week, and at least twice as many units of Y as of X must be produced each week. Each unit of X requires 30 minutes of labour, and each unit of Y requires two hours of labour. There are 5,000 hours of labour available each week.

Which of the following is the correct set of constraints?

A	0.5x + 2y	≤	5,000
	x	≥	50
	y	≤	2x
B	x + 4y	≤	5,000
	x	≥	50
	y	≥	2x
C	0.5x + 2y	≤	5,000
	x	≥	50
	y	≥	100
D	0.5x + 2y	≤	5,000
	x	≥	50
	y	≥	2x

Test Your Understanding 3

An office manager wishes to minimise the cost of telephone calls made. 40% of calls in peak hours cost $1 each and the remainder of such calls cost $1.50 each. 30% of calls at other times cost 80c each, 50% of them cost 90c each, and 20% of them cost $1 each. These proportions cannot be varied, though the total numbers of calls made in peak hours and of calls made at other times can be.

If x equals the number of calls made each day in peak hours, and y equals the number of calls made at other times, write the manager's objective function into the following box:

Test Your Understanding 4

The shadow price of a binding constraint is:

A The decrease in contribution which occurs when increasing the constraint limit by one unit

B The premium (over and above the normal price) that the company would be willing to pay to suppliers for supplying one more unit of the binding constraint

C The contribution gained from being able to produce one more unit of the most profitable product

D The cost of acquiring one more unit of the binding constraint from suppliers

Test Your Understanding 5

Direct labour is currently paid at a rate of $40 per hour. Direct labour is a scarce resource however the workforce has agreed to work additional hours but the rate is currently in negotiation. Each unit will require 2 hours of labour.

The shadow price of labour is $12 per hour.

What is the maximum amount per hour that the organisation would pay for the extra hours?

A $12

B $40

C $52

D $64

Test Your Understanding 6

QT manufactures two products, X and Y. It has created a linear programme problem and formulated the objective function as follows:

Maximise contribution = 20x + 5y

Where

X = Number of product X produced

Y = Number of product Y produced

QT has determined that two materials, A and B, form the binding constraints. The constraints have been represented by the following formulae:

(A) 5x + 2y = 11,000 kgs
(B) 10x + 5y = 25,000 kgs

The solution to the linear programme formulation provided a contribution of $35,000. However, a new market supplier for material A has been found and, although the supplier is more expensive than existing suppliers, this may alleviate the material A constraint.

The shadow price for material A is $_____

Test Your Understanding 7

Scenario

HJK is a light engineering company which produces a range of components, machine tools and electronic devices for the motor and aircraft industry. It employs about 1,000 people in 12 main divisions, one of which is the alarm systems division.

Alarm systems division

HJK produces two types of alarm system, one for offices and homes (X) and the other for motor vehicles (Y), on the same equipment. For financial reasons, it is important to minimise the costs of production. To match the current inventory and demand position, at least 100 alarm systems in total are required each week, but the quantity of one type must not exceed twice that of the other. The inputs necessary for the manufacture of one alarm system are given below, together with the availability of resources each week:

Type	*Plating*	*Circuitry*	*Assembly*
X	3 feet	4 units	20 mins
Y	2 feet	8 units	8 mins
Totals available each week	420 feet	800 units	34 hours

The management accountant estimates that the unit costs of production are $100 for X and $80 for Y. Past experience suggests that all alarms can be sold. At present, 75 of each alarm system are produced each week.

Tasks:

(a) State the objective function and the constraints for the production of alarm systems AND use a graphical method to find the optimal product mix.

(b) Explain briefly any points of significance for management.

(Time Allowed: 30 minutes)

Test your understanding answers

Example 1

	Available	Required for order	Remaining
Material A	1,200	100	1,100
Material B	1,500	140	1,360
Labour	2,000	240	1,760

Required for order:

Material A: (20*2) + (20*3) = 100

Material B: (20*5) + (20*2) = 140

Labour: (20*7) + (20*5) = 240

(1) Define variables

Let A be the number of Alphas made **after** the customer order

Let B be the number of Betas made after the customer order.

(2) Objective function

The objective is to maximise contribution C, with C = \$8A + \$8B

(3) Constraints

Material A: 2A + 3B <1,100

Material B: 5A + 2B <1,360

Labour: 7A + 5B < 1,760 and A,B ≥ 0

Test Your Understanding 1

Multiply (i) by 4 and (ii) by 3:

$8X + 12Y = 760$ (iii)
$21X + 12Y = 1020$ (iv)

Take equation (iii) away from equation (iv):

$13X = 260$

$X = 260 \div 13 = 20$

Substitute $X = 20$ in (ii):

$140 + 4Y = 340$
$4Y = 340 - 140 = 200$
$Y = 200 \div 4 = 50$

Check in (i):

$(2 \times 20) + (3 \times 50) = 40 + 150 = 190$

The solution is $X = 20$, $Y = 50$

Test Your Understanding 2

D

Test Your Understanding 3

Calculate the weighted average cost per call:

Peak hours ($1 × 0.40) + ($1.50 × 0.60) = $1.30

Other times ($0.80 × 0.30) + ($0.90 × 0.50) + ($1 × 0.20) = $0.89

Hence the objective is to

minimise 130x + 89y

Test Your Understanding 4

B

Option A is incorrect because a shadow price would represent the *increase* in contribution that could be earned from having more of the scarce resource.

Option C is incorrect because linear programming only works if product units are divisible. Contribution is likely to be stated per unit rather than per resource used. For example, labour would have a shadow price per hour rather than per unit.

Option D is incorrect because the shadow price may be very different from the price that is quoted by suppliers. The shadow price would allow the company to make a decision as to whether the purchase of extra supplies is a good decision.

Option B is the correct definition of a shadow price.

Test Your Understanding 5

C

The shadow price represents the highest acceptable premium (over and above the normal wage rate) that the organisation would be willing to pay.

The maximum overall rate that it would pay would therefore be the normal rate of $40 per hour plus the shadow price of $12 = $52 per hour.

Test Your Understanding 6

The shadow price for material A is **$10**

To calculate the shadow price of material A we add one more unit of material A to the constraint formula so that the two constraint formulae become:

(A) 5x + 2y	=	11,001 kgs
(B) 10x + 5y	=	25,000 kgs

Multiplying the first constraint by 5 and the second constraint by 2 in order to solve these simultaneous equations gives us:

(A) 25x + 10y	=	55,005 kgs
(B) 20x + 10y	=	50,000 kgs

Solving this provides the optimal quantity of each product:

x	=	1,001 units
y	=	2,998 units

The new total contribution is calculated as follows:

	Units	*Contribution per unit*	*Total contribution*
X	1,001	$20	$20,020
Y	2,998	$5	$14,990
Total			$35,010

The original contribution was $35,000.

Therefore, the increase in contribution from one kilogramme of material A is $10 – this is its shadow price. The company should be prepared to pay up to $10 extra per kilogramme to the new supplier.

Test Your Understanding 7

(a) Let x = number of alarm systems for offices and home

Let y = number of alarm systems for motor vehicles

Objective function:

Minimise cost = 100x + 80y

Subject to:

Minimum production	$x + y$	$\geq$	100
	x	$\leq$	$2y$
	y	$\leq$	$2x$
Plating	$3x + 2y$	$\leq$	420
Circuitry	$4x + 8y$	$\leq$	800
Assembly	$20x + 8y$	$\leq$	2,040
Non-negativity	x,y	$\geq$	0

Workings for the graph

We are going to be drawing a number of straight lines. We need two points to define a straight line. The simplest thing to do in most cases is to make x = 0 and calculate what y must be to fit the equation and then make y = 0 and calculate what x must be.

x + y = 100		x = 2y		y = 2x	
x	y	x	y	x	y
0	100	0	0	0	0
100	0	200	100	100	200

3 x + 2y = 420		4x + 8y = 800		20x + 8y = 2040	
x	y	x	y	x	y
0	210	0	100	0	255
140	0	200	0	102	0

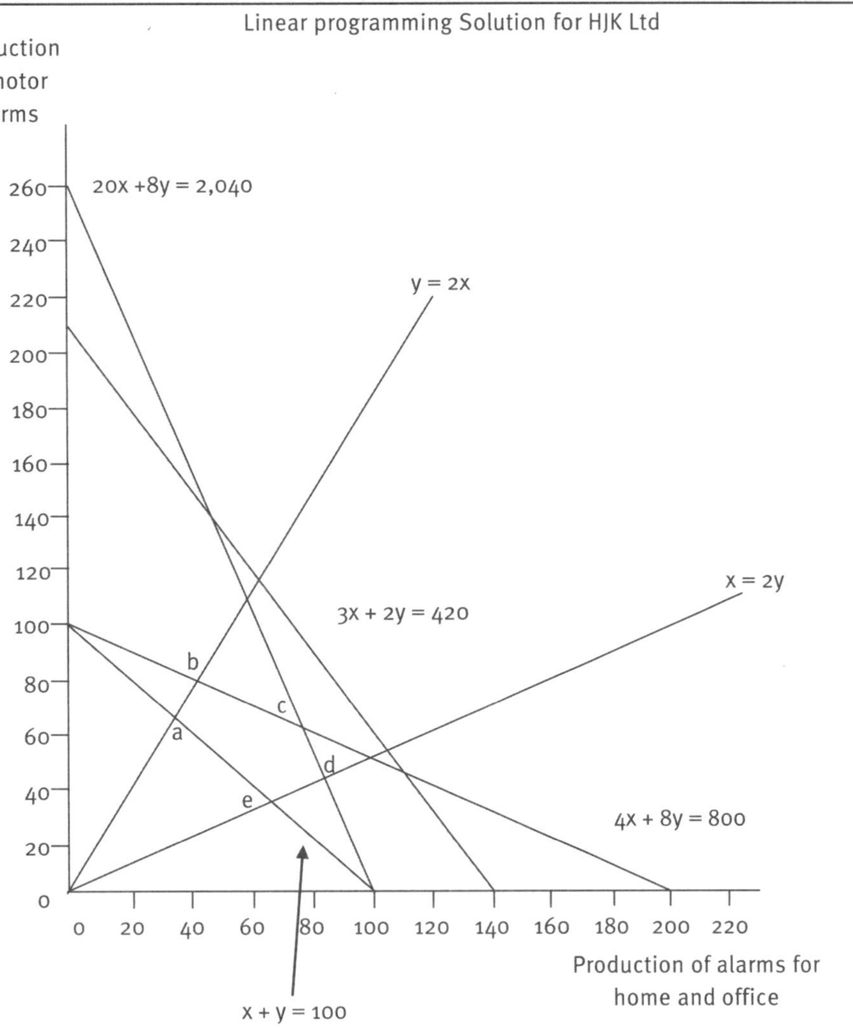

Solving the graph

We are trying to minimise cost, So we want to produce as little x as possible, i.e. we want to be as far to the left as possible and we want to produce as little y as possible, i.e. we want to be as far down on the graph as possible.

We can therefore eliminate some of the possible solutions. The optimum solution has to be on a corner, i.e. has to be on an intersection of two lines, so the possible solutions are either nodes (a), (b), (c), (d) or (e) (on the graph over the page), We can see, however, that node (b) is not as good as node (a) because node (a) is both lower down the graph and to the left of node (b) and therefore represents less x and less y and less cost.

Similarly, node (c) is not as good as node (e). (Node (e) is lower down the graph and to the left of node (c) and therefore represents less x and less y and therefore less cost.) Finally node (d) is not as good as node (e) for the same reasons.

So, the optimum solution is either node (a) or (node (e).

Node (a) lies on two lines:

x + y	=	100
y	=	2x

This gives a solution of 33.33 units of x and 66.67 units of y.

Cost = (33.33 × \$100) + (66.67 × \$80) = \$8,667

Node (e) lies on 2 lines:

x + y	=	100
x	=	2y

This gives a solution of 66.67 units of x and 33.33 units of y.

Cost = (66.67 × \$100) + (33.33 × \$80) = \$9,333

Therefore the optimum solution is to produce 33.33 units of X and 66.67 units of Y. This minimises cost at \$8,667.

(b) Management should question why HJK is trying to minimise cost. HJK Ltd is a commercial organisation and therefore its objective should be to maximise profit, not minimise cost.

The second most interesting point is that the current production plan is not feasible. It breaks the constraint for circuitry, i.e. 75 home and office alarms need 4 units each = 300 units in total and 75 motor vehicle alarms need 8 units each = 600 in total and 900 units as a grand total. This exceeds the available amount of 800.

chapter

8

Variance analysis: calculations

Chapter learning objectives

Lead	**Component**
A1. discuss costing methods and their results.	(c) Apply standard costing methods including the reconciliation of budgeted and actual profit margins.

1 Chapter overview diagram

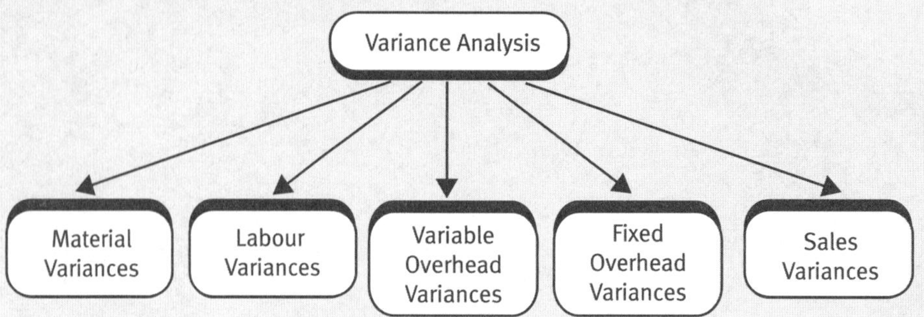

2 Standard costing and variance analysis

Standard costing is a technique which establishes predetermined estimates of the costs of products and services and then compares these predetermined costs with actual costs as they are incurred. The predetermined costs are known as standard costs and the difference between the standard cost and actual cost is known as a variance.

The process by which the total difference between actual cost and standard is broken down into its different elements is known as **Variance Analysis**.

A variance is the difference between actual results and the budget or standard.

Taken together, cost and sales variances can be used to explain the difference between the budgeted profit for a period and the actual profit.

When actual results are *better than* expected results, a **favourable (F)** variance occurs.

When actual results are *worse than* expected results, an **adverse variance (A)** occurs.

Variance groups

Variances can be divided into three main groups:

- sales variances
- variable cost variances
  - material variances
  - labour variances
  - variable overhead variances
- fixed overhead variances

Further explanation of standard costing

Whenever identical operations are performed or identical products are manufactured many times over, it should be possible to decide in advance not merely what they are *expected to cost*, but also what they *ought to cost*.

Similarly, when a standard service is provided many times over, it should be possible to establish in advance how the service should be provided, how long it should take and how much it should cost.

- A **standard** is 'a benchmark measurement of resource usage or revenue or profit generation, set in defined conditions' (CIMA *Official Terminology*).
- A **standard cost** for a product or service is a predetermined (planned) unit cost, based on a standard specification of the resources needed to supply it and the costs of those resources.

  A standard cost is based on technical specifications for the materials, labour time and other resources required and the prices and rates for the materials and labour.

  Standard costs can be prepared using either absorption costing or marginal costing.

- A **standard price** for a product or service is the expected price for selling the standard product or service. When there is a standard sales price and a standard cost per unit, there is also a **standard profit per unit** (absorption costing) or **standard contribution per unit** (marginal costing).

Types of standard

There are four main types of standard:

Attainable standards

- They are based upon efficient (but not perfect) operating conditions.
- The standard will include allowances for normal material losses, realistic allowances for fatigue, machine breakdowns, etc.
- These are the most frequently encountered type of standard.
- These standards may motivate employees to work harder since they provide a realistic but challenging target.

Basic standards

- These are long-term standards which remain unchanged over a period of years.
- Their sole use is to show trends over time for such items as material prices, labour rates and efficiency and the effect of changing methods.
- They cannot be used to highlight current efficiency.
- These standards may demotivate employees if, over time, they become too easy to achieve and, as a result, employees may feel bored and unchallenged.

Current standards

- These are standards based on current working conditions.
- They are useful when current conditions are abnormal and any other standard would provide meaningless information.
- The disadvantage is that they do not attempt to motivate employees to improve upon current working conditions and, as a result, employees may feel unchallenged.

Ideal standards

- These are based upon perfect operating conditions.
- This means that there is no wastage or scrap, no breakdowns, no stoppages or idle time; in short, no inefficiencies.
- In their search for perfect quality, Japanese companies use ideal standards for pinpointing areas where close examination may result in large cost savings.
- Ideal standards may have an adverse motivational impact since employees may feel that the standard is impossible to achieve.

Variance analysis

Variances can be calculated for both costs and sales. Cost variances analyse the difference between actual costs and standard costs. Sales variances analyse the difference between actual and budgeted sales prices and sales volumes.

Where standard costing is used, variance analysis can be an important aspect of performance measurement and control. It is defined in the CIMA Official Terminology as 'the evaluation of performance by means of variances, whose timely reporting should maximise the opportunity for managerial action'.

Variance reports comparing actual results with the standards or budget are produced regularly, perhaps monthly.

The difference between budgetary control & variance analysis

Budgetary control is concerned with controlling total costs, whereas standard costing and variance analysis are concerned with unit costs.

In order to use standard costing, a standard unit must be made or a standard action be performed. Budgetary control is more flexible and can be used to control costs even when a wide variety of activities are undertaken.

One disadvantage of using budgetary control is that whilst it limits expenditure it does not provide a basis for measuring the efficiency of that expenditure.

A standard costing system is integrated with the actual accounting system whereas budgetary control operates as a reporting system external to the accounting system.

Budgetary control is often used for discretionary items such as research and development, advertising and non-activity related costs such as administration.

In manufacturing organisations it is likely that the output units will be homogenous and easily measured, whereas in non-manufacturing (service organisations) there are likely to be various forms of output which may not be easy to measure.

3 Sales variances

The difference between a budgeted profit and the actual profit achieved in a period is explained by both cost variances and sales variances. Cost variances explain the differences between actual costs and budgeted or standard costs. Sales variances explain the effect of differences between:

- actual and standard sales prices, and
- budgeted and actual sales volumes.

Sales price variance

A sales price variance shows the effect on profit of a 'change in revenue caused by the actual selling price differing from that budgeted' *(CIMA Official Terminology)*. It is calculated as the difference between:

(a) Standard selling price multiplied by the actual number of units sold, and

(b) Actual selling price multiplied by the actual number of units sold.

Proforma

Sales price variance		$
Units sold should have sold for	(actual sales units × standard sales price per unit)	X
They did sell for	(actual sales revenue)	Y
Sales price variance		X–Y

This variance is favourable if actual sales revenue is higher than sales at the standard selling price, and adverse if actual sales revenue is lower than standard.

Sales volume variance

The sales volume variance is a 'measure of the effect on contribution/profit of not achieving the budgeted volume of sales' *(CIMA Official Terminology)*. It is the difference between actual and budgeted sales volumes valued at either standard profit, in an absorption costing system, or standard contribution in a marginal costing system.

Proforma

A sales volume variance measured in units has to be calculated first. The variance is favourable if actual sales volume is higher than budgeted sales volume, and adverse if actual sales volume is lower than budget.

Sales volume variance	**Units of sale**
	Units
Actual sales volume	X
Budgeted sales volume	Y
Sales volume variance	X–Y

The variance in units can then be valued in one of three ways:

- at the **standard profit per unit** – if using absorption costing
- at the **standard contribution per unit** – if using marginal costing
- at the **standard revenue per unit** – this is rarely used and you should only do so if it was specifically asked for in an exam question.

Example 1

Walter Dean Ltd has budgeted sales of 400 units at $25 each. The variable costs are expected to be $18 per unit, and there are no fixed costs.

The actual sales were 500 units at $20 each and costs were as expected.

Calculate the selling price variance and the sales volume contribution variance.

Example 2

The following data is available for the most recent month of sales:

	Budget	**Actual**
Sales units	320	380
Selling price per unit	$45	$42
Total cost per unit	$23	$22
Variable cost per unit	$17	$15

Calculate the sales variances, calculating the sales volume variance using absorption costing, marginal costing and standard revenue per unit.

4 Direct material cost variances

This section has three variances. The direct material total variance, which shows the total difference in the amount spent on materials, and this can also be split into two further components – the materials price and materials usage variances.

Direct material total variance

The difference between:

(a) the standard direct material cost of the actual production and

(b) the actual direct material cost.

Proforma

Direct material total variance		$
Actual quantity of output	should cost (standard)	X
	did cost	Y
Total cost variance		X–Y

Example 3

James Marshall Ltd makes a single product with the following budgeted material costs per unit:

2 kg of material A at $10/kg

Actual details:

Output 1,000 units
Material purchased and used 2,200 kg
Material cost $20,900

Calculate the direct material total variance.

A total material variance actually conveys very little useful information. It needs to be analysed further. It can be analysed into two sub-variances:

(1) a direct material price variance, i.e. paying more or less than expected for materials and

(2) a direct material usage variance, i.e. using more or less material than expected.

CIMA definitions

The total direct material variance is defined as:

> *measurement of the difference between the standard material cost of the output produced and the material cost incurred. (CIMA Official Terminology).*

The material price variance is defined as:

> *the difference between the actual price paid for purchased materials and their standard cost. (CIMA Official Terminology).*

The material usage variance is defined as a variance which:

> *measures efficiency in the use of material, by comparing standard material usage for actual production with actual material used, the difference is valued at standard cost. (CIMA Official Terminology).*

Direct material price variance

It is calculated as the difference between:

(a) standard purchase price per kg (or per litre for liquids) and

(b) actual purchase price

multiplied by the actual quantity of material purchased or used.

Note that the material price variance can be calculated either at the time of purchase or at the time of usage.

Proforma

Direct materials price variance		$
Actual quantity of materials	should cost (standard)	X
	did cost (actual)	Y
		–––
Direct materials price variance		X–Y
		–––

The impact of inventory valuation

If inventory is valued at standard cost, then the calculation should be performed using the quantity of materials *purchased*. This will ensure that all of the variance is eliminated as soon as purchases are made and the inventory will be held at standard cost.

If inventory is valued at actual cost, then the calculation should be performed using the quantity of materials *used*. This means that the variance is calculated and eliminated on each item of inventory as it is used up. The remainder of the inventory will then be held at actual price, with its price variance still 'attached', until it is used and the price variance is calculated.

Direct material usage variance

The difference between:

(a) the standard quantity of material specified for the actual production and

(b) the actual quantity used

multiplied by the standard purchase price.

Proforma

Direct materials usage variance		$
Actual output produced	should use (standard quantity)	X
	did use (actual quantity)	Y
Direct materials usage variance	(in material quantity)	X–Y
× standard price	(per unit of material)	$P
Direct materials usage variance		$P × (X–Y)

Example 4

For example 3, calculate the price and usage variances for materials.

An alternative method

Using the data in Example 3, calculate the same variances for materials using the following format:

SQSP			
	Usage variance		
AQSP			Total variance
	Price variance		
AQAP			

Where SQ means Standard Quantity
SP means Standard Price
AQ means Actual Quantity
and AP means Actual Price

Standard Quantity means the standard quantity of the actual output.

Note: This assumes purchases = issues and/or the price variance is calculated at the time of issue.

					$	
SQSP						
	2 kg/unit x 1,000 units	x	$10/kg	=	20,000	Usage
AQSP						$2,000 A
	2,200 kg	x	$10/kg	=	22,000	
AQAP						$1,100 F
		x		=	20,900	Price

5 Direct labour cost variances

This section has four variances. The direct labour total cost variance, which shows the impact of any overall change in the amount spent on labour, and this can also be split into two further components – the labour rate and labour efficiency variances. In some scenarios we might also see a labour idle time variance.

Direct labour total variance

The difference between:

(a) the standard direct labour cost of the actual production and

(b) the actual cost of direct labour.

Proforma

Direct labour total variance		$
Actual quantity of output	should cost (standard)	X
	did cost	Y
Total cost variance		X–Y

A total labour variance can also be analysed further. It can be analysed into two sub-variances:

(1) a direct labour rate variance, i.e. paying more or less than expected per hour for labour and

(2) a direct labour efficiency variance, i.e. using more or less labour hours per unit than expected.

CIMA definitions

The total direct labour variance is defined as one which:

indicates the difference between the standard direct labour cost of the output which has been produced and the actual direct labour cost incurred.
(CIMA Official Terminology).

The direct labour rate variance is defined as one which:

indicates the actual cost of any change from the standard labour rate of remuneration.
(CIMA Official Terminology).

The direct labour efficiency variance is defined as:

standard labour cost of any change from the standard level of labour efficiency.
(CIMA Official Terminology).

Direct labour rate variance

The difference between:

(a) standard rate per hour and the

(b) actual rate per hour

multiplied by the actual hours that were paid for.

Proforma

Direct labour rate variance		$
Number of hours paid	should cost/hr (standard)	X
	did cost (actual)	Y
Direct labour rate variance		X–Y

Direct labour efficiency variance

The difference between:

(a) the standard hours specified for the actual production and

(b) the actual hours worked

multiplied by the standard hourly rate.

Proforma

Direct labour efficiency variance:		**Hours**
Actual output produced	should take (standard hours)	X
	did take (actual hours)	Y
Direct labour efficiency variance	(in hours)	X–Y
× standard rate per hour		$P
Direct labour efficiency variance		$P × (X–Y)

Example 5

Ivan Korshunov provides a pension consultancy service and has the following budgeted/standard information:

Budgeted services	1,000
Labour hours per unit	3
Labour rate per hour	$80

Actual results:

Number of services provided	1,100
Hours paid for and worked	3,400 hours
Labour cost	$283,000

Calculate rate and efficiency variances for labour.

Idle time and idle time variances

During a period, there might be idle time, when the work force is not doing any work at all.

When idle time occurs, and if it is recorded, the efficiency variance should be separated into two parts:

- an idle time variance
- an efficiency variance during active working hours.

If there is no standard idle time set, then **the idle time variance is always adverse**, because it represents money 'wasted'.

Idle time definition

The purpose of an efficiency variance should be to measure the efficiency of the work force in the time they are actively engaged in making products or delivering a service.

The direct labour idle time variance is defined as:

> *this variance occurs when the hours paid exceed the hours worked and there is an extra cost caused by this idle time. Its computation increases the accuracy of the labour efficiency variance.*
>
> *(CIMA Official Terminology).*

Illustration 1

A product has a standard direct labour cost of $15, consisting of 1.5 hours of work for each unit at a cost of $10 per hour. During April, 100 units were produced. The direct labour workers were paid $2,000 for 160 hours of attendance, but the idle time records show that 30 hours in the month were recorded as idle time.

(a) We can record an idle time variance of 30 hours (A). This is costed at the standard rate per hour, $10, to give an idle time variance of $300(A).

(b) The efficiency variance should then be calculated using the active hours worked, not the total hours paid for.

Direct labour efficiency variance

		Hours
Actual output produced	should take (standard hours)	
100 units	1.5 hrs per unit	150
	did take (160 hrs – 30 hrs)	130
Direct labour efficiency variance	(in hours)	20 F
× standard rate per hour		$10/hr
Direct labour efficiency variance		$200 F

Example 6

Melanie Mitchell Ltd makes a single product with the following information:

Budget/Standard

Output	1,000 units
Hours	6,000
Labour cost	$42,000

Actual

Output	900 units
Hours paid	5,500
Hours worked	5,200
Labour cost	$39,100

Calculate appropriate variances for labour

Expected idle time

Some organisations may experience idle time on a regular basis. For example, if demand is seasonal or irregular, but the organisation wishes to maintain and pay a constant number of workers, they will experience a certain level of 'expected' or 'normal' idle time during less busy periods.

In this situation the standard labour rate may include an allowance for the cost of the expected idle time. Only the impact of any unexpected or abnormal idle time would be included in the idle time variance. If actual idle time is greater than standard then the variance is adverse; if it is less than standard then it would be favourable.

Example

LBC offer a public bus service for local journeys at a popular holiday resort. It experiences seasonal demand for its product. During the next period the company expects that there will be an average level of idle time equivalent to 20% of hours paid. The company's standard labour rate is $9 per hour before the adjustment for idle time payments.

The standard time for each journey is 3 active (productive) hours.

Actual results for the period were as follows:

Number of journeys	3,263
Actual hours paid for	14,000
Actual active (productive) hours	10,304

Required:

Calculate the following variances for the period:

(i) the idle time variance

(ii) the labour efficiency variance.

Solution

The basic standard rate per hour must be increased to allow for the impact of the idle time:

$$\text{Standard rate per hour worked} = \frac{\$9.00}{0.8} = \$11.25$$

The variances can now be evaluated at this increased hourly rate.

Idle time variance

	Hours
Expected idle time = 20% × 14,000 hours paid	2,800
Actual idle time = 14,000 – 10,304 hours	3,696
Variance (hours)	896 A
Standard rate per hour worked	$11.25
Idle time variance	$10,080 A

Labour efficiency variance

	Hours
3,263 journeys should have taken (×3)	9,789
But did take (productive hours)	10,304
Variance (hours)	515 A
Standard rate per hour worked	$11.25
Labour efficiency variance	$5,794 A

6 Variable overhead variances

Variable overhead variances are similar to direct materials and direct labour cost variances.

- In standard product costing, a variable production overhead total variance can be calculated, and this can be analysed into an expenditure variance and an efficiency variance.
- With service costing, a variable overhead total variance can be calculated, but this might not be analysed any further.

Since variable production overheads are normally assumed to vary with labour hours worked, **labour hours are used in calculations**. This means, for example, that the variable production overhead efficiency variance uses exactly the same hours as the direct labour efficiency variance.

Details on the variances

Variable production overhead total variance

The difference between:

(a) the standard variable overhead cost of the actual production and

(b) the actual cost of variable production overheads.

Variable production overhead total variance		$
Actual quantity of output	should cost (standard)	X
	did cost	Y
Total variance		X–Y

A total variable production overhead variance can also be analysed further. It can be analysed into two sub-variances:

(1) a variable production overhead expenditure variance, i.e. paying more or less than expected per hour for variable overheads and

(2) a variable production overhead efficiency variance, i.e. using more or less variable overheads per unit than expected.

The official CIMA definitions are as follows:

The variable production overhead total variance is defined as one which:

measures the difference between the variable overhead that should be used for actual output and variable production overhead actually used.

(CIMA Official Terminology).

The variable production overhead expenditure variance is defined as one which:

indicates the actual cost of any change from the standard rate per hour. Hours refer to either labour or machine hours depending on the recovery base chosen for variable production overhead.

(CIMA Official Terminology).

The variable production overhead efficiency variance is defined as the:

standard variable overhead cost of any change from the standard level of efficiency.

(CIMA Official Terminology).

Variable production overhead expenditure variance

		$
Number of hours worked	should cost/hr (standard)	X
	did cost (actual)	Y
Variable production overhead expenditure variance		X–Y

Variable production overhead efficiency variance

		Hours
Actual output produced	should take (standard hours)	X
	did take (actual hours)	Y
Efficiency variance	(in hours)	X–Y
× standard variable overhead rate per hour		$P
Variable production overhead efficiency variance		$P × (X–Y)

Example 7

The budgeted output for KB for May was 1,000 units of product A. Each unit requires 2 direct labour hours. Variable overheads are budgeted at $3 per labour hour.

Actual results:

Output	900 units
Labour hours worked	1,980 hours
Variable overheads	$5,544

Calculate appropriate variances for variable overheads.

Alternative method

Using the same example, calculate appropriate variances for variable overhead using the following format:

SHSR
} Efficiency variance
AHSR
} Expenditure variance
AHAR

} Total variance

Where	SH	means Standard Hours
	SR	means Standard Rate
	AH	means Actual Hours
and	AR	means Actual Rate

Standard Hours means the standard hours of the actual output.

					$	
SHSR	2 hrs/unit x 900 units	x	$3/hr	=	5,400	Efficiency $540 A
AHSR	1,980 hrs	x	$3/hr	=	5,940	
AHAR				=	5,544	$396 F Expenditure

Idle time variances and variable production overhead

The analysis of variable production overhead variances is affected by the existence of idle time. It is usually assumed that variable production overhead is incurred during active hours only.

The variable production overhead efficiency variance is calculated in the same way that the direct labour efficiency variance is calculated when there is idle time.

The variable production overhead expenditure variance, when there is idle time, is the difference between:

- the standard variable overhead cost of the active hours worked, and
- the actual variable overhead cost.

Example 8

Extracts from the standard cost card of a product are as follows:

		$/unit
Direct labour	2 hours × $15 per hour	30
Variable production overhead	2 hours × $4 per hour	8

During May, 200 units were produced. The direct labour workers were paid $6,600 for 440 hours of work, but the idle time records show that 20 hours in the month were recorded as idle time. Actual variable production overhead expenditure incurred was $1,530.

Calculate the labour and variable overhead variances.

7 Fixed production overhead cost variances

Fixed production overhead total variance

The amount of overhead absorbed for each unit of output is the standard fixed overhead cost per unit. The total cost variance is therefore calculated as follows:

The difference between:

(a) the standard fixed production overhead cost absorbed by the actual production (i.e. the amount of fixed overhead actually absorbed into production using the standard absorption rate), and

(b) the actual fixed production overheads incurred.

Proforma

Fixed production overhead total variance		$
Overheads absorbed	(Actual output × standard fixed production overhead absorption rate)	X
Actual fixed overhead incurred		Y
Fixed production overhead total cost variance		X Y

Under/over-absorption

In standard absorption costing, the total cost variance for fixed production overhead variances is the amount of over-absorbed or under-absorbed overhead. Over-absorbed overhead is a favourable variance, and under-absorbed overhead is an adverse variance.

Under/over-absorption is the difference between the overheads incurred and the overheads absorbed.

The under/over-absorption occurs because the OAR is based upon two predictions – the budgeted fixed overhead and the budgeted level of activity. If either or both predictions are wrong there will be under/over-absorption and there will be a fixed overhead total variance.

- If the actual expenditure is different from the budgeted expenditure there is an expenditure variance and
- If the actual production is different from the budgeted production there is a volume variance. A fixed production overhead volume variance represents the amount of fixed overhead that has been under- or over-absorbed due to the fact that actual production volume differed from the budgeted production volume.

Fixed production overhead expenditure variance

The difference between:

(a) budgeted fixed production overhead and

(b) actual fixed production overhead.

Proforma

Fixed production overhead expenditure variance	$
Budgeted fixed overhead	X
Actual fixed production overhead incurred	Y
Fixed production overhead expenditure variance	X–Y

An expenditure variance can be calculated for fixed production overhead. A similar variance can be calculated (if required) for other fixed overhead costs:

- a fixed administration overhead expenditure variance
- a fixed sales and distribution overhead expenditure variance.

Fixed production overhead volume variance

The volume variance is calculated as the difference between:

(a) Budgeted output in units and
(b) Actual output in units

multiplied by the standard fixed overhead cost per unit.

The fixed overhead volume variance does not occur in a marginal costing system.

Proforma

Fixed production overhead volume variance

		Units
Actual output produced		X
Budgeted output		Y
Volume variance	(in units)	X–Y
× standard fixed overhead rate per unit		$F
Fixed production overhead volume variance		$F × (X–Y)

You may be aware that the fixed production overhead volume variance can be sub-divided into a fixed production overhead capacity and fixed production overhead efficiency (explained later).

Example 9

The following data relates to the fixed production overhead costs of producing widgets in March:

Budgeted fixed production overhead expenditure	$4,375
Budgeted production volume (widgets)	1,750 units
Standard fixed production overhead cost:	
(0.25 hours @ $10 per hour)	$2.50
Number of widgets produced in March	1,800 units
Actual fixed production overhead expenditure	$4,800

Required:

Calculate the fixed production overhead expenditure and volume variances in March.

It has been shown in an earlier chapter that, where products take different times to produce, it is not always suitable to have fixed overheads allocated on a per unit basis. A labour hour basis may be more suitable, for example.

It may therefore be necessary to work out the fixed overhead volume variance based on the fixed overhead absorption rate **per hour**, rather than the rate per unit. This is needed when an organisation has more than one product and an absorption rate per unit is not appropriate.

The variance is calculated by comparing the cost of the standard hours for actual production with the total budgeted fixed overhead.

Illustration

A cosmetic dental practice offers two types of treatment, teeth whitening and teeth straightening. The treatments last for varying amounts of time and fixed overheads are allocated to treatments based on labour hours spent on the treatment. In the month of September total fixed overheads were budgeted to be $40,000 and the services were budgeted to have the following total labour hours:

Service	Whitening	Straightening
Budgeted hours	460	540

During September there were 190 teeth straightening treatments which took on average 2.8 hours per treatment compared to a standard time of 3 hours per treatment.

Calculate the fixed overhead volume variance for the teeth straightening service for September.

Solution

The fixed overhead absorption rate per hour is:

= $40,000 (460 hours + 540 hours) = $40 per hour

The budgeted overhead cost for the teeth straightening treatment is:

= 540 hours × $40 per hour = $21,600

The standard cost of the standard hours worked is:

= 190 treatments × 3 hours per treatment × $40 per hour = $22,800

The variance = $22,800 – $21,600 = $1,200 Favourable

Fixed overhead capacity and efficiency variances

In absorption costing systems, if the fixed overhead is absorbed based on **hours**, then the fixed overhead volume variance can be subdivided into capacity and efficiency variances.

- The capacity variance measures whether the workforce worked more or fewer hours than **budgeted** for the period:

	$
Actual hours × FOAR per hour	X
Less Budgeted expenditure	(X)
Fixed overhead capacity variance	X

The efficiency variance measures whether the workforce took more or less time than **standard** in producing their output for the period:

	$
Standard hours for actual production × FOAR per hour	X
Less Actual hours × FOAR per hour	(X)
Fixed overhead efficiency variance	X

Together, these two sub-variances explain why the level of activity was different from that budgeted, i.e. they combine to give the fixed overhead volume variance.

Example 10

The following information is available for a company for Period 4.

Fixed production overheads	$22,960
Units	6,560

The standard time to produce each unit is 2 hours

Actual

Fixed production overheads	$24,200
Units	6,460
Labour hours	12,600 hrs

Required:

Calculate the following:

(a) fixed overhead absorption rate per hour

(b) fixed overhead capacity variance

(c) fixed overhead efficiency variance

(d) fixed overhead volume variance.

Marginal costing fixed production overhead variances

In marginal costing, fixed production overheads are not absorbed into the cost of production. For this reason, there is no fixed production overhead volume variance.

The only fixed production overhead variance reported in standard marginal costing is a fixed production overhead expenditure variance. This is the difference between actual and budgeted fixed production overhead expenditure, as described above for absorption costing.

8 Operating statement

An operating statement is a top-level variance report, reconciling the budgeted and actual profit for the period.

An operating statement starts off with the expected figure, e.g. budgeted or standard profit or contribution or cost, etc. and ends up with the corresponding actual figure. In between we list all the appropriate variances in as much detail as possible.

The format will be similar to the following, the numbers have no significance. They are purely for illustration purposes.

Operating Statement for Period 12

		$	$	$
Budgeted gross profit				100,000
Sales volume profit variance				15,000F
Budgeted profit from actual sales volume				115,000
Sales price variance				28,750F
				143,750
		Adverse	**Favourable**	
Cost variances				
Direct material A	Price	3,100		
	Usage		10,000	
Direct material B	Price		3,050	
	Usage		7,500	
Direct labour	Efficiency		7,000	
	Rate		12,000	
	Idle time		3,000	
Variable overhead	Efficiency	4,000		
	Expenditure		3,500	
Fixed Prod overhead	Expenditure		11,500	
	Volume	30,400		
		37,500	57,550	20,050F
Actual gross profit				163,800

In some questions the usage variance will be sub-divided into mix and yield variances. This is covered in the chapter on 'Advanced Variances' later in the text.

Variance reporting

Variances should be reported to management at the end of each control period, for example at the end of each month. There might be a hierarchy of control reports:

- a top level report reconciling budgeted and actual profit should be prepared for senior management
- variance reports might be prepared for individual managers with responsibility for a particular aspect of operations.

For example, regional sales managers might be sent variance reports showing sales price and sales volume variances for their region. Production managers might be sent variance reports relating to materials usage, labour efficiency and other items of expenditure under their control. Similarly, detailed reports on overhead expenditure variances might be sent to the managers responsible for departmental spending.

Variance reports should be provided as soon as possible after the end of each control period, since there is a risk that variance information might be considered 'out of date' if it is received several weeks after the control period has ended.

Example 11

SM is a manufacturing company which produces a variety of products. The following information relates to one of its products – Product W:

Standard cost data

		$	$
Selling price			100
Direct Material X	5 kg	15	
Direct Material Y	4 kg	20	
Direct labour	@ $8/hr	24	
Variable overheads		18	
Fixed overheads		6	
			83
Profit per unit			17

The budgeted production is 24,000 units per annum evenly spread throughout the year, with each calendar month assumed to be equal. March is a bad month in terms of sales revenue and it is expected that sales will only be 1,700 units during the month. Fixed overheads were expected to be $144,000 per year and are absorbed on a labour hour basis.

Actual results for the month of March were that sales were 2,200 units at a price of $90. There was no change in inventory of finished goods or raw materials.

The purchases during the month were 11,300 kg of material X at $2.80 per kg and 8,300 kg of material Y at $5.30 per kg.

4,800 labour hours were worked at a rate of $8.10 per hour and 1,600 hours at $8.30.

The actual variable overheads for the period were $33,000 and the fixed overheads were $12,500.

The company uses an absorption costing system and values its raw materials at standard cost.

Required:

Calculate appropriate variances for the month of March in as much detail as possible and present an operating statement reconciling budgeted profit with actual profit.

You are not required to calculate mix or yield variances as Sam Mendes Ltd does not sub-analyse the material usage variance.

Variances in service industries

In the exam, you are just as likely to encounter service industries as manufacturers. These could be law firms, healthcare providers, accountants, banks etc. The calculations, however, will still follow the same principles as in manufacturing.

Illustration

The standard cost schedule for hospital care for a minor surgical procedure is shown below.

Staff: patient ratio is 0.75:1

		$
Nursing costs	2 days × 0.75 × $320 per day	480
Space and food costs	2 days × $175 per day	350
Drugs and specific materials		115
Hospital overheads	2 days × $110 per day	220
Total standard cost		1,165

The actual data for the hospital care for one patient having the minor surgical procedure showed that the patient stayed in hospital for three days. The cost of the drugs and specific materials for this patient was $320. There were 0.9 nurses per patient on duty during the time that the patient was in hospital. The daily rates for nursing pay, space and food, and hospital overheads were as expected.

Prepare a statement that reconciles the standard cost with the actual costs of hospital care for this patient. The statement should contain FIVE variances that will give useful information to the manager who is reviewing the cost of hospital care for minor surgical procedures.

Solution

		$	$
Standard cost for 2-day procedure			1,165
Length of stay variances:			
Nursing costs	1 day × 0.75 × $320 per day	240A	
Space and food costs	1 day × $175 per day	175A	
Hospital overheads	1 day × $110 per day	110A	
		——	525 A
Standard cost for 3-day stay			1,690
Drug and specific cost variances			205 A
Nursing staff variance	3 days × (0.90 – 0.75) × $320 per day		144 A
Actual cost			2,039

Calculating actual data from standard cost details and variances

An excellent way of testing whether you really understand the reasons for and the calculation of operating variances is to 'work backwards' from standard cost data and variances to arrive at the actual results.

Example on working backwards

Q operates a system of standard costing and in respect of one of its products, which is manufactured within a single cost centre, the following information is given.

For one unit of product the standard material input is 16 litres at a standard price of $2.50 per litre. The standard labour rate is $5 per hour and 6 hours are allowed to produce one unit. Fixed production overhead is absorbed at the rate of 120% of direct labour cost. During the last 4 weeks accounting period the following occurred.

- The material price variance was extracted on purchase and the actual price paid was $2.45 per litre.
- Total direct labour cost was $121,500.
- Fixed production overhead cost incurred was $150,000.

Variances included:

	Favourable	*Adverse*
	$	$
Direct material price	8,000	
Direct material usage		6,000
Direct labour rate		4,500
Direct labour efficiency	3,600	
Fixed production overhead expenditure		6,000

Required:

Calculate the following for the 4-week period:

(a) budgeted output in units

(b) number of litres purchased

(c) number of litres used above standard allowed

(d) actual units produced

(e) actual hours worked

(f) average actual direct labour rate per hour.

Solution

The best thing to do as a first step is to pull together all of the standard cost information to calculate a standard cost per unit.

	$
Direct material (16 litres × 2.5 per litre)	40
Direct labour (6 hours × $5 per hour)	30
Fixed production overhead ($30 × 120%)	36
Total	106

Calculating the required figures is now just a series of exercises in logic. These exercises can seem difficult to the novice – but the logic becomes simple and obvious with familiarity.

(a) If actual fixed production overhead was $150,000 and the fixed production overhead expenditure variance was $6,000 adverse, then it follows that the budget fixed overhead was $144,000. From this it follows that the budget must have been 4,000 units (that is, $144,000 budgeted overhead/$36 standard overhead cost per unit).

(b) If the standard material purchase price was $2.50 per litre and the actual purchase price was $2.45, then it follows that the material price variance is $0.05 per litre favourable. We are told that the material price variance was $8,000 favourable, so it follows that 160,000 litres must have been purchased (that is, $8,000 price variance/$0.05 price variance per litre).

(c) If the direct material usage variance was $6,000 adverse and the standard price of materials is $2.50 per litre, then it follows that the number of litres used above the standard allowance is 2,400 ($6000/$2.50 per litre).

(d) If the actual direct labour cost was $121,500 and labour cost variances totalling $900 adverse ($4,500 adverse rate plus $3,600 favourable efficiency) were experienced, then the standard labour cost for the output achieved was $120,600. It follows that the units produced were 4,020 (that is, $120,600 standard labour cost/$30 standard labour cost per unit).

(e) The total hours actually worked is 24,120 standard hours worked (that is, 4,020 units produced at 6 standard hours per unit) minus the 720-hour favourable labour efficiency variance (that is, $3,600 efficiency variance/$5 standard rate per hour). This gives a total of 23,400 actual hours worked.

(f) If the actual labour cost was $121,500 and the actual hours worked was 23,400, then it follows that the actual wage rate per hour was $5.1923.

9 Variance analysis using ABC costing

As part of variance analysis managers will need to establish standard costs. Activity based costing is one method for determining costs and hence will have implications of some of the variances calculated.

Compared to traditional absorption costing, the use of ABC is most likely to impact overhead variances.

Typically, standard costs can be compared to actual and an overhead expenditure and efficiency variance calculated.

Illustration

An ABC approach to the analysis of overhead costs is possible. This follows the ABC logic that all overheads are variable if one understands what they vary with. Let us illustrate the approach with a simple example.

Example

XX produces the Unit and all overheads are associated with the delivery of Units to its customers. Budget details for the period include $8,000 overheads, 4,000 Units output and 40 customer deliveries. Actual results for the period are $7,800 overheads, 4,200 Units output and 38 customer deliveries.

The overhead cost variance for the period is

	$	
Actual cost	7,800	
Standard cost (4,200 units × $2 per unit)	8,400	
Cost variance	600	F

Applying the traditional fixed overhead cost variance analysis gives the following result:

		$	
Volume variance	($8,400 standard – $8,000 budget)	400	F
Expenditure variance	($8,000 budget – $7,800 actual)	200	F
Cost variance		600	F

Adopting an ABC approach gives the following result:

		$	
Efficiency variance	(42 standard – 38 actual deliveries) × $200	800	F
Expenditure variance	[(38 deliveries × $200) – $7,800]	200	A
Cost variance		600	F

The ABC approach is based on an assumption that the overheads are essentially variable (but variable with the delivery numbers and not the Units output). The ABC cost variances are based on a standard delivery size of 100 Units and a standard cost per delivery of $200. Both of these figures are derived from the budget. The activity variance reports the cost impact of undertaking more or less activities than standard, and the expenditure variance reports the cost impact of paying more or less than standard for the actual activities undertaken.

10 Chapter summary

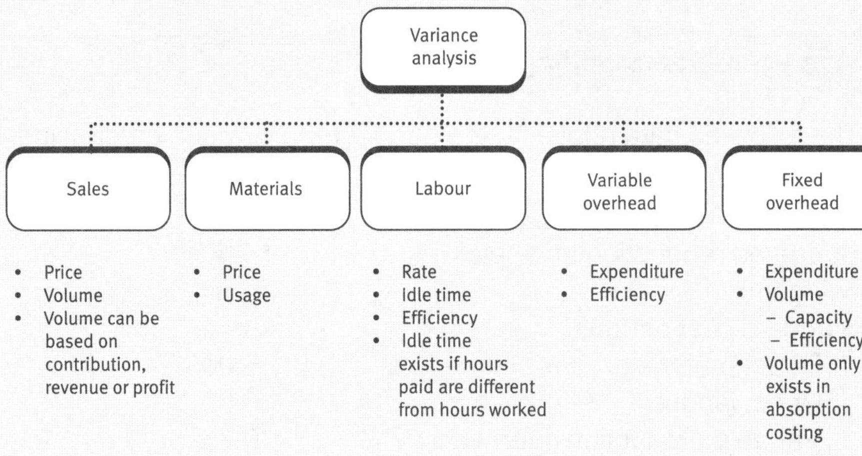

- Price
- Volume
- Volume can be based on contribution, revenue or profit

- Price
- Usage

- Rate
- Idle time
- Efficiency
- Idle time exists if hours paid are different from hours worked

- Expenditure
- Efficiency

- Expenditure
- Volume
  - Capacity
  - Efficiency
- Volume only exists in absorption costing

11 Practice questions

Test your understanding 1

The following data relates to the budget for a company producing widgets in March:

Budgeted production and sales (widgets)	1,750 units
Standard cost per unit:	$
Direct materials	6.00
Direct labour	3.00
Variable production overhead	0.75
Fixed production overhead	2.50
	12.25
Standard sales price	18.25
Standard profit per unit	6.00
Number of widgets produced and sold in March	1,800 units
Actual sales revenue	$32,300

Required:

Calculate the sales price and sales volume profit variance. What would be the sales volume contribution variance if standard marginal costing were used?

Test your understanding 2

Major Caldwell makes and sells a single product. Each unit of the product requires 3 kg of material at $4 per kg.

The actual details for last period were that 1,200 units of finished goods were produced, 3,600 kg of material were purchased for $14,800 and 3,520 kg were used.

Major Caldwell maintains its raw materials account at standard.

Calculate appropriate variances for materials.

Test your understanding 3

The standard direct material and labour costs for a product are:

		$
Direct material A	2 kg × $ 4/kg	8
Direct material B	0.5 litres × $6/ltr	3
Direct labour	0.75 hours × $12 per hour	9
		20

During November, the company made 3,200 units and sold 2,900. Actual production costs were:

		$
Direct material A	6,100 kgs	25,000
Direct material B	1,750 litres	11,600
Direct labour	2,200 hours paid (only 2,000 hours worked)	28.000

Required:

Calculate the following variances:

- direct materials price
- direct materials usage
- direct labour rate
- direct labour idle time
- direct labour efficiency.

Test your understanding 4

Jack Doherty makes a single product with the following standard cost details per unit.

				$
Direct materials	5 kg	@	$4/kg	20
Direct labour	4 hrs	@	$6/hr	24

Actual results were that 1,000 units were produced and sold. The actual hours paid for were 4,100 and the hours worked were 3,900. The actual labour cost was $27,060. The number of kg purchased in the month was 5,200 kg for $21,320 and the number of kg used was 4,900 kg. The company calculates the material price variance at the time of purchase.

Calculate appropriate variances for materials and labour.

Test your understanding 5

Col. Axelrod makes and sells a single product with the following information:

Std/Budget

Output	1,000 units
Material	3,000 kg @ $5/kg
Labour	5,000 hours @$6/hr

Actual

Output	1,100 units		
Material	Purchased Used	3,600 kg 3,400 kg	for $18,720
Labour hrs	Paid for Worked	5,200 hrs 4,900 hrs	for $32,760

Col. Axelrod Ltd maintains its raw material account at standard cost. Calculate the variances for materials and labour.

Test your understanding 6

IR hospital provides surgical treatments which require 3 standard hours per treatment. Fixed overheads are budgeted at $12,000 and are absorbed on a labour hour basis. The hospital budgeted to provide 1,000 treatments during March.

Actual results:

Treatments	1,100
Labour hours	3,080 hours
Overheads incurred	$13,000

Calculate appropriate variances for fixed overhead.

Test your understanding 7

The electronic crime division of a local police station had the following information for Period 4:

Budget	
Fixed overheads	$22,960
Reported crimes	6,560
The standard time to deal with each crime is 2 hours.	
Actual	
Fixed overheads	$24,200
Reported crimes	6,460
Labour hours	12,600 hrs

Required:

If the division uses an absorption costing system, calculate the following:

(a) FOAR per labour hour

(b) Fixed overhead expenditure variance

(c) Fixed overhead capacity variance

(d) Fixed overhead efficiency variance

(e) Fixed overhead volume variance.

Test your understanding 8

Last month, 40,000 production hours were budgeted in CTD, and the budgeted fixed production overhead cost was $250,000. Actual results show that 38,000 hours were worked and paid, and the standard hours for actual production were 35,000. CTD operates a standard absorption costing system.

What was the fixed production overhead capacity variance for last month?

A $12,500 Adverse

B $12,500 Favourable

C $31,250 Adverse

D $31,250 Favourable

Test your understanding 9

Scenario

Malcolm Reynolds makes and sells a single product, Product Q, with the following standard specification for materials:

	Quantity	Price per kg
	kg	$
Direct material X	12	40
Direct material Y	8	32

It takes 20 direct labour hours to produce one unit with a standard direct labour cost of $10 per hour.

The annual sales/production budget is 2,400 units evenly spread throughout the year. The standard selling price was $1,250 per unit.

The budgeted production overhead, all fixed, is $288,000 and expenditure is expected to occur evenly over the year, which the company divides into 12 calendar months. Absorption is based on direct labour hours.

For the month of October the following actual information is provided.

	$	$
Sales (220 units)		264,000
Cost of sales		
Direct materials used	159,000	
Direct wages	45,400	
Fixed production overhead	23,000	
		227,400
Gross profit		36,600
Administration costs	13,000	
Selling and distribution costs	8,000	
		21,000
Net profit		$15,600

Costs of opening inventories, for each material, were at the same price per kilogram as the purchases made during the month but there had been changes in the materials inventory levels, viz.:

	1 October	**30 October**
	kg	kg
Material X	680	1,180
Material Y	450	350

Material X purchases were 3,000 kg at $42 each.

Material Y purchases were 1,700 kg at $30 each.

The number of direct labour hours worked was 4,600 and the total wages incurred $45,400.

Work-in-progress inventories and finished goods inventories may be assumed to be the same at the beginning and end of October.

Tasks:

(a) to prepare a standard product cost for one unit of product Q showing the standard selling price and standard gross profit per unit

(b) to calculate appropriate variances for the materials, labour, fixed production overhead and sales, noting that it is company policy to calculate material price variances at time of issue to production and that Malcom Reynolds does not calculate mix and yield variances

(c) to prepare a statement for management reconciling the budgeted gross profit with the actual gross profit.

Test your understanding 10

Gooch makes a single product and operates a standard costing system. The following variances, standard costs and actual results relate to period 6:

Variances

	Favourable	Adverse
Direct material price variance		1,012
Direct material usage variance		1,380
Direct labour rate variance		920
Direct labour efficiency variance	3,680	
Variable overhead expenditure variance		1,288
Variable overhead efficiency variance	920	

Standard cost data

		$/unit
Direct materials	2 kg @ $3/kg	6
Direct labour	3 hrs @ $8/hr	24
Variable overheads	3 hrs @ $2/hr	6
Fixed overheads	3 hrs @ $4/hr	12
		$48

Fixed overheads were budgeted at $24,000 and the budgeted profit per unit was 20% of the selling price. Budgeted sales were 1,900 units.

Actual results

Material purchased and used	$16,192
Labour cost	$52,440
Variable overhead cost	$14,168
Fixed overhead cost	$23,500

Selling price per unit was $3 lower than budget and there was no change in inventory levels.

You are required to calculate the:

(a) actual output
(b) actual material price per kg
(c) labour hours worked
(d) fixed overhead volume variance
(e) fixed overhead expenditure variance
(f) sales volume profit variance
(g) selling price variance
(h) budgeted profit
(i) actual profit.

Test your understanding 11

Scenario

RBF Transport, a haulage contractor, operates a standard costing system and has prepared the following report for April 20X0:

Operating statement

		$	$	$
Budgeted profit				8,000
Sales volume profit variance				880 (A)
				7,120
Selling price variance				3,560 (F)
				10,680
Cost variances		*A*	*F*	
Direct labour	– rate		1,086	
	– efficiency	240		
Fuel	– price	420		
	– usage	1,280		
Variable overhead	– expenditure		280	
	– efficiency	180		
Fixed overhead	– expenditure		400	
	– volume	1,760		
		3,880	1,766	2,114 (A)
Actual profit				8,566

The company uses delivery miles as its cost unit, and the following details have been taken from the budget working papers for April 20X0:

(1) Expected activity	200,000 delivery miles
(2) Charge to customers	$0.30 per delivery mile
(3) Expected variable cost per delivery mile:	
Direct labour (0.02 hours)	$0.08
Fuel (0.1 litres)	$0.04
Variable overhead (0.02 hours)	$0.06

The following additional information has been determined from the actual accounting records for April 20X0.

- Fixed overhead cost $15,600
- Fuel price $0.42 per litre
- Direct labour hours 3,620

Tasks:

(a) Calculate for April 20X0:
   (i) the actual number of delivery miles
   (ii) the actual direct labour rate per hour
   (iii) the actual number of litres of fuel consumed
   (iv) the actual variable overhead expenditure.

(b) State TWO possible causes of the fuel usage variance.

(Time allowed for part (b): 5 minutes)

(c) Prepare a report, addressed to the transport operations manager, explaining the different types of standard which may be set, and the importance of keeping standards meaningful and relevant.

(Time allowed for part (c): 15 minutes)

Test your understanding 12

Flexed budgets for the cost of medical supplies in a hospital, based on a percentage of maximum bed occupancy, are shown below:

Bed occupancy	82%	94%
Medical supplies cost	$410,000	$429,200

During the period, the actual bed occupancy was 87% and the total cost of the medical supplies was $430,000.

Identify the medical supplies expenditure variance:

A $5,000 adverse

B $12,000 adverse

C $5,000 favourable

D $12,000 favourable

Test your understanding 13

A company has a sales budget of $145,000 per month for the financial year January to December. However, by the end of May, the cumulative sales variances for the year to date are:

Sales price variance $30,000 (A)

Sales volume contribution variance $16,000 (A)

The standard contribution/sales ratio is 40%. The marketing department has now estimated that sales for the next three months will be $120,000 per month, but for the rest of the year, monthly sales should rise to $148,000.

Required:

Prepare a statement as at the end of May that compares budgeted and forecast sales revenue and contribution for the year as a whole. Ignore variable cost variances.

Test your understanding 14

A company uses standard marginal costing. Last month the standard contribution on actual sales was $44,000 and the following variances arose:

Total variable costs variance	$6,500 Adverse
Sales price variance	$2,000 Favourable
Sales volume contribution variance	$4,500 Adverse

What was the actual contribution for last month?

A $33,000

B $35,000

C $37,500

D $39,500

Test your understanding 15

A company has prepared an activity-based budget for its stores department. One activity concerns inventory counts which has an activity based cost driver of $800 per inventory count (based on a budgeted activity of 50 counts per year).

During the year there were 52 counts and the actual cost for inventory counts was $40,560.

To the nearest $, the value of the variance for inventory counts in the year was $_____

Test your understanding 16

One activity for the tax department of a large accountancy firm is to perform follow-up visits to clients to investigate and resolve issues that have arisen as part of its tax work for that client. Information for this activity for the year was as follows:

	Budget	Actual
Clients	2,000	2,100
Follow up visits	4,000	3,600
Activity cost	$180,000	$168,000

Required:

Calculate the overhead expenditure variance and the overhead efficiency variance for the follow up activity.

Test your understanding answers

Example 1

Selling price variance

	$
Standard selling price	25
Actual selling price	20
	5 A
× Actual no of units sold	× 500
	2,500 A

Sales volume contribution variance

	Units
Budgeted sales	400
Actual sales	500
	100 F
× Standard contribution per unit	× $7
	$700 F

In this scenario there are no fixed costs, so the answer is the same whether we are using marginal or absorption costing.

Example 2

Sales price variance		$
Units sold should have sold for	(380 units × $45 per unit)	17,100
They did sell for	(actual sales revenue)	15,960
Sales price variance		1,140 (A)

Absorption costing

Sales volume profit variance	**Units**	
Actual sales volume	380	
Budgeted sales volume	320	
Sales volume variance	60	(F)
× standard profit per unit ($45 – $23)	× $22	
Sales volume profit variance	$1,320	(F)

Marginal costing

Sales volume contribution variance	**Units**	
Actual sales volume	380	
Budgeted sales volume	320	
Sales volume variance	60	(F)
× standard contribution per unit ($45 – $17)	× $28	
Sales volume contribution variance	$1,680	(F)

Standard revenue per unit

Sales volume revenue variance	**Units**	
Actual sales volume	380	
Budgeted sales volume	320	
Sales volume variance	60	(F)
× standard selling price per unit	× $45	
Sales volume revenue variance	$2,700	(F)

Example 3

Direct material total variance

	$
Standard cost of actual output	
2 kg × 1,000 units × $10/kg	20,000
Actual cost	20,900
	900 A

Example 4

Direct materials price variance:		$
Actual quantity of materials	should cost (standard)	
2,200 kgs	$10/kg	22,000
	did cost (actual)	20,900
Direct materials price variance		1,100 F

Direct materials usage variance:		$
Actual output produced	should use (standard quantity)	
1,000 units	2 kgs/unit	2,000
	did use (actual quantity)	2,200
Direct materials usage variance	(in material quantity)	200 A
× standard price	(per unit of material)	$10
Direct materials usage variance		2,000 A

Example 5

Direct labour rate variance:		$
Number of hours worked	should cost/hr (standard)	
3,400 hours	$80/hr	272,000
	did cost (actual)	283,000
Direct labour rate variance		11,000 A

Direct labour efficiency variance:		**Hours**
Actual services provided 1,100	should take (standard hours)	3,300
	3 hrs per service	
	did take (actual hours)	3,400
Direct labour efficiency variance	(in hours)	100 A
× standard rate per hour		$80/hr
Direct labour efficiency variance		$8,000 A

Example 6

				$	
SHSR	6 hrs/unit x 900 units	x	$7/hr	= 37,800	Efficiency $1,400 F
AHSR	5,200 hrs	x	$7/hr	= 36,400	

The efficiency variance looks at whether people **WORK** fast or slow and looks at hours **WORKED**.

				$	
AHSR	5,500 hrs	x	$7/hr	= 38,500	$600 A Rate
AHAR				= 39,100	

The rate variance looks at the rate of **PAY** so it looks at the hours **PAID**.

Idle time variance

(5,500 – 5,200) × $7 per hour $2,100 A

Or the idle time variance is simply the difference between the $38,500 and the $36,400 above = $2,100 A.

Example 7

Variable production overhead expenditure variance:		$
Number of hours worked	should cost/hr (standard)	
1,980 hours	$3/hour	5,940
	did cost (actual)	5,544
Variable production overhead expenditure variance		396 F

Variable production overhead efficiency variance:		**Hours**
Actual output produced	should take (standard hours)	
900 units	2 hours/unit	1,800
	did take (actual hours)	1,980
Efficiency variance	(in hours)	180 A
× standard variable overhead rate per hour		$3
Variable production overhead efficiency variance		$540 A

Example 8

(a) The idle time variance is 20 hours × $15 = $300 (A).

(b) The efficiency variances are then calculated based on the active hours worked, not on the total hours paid for.

Efficiency variances:		**Hours**
Actual output produced	should take	
200 units	(standard hours)	400
	2 hours/unit	
	did take (440 – 20)	420
Efficiency variance	(in hours)	20 A
× standard direct labour rate per hour		$15
Direct labour efficiency variance		$300 A
× standard variable overhead rate per hour		$4
Variable production overhead efficiency variance		$80 A

(c) The variable production overhead expenditure variance is based on active hours only, since variable production overhead cost is not incurred during idle time.

Variable production overhead expenditure variance:		$
Number of hours worked	should cost/hr (standard)	
420 hours	$4/hour	1,680
	did cost (actual)	1,530
Variable production overhead expenditure variance		150 F

Example 9

Fixed production overhead expenditure variance:		$	
Budgeted fixed overhead		4,375	
Actual fixed overhead incurred		4,800	
Fixed production overhead expenditure variance		425	(A)
Fixed production overhead volume variance:		**Units**	
Actual output produced		1,800	
Budgeted output		1,750	
Volume variance	(in units)	50	
× standard fixed overhead rate per unit		$2.50	
Fixed production overhead volume variance		$125	(F)

Example 10

(a) FOAR = $22,960/(6,560 units × 2 hours) = $1.75 per hour

(b)	Actual hours × FOAR 12,600 × $1.75	$22,050
	Less Budgeted expenditure	($22,960)
	Capacity variance	$910 (A)
(c)	Standard hours × FOAR 6,460 × 2 × $1.75	$22,610
	Less Actual hours × FOAR 12,600 × $1.75	($22,050)
	Efficiency variance	$560 (F)

(d) The fixed overhead volume variance is the sum of the capacity and efficiency variances, i.e.

$910 (A) + $560 (F) = 350 (A).

This can be proved as follows:

Standard hours × FOAR per hour (6,460 × 2 hours × $1.75)	$22,610
Less: Budgeted expenditure	($22,960)
Total variance	$350(A)

Example 11

Standard product cost

		$	$
Standard selling price			100
Material X	5 kg @ $3/kg	15	
Material Y	4 kg @ $5/kg	20	
Direct labour	3 hrs @ $8/hr	24	
Variable overheads	3 hrs @ $6/hr	18	
Fixed overheads (W1)	3 hrs @ $2/hr	6	
			83
Standard profit per unit			17

Material X variances

				$	
SQSP					
5 kg/unit x 2,200 units	x	$3/kg	=	33,000	Usage $900 A
AQSP					
11,300 kg	x	$3/kg	=	33,900	
AQAP					$2,260 F
11,300 kg	x	$2.8/kg	=	31,640	Price

Material Y variances

				$	
SQSP					
4 kg/unit x 2,200 units	x	$5/kg	=	44,000	Usage $2,500 F
AQSP					
8,300 kg	x	$5/kg	=	41,500	
AQAP					$2,490 A
8,300 kg	x	$5.30/kg	=	43,990	Price

Fixed overhead expenditure variance

	$
Budgeted cost	12,000
Actual cost	12,500
	500 A

Fixed overhead volume variance

	Units
Budgeted output	2,000
Actual output	2,200
	200 F
× Std fixed overhead cost per unit	× $6
	$1,200 F

Sales volume profit variance

	Units
Budgeted sales	1,700
Actual sales	2,200
	500 F
× Std profit per unit	× $17
	$8,500 F

Sales price variance

	$
Std selling price	100
Actual selling price	90
	10 A
× Actual no of units sold	× 2,200
	$22,000 A

Operating statement

	$	$	$
Budgeted gross profit (W2)			28,900
Sales volume profit variance			8,500 F
Budgeted profit on actual sales			37,400
Selling price variance			22,000 A
			15,400

		Favourable	Adverse	
Cost variances				
Material X	Usage		900	
	Price	2,260		
Material Y	Usage	2,500		
	Price		2,490	
Direct labour	Efficiency	1,600		
	Rate		960	
Variable overhead	Efficiency	1,200		
	Expenditure	5,400		
Fixed prod overhead	Expenditure		500	
	Volume	1,200		
		14,160	4,850	9,310 F
Actual profit (W3)				24,710

Workings

(W1) Budgeted fixed overheads are $144,000 per year and the budgeted output is 24,000 units for the year. Thus the budgeted/standard fixed cost per unit is $6.

The overheads are absorbed on direct labour hours and each unit takes 3 hours. Therefore the budgeted/standard fixed overhead is $2 per hour ($6 ÷ 3 hours).

(W2) Budgeted profit = $17 per unit × Budgeted **sales** of 1,700 units = $28,900.

(W3)

		$	$
Sales	2,200 units × $90		198,000
Material X	11,300 kg × $2.80/kg	31,640	
Material Y	8,300 kg × $5.30/kg	43,990	
Direct labour	(4,800 hrs × $8.10) + (1,600 hrs × $8.30)	52,160	
Variable overhead		33,000	
Fixed overhead		12,500	
			173,290
Actual profit			24,710

Test your understanding 1

Sales price variance:		$
Units sold should have sold for	(1.800 units × $18.25 per unit)	32,850
They did sell for	(actual sales revenue)	32,300
Sales price variance		550 (A)

Sales volume variance	**Units**
Actual sales volume	1,800
Budgeted sales volume	1,750
Sales volume variance	50
× standard profit per unit	× $6
Sales volume profit variance	$300 (F)

Marginal costing

The contribution per unit is $8.50 ($18.25 – 6.00 – 3.00 – 0.75)

Sales volume variance	**Units**
Actual sales volume	1,800
Budgeted sales volume	1,750
Sales volume variance	50
× standard contribution per unit	× $8.50
Sales volume contribution variance	$425 (F)

Test your understanding 2

					$	
SQSP						
	3 kg/unit x 1,200 units	x	$4/kg	=	14,400	Usage $320 F
AQSP						
	3,520 kg	x	$4/kg	=	14,080	

For a **USAGE** variance the quantity must be the quantity **USED**

					$	
AQSP						
	3,600 kg	x	$4/kg	=	14,400	$400 A Price
AQAP						
				=	14,800	

As the price variance is calculated at the time of **PURCHASE** then the quantity must be the quantity **PURCHASED** and we had to use the more complicated format.

Test your understanding 3

Direct material A price variance:		$	
Actual quantity of materials	should cost (standard)		
6,100 kgs	$4/kg	24,400	
	did cost (actual)	25,000	
Direct material A price variance		600	A

Direct material A usage variance:		$	
Actual output produced	should use (standard quantity)		
3,200 units	2 kgs/unit	6,400	
	did cost (actual quantity)	6,100	
Direct materials price variance	(in material quantity)	300	F
× standard price	(per unit of material)	$4	
Direct material A usage variance		1,200	F

Direct material B price variance:		$	
Actual quantity of materials	should cost (standard)		
1,750 ltrs	$6/ltr	10,500	
	did cost (actual)	11,600	
Direct material B price variance		1,100	A

Direct material B usage variance:		$	
Actual output produced	should use (standard quantity)		
3,200 units	0.5 ltrs/unit	1,600	
	did cost (actual quantity)	1,750	
Direct materials usage variance	(in material quantity)	150	A
× standard price	(per unit of material)	$6	
Direct material B usage variance		900	A

Direct labour rate variance:

		$
Number of hours paid	should use/hr (standard)	
2,200 hours	$12/hr	26,400
	did cost (actual)	28,000
Direct labour rate variance		1,600 A

Idle time variance:

There are 200 hours of idle time. At a standard cost of $12 per hour, this gives an idle time variance of

= 200 hours × $12/hour
= $2,400 A

Direct labour efficiency variance:

		$
Actual output produced	should use (standard hours)	
3,200 units	0.75 hrs per unit	2,400
	did take (actual hours)	2,000
Direct labour efficiency variance	(in hours)	400 F
× standard rate per hour		$12/hr
Direct labour efficiency variance		$4,800 F

Test your understanding 4

Material variances

					$	
SQSP						
	5 kg/unit x 1,000 units	x	$4/kg	=	20,000	Usage
AQSP						$400 F
	4,900 kg	x	$4/kg	=	19,600	

For a **USAGE** variance the quantity must be the quantity **USED**

					$	
AQSP						
	5,200 kg	x	$4/kg	=	20,800	$520 A
AQAP						Price
				=	21,320	

As the price variance is calculated at the time of **PURCHASE** then the quantity must be the quantity **PURCHASED** and we had to use the more complicated format.

Labour variances

					$	
SHSR						
	4 hrs/unit x 1,000 units	x	$6/hr	=	24,000	Efficiency
AHSR						$600 F
	3,900 hrs	x	$6/hr	=	23,400	

The efficiency variance looks at whether people **WORK** fast or slow and looks at hours **WORKED**.

					$	
AHSR						
	4,100 units	x	$6/hr	=	24,600	$2,460 A
AHAR						Rate
				=	27,060	

The rate variance looks at the rate of **PAY** so it looks at the hours **PAID**.

Idle time variance

(4,100 – 3,900) × $6 per hour $1,200 A

Or the idle time variance is simply the difference between the $23,400 and the $24,600 above = $1,200 A.

Test your understanding 5

Material variances

					$	
SQSP	3 kg/unit x 1,100 units	x	$5/kg	=	16,500	Usage
AQSP	3,400 kg	x	$5/kg	=	17,000	$500 A

For a **USAGE** variance the quantity must be the quantity **USED.**

					$	
AQSP	3,600 kg	x	$5/kg	=	18,000	$720 A
AQAP				=	18,720	Price

As the price variance is calculated at the time of **PURCHASE** then the quantity must be the quantity **PURCHASED** and we had to use the more complicated format.

Labour variances

					$	
SHSR	5 hrs/unit x 1,100 units	x	$6/hr	=	33,000	Efficiency
AHSR	4,900 hrs	x	$6/hr	=	29,400	$3,600 F

The efficiency variance looks at whether people **WORK** fast or slow and looks at hours **WORKED**.

					$	
AHSR	5,200 hrs	x	$6/hr	=	31,200	$1,560 A
AHAR				=	32,760	Rate

The rate variance looks at the rate of **PAY** so it looks at the hours **PAID**.

Idle time variance

(5,200 – 4,900) × $6 per hour $1,800 A

Or the idle time variance is simply the difference between the $29,400 and the $31,200 above = $1,800 A.

Test your understanding 6

Fixed overhead total variance

	$
Standard cost of actual output	
$12/unit × 1,100 treatments	13,200
Actual cost	13,000
	200 F

Fixed overhead expenditure variance

	$
Budgeted cost	12,000
Actual cost	13,000
	1,000 A

Fixed overhead volume variance

	Units
Budgeted treatments	1,000
Actual treatments	1,100
	100 F
× Std fixed overhead cost per treatment	×12
	$1,200 F

Under-/over-absorption

	$
Overheads incurred	13,000
Overheads absorbed	
$4/direct labour hour × (3 hours × 1,100 treatments)	13,200
Over-absorption	200

The overhead absorption rate is based on direct labour hours and =

$$\frac{\text{Budgeted overheads}}{\text{Budgeted level of activity}}$$

$$\text{OAR} = \frac{\$12{,}000}{1{,}000 \text{ treatments} \times 3 \text{ hrs}} \quad \$4/\text{direct labour hour}$$

It would now be very natural to calculate the overheads absorbed by multiplying the OAR by the actual number of hours, i.e. 3,080, but in a standard costing system, the overheads are absorbed on the standard hours, not the actual hours.

The standard hours are the standard hours of actual output, 3 hours × 1,100 units = 3,300 hours.

Fixed overhead capacity variance

Actual hours × FOAR 3,080 hours × $4	$12,320
Less Budgeted expenditure	($12,000)
Capacity variance	$320 (F)

Fixed overhead efficiency variance

Standard hours × FOAR 3,300 hours × $4	$13,200
Less Actual hours × FOAR 3,080 × $4	($12,320)
Efficiency variance	$880 (F)

Test your understanding 7

(a) FOAR = \$22,960 ÷ (6,560 units × 2 hours per reported crime) = \$1.75 per hour

(b) **Fixed overhead expenditure variance**

	\$
Budgeted fixed overhead	22,960
Actual fixed overhead	24,200
Variance	1,240 A

Fixed overhead expenditure variance – three line method

AH AR = \$24,200

Var. = \$1,240 A

BH SR = \$22,960

(c) **Fixed overhead capacity variance**

	Hours
Budgeted hours worked = 2 hours × 6,560 reported crimes	13,120
Actual hours worked	12,600
Variance	520 A

Variance in \$ = 520A hours × **standard FOAR** \$1.75/hr = \$910 A

Fixed overhead capacity variance – three line method

BH SR = \$22,960

Variance = \$910 A

AH SR = 12,600 × \$1.75 = \$22,050

(d) **Fixed overhead efficiency variance**

	Hours
Actual 6,460 crimes, **should** take 2 hours per reported crime	12,920
Actual 6,460 crimes, did take	12,600
Variance	320 F

Variance in \$ = 320F hours × **standard FOAR** per hour \$1.75 = \$560 F

Fixed overhead efficiency variance – alternative method

AH SR = 12,600 × $1.75 = $22,050

Variance = $560 F

SH SR = (6,460 × 2) × $1.75 = $22,610

(e) **Fixed overhead volume variance**

	Units
Budgeted reported crimes	6,560
Actual reported crimes	6,460
Variance	100 A

Variance in $ = 100 A reported crimes × **standard hours** of 2 × **standard FOAR** per hour $1.75 = $350 A

Fixed overhead volume variance – alternative method

BH SR = $22,960

Variance = $350 A

SH SR = (6,460 × 2) × $1.75 = $22,610

Note: The fixed overhead volume variance of $350A is the total of the capacity and efficiency variances ($910 A + $560 F).

Test your understanding 8

A

	$
Actual hours × FOAR per hour	
38,000 × $250,000/40,000 hours	$237,500
Budgeted expenditure	$250,000
Capacity variance	$12,500 (A)

Test your understanding 9

(a) Standard product cost

		$	$
Standard selling price			1,250
Material X	12 kg @ $40/kg	480	
Material Y	8 kg @ $32/kg	256	
Direct labour	20 hrs @ $10/hr	200	
Production overhead (W1)		120	
			1,056
Standard gross profit			194

(b) Material X variances

				$	
SQSP 12 kg/unit x 220 units	x	$40/kg	=	105,600	Usage $5,600 F
AQSP 2,500 kg (W2)	x	$40/kg	=	100,000	
AQAP 2,500 kg	x	$42/kg	=	105,000	$5,000 A Price

Material Y variances

				$	
SQSP 8 kg/unit x 220 units	x	$32/kg	=	56,320	Usage $1,280 A
AQSP 1,800 kg (W2)	x	$32/kg	=	57,600	
AQAP 1,800kg	x	$30/kg	=	54,000	$3,600 F Price

Direct labour variances

				$	
SHSR 20 hrs/unit x 220 units	x	$10/hr	=	44,000	Efficiency $2,000 A
AHSR 4,600 hrs	x	$10/hr	=	46,000	
AHAR			=	45,400	$600 F Rate

Fixed Overhead Expenditure variance

	$
Budgeted Cost (W3)	24,000
Actual Cost	23,000
	1,000 F

Fixed overhead volume variance

	Units
Budgeted output (2,400 units p.a. ÷ 12 months)	200
Actual output	220
	20 F
× Std fixed overhead cost per unit	×120
	$2,400 F

This can be sub-divided into the efficiency and capacity variances:

Fixed overhead efficiency variance

	Hours
Standard hours for actual production	4,400
Less Actual hours	(4,600)
Fixed overhead efficiency variance – hours	200 A
FOAR	$6
	1,200 A

Fixed overhead capacity variance

	$
Actual hours × FOAR per hour (4,600 hours × $6 per hour)	27,600
Less Budgeted expenditure ($288,000/12 months)	(24,000)
Fixed overhead capacity variance	3,600 F

Sales price variance

	$
Std selling price	1,250
Actual selling price ($264,000/220 units)	1,200
	50 A
× Actual no of units sold	× 220
	$11,000 A

Selling volume profit variance

	Units
Budgeted sales	200
Actual sales	220
	20 F
× Std profit per unit	× 194
	$3,880 F

(c) **Operating statement**

		$	$	$
Budgeted gross profit (W4)				38,800
Sales volume profit variance				3,880 F
Standard profit on actual sales				42,680
Sales price variance				11,000 A
				31,680
		Favourable	**Adverse**	
Cost variances				
Material X	Usage	5,600		
	Price		5,000	
Material Y	Usage		1,280	
	Price	3,600		
Direct labour	Efficiency		2,000	
	Rate	600		
Fixed prod overhead	Expenditure	1,000		
	Efficiency		1,200	
	Capacity	3,600		
		14,400	9,480	4,920 F
Actual gross profit				36,600

Workings:

(W1) Fixed over head per unit = $288,000/2,400 units = $120 per unit. With labour taking 20 hours per unit this equates to a FOAR of $6 per hour

(W2)

	Material X	Material Y
	Kg	Kg
Op inventory	680	450
+ Purchases	3,000	1,700
	3,680	2,150
– Cl inventory	1,180	350
Materials issued/used	2,500	1,800

(W3) Budgeted fixed overhead per month = $288,000/12 = $24,000

(W4) Budgeted profit = 200 units × $194 = $38,800

Test your understanding 10

(a) This is a 'backwards' question. Rather than calculating the variances ourselves, we have been given some of them. We have to find some other information which is missing. We will use the variances to work backwards to find that missing information.

The starting point is usually to find a variance which mentions the missing information, i.e. for part (a) we are asked for the actual output. We need to find a variance which mentions the actual output somewhere along the line.

One set of variances which would work are the material variances. The first line of the format is SQSP, where SQ is the standard quantity of the **actual output**.

We plug in the information that we know, and we can then work backwards to find the missing information.

Material variances

				$	
SQSP					
2 kg/unit x ? units	x	$3/kg	=	?	Usage $1,380 A
AQSP					
? kg	x	$3/kg	=	?	
AQAP					$1,012 A Price
? kg	x	$?/kg	=	16,192	

We know that AQAP is 16,192 and we know that the price variance is 1,012 A, so we can work backwards to find AQSP.

AQSP = 16,192 - 1,012 = 15,180

Material variances

				$	
SQSP					
2 kg/unit x ? units	x	$3/kg	=	?	Usage $1,380 A
AQSP					
? kg	x	$3/kg	=	15,180 Bal 1	
AQAP					$1,012 A Price
? kg	x	$?/kg	=	16,192	

Now, we know AQSP is 15,180 and the usage variance is 1,380 A, so we can work backwards to find SQSP.

SQSP = 15,180 - 1380 A = 13,800

Material variances

				$	
SQSP					
2 kg/unit x ? units	x	$3/kg	=	13,800 Bal 2	Usage $1,380 A
AQSP					
? kg	x	$3/kg	=	15,180 Bal 1	
AQAP					$1,012 A Price
? kg	x	$?/kg	=	16,192	

Finally, for the first line, we know SQSP, i.e. we know 2 kg x something x $3/kg = 13,800. We can work backwards to find the actual output.

Actual output = 13,800 ÷ 2kg ÷ $3/kg = 2,300 units

Material variances

				$	
SQSP					
2 kg/unit x 2,300 Bal 3 units	x	$3/kg	=	13,800 Bal 2	Usage $1,380 A
AQSP					
? kg	x	$3/kg	=	15,180 Bal 1	
AQAP					$1,012 A Price
? kg	x	$?/kg	=	16,192	

(b) We have already worked out a lot of the figures that we need for the material variances. We can carry on from where we left off in part (a).

Material variances

				$	
SQSP					
2 kg/unit x 2,300 [Bal 3] units	x	$3/kg	=	13,800 [Bal 2]	Usage $1,380 A
AQSP					
? kg	x	$3/kg	=	15,180 [Bal 1]	
AQAP					$1,012 A Price
? kg	x	$?/kg	=	16,192	

For the second line, we know AQSP = 15,180, i.e. we know that AQ x 3 = 15,180.

Actual quantity = 15,180 ÷ 3 = 5,060 kg

AQ appears on both the second line and the third line, so we can write 5,060 kg on both lines.

Material variances

				$	
SQSP					
2 kg/unit x 2,300 [Bal 3] units	x	$3/kg	=	13,800 [Bal 2]	Usage $1,380 A
AQSP					
5,060 [Bal 4] kg	x	$3/kg	=	15,180 [Bal 1]	
AQAP ⇩					$1,012 A Price
5,060 [Bal 4] kg	x	$?/kg	=	16,192	

Finally for the third line, AQAP = 5,060 Kg x something = 16,192

Actual price = 16,192 ÷ 5,060 = $3.20 per kg.

Material variances

				$	
SQSP					
2 kg/unit x 2,300 [Bal 3] units	x	$3/kg	=	13,800 [Bal 2]	Usage $1,380 A
AQSP					
5,060 [Bal 4] kg	x	$3/kg	=	15,180 [Bal 1]	
AQAP ⇩					$1,012 A Price
5,060 [Bal 4] kg	x	$3.20/kg [Bal 5]	=	16,192	

(c) **Labour variances**

				$	
SHSR					
3 hrs/unit x 2,300 units	x	$8/hr	=	55,200	Efficiency $3,680 F
AHSR					
? hrs	x	$8/hr	=	?	
AHAR					$920 A Rate
? hrs	x	$?/hr	=	52,440	

To find out the labour hours we can use the labour variances format. We can find AHSR by subtracting the efficiency variance of 3,680 F from SHSR to get 51,520 or by adding the adverse rate variance of 920 to AHAR.

Once we know that AHSR is $51,520, we know that something x $8/hr = $51,520.

Actual hours = 51,520 ÷ 8 = 6,440 hours

Labour variances

				$	
SHSR					
3 hrs/unit x 2,300 units	x	$8/hr	=	55,200	Efficiency $3,680 F
AHSR					
6,440 [Bal 2] hrs	x	$8/hr	=	51,520 [Bal 1]	
AHAR					$920 A rate
? hrs	x	$?/hr	=	52,440	

(d) **Fixed overhead volume variance**

	Units
Budgeted output	2,000
Actual output	2,300
	300F
× Std fixed overhead cost per unit	× 12
	$3,600F

(e) **Fixed overhead expenditure variance**

	$
Budgeted cost	24,000
Actual cost	23,500
	500 F

(f) **Sales volume profit variance**

		Units
Budgeted sales		1,900
Actual sales		2,300
		400 F
× Std profit per unit		× 12
	=	$4,800 F

The profit margin is 20% of selling price. A profit margin of 20% is the same as a mark-up of 25%. Thus we know standard cost to be $48 per unit, standard profit must be 25% of that, must be $12 per unit.

(g) **Selling price variance**

		$
Std selling price		60
Actual selling price		57
		3 A
× Actual no of units sold		× 2,300
	=	6,900 A

We know that standard cost is $48 per unit and we the standard profit (from part (f)) is $12. Therefore standard selling price = $48 + $12 = $60.

(h) Budgeted profit = 1,900 units × $12 per unit = $22,800.

(i)

		$	$
Sales	2,300 units × $57		131,100
Direct material		16,192	
Direct labour		52,440	
Variable overhead		14,168	
Fixed overhead		23,500	
			106,300
Actual profit			24,800

Test your understanding 11

Key answer tips

This is a very good test of the depth of your knowledge of variances. The basic technique is to set out your normal computations of the variances, putting in the figures you know and working back to those you don't. Often the results from one will be needed in another, so do all the related variances together.

(a) (i) Budgeted fixed overhead cost/mile =

$$= \frac{(\$15,600 + \$400)}{200,000} = \$0.08/\text{mile}$$

Volume variance = $1,760 (A)

Volume difference = $1,760 ÷ $0.08

= 22,000 miles(A)

Actual miles = 200,000 – 22,000

178,000

(ii)

$$\text{Standard rate/hr} = \frac{\$0.08}{0.02}$$

= $4/hour

Rate variance = $1,086 (F)

$$= \frac{\$1,086}{3,260} = \$0.30/\text{hr (F)}$$

Actual rate $4.00 – $0.30 = $3.70/hr

(iii)

Standard price/litre = $\dfrac{\$0.04}{0.1}$

= \$0.40/litre

Actual price/litre = \$0.42/litre

Price variance/litre = \$0.02 (A)

Total price variance = \$420 (A)

Actual number of litres = $\dfrac{\$420}{\$0.02}$ = 21,000

(iv) **Variable overhead variances**

			$		
SHSR					
0.02 hrs × 178,000 delivery miles	×	\$3/hr	= 10,680		Efficiency \$180 A
AHSR	×	\$3/hr	= ?		
AHAR			= ?		\$280 F Expenditure

We know all the above infor mation, but are trying to find the missing information represented by question marks. In particular we are trying to find the bottom question mark, the actual hours at the actual rate, i.e. the actual variable overhead expenditure. We can do this in one step or two. Taking it in two steps, we can find the middle question mark:

SHSR					
0.02 hrs × 178,000 delivery miles	×	\$3/hr	= 10,680		Efficiency \$180 A
AHSR	×	\$3/hr	= 10,860	Bal 1	
AHAR			= ?		\$280 F Expenditure

And then, the bottom question mark:

SHSR					
0.02 hrs × 178,000 delivery miles	×	\$3/h	= 10,680		Efficiency \$ 180 A
AHSR	×	\$3/hr	= 10,860	Bal 1	
AHAR			= 10,580	Bal 2	\$280 F Expenditure

The actual variable overhead expenditure is \$10,580

(b) Two possible causes of an adverse fuel usage variance are:

(i) Spillage of fuel occurred on filling vehicle fuel tanks.

(ii) Vehicles are in need of servicing and as a result fuel usage is excessive.

(c) **To:** Transport Operations Manager

From: Management Accountant

Date: XX – XX – XX

Subject: Standard costs

Introduction

This report explains the type of standard cost which may be set and importance of keeping standards meaningful and relevant.

Types of standard

A standard cost is a prediction of the cost per unit expected in a future period. It is dependent on estimates of resource requirements per output unit and the price to be paid per resource unit.

There are three types of standard which may be set and these are often referred to as:

- current standard
- attainable standard; and
- ideal standard.

The current standard uses existing efficiency and achievement levels as the standard for the future period. This does not encourage improvement and may also allow existing inefficiencies to continue unnoticed.

The attainable standard sets a target which requires improvements in performance if it is to be achieved, but these are small and are considered to be achievable (or attainable). This form of standard is believed to be the best motivator to a manager.

The ideal standard assumes a perfect working environment (which never exists for a prolonged period). This is impossible to achieve.

Keeping standards useful

Standards are useful as a basis for performance evaluation. If such comparisons are to be valid the standard must reflect the current method of working AND resource prices which are realistic. If standards are not kept up to date they are no longer meaningful and thus their usefulness is reduced.

Conclusion

I recommend that attainable standards should be used, and that they should be reviewed regularly. Please contact me if you wish to discuss this further.

Test your understanding 12

B

Contribution margin	=	$\frac{429{,}200 - 410{,}000}{94\% - 82\%}$
	=	\$1,600 for every 1% change
Budget for 87% occupancy	=	\$429,200 – (7 × 1600)
	=	\$418,000
Medical expenditure variance	=	418,000 – 430,000
	=	\$12,000 Adverse

Test your understanding 13

	$
Sales volume (contribution) variance	16,000 (A)
Standard contribution/sales ratio:	40%
Sales volume variance in sales revenue	40,000 (A)
Sales price variance	30,000 (A)
Budgeted sales for the first 5 months (× 145,000)	725,000
Actual sales revenue for the first five months	655,000
Expected sales for the next 3 months (× 120,000)	360,000
Expected sales for the final 4 months (× 148,000)	592,000
Forecast sales for the year	**1,607,000**

	$
Forecast sales for the year (actual revenue)	1,607,000
Cumulative sales price variances	30,000 (A)
Forecast sales at standard sales prices	1,637,000
Standard contribution/sales ratio	40%
Forecast contribution at standard sales price	$654,800
Cumulative sales price variances	$30,000(A)
Forecast contribution at actual sales prices	$624,800

Statement of budgeted and forecast annual results, as at end May

	Budget	*Forecast*	*Variance*
	$	$	$
Sales revenue (145,000 × 12)	1,740,000	1,607,000	133,000 (A)
Contribution (1,740,000 × 40%)	696,000	624,800	71,200 (A)

Test your understanding 14

D $39,500

Standard contribution on actual sales	$44,000
Add: Favourable sales price variance	$2,000
Less: Adverse total variable costs variance	($6,500)
Actual contribution	$39,500

Test your understanding 15

Activity	*Expected cost*	*Actual cost*	*Variance*
	$	$	$
Inventory counts (based on 52 counts)	41,600	40,560	**1,040** (F)

Test your understanding 16

Variable overhead expenditure variance

		$
3,600 actual visits should cost	($180,00/4,000 visits =) $45 per visit	162,000
3,600 actual visits did cost		168,000
Variance		$6,000 A

Variable overhead efficiency variance

		Visits
2,100 actual clients should require	(4,000 visits/2,000 clients =) 2 visits per client	4,200
2,100 actual clients did require		3,600
Variance		600 F

Variance = 600 F visits × standard cost of $45 per visit = $27,000 F

chapter

9

Variance analysis: discussion elements

Chapter learning objectives

Lead	Component
A1. discuss costing methods and their results.	(d) Interpret material, labour, variable overhead, fixed overhead and sales variances. (e) Explain the advantages and disadvantages of standard costing in various sectors and its appropriateness in the contemporary business environment.

1 Chapter overview diagram

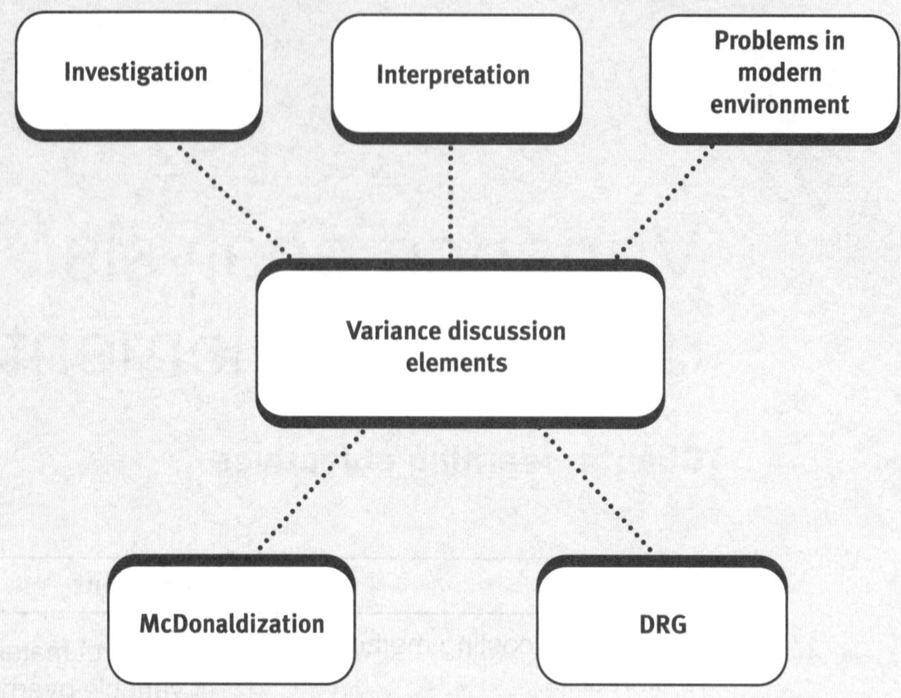

2 Variance investigation

Variances arise naturally in standard costing because a standard cost is a long term average cost. In any period actual costs may be higher or lower than standard but in the long run these should cancel out if the process is under control.

Variances may also arise because of:

- poor budgeting
- poor recording of cost
- operational reasons (the key emphasis in exam questions)
- random factors.

It is important to identify the reason for a variance so that appropriate action can be taken, but time and effort will be wasted if all variances are investigated as many will arise as a normal part of the process.

When should a variance be investigated?

Factors to consider include the following:

- the size of the variance
- the likelihood of the variance being controllable or its cause already known
- the likely cost of an investigation
- the interrelationship of variances
- the type of standard that was set.

Investigating variances

Factors to consider

- The size of the variance. Costs tend to fluctuate around a norm and therefore 'normal' variances may be expected on most costs. The problem is to decide how large a variance must be before it is considered 'abnormal' and worthy of investigation.
  A rule of thumb may be established that any variance which exceeds, say, 5 per cent of its standard cost may be worthy of investigation. Alternatively control limits may be set statistically and if a cost fluctuates outside these limits it should be investigated.
- The likelihood of the variance being controllable or its cause already known. Managers may know from experience that certain variances may not be controllable even if a lengthy investigation is undertaken to determine their causes. They may also be immediately aware of the cause of a variance. For example, it may be argued that a material price variance is less easily controlled than a material usage variance because it is heavily influenced by external factors. The counter-argument to the latter is that a materials price variance may be caused by external market factors (uncontrollable) or the quality of procurement management – and one doesn't know which is the cause until it is investigated.
- The likely cost of an investigation. This cost would have to be weighed against the cost which would be incurred if the variance were allowed to continue in future periods.
- The interrelationship of variances. Adverse variances in one area of the organisation may be interrelated with favourable variances elsewhere. For example, if cheaper material is purchased this may produce a favourable material price variance. However, if the cheaper material is of lower quality and difficult to process, this could result in adverse variances for material usage and labour efficiency.

- The type of standard that was set. A standard that is set at an unachievable level (for example, one where labour must always work at 100% efficiency) will almost always result in some adverse variances, because of unavoidable illnesses, for example. Managers must decide on the 'normal' level of adverse variance which they would expect to see.

  Another example is where a standard price is set at an average rate for the year. Assuming that inflation or a known upward trend exist, favourable price variances might be expected at the beginning of the year, to be offset by adverse price variances towards the end of the year as actual prices begin to rise.

Variance investigation techniques

Reporting by exception

Variance reports might identify significant variances. This is a form of reporting by exception, in which particular attention is given to the aspects of performance that appear to be exceptionally good or bad.

Alternatively, a rule might be applied generally that any adverse variance or favourable variance should be investigated if it exceeds more than a given percentage amount of the standard cost. For example, a rule might be applied that all adverse variances exceeding 5% of standard cost should be investigated and all favourable variances exceeding 10% of the standard should also be investigated.

Cumulative variances and control charts

An alternative method of identifying significant variances is to investigate the cause or causes of a variance only if the cumulative total for the variance over several control periods exceeds a certain limit.

The reason for this approach is that variances each month might fluctuate, with adverse variances in some months and favourable variances in the next. Provided that over time, actual results remain close to the standard, monthly variances might be acceptable.

For example, actual fixed overhead expenditure will not be exactly the same every month. Budgeted monthly expenditure, on the other hand, might be calculated by dividing the budgeted annual expenditure by 12. Consequently, there will inevitably be favourable or adverse expenditure variances from one month to the next, although over the course of the financial year, actual and budgeted expenditure should be the same.

This approach to identifying significant variances can be illustrated by the concept of a variance control chart. Variances should only be investigated when the cumulative total of variances exceeds predetermined control limits.

Setting the control limits

The control limits used as a basis for determining whether a variance should be investigated may be set statistically based on the normal distribution.

Using historical data a standard can be set as an expected average cost and a standard deviation can also be established. By assuming that a cost conforms to the normal distribution a variance will be investigated if it is statistically significant and has not arisen according to chance.

- If a company has a policy to investigate variances that fall outside the range that includes 95% of outcomes, then variances which exceed 1.96 standard deviations from the standard would be investigated.
- If a company has a policy to investigate variances that fall outside the range that includes 99% of outcomes, then variances which exceed 2.58 standard deviations from the standard would be investigated.

For control purposes, management might need to establish why a particular variance has occurred. Once the reason for the variance has been established, a decision can then be taken as to what control measures, if any, might be appropriate:

- to prevent the adverse variance continuing in the future, or
- to repeat a favourable variance in the future, or
- to bring actual results back on course to achieve the budgeted targets.

3 Interpretation of variances

Possible operational causes of variances are as follows:

Material price

(1) Using a different supplier, who is either cheaper or more expensive.

(2) Buying in larger-sized orders, and getting larger bulk purchase discounts. Buying in smaller-sized orders and losing planned bulk purchase discounts.

(3) An unexpected increase in the prices charged by a supplier.

(4) Unexpected buying costs, such as high delivery charges.

(5) Efficient or inefficient buying procedures.

(6) A change in material quality, resulting in either higher or lower purchase prices.

Material usage

(1) A higher-than-expected or lower-than-expected rate of scrap or wastage.

(2) Using a different quality of material (higher or lower quality) could affect the wastage rate.

(3) Defective materials.

(4) Better quality control.

(5) More efficient work procedures, resulting in better material usage rates.

(6) Changing the materials mix to obtain a more expensive or less expensive mix than the standard.

Labour rate

(1) An unexpected increase in basic rates of pay.

(2) Payments of bonuses, where these are recorded as direct labour costs.

(3) Using labour that is more or less experienced (and so more or less expensive) than the 'standard'.

(4) A change in the composition of the work force, and so a change in average rates of pay.

Labour efficiency

(1) Taking more or less time than expected to complete work, due to efficient or inefficient working.

(2) Using labour that is more or less experienced (and so more or less efficient) than the 'standard'.

(3) A change in the composition or mix of the work force, and so a change in the level of efficiency.

(4) Improved working methods.

(5) Industrial action by the work force: 'working to rule'.

(6) Poor supervision.

(7) Improvements in efficiency due to a 'learning effect' amongst the work force.

(8) Unexpected lost time due to production bottlenecks and resource shortages.

Overhead variances

(1) Fixed overhead expenditure adverse variances are caused by spending in excess of the budget. A more detailed analysis of the expenditure variance would be needed to establish why actual expenditure has been higher or lower than budget.

(2) The fixed overhead volume variance (and therefore the capacity and efficiency variance) is caused by changes in production volume (which in turn might be caused by changes in sales volume or through increased labour productivity).

(3) Variable production overhead expenditure variances are often caused by changes in machine running costs (for example, if electricity rates have changed).

(4) Variable production overhead efficiency variances: the causes are similar to those for a direct labour efficiency variance.

Sales price

(1) Higher-than-expected discounts offered to customers to persuade them to buy, or due to purchasing in bulk.

(2) Lower-than-expected discounts, perhaps due to strength of sales demand.

(3) The effect of low-price offers during a marketing campaign.

(4) Market conditions forcing an industry-wide price change.

Sales volume

(1) Successful or unsuccessful direct selling efforts.

(2) Successful or unsuccessful marketing efforts (for example, the effects of an advertising campaign).

(3) Unexpected changes in customer needs and buying habits.

(4) Failure to satisfy demand due to production difficulties.

(5) Higher demand due to a cut in selling prices, or lower demand due to an increase in sales prices.

4 Possible interdependence between variances

In many cases, the explanation for one variance might also explain one or more other variances in which case the variances are inter-related.

For control purposes, it might therefore be necessary to look at several variances together and not in isolation.

Some examples of interdependence between variances are listed below.

- Using cheaper materials will result in a favourable material price variance, but using the cheaper material in production might increase the wastage rate (adverse material usage) and cause a fall in labour productivity (adverse labour and variable overhead efficiency).

  A more expensive mix of materials (adverse mix variance) might result in higher output yields (favourable yield variance). Mix and yield variances are covered in the next chapter.
- Using more experienced labour to do the work will result in an adverse labour rate variance, but productivity might be higher as a result (favourable labour and variable overhead efficiency).
- Changing the composition of a team might result in a cheaper labour mix (favourable mix variance) but lower productivity (adverse yield variance).
- Workers trying to improve productivity (favourable efficiency variance) in order to win a bonus (adverse rate variance) might use materials wastefully in order to save time (adverse materials usage).
- Cutting sales prices (adverse sales price variance) might result in higher sales demand from customers (favourable sales volume variance).

5 The controllability principle

Controllability means the extent to which a specific manager can control costs or revenues or any other item (such as output quality). The controllability principle is that a manager should only be made accountable and responsible for costs and revenues that he or she can control directly.

In variance reporting, this means that variances should be reported to the managers who are in a position to control the costs or revenues to which the variances relate.

Composite variances

Sometimes a variance might be caused by a combination of two factors. The variance is a composite variance, because it is the result of the two factors combined. To apply the controllability principle, the variance should be reported to each of the managers who are in a position to control one of the factors.

6 Standard costing in the modern manufacturing environment

Standard costing may be inappropriate in the modern production environment because:

- products in these environments tend not to be standardised
- standard costs become outdated quickly
- production is highly automated
- modern environments often use ideal standards rather than current standards
- the emphasis is on continuous improvement so preset standards become less useful
- variance analysis may not give enough detail
- variance reports may arrive too late to solve problems.

Further explanation

Non-standard products

Standard product costs apply to manufacturing environments in which quantities of an identical product are output from the production process. They are not suitable for manufacturing environments where products are non-standard or are customised to customer specifications.

Standard costs become outdated quickly

Shorter product life cycles in the modern business environment mean that standard costs will need to be reviewed and updated frequently. This will increase the cost of operating a standard cost system but, if the standards are not updated regularly, they will be of limited use for planning and control purposes. The extra work involved in maintaining up-to-date standards might limit the usefulness and relevance of a standard costing system.

Production is highly automated

It is doubtful whether standard costing is of much value for performance setting and control in automated manufacturing environments. There is an underlying assumption in standard costing that control can be exercised by concentrating on the efficiency of the workforce. Direct labour efficiency standards are seen as a key to management control. However, in practice, where manufacturing systems are highly automated, the rates of production output and materials consumption, are controlled by the machinery rather than the workforce.

Ideal standard used

Variances are the difference between actual performance and standard, measured in cost terms. The significance of variances for management control purposes depends on the type of standard cost used. JIT and TQM businesses often implement an ideal standard due to the emphasis on continuous improvement and high quality. Therefore, adverse variances with an ideal standard have a different meaning from adverse variances calculated with a current standard.

Emphasis on continuous improvement

Standard costing and adherence to a preset standard is inconsistent with the concept of continuous improvement, which is applied within TQM and JIT environments.

Detailed information is required

Variance analysis is often carried out on an aggregate basis (total material usage variance, total labour efficiency variance and so on) but in a complex and constantly changing business environment more detailed information is required for effective management control.

Monitoring performance is important

Variance analysis control reports tend to be made available to managers at the end of a reporting period. In the modern business environment managers need more 'real time' information about events as they occur.

Addressing the criticisms

An organisation's decision to use standard costing depends on its effectiveness in helping managers to make the correct planning and control decisions. Many of the above criticisms can be addressed by adaptations to traditional standard costing systems.

- Standard costs must be updated regularly if they are to remain useful for control purposes.
- The use of demanding performance standards can help to encourage continuous improvement.
- The standard costing system can be adapted to produce a broader analysis of variances that are less aggregated.

- It is possible to place less emphasis on labour cost variances and focus more on variances for quality costs, variable overhead costs, and so on.
- Real time information systems have been developed which allow for corrective action to be taken sooner in response to reported variances.
- Standard costing may still be useful even where the final product or service is not standardised. It may be possible to identify a number of standard components and activities for which standards may be set and used effectively for planning and control purposes.

7 McDonaldization

An area where standard costing becomes very useful is in industries where McDonaldization might apply. (The concept of McDonaldization comes from the successes of the fast food company).

In essence, McDonaldization is the **process of rationalisation**, albeit taken to extreme levels. One of the fundamental aspects of McDonaldization is that almost any task can (and should) be rationalised.

The process of McDonaldization takes a task and breaks it down into smaller tasks. This is repeated until all tasks have been broken down to the smallest possible level. The resulting tasks are then rationalised to find the single most efficient method for completing each task. All other methods are then deemed inefficient and discarded.

The impact of McDonaldization is that **standards can be more accurately set and assessed**. Managers know, with a high degree of accuracy, how much time and cost should go into each activity.

Although the principles are perhaps best understood by applying them to the way McDonalds has operated, it is important to remember that they can be applied to many other services, such as hairdressing, dentistry, or opticians' services.

More details

The term was defined by George Ritzer (1996) as 'the process by which the principles of the fast-food restaurant are coming to dominate more and more sectors of American society, as well as the rest of the world'.

Ritzer identified four dimensions to McDonaldization which are critical to the success of the model.

(1) **Efficiency**. This means choosing the optimum means to achieve a given end. Consumers should be able to get what they need more quickly and with less effort. Workers should perform tasks more quickly and with less effort. In McDonalds, for example, drinks dispensers, automatic coffee brewers, microwave ovens, automatic potato peelers, dishwashers and pre-programmed cash registers have saved time, reduced the need for human input and reduced the scope for error.

(2) **Calculability**. This means the ability to produce and obtain large quantities of something very quickly. A problem with fast high-volume production is that quality might suffer consequently non-human technologies should be used as much as possible to perform tasks. Quantity has become equivalent to quality, a lot of something, or the quick delivery of it, means that it must be good.

(3) **Control**. There should be effective controls over both employees and customers. In McDonalds restaurants, for example, customers are expected to clear their own tables after eating.

(4) **Predictability**. Customers (and employees) should know exactly what they are going to get at any service point anywhere in the world. In the case of McDonalds, for example, the predictability of what customers get in any outlet has been a significant factor in expansion through franchising.

Other principles on which McDonaldization is based are that:

- When goods and services are more uniform in quality, quality will be better.
- Standardisation of services is less expensive than customisation.
- Customers like familiarity, and feel that it is safer to do things within a controlled regime.
- People like to be treated in the same way as everyone else.

Features of the McDonalds service, which are probably familiar to you, are automation, speed, the use of disposable paper products and plastic wraps, pre-sliced cheese and packs of tomato ketchup, getting customers to do the work and having a limited menu of items with a short preparation time. Customers feel they are getting a good deal in terms of generous portions for a reasonable price and in a short time.

The relevance of standard costing to services of this nature should be apparent. Management should be able to set accurate standards for what is takes, in terms of materials and time, to provide standard items to customers. This in turn means that costs are both minimised and predictable, and with predictable costs, it becomes possible to set prices that customers see as fair (or even better) and still make a large profit.

8 Diagnostic related groups

One specific area where standard costing currently appears to be flourishing is in healthcare management. For the purposes of remunerating healthcare providers and evaluating the performance of those providers, it is often deemed necessary to determine the standard cost of providing healthcare to persons suffering from specific medical conditions.

One response to this is the use of the diagnostic reference (or related) group (DRG) otherwise known as the healthcare resource group or case mix group. The medical conditions from which patients admitted to hospital are suffering can be classified into DRGs.

Patients within a given DRG all suffer from broadly the same medical condition and will receive broadly the same treatment. Diagnostic reference groups are another application of standards in a service industry.

Hospitals will get paid a 'standard cost' for each treatment they provide and their efficiency and performance can be measured against standard treatment times etc.

More details

DRGs have been defined as 'systems for classifying patient care by relating common characteristics such as diagnosis, treatment and age to an expected consumption of hospital resources and length of stay. Its aim is to provide a framework for specifying care mix and to reduce hospital costs' (www.online-medical-dictionary.org).

The concept was developed in US healthcare in the early 1980s as a means of controlling the costs of the Medicare health service. In broad terms, patients are placed into one of several standard categories of condition and treatment, and the amount that Medicare will pay the hospitals providing the treatment is based on a standard price for that category.

Most practical applications of this approach involve the adoption of between 600 and 800 DRGs. Healthcare funders (insurance companies or the NHS) may undertake to pay a given amount per day to a hospital for the treatment of patients within a particular DRG. That per day rate will be determined with reference to the standard cost of treating a patient within the DRG – having regard to the resources required and the amount that the hospital has to pay for those resources. At the same time, the performance of a hospital may be evaluated by comparing its actual per day costs for given DRGs with the relevant standards. If a hospital incurs a cost of $5,000 per day for treating a patient requiring a liver transplant and the standard cost (or benchmark cost) is $4,000 per day, then this comparison offers a comment on the efficiency of the hospital concerned. Similarly, if a hospital takes 23 days to treat a particular DRG and the standard is 19 days, then this also is a comment on its efficiency.

However, the DRG approach is not without its critics. The clinical treatments available for any illness are varied. In the case of heart disease they range from a heart transplant at one extreme to merely counselling on lifestyle and diet at the other extreme. Each patient is different having regard to the detailed nature of the disease, its degree of progression and their own strength and state of general health. The clinician should evaluate each patient individually and decide on the programme of surgery, drugs and lifestyle counselling that is appropriate in each case. However, if a hospital is paid a fixed daily rate for treating a patient in a given DRG, then the clinician will be most reluctant to provide treatment above or below the standard package for that DRG. If treatment is provided above standard, then the hospital will not be paid any additional fee, and treatment below standard may result in unpleasant accusations of malpractice being levelled by both patients and funding providers.

The logic of the DRG approach is that each patient who presents with a given set of symptoms is offered a standard package of treatments – which may not always be entirely appropriate. A clinician may be tempted simply to offer the standard package to each patient in a DRG even though he or she may suspect that package to be inadequate in some cases and excessive in others. In effect, the approach may induce a degree of McDonaldisation with all patients served the medical equivalent of a Big-Mac. Unless great sensitivity is exercised in its application, the use of DRGs may result in clinical practice being distorted by what is essentially a financial control system.

9 Chapter summary

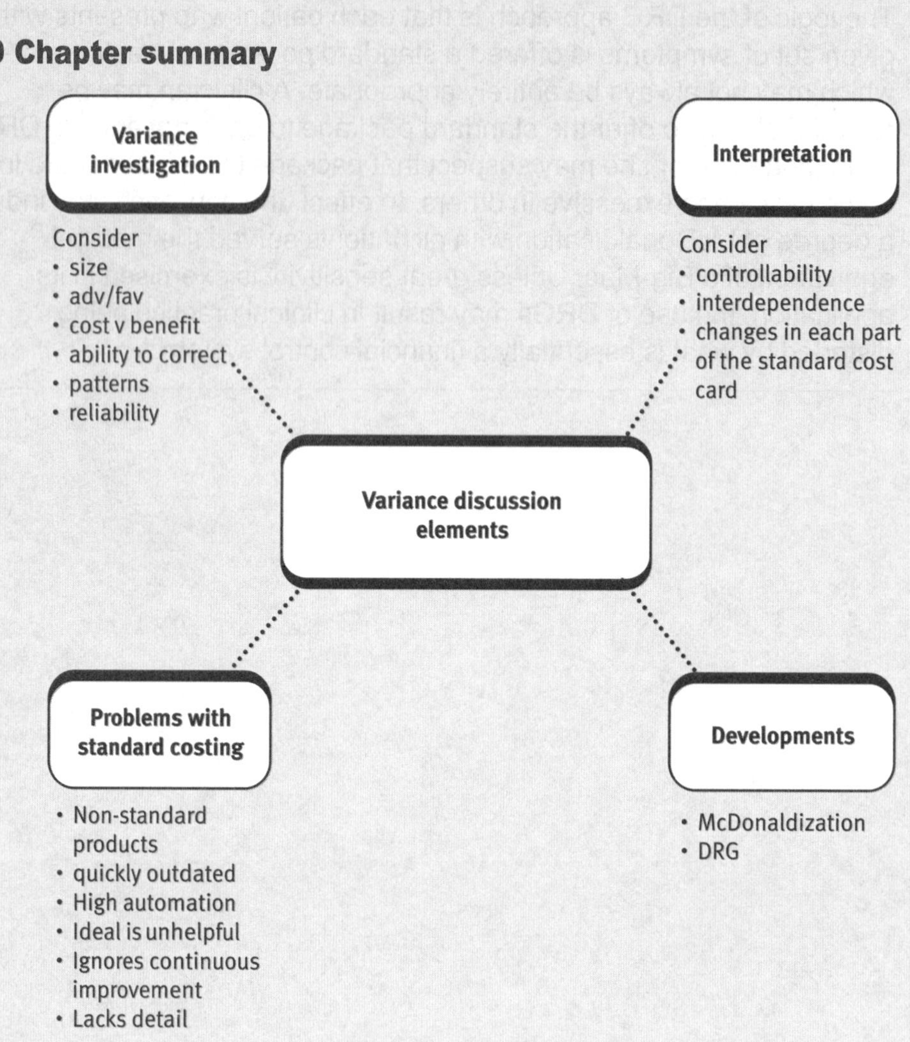

10 Practice questions

Test your understanding 1

Describe whether standard costing applies in both manufacturing and service businesses and how it may be affected by modern initiatives of continuous performance improvement and cost reduction.

(Time allowed: 10 minutes)

Test your understanding 2

ML produces a single product for which the following data are given:

Standards per unit of product:

Direct material	4 kg at $3 per kg
Direct labour	2 hours at $6.40 per hour

Actual details for given financial period:

Output produced in units		38,000
Direct materials:		$
purchased	180,000 kg for	504,000
issued to production	154,000 kg	
Direct labour	78,000 hours worked for	546,000

There was no work in progress at the beginning or end of the period.

From this information the following variances have been calculated:

Variance	**Favourable**	**Adverse**
	$	$
Direct labour efficiency		12,800
Direct labour rate		46,800
Direct materials usage		6,000
Direct materials price (based on issues to production)	30,800	

State whether in each of the following cases, the comment given and suggested as the possible reason for the variance, is consistent or inconsistent with the variance calculated:

(place a tick in the appropriate column)

Variance	**Consistent?**	**Inconsistent?**
Direct labour efficiency variance: the efficiency of labour was commendable		
Direct labour rate variance: the union negotiated wage increase was $0.60 per hour lower than expected		
Direct materials usage variance: material losses in production were less than had been allowed for in the standard		
Direct materials price variance: the procurement manager has ignored the economic order quantity and, by obtaining bulk quantities, has purchased material at less than the standard price		

Test your understanding 3

A dental practice uses standard costing and variance analysis. Match the variance to the most likely cause:

Variance:

(a) adverse materials price

(b) adverse labour efficiency

(c) favourable fixed overhead volume

(d) adverse sales price

Potential causes:

(i) more dental treatments were carried out than was budgeted

(ii) new competition entered the market

(iii) new dentists were recruited

(iv) new suppliers were used

Test your understanding 4

Explain the factors that should be considered before deciding to investigate a variance.

(Time allowed: 10 minutes)

Test your understanding 5

Explain how McDonaldization might be used for a dental practice offering standard treatments to patients. The practice has around 40 dentists in operation across 8 sites spread around a major city.

(Time allowed: 10 minutes)

Test your understanding answers

Test your understanding 1

Standard costing is most suited to organisations whose activities consist of a series of common or repetitive operations. Typically, mass production manufacturing operations are indicative of its area of application. It is also possible to envisage operations within the service sector to which standard costing may apply, though this may not be with the same degree of accuracy of standards which apply in manufacturing. For example, hotels and restaurants often use standard recipes for preparing food, so dealing with conference attendance can be like a mass production environment. Similarly, banks will have common processes for dealing with customer transactions, processing cheques, etc. It is possible therefore that the principles of standard costing may be extended to service industries.

In modern manufacturing and service businesses, continuous improvement and cost reduction are topical. In order to remain competitive it is essential that businesses address the cost levels of their various operations. To do this they have to deal with the costing of operations. But the drive to 'cost down' may mean in some cases that standards do not apply for long before a redesign or improvement renders them out of date. In such a setting an alternative to the use of standard costs is to compare actual costs with those of the previous operating period. We have seen above that a standard costing system has a variety of purposes. It is for management to judge their various reasons for employing standard costing and, consequently, whether their aims of continuous improvement and cost reduction render the system redundant.

Test your understanding 2

(i) Direct labour efficiency variance: Inconsistent. The workforce were inefficient.

(ii) Direct labour rate variance: Inconsistent. In fact the wage increase was $0.60 per hour higher than expected.

(iii) Direct materials usage variance: Inconsistent. If the losses had been less than expected then the usage variance would have been favourable.

(iv) Direct materials price variance: Consistent. A bulk purchase discount should lead to cheaper materials and hence a favourable material price variance.

Test your understanding 3

Variance	**Most likely cause**
adverse materials price	new suppliers were used
adverse labour efficiency	new dentists were recruited
favourable fixed overhead volume	more dental treatments were carried out than was budgeted
adverse sales price	new competition entered the market

Test your understanding 4

The factors that should be considered before deciding to investigate a variance include the following:

- The size of the variance, both in absolute terms and as a percentage of the standard cost.
- The trend in the variance. If the variance fluctuates from adverse to favourable and back again then over a period of time the trend in the variance might be insignificant and the cause is thus not worthy of investigation.
- The cost of conducting an investigation should be balanced against the likely benefit to be derived from the investigation.
- The likelihood of the variance being controllable. For example, certain price variances may be due to movements in external market prices which are outside the control of the organisation's management.
- The interrelationship of variances. An adverse material usage variance might be directly related to a favourable materials price variance due to lower quality material being purchased, leading to high wastage.
- The type of standard that was set. For example an ideal standard is likely to result in adverse efficiency variances and a price standard that was set as an average for a period might produce favourable variances early in the period, followed by adverse variances later in the period.

Test your understanding 5

McDonaldization aims at finding the quickest and cheapest ways to produce a product or provide a service. Once this aim is achieved then all other alternative methods are ignored.

The method becomes the standard and allows management to set accurate standards for the provision of this product or service. In a dental practice different ways of providing treatment could be considered. Once the quickest and cheapest method is determined then codes of conduct and a universal standard could be applied to ensure that the treatment is provided in exactly the same way to all patients. Any deviations from this would lead to a variance that would have to be explained by the individual dentist.

chapter

10

Advanced variances

Chapter learning objectives

Lead	Component
A1. Discuss costing methods and their results.	(c) Apply standard costing methods including the reconciliation of budgeted and actual profit margins, distinguishing between planning and operational variances.

1 Chapter overview diagram

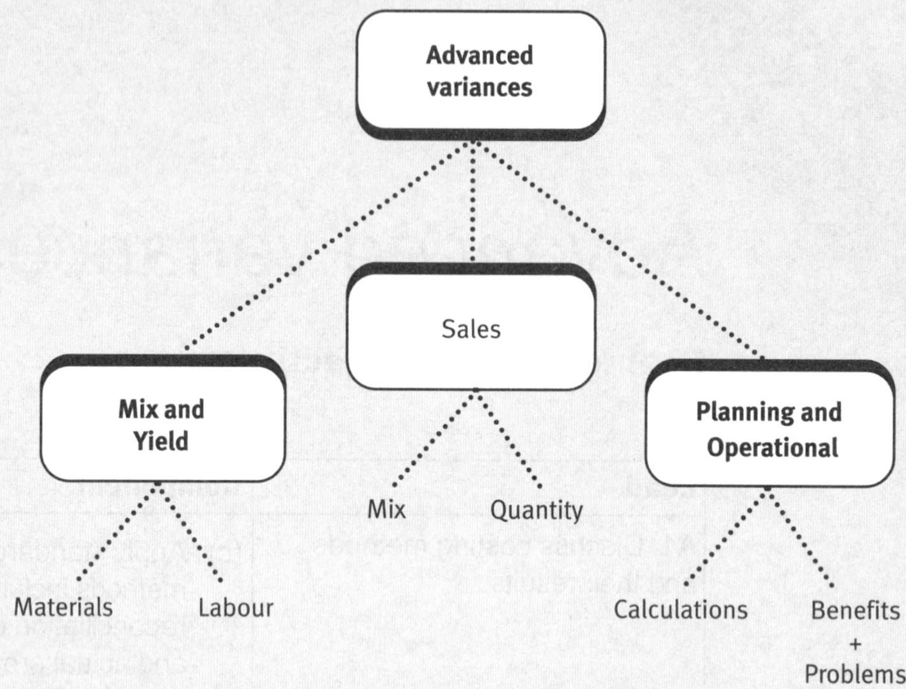

2 Advanced material variances – mix and yield

In many industries, particularly process industries, input consists of more than one type of material and it is possible to vary the mix. In many cases this would then affect the quantity of output produced. To analyse this the usage variance can be broken down into mix and yield variances.

Material mix variance

The material mix variance arises when the mix of materials used differs from the predetermined mix included in the calculation of the standard cost of an operation.

Material yield variance

The material yield variance arises when there is a difference between the standard output for a given level of input and the actual output attained.

Further details

The meaning of the mix variance

For materials and labour variances, a mix variance measures whether the actual mix that occurred was more or less expensive than the standard mix. If the mixture is varied so that a larger than expected proportion of a more *expensive* material is used there will be an *adverse* variance. When a larger than expected proportion of a *cheaper* material is included in the mix, then a *favourable* variance occurs.

For example, suppose that a product consists of two materials, X and Y, the standard mix of the two items is 50:50, and material X is much more expensive than material Y.

- If the actual mix used to make the product contains more than 50% of X and less than 50% of Y, the actual mix will be more expensive than the standard mix, because it includes a bigger-than-standard proportion of the expensive material. The mix variance will be adverse.
- Similarly, if the actual mix used to make the product contains less than 50% of X and more than 50% of Y, the actual mix will be less expensive than the standard mix, and the mix variance will be favourable.

The meaning of the yield variance

A materials yield variance is similar to a materials usage variance. However, instead of calculating a usage variance for each material separately, a single yield variance is calculated for all the materials as a whole. The yield variance is calculated first of all in terms of units of material, and is converted into a money value at the weighted average standard cost per unit of material.

When a mix variance is calculated, it is assumed that the mix of materials or labour can be controlled.

- The material yield should therefore be assessed for all the materials combined, not for each item of material separately.
- Similarly, the labour yield variance should be assessed for the labour team as a whole, not for each grade of labour separately.

The yield variance then tells us the effect of varying the total input of a factor of production (e.g. materials or labour) while holding constant the input mix (the proportions of the types of materials or labour used) and the weighted average unit price of the factor of production.

3 Calculating mix and yield variances

There are two different methods for calculating the mix variance mentioned in the syllabus – the individual units method and the weighted average method.

The individual units method is easier to calculate and understand (so you should use this in the exam if you have a choice), but the weighted average is technically superior.

Both methods produce exactly the same total figure for the mix variance.

Both methods compare the actual mix of materials with the standard mix.

- The actual mix = the actual quantities of materials used (for each material individually and in total).
- The standard mix = the actual total quantity of materials used, with the total divided between the individual materials in the standard proportions.
- The mix variance in units of material is the difference between the actual mix and the standard mix. A mix variance is calculated for each individual material in the mix.

Materials mix – individual units method

(1) Write down the actual input. (This is the **actual mix**.)

(2) Take the actual input in total and push it down one line and then work it back in the standard proportions. (This is the **standard mix**.)

(3) Calculate the difference between the standard mix (line 2) and the actual mix (line 1). This is the mix variance in terms of physical quantities and must add up to zero in total. (If you use a higher than expected proportion of one material, you must use a lower than expected proportion of something else!)

(4) Multiply by the standard price per kg.

(5) This gives the mix variance in financial terms.

	Material A	Material B	Total
	Kg	Kg	Kg
1 Actual input	N	N	NN
			⇓
2 Actual input in std proportions	N	N	⇐ NN
	—	—	—
3 Difference in quantity	N	N	
4 × Std price	× $N	× $N	
5 Mix variance	$N	$N	$N
	—	—	—

Materials mix – weighted average method

The format is similar to that used for the individual units method, except that once the difference in quantity has been calculated, instead of multiplying by the individual material price, we multiply by the difference between the individual price and the weighted average price.

Calculate the weighted average std cost of the materials. (This is needed for step 4). *You have to be very careful here. This weighted average is the weighted average cost per kg of input as we are just about to compare* ***inputs****.*

Further details on the weighted average method

The individual units method is easier to understand, but is slightly flawed. The weighted average method is theoretically superior.

The detailed stages in the calculation are as follows:

(1) Write down the actual usage. (This is the **actual mix**.)

(2) Take the actual usage in total and push it down one line and then work it back in the standard proportions. (This is the **standard mix**.)

(3) Calculate the difference between the standard mix (line 2) and the actual mix (line 1). This is the mix variance in terms of kgs or litres and must add up to zero in total. (If you use a higher proportion of one type of material, you must use a lower proportion of another type!)

Remember what a mix variance means – using a higher proportion of an expensive type of material is adverse, but using a higher proportion of a cheaper type of material would actually be regarded as a good thing.

We have just found out for each type of material whether we have used a higher or lower proportion of that material. In order to decide whether the variance is favourable or adverse we need to know whether that type of material is cheap or expensive. We determine this by comparing the individual costs of material with the weighted average rate.

(4) Determine for each type of material whether it is cheap or expensive compared to a weighted average price.

(5) Multiply the results from line 3 and line 4.

(6) This gives the mix variance in financial terms.

	Material A	**Material B**		**Total**
	Kgs	Kgs		Kgs
1 Actual usage	N	N		NN
				⇓
2 Actual usage in std proportions	N	N	⇐	NN
	—	—		—
3 Difference in quantity	N	N		
4 × Difference in rate	x $N	x $N		
(weighted average std cost – individual material cost)				
	—	—		—
5 Mix variance	$N	$N		$N
	—	—		—

Yield variance

The yield variance only happens in total (CIMA and the examiner do not consider individual yield variances to be meaningful). The yield variance is calculated in the **same way under both methods**.

(1) Calculate the **standard yield**. This is the expected output from the actual input.

(2) Compare this to **actual yield**.

(3) The difference is the yield variance in physical terms.

(4) To express the variance in financial terms we multiply by the standard cost. One thing to be careful of however is that the yield variance considers outputs and so the standard cost is the standard cost per kg **of output**.

(5) This gives the yield variance in financial terms.

		Kg
1	Standard yield of actual input	N
2	Actual yield	N
		—
3		N
4	× Std cost per kg of output	× $N
		—
		$N
		—

Alternative yield valuation method

There are two approaches to calculating and valuing the yield variance. Both give the same answer and both are acceptable in the exam. You will see different TYU's in this chapter using different approaches, but it is probably best for the exam to learn one method and stick to using that method.

Here is an illustration of both methods:

Illustration

A company produces a product with the following inputs in each batch:

Material	**Input (kg)**	**Cost per kg**	**Total cost ($)**
X	0.90	$0.05	0.0450
Y	0.10	$0.21	0.0210
Z	0.05	$0.29	0.0145
Total	**1.05**		**0.0805**

These inputs will provide 1 kg of output.

The actual results show:

Input = 22,880 kgs

Output = 21,500 kgs.

Use this information to calculate the materials yield variance.

Solution

There are two possible approaches to the calculation:

(i) value materials at the **cost per output**

The yield variance is based on an **output** measure.

Therefore the cost is $0.0805/1 kg = $0.0805

Now adjust the input to **calculate the expected output** (i.e. 22,880 kgs input should have produced (22,880/1.05) 21,790.5 kgs)

The yield variance =

(actual yield – standard yield) × standard cost per output
(21,500 – 21,790.5) × 0.0805

= $23.38 A

(ii) value materials at the **cost per input**

The yield variance is based on an **input** measure.

Therefore the cost is $0.0805/1.05 kg = $0.0766

Now adjust the output to **calculate the expected input** (i.e. to get 21,500 kgs out, we should have put in (21,500 × 1.05) 22,575 kgs)

The yield variance =

(actual yield – standard yield) × standard cost per input
(22,880 – 22,575) × 0.0766

= $23.38 A

Both techniques give the same answer, so either approach is acceptable.

Example 1

Hordru Ltd operates a standard costing system.

The standard direct material mix to produce 1,000 kilos of output is as follows:

Material grade	Input quantity	Standard price per kilo input
	(kilos)	$
A	600	1.10
B	240	2.40
C	360	1.50

During April the actual output of the product was 21,000 kilos.

The actual materials issued to production were:

Material grade	Quantity (kilos)
A	14,000
B	5,500
C	5,500

Required:

(a) Calculate material mix variances for each material grade and in total, using individual material prices per kilo as the variance valuation base.

(b) Calculate material mix variances for each material grade and in total, using the budgeted weighted average material price per kilo as the variance valuation base.

(c) Calculate the materials yield variance.

Using mix and yield variances

Mix variances might be calculated when there is a mix of two or more items, and the mix is regarded as **controllable** by management.

- Two or more materials might be used in making a product or providing a service. If standard costing is used and the mix of the materials is seen as controllable, a materials mix variance and a materials yield variance can be calculated. These provide a further analysis of the materials usage variance.
- Two or more different types of labour might be used to make a product or provide a service. If standard costing is used and the labour mix in the team is seen as controllable, a labour mix variance and a labour yield variance can be calculated. These provide a further analysis of the labour efficiency variance.

If the mix cannot be controlled, it is inappropriate to calculate a mix and yield variance. Instead, a usage variance should be calculated for each individual material or an efficiency variance should be calculated for each individual type or grade of labour. *In other words, if the mix cannot be controlled, the usage or efficiency variance should not be analysed into a mix and yield variance.*

The weighted average method for the mix variance is seen as being superior to the individual units method. It is easier to see the impact of each individual product or service when it is measured against the average price. If one product is more expensive than another for example, it will show as a negative in the calculation (i.e. when we calculate weighted average price less individual product standard price). The weighted average method provides better variances for control purposes. For example, if we look at Material A in Example 1, the company has used more of the material than it should have done. Using the individual units method we see an adverse variance for Material A in the mix calculation. But what the weighted average method shows is that Material A is relatively cheap ($1.10) when compared to the average price of materials ($1.48), and using more of this material is therefore better for the company's costs and this should be recorded as a favourable variance.

4 Advanced labour variances – mix and yield

Labour mix variance

The labour mix variance arises when the mix of labour used differs from the predetermined mix included in the calculation of the standard cost of an operation. If the mixture is varied so that a larger than expected proportion of a higher grade of labour is used there will be an *adverse* variance. When a larger than expected proportion of a *lower grade of labour* is included in the mix, then a *favourable* variance occurs.

Labour yield variance

The labour yield variance arises when there is a difference between the standard output for a given level of input (measured in terms of hours) and the actual output attained.

Calculations

These are **calculated in exactly the same way as the material mix and yield variances** except that the situation will involve different grades of labour instead of different types of material.

Calculations

Labour mix variance – individual units method

A labour mix variance is sometimes called a team composition variance. It measures whether the actual composition of the labour team was more or less expensive than the standard mix.

(1) Write down the actual hours. (This is the **actual mix**.)

(2) Take the actual hours in total and push it down one line and then work it back in the standard proportions. (This is the **standard mix**.)

(3) Calculate the difference between the standard mix (line 2) and the actual mix (line 1). This is the mix variance in terms of hours and must add up to zero in total. (If you use a higher proportion of one type of labour, you must use a lower proportion of another type!)

(4) Multiply by the standard rate per hour.

(5) This gives the mix variance in financial terms.

	Skilled Labour	Unskilled Labour		Total
	Hrs	Hrs		Hrs
1 Actual hours	N	N		NN
				⇓
2 Actual hours in std proportions	N	N	⇐	NN
	—	—		—
3 Difference in quantity	N	N		
4 × Std rate	× $N	× $N		
5 Mix variance	$N	$N		$N
	—	—		—

Labour mix variance – weighted average method

The format is similar to that used for the individual units method, except that once the difference in quantity has been calculated, instead of multiplying by the individual labour rate, we multiply by the difference between the individual standard rate and the weighted average standard rate.

Calculate the weighted average standard cost of the labour. (This is needed for step 4). *You have to be very careful here. This weighted average is the weighted average cost per hour as we are just about to compare* ***inputs****.*

(1) Write down the actual hours. (This is the **actual mix**.)

(2) Take the actual hours in total and push it down one line and then work it back in the standard proportions. (This is the **standard mix**.)

(3) Calculate the difference between the standard mix (line 2) and the actual mix (line 1). This is the mix variance in terms of hours and must add up to zero in total. (If you use a higher proportion of one type of labour, you must use a lower proportion of another type!)

Remember what a mix variance means – using a higher proportion of an expensive grade of labour is adverse, but using a higher proportion of a cheap grade would actually be regarded as a good thing.

We have just found out for each grade of labour whether we have used a higher or lower proportion of that grade. In order to decide whether the variance is favourable or adverse we need to know whether that grade of labour is cheap or expensive. We determine this by comparing the individual labour rate with the weighted average rate.

(4) Determine for each grade of labour whether it is cheap or expensive compared to a weighted average price.

(5) Multiply the results from line 3 and line 4.

(6) This gives the mix variance in financial terms.

	Skilled Labour	**Unskilled Labour**		**Total**
	Hrs	*Hrs*		*Hrs*
1 Actual hours	N	N		NN
				⇓
2 Actual hours in std proportions	N	N	⇐	NN
	—	—		—
3 Difference in quantity	N	N		
4 × Difference in rate	x $N	x $N		
(weighted average std rate – individual labour std rate)				
	—	—		—
5 Mix variance	$N	$N		$N
	—	—		—

Labour yield variance

A labour yield variance is sometimes called a team productivity variance. It measures the efficiency of the team as a whole, rather than the efficiency of each grade of labour separately.

The yield variance is calculated in the same way under both methods. Again it only happens in total (CIMA and the examiner do not consider individual yield variances to be meaningful) and is calculated in the same way as the materials yield variance.

(1) Calculate the **standard yield**. This is the expected output from the actual input.

(2) Compare this to **actual yield**.

(3) The difference is the yield variance in hours.

(4) To express the variance in financial terms we multiply by the standard cost. One thing to be careful of however is that the yield variance considers outputs and so the standard cost is the standard cost per hour **of output**.

(5) This gives the yield variance in financial terms.

		hrs
1	Standard yield of actual hours	N
2	Actual yield	N
		–
3		N
4	× std cost per hour of output	× N
		N

Labour variances in service industries

Labour is likely to be a key factor in service industries. Industries such as consultancy, accountancy, law and construction are likely to use more than one grade of labour. There may be a split between skilled, semi-skilled and unskilled staff. The labour mix and yield variances therefore become crucial in these organisations.

Illustration

A management consulting company had budgeted the staff requirements for a particular job as follows:

	$
40 hours of senior consultant at $100 per hour	4,000
60 hours of junior consultant at $60 per hour	3,600
Budgeted staff cost for job	7,600

The actual hours recorded were:

	$
50 hours of senior consultant at $100 per hour	5,000
55 hours of junior consultant at $60 per hour	3,300
Actual staff cost for job	8,300

The junior consultant reported that for 10 hours of the 55 hours recorded there was no work that she could do.

Calculate the following variances:

- idle time variance
- labour mix variance using the weighted average method
- labour yield variance.

Solution

Idle time variance

The idle time variance is the difference between the actual hours worked and the actual hours paid for, then multiplied by the standard labour rate per hour. The junior consultant (paid $60 per hour) has stated that there were 10 of her hours which were idle time.

Idle time variance = 10 hours $60 per hour = $600 A

Mix variance

	Senior Consultant hours	*Junior Consultant hours*	*Total hours*
Actual hours	50	45	95
Actual hours in standard proportions (4:6)	38	57	95
Difference in hours	12	–12	
× Difference in rate			
(weighted average std rate – individual labour std rate)			
× ($76 – $100)	× –$24		
× ($76 – $60)		× $16	
Mix variance	$288 A	$192 A	$480 A

Note that the junior labour variance is adverse because the company has used less of the cheaper source of labour than expected. This will harm profits.

Yield variance

Standard hours for the job	100
Actual hours for the job	95
Variance in hours	5 F
× Std cost per hour of output	× 76
Yield variance	$380 F

Note: The mix and yield variances focus on hours worked rather than hours paid.

Limitations of mix variances

Mix and yield variances can provide useful control information, but only where the mix of materials or labour is controllable, and where the information about total yield is more useful than usage/efficiency variances for the individual materials or labour grades separately.

Using mix variances also has some other limitations.

- It is often found that the mix and yield variances are interdependent, and one variance cannot be assessed without also considering the other. For example, the inefficiency of a team (adverse labour yield variance) could be explained by the fact that the team has a larger-than-expected proportion of inexperienced, cheaper employees (favourable labour mix variance).
- If management is able to achieve a cheaper mix of materials or labour, without affecting yield, the standard becomes obsolete. The cheaper mix should become the new standard mix.
- Control measures to improve the mix by making it cheaper are likely to affect the quality of the output or the work done. Analysing mix and yield variances for control purposes does not take quality issues into consideration.
- Mix and yield variances are based on standard prices for material and standard rates for labour. Actual prices/rates may differ from standard and this will be measured using the material price/labour rate variances. For an overall assessment of performance these will also have to be taken into consideration.

Sales mix and quantity

The sales volume variance can be analysed into mix and quantity components using the same logic encountered in regard to materials usage and labour efficiency variances.

Note: No valid information would be obtained if these variances are calculated in relation to products sold to different markets since the factors which influence demand and preferences in these markets would be different. For example, no meaningful information would result if these variances were calculated by Matressmen, a company who make beds as well as an android tablet. But it might prove very useful to, say, a movie franchise which may set targets for a mix of cinema ticket sales, disc sales, streaming sales and merchandising sales. The franchise might, for example, expect 30% of sales to come from merchandising. The sales mix variance then becomes very useful to the franchise.

Illustration on sales mix and quantity

A furniture company manufactures high quality dining room furniture that is sold to major retail stores.

Extracts from the budget for last year are given below:

	Tables	*Chairs*	*Sideboards*
Sales quantity (units)	8,000	26,000	6,000
Average selling price	$2,200	$320	$2,800
Direct material cost per unit	$1,000	$160	$1,200
Direct labour cost per unit	$400	$60	$600
Variable overhead cost per unit	$40	$6	$60

The budgeted direct labour cost per hour was $20.

Actual results for last year were as follows:

	Tables	*Chairs*	*Sideboards*
Sales quantity (units)	7,200	31,000	7,800
Average selling price	$2,400	$310	$2,500
Direct material cost per unit	$1,100	$150	$1,300
Direct labour cost per unit	$450	$60	$600
Variable overhead cost per unit	$60	$8	$80

The actual direct labour cost per hour was $18.75. Actual variable overhead cost per direct labour hour was $2.50. The company operates a just-in-time system for purchasing and production and does not hold any inventory.

Required:

Calculate the following variances for the furniture company for last year:

(i) the sales mix contribution variance

(ii) the sales quantity contribution variance

and explain the meaning of the variances calculated.

Solution

In order to perform the calculations we need to calculate the contribution per unit of each product:

	Tables	*Chairs*	*Sideboards*
	$ per unit	$ per unit	$ per unit
Average selling price	2,200	320	2,800
Direct material cost per unit	1,000	160	1,200
Direct labour cost per unit	400	60	600
Variable overhead cost per unit	40	6	60
Contribution	760	94	940

Sales mix contribution variance

Product	**Actual sales quantity**	**Actual sales at budget mix**	**Difference**	**Variance from weighted average contribution per unit**	**Mix variance** ($000)
Tables	7,200	9,200	2,000 A	$760 – $354.10	811.80 A
Chairs	31,000	29,900	1,100 F	$94 – $354.10	286.11 A
Sideboards	7,800	6,900	900 F	$940 – $354.10	527.31 F
	46,000	46,000			570.60 A

Or alternatively:

Product	Actual sales quantity	Actual sales at budget mix	Difference	Contribution	Mix variance ($000)
Tables	7,200	9,200	2,000 A	$760	1,520.00 A
Chairs	31,000	29,900	1,100 F	$94	103.40 F
Sideboards	7,800	6,900	900 F	$940	846.00 F
	46,000	46,000			570.60 A

Sales quantity contribution variance

Product	Budget sales quantity	Actual sales at budget mix	Difference	Contribution	Mix variance ($000)
Tables	8,000	9,200	1,200 F	$760	912.00 F
Chairs	26,000	29,900	3,900 F	$94	366.60 F
Sideboards	6,000	6,900	900 F	$940	846.00 F
	40,000	46,000			2,124.60 A

Or alternatively:

Product	Budget sales quantity	Contribution	Mix variance ($000)
Tables	8,000	$760	6,080
Chairs	26,000	$94	2,444
Sideboards	6,000	$940	5,640
	40,000		14,164

Weighted average contribution = $14,164k/40,000 = $354.10
Sales quantity contribution variance = (46,000 – 40,000) × $354.10 = $2,124.6 F

Variance interpretation

The sales quantity contribution variance and the sales mix contribution variance explain how the sales volume contribution variance has been affected by a change in the total quantity of sales and a change in the relative mix of products sold. From the figures calculated for the sales quantity contribution variance in part (a) we can say that the increase in total quantity sold would have earned an additional contribution of $2,124,600, if the actual sales volume had been in the budgeted sales mix.

The sales mix contribution variance shows that the change in the sales mix resulted in a reduction in profit of $570,600. The change in the sales mix has resulted in a relatively higher proportion of sales of chairs which is the product that earns the lowest contribution and a lower proportion of tables which earn a contribution significantly higher than the weighted average contribution. The relative increase in the sale of sideboards however, which has the highest unit contribution, has partially offset the switch in mix to chairs.

Benefits and problems of mix and quantity variances

Benefits

- The sales mix variance can allow an organisation identify trends in sales of individual elements of its total product sales. For example, they may find that although overall sales are improving (as suggested by the sale quantity or sales volume variance being favourable, that one individual product has shown a period-on-period decline in volume).
- The sales quantity variance can be used to indicate changes in the size of the market and/or the change in the market share for an organisation.
- The sales mix variance may indicate future directions for sales strategies – organisations would aim to repeat any favourable variances by identifying and exploiting their causes.
- The sales mix variance can be used to gauge the success or failure of new marketing campaigns. For example, if an organisation were to launch a special edition of its product, it might be able to determine the impact that this has on its profits as well as any adverse impact it might have had on sales of its regular product.

- Responsibility accounting is improved when the sales volume variance is split between the sales mix and quantity variance as different managers might be responsible for different elements of sales. The sales quantity variance, for example, will indicate whether the sales team have performed well overall, whereas the mix variance will then provide information on the success of those responsible for applying the mix of sales.

Problems

- Like any variance, it will be important for the user to consider the controllability of the variance before making performance review decisions based on the output. For example, an adverse sales quantity variance might have been caused by an uncontrollable change in government restrictions on sales of the product, rather than having being caused by the actions of the sales team/manager.
- Likewise, variances should be considered as a whole rather than on an individual basis due to their interdependence. Managers would have to be aware, for example, that sales volume variances might be affected by decisions taken in production (such as a change in materials or labour used).
- The sales mix variance is only relevant if the products have some sort of relationship between them. Examples of this are:
  - the products are of the same type but of a different variety (for example, where there are 'normal' and 'special' editions of a product
  - the products are complementary (for example, where a company sells both ebooks and ereaders)
  - the products can be substituted for each other (for example, a company might sell European and Asian holidays).
- It can sometimes be difficult to apply these techniques in organisations which have very broad product ranges. It can be difficult to determine which products are complementary, which are substitutes etc. and often computer based techniques are needed to perform the detailed calculations.

Overall, these can be complex calculations that might only apply for certain organisations. But for managers who can interpret these well, sales mix and quantity variance analysis can provide vital information on sales trends, marketing effects, marketing position and variance responsibility.

5 Planning and operational variances

One reason that a variance may arise may be that the original plan has subsequently been found to be inappropriate. This might arise, for example, if suppliers have increased the cost of raw materials and this has not been accounted for in the original standard cost card. In that case the total variance must be split into two constituent parts:

- the **planning variance** – this is the part of the variance caused by an inappropriate original (ex-ante) standard, and
- the **operational variance** – this is the part of the variance attributable to decisions taken within the business that has caused a change between the revised (ex-post) standard and the actual results.

Further explanation

Forecasts by their nature are unreliable, and yet most standards are set on a forecast basis, i.e. ***ex ante*** or before the event. A planning variance arises from an inability to make exact predictions of future costs and revenues at the budgeting stage.

If it were possible to set standards with the benefit of hindsight, i.e. ***ex post*** or after the event managers would be able to see more clearly what amount of variances was genuinely attributable to operating performance (***operational variances***) and what amount to difficulties or errors in setting the original standard (***planning variances***). Such information should improve operational control and may also provide guidance for the improvement of planning procedures.

The planning variance is usually regarded as uncontrollable and has arisen because the original standard was not reflective of the attainable standard. The operational variance is controllable.

Operational variances

Operational variances are variances that are assumed to have occurred due to operational factors. These are materials price and usage variances, labour rate and efficiency variances, variable overhead expenditure and efficiency variances, fixed overhead expenditure variances, and sales variances.

Operational variances are calculated with the 'realistic' ex post standard. They are calculated in exactly the same way as described in earlier chapters, the only difference being that the ex post standard is used, not the original standard.

Planning variances

A planning variance measures the difference between the budgeted and actual profit that has been caused by errors in the original standard cost. It is the difference between the ex ante and the ex post standards.

- A planning variance is **favourable** when the ex post standard cost is lower than the original ex ante standard cost.
- A planning variance is **adverse** when the ex post standard cost is higher than the original ex ante standard cost.

Controllability and responsibility

Management will wish to draw a distinction between these two variances in order to gain a realistic measure of operational efficiency. As planning variances are self-evidently not under the control of operational management, it cannot be held responsible for them, and there is thus no benefit to be gained in spending time investigating such variances at an operational level. Planning variances may arise from faulty standard-setting, but the responsibility for this lies with senior, rather than operational management.

Example 2

A government department is responsible for awarding entry visas for overseas residents wishing to enter the country. Details of actual and budget labour costs for the department for period 9 are:

	Budget	**Actual**
Applications	500	550
Labour hours	1,000	1,200
Labour cost ($)	5,000	5,100

However, a relaxation in the government's legal entry checks for overseas residents subsequent to the preparation of the budget resulted in a 25% increase in standard labour efficiency, such that it is now possible to assess 5 applications instead of 4 applications using 8 hours of labour – giving a revised standard labour requirement of 1.6 hours (thus $8 labour cost) per application.

Required:

Calculate all relevant labour variances for the period.

Example 3

Big set up a factory to manufacture and sell 'Advance', a new consumer product. The first year's budgeted production and sales were 1,000 units. The budgeted sales price and standard costs for 'Advance' were as follows:

	$	$
Standard sales price per unit		200
Standard costs per unit		
Raw materials (10 kg at $10)	100	
Labour (6 hours at $8)	48	
		(148)
Standard contribution per unit		52

Actual results for the first year were as follows:

	$000	$000
Sales (1,000 units)		316
Production costs (1,000 units)		
Raw materials (10,800 kg)	194.4	
Labour (5,800 hours)	69.6	
		(264)
Actual contribution (1,000 units)		52

The managing director made the following observations on the actual results:

In total, the performance agreed with budget; nevertheless, in every aspect other than volume, there were large differences.

Sales were made at what was felt to be the highest feasible price, but we now feel that we could have sold for $330 with no adverse effect on volume. Labour costs rose dramatically with increased demand for the specialist skills required to produce the product, and the general market rate was $12.50 per hour – although we always paid below the general market rate whenever possible.

The raw material cost that was expected at the time the budget was prepared was $10 per kilogram. However, the market price relating to efficient purchases of the material during the year was $17 per kilogram.

It is not proposed to request a variance analysis for the first year's results. In any event, the final contribution was equal to that originally budgeted, so operations must have been fully efficient.

Required:

Despite the managing director's reluctance to calculate it, produce an operating statement for the period ignoring the impact of any planning variances.

Calculate the impact of the planning variances for the business.

6 Causes of planning variances

There must be a good reason for deciding that the original standard cost is unrealistic. Deciding in retrospect that expected costs should be different from the standard should not be an arbitrary decision, aimed perhaps at shifting the blame for poor results from poor operational management to poor cost estimation.

A good reason for a change in the standard might be:

- a change in one of the main materials used to make a product or provide a service
- an unexpected increase in the price of materials due to a rapid increase in world market prices (for example, the price of oil or other commodities)
- a change in working methods and procedures that alters the expected direct labour time for a product or service
- an unexpected change in the rate of pay to the work force.

More than one planning error

A situation might occur where the difference between the standards is in two (or more) items.

In these circumstances, the rules for calculating planning and operational variances are as follows:

- Operational variances are calculated against the most up-to-date revision
- The total planning variance will be the difference between the original standard or budget and the most up-to-date revision. This can then be further divided between each individual planning error.

For example, the original standard cost for a product was $4 per kg and the actual cost was $6 per kg. Two planning variances were discovered. Firstly, the accountant had assumed that a bulk discount on purchases would arise but this was never likely, and it meant that the standard should have been set at $4.60 per kg,. Secondly, a worldwide shortage of materials led to an industry wide increase of $1 per kg to the cost of materials. This means that the most up-to-date standard cost would have been $5.60 per kg. The operational variance would therefore be $0.40 ($6 – $5.60)per kg adverse and the total planning variance would be $1.60 ($5.60 – $4) per kg. The planning variance could then be split between the two effects: there is a $0.60 per kg adverse variance caused by the failure to gain the bulk discount, and a $1 per kg adverse variance caused by the market conditions.

7 Benefits and problems of planning variances

Benefits	Problems
• More useful	• Subjective
• Up-to-date	• Time consuming
• Better for motivation	• Can be manipulated
• Assesses planning	• Can cause conflict

More details

Benefits of planning and operational variances

(1) In volatile and changing environments, standard costing and variance analysis are more useful using this approach.

(2) Operational variances provide up to date information about current levels of efficiency.

(3) Operational variances are likely to make the standard costing system more acceptable and to have a positive effect on motivation.

(4) It emphasises the importance of the planning function in the preparation of standards and helps to identify planning deficiencies.

Problems of planning and operational variances

(1) There is an element of subjectivity in determining the ex-post standards as to what is 'realistic'.

(2) There is a large amount of labour time involved in continually establishing up to date standards and calculating additional variances.

(3) There is a great temptation to put as much as possible of the total variances down to outside, uncontrollable factors, i.e. planning variances.

(4) There can then be a conflict between operating and planning staff. Each laying the blame at each other's door.

On the face of it, the calculation of operational and planning variances is an improvement over the traditional analysis. However, you should not overlook the considerable problem of data collection for the revised analysis: where does this information come from, and how can we say with certainty what should have been known at a particular point in time?

8 Chapter summary

Advanced variances

Mix and Yield

- Mix is adverse if we use more of the expensive material/ labour
- Yield is adverse if we use more materials/ labour overall

Planning and Operational

- Planning variance = original standard – revised standard
- Operational variance = revised standard – actual results

Sales mix and quantity

- analyses the sales volume variance
- mix is adverse if we sell less of the more profitable product

9 Practice questions

Test your understanding 1

A company manufactures a chemical using two components, A and B. The standard information for one unit of the chemical are as follows:

		$
Material A	10 kg at $4 per kg	40
Material B	20 kg at $6 per kg	120
		160

In a particular period, 160 units of the chemical were produced, using 1,000 kgs of material A and 1,460 kgs of material B.

Required:

Calculate the material usage, mix and yield variances for each material.

Test your understanding 2

Buzz Lightyear Ltd makes a single product, of which the standard labour input per unit is:

Skilled labour	6 hrs @ $12/hr
Unskilled labour	4 hrs @ $7/hr

During Period 1:

1,000 units were produced

5,250 hours of skilled labour were used and

5,250 hours of unskilled labour were used

Calculate the labour mix variances for each grade of labour and the labour yield variance in total.

Use both the weighted average method and the individual units method.

Test your understanding 3

Leopard Airlines has estimated that on any flight, the free drinks consumed by passengers will be *(for every 10 passengers)*:

	Number of drinks	**Cost per drink**	**Total cost $**
Low cost	5	$0.25	1.25
Medium cost	8	$0.50	4.00
High cost	12	$1.00	12.00
	25		17.25

On a flight to Bermuda with 300 passengers on board, the actual number of free drinks consumed was as follows:

	Number of drinks
Low cost	215
Medium cost	280
High cost	355
	850

Calculate the materials mix and yield variances for this flight.

Test your understanding 4

Product XYZ is made by mixing three materials (X, Y and Z). There is an expected loss of 20% of the total input. The budgeted and actual results for Period 1 are shown below. There were no opening or closing inventories of any materials or of the finished product.

	Budget	Actual
Output of XYZ	**800 kg**	**960 kg**
Material		
X	500 kg @ $5.00 per kg	600 kg @ $4.70 per kg
Y	300 kg @ $6.00 per kg	380 kg @ $6.50 per kg
Z	200 kg @ $7.00 per kg	300 kg @ $7.10 per kg
Total input	**1,000 kg**	**1,280 kg**

Calculate for Period 1:

(i) the total materials mix variance

(ii) the total materials yield variance.

Test your understanding 5

A beauty salon offers two types of treatment, Standard and Deluxe, details for the current period as follows:

	Standard mix (treatments)	**Standard profit** ($ per treatment)	**Average profit** ($ per treatment)
Standard	2	5	
Deluxe	3	6	
Total	5	((2×5)+(3×6))/5	5.60

Budget sales – 200 units Standard and 300 units Deluxe

Actual sales – 180 units Standard and 310 units Deluxe

Required:

(a) calculate the sales quantity profit variance

(b) calculate the sales mix profit variance using the individual method

(c) calculate the sales mix profit variance using the weighted average method.

Test your understanding 6

Pan-Ocean Chemicals has one product, which requires inputs from three types of material to produce batches of Synthon. Standard cost details for a single batch are shown below:

Material type	Standard quantity (kgs)	Standard price per kg ($)
S1	8	0.30
S2	5	0.50
S3	3	0.40

A standard loss of 10% of input is expected. Actual output was 15,408 kgs for the previous week. Details of the material used were:

Material type	Quantity (kgs)
S1	8,284
S2	7,535
S3	3,334

Required:

Calculate the individual material mix and yield and the total usage variance.

Test your understanding 7

The following data relates to Skilled Labour Grade ST1

Standard labour hours per unit	5 hours
Standard labour rate	$10 per hour
Actual production	250 units
Actual labour hours	1,450 hours
Actual labour cost	$13,050

During the month there was an unforeseen shortage of the Skilled Labour Grade ST1. Semi skilled workers (Grade ST2) were hired. As a consequence of this, the standard time was revised to 6 hours per unit.

Required:

Calculate labour rate and efficiency variances using a planning and operational approach.

Test your understanding 8

Holmes Ltd uses one raw material for one of their products. The standard cost per unit at the beginning of the year was $28, made up as follows:

Standard material cost per unit = 7 kg per unit at $4 per kg = $28.

In the middle of the year the supplier had changed the specification of the material slightly due to problems experienced in the country of origin, so that the standard had to be revised as follows:

Standard material cost per unit = 8 kg per unit at $3.80 per kg = $30.40.

The actual output for November was 1,400 units. 11,000 kg of material was purchased and used at a cost of $41,500.

Calculate

(a) material price and usage variances using the traditional method

(b) the planning and operational material variances.

Test your understanding 9

WC is a company that installs kitchens and bathrooms for customers who are renovating their houses. The installations are either pre-designed 'off-the-shelf' packages or highly customised designs for specific jobs.

The company operates with three divisions: Kitchens, Bathrooms and Central Services. The costs of the Central Services division, which are thought to be predominantly fixed, include those incurred by the design, administration and finance departments. The Central Services costs are charged to the other divisions based on the budgeted Central Services costs and the budgeted number of jobs to be undertaken by the other two divisions.

The budgeting and reporting system of WC is not very sophisticated and does not provide much detail for the Directors of the company. The budgeted details for last year were:

	Kitchens	**Bathrooms**
Number of jobs	4,000	2,000
	$	$
Average price per job	10,000	7,000
Average direct costs per job	5,500	3,000
Central services recharge per job	2,500	2,500
Average profit per job	2,000	1,500

The actual results were as follows:

	Kitchens	**Bathrooms**
Number of jobs	2,600	2,500
	$	$
Average price per job	13,000	6,100
Average direct costs per job	8,000	2,700
Central services recharge per job	2,500	2,500
Average profit per job	2,500	900

The actual costs for the Central Services division were $17.5 million.

Required:

(a) Calculate the budgeted and actual profits for both the Kitchen and Bathroom division and for the whole company for the year.

(b) Calculate the sales price variances and the sales mix profit and sales quantity profit variances.

(c) Prepare a statement that reconciles the budgeted and actual profits and shows appropriate variances in as much detail as possible.

(d) Using the statement that you prepared in part (c) above, discuss the performance of the company for the year.

Test your understanding 10

The expected contribution per unit of the product manufactured by ATS is $26, ascertained as below:

		$	$
Selling price			110
Material	8 kg × $3/kg	24	
Labour	6 hours × $10/hour	60	
		—	
			84
			—
Contribution/unit			26
			—

The expected contribution was $31,200. The actual contribution was $38,800 as shown below:

		$	$
Actual sales revenue	1,000 units @ $135		135,000
Actual material cost	7,800 kg × $4/kg	31,200	
Actual labour cost	6,250 hours × $10.40/hour	65,000	
		———	
			96,200
			———
Actual contribution			38,800
			———

The Sales Director made the policy decision to sell at $5 above the prevailing market price of $125, suggesting that if they did suffer a decrease in volume, ATS would still be better off. It was also accepted that an efficient purchasing officer could have purchased at around $4.50 per kg.

There was no inventory movement of either materials or finished goods in the period.

Required:

Prepare a variance statement which would be most helpful to the management of ATS, which clearly takes planning and operational variances into consideration.

Test your understanding 11

A company budgeted to make and sell 2,000 units of its only product, for which the standard marginal cost is:

		$
Direct materials	4 kilos at $2 per kilo	8
Direct labour	3 hours at $6 per hour	18
		26

The standard sales price is $50 per unit and the standard contribution $24 per unit. Budgeted fixed costs were $30,000, giving a budgeted profit of $18,000.

Due to severe material shortages, the company had to switch to a less efficient and more expensive material, and it was decided in retrospect that the realistic (ex post) standard direct material cost should have been 5 kilos at $3 per kilo = $15 per unit.

Actual results were as follows:

Actual production and sales: 2,400 units

		$	$
Sales revenue			115,000
Direct materials	12,300 kilos at $3 per kilo	36,900	
Direct labour	7,500 hours at $6.10 per hour	45,750	
Total variable costs			82,650
Actual contribution			32.350
Actual fixed costs			32,000
Actual profit			350

Required:

Prepare an operating statement with planning and operational variances that reconciles the budgeted and actual profit figures.

Test your understanding 12

Scenario

It might be argued that only operational variances have significance for performance measurement. Planning variances cannot be controlled and so have little or no value for performance reporting.

Task:

State briefly, with your reason(s), whether you agree with this point of view.

(Time allowed: 10 minutes)

Test your understanding 13

Scenario

FB makes and sells a single product. The standard cost and revenue per unit are as follows:

		$
Selling price		400
Direct material A	5 kg at $25 per kg	125
Direct material B	3 kg at $22 per kg	66
Direct labour	3 hours at $10 per hour	30
Variable overheads	3 hours at $7 per hour	21
Standard contribution		158

The budgeted production and sales for the period in question were 10,000 units.

The mix of materials can be varied and therefore the material usage variance can be sub-divided into mix and yield variances.

For the period under review, the actual results were as follows:

Production and sales		9,000 units
		$
Sales revenue		4,455,000
Material cost	A – 35,000 kg	910,000
	B – 50,000 kg	1,050,000
Labour cost	30,000 hours	385,000
Variable overhead		230,000

The general market prices at the time of purchase for material A and material B were \$21 per kg and \$19 per kg respectively.

There were no opening or closing inventories during the period.

Tasks:

(a) Prepare a statement detailing the variances (including planning and operational, and mix and yield variances) which reconciles the budgeted contribution and the actual contribution.

(b) Explain the results and usefulness to FB of the planning and operational, and mix and yield variances that you have calculated in your answer to part (a).

(Time allowed for part (b): 15 minutes)

Test your understanding answers

Example 1

(a) **Mix variance (individual units method)**

		Material A	Material B	Material C	Total
		Kg	Kg	Kg	Kg
1	Actual input	14,000	5,500	5,500	25,000
2	Actual input in std proportions				⇓
	50%:20%:30%	12,500	5,000	7,500	⇐ 5,000
3	Difference in quantity	1,500 A	500 A	2,000 F	
4	× Std price	× 1.10	× 2.40	× 1.50	
5	Mix variance	$1,650 A	$1,200 A	$3,000F	$150 F

(b) **Mix variance (weighted average method)**

$$\text{Weighted average std cost} = \frac{(600 \times 1.10) + (240 \times 2.40) + (360 \times 1.50)}{1{,}200 \text{ kg}} = \$1.48/\text{kg}$$

	Material A	Material B	Material C	Total
	Kg	Kg	Kg	Kg
1 Actual input	14,000	5,500	5,500	25,000
2 Actual input in std proportions				⇓
50%:20%:30%	12,500	5,000	7,500	⇐25,000
3 Difference in quantity	1,500	500	– 2,000	
4 × Difference in price (weighted av. std price – Ind. material std price)				
× (1.48 – 1.10)	× 0.38			
× (1.48 – 2.40)		× – 0.92		
× (1.48 – 1.50)			– 0.02	
5 Mix variance	$570 F	$460 A	$40 F	$150 F

(c) **Yield variance**

This is calculated in exactly the same way under both methods.

$$\text{Std cost per kg of output} = \frac{(600 \times 1.10) + (240 \times 2.40) + (360 \times 1.50)}{1,000 \text{ kg}} = \$1.776/\text{kg}$$

		Kg
1	Std yield $25,000 \times \frac{1,000}{1,200}$	20,833.33
2	Actual yield	21,000
3		166.67 F
4	× Std price/cost per kg of output	× 1.776
	Yield variance	296 F

Example 2

The total labour cost variance for period 9 is $400 favourable (i.e. $5,500 standard cost less $5,100 actual cost). This may be analysed as follows:

Planning variance:

Original (ex-ante) standard less the revised (ex-post) labour cost
(550 applications × $10) – (550 applications × $8) = $1,100 favourable

Operational variances:

Labour efficiency:

(standard (ex-post) hours less actual hours) × standard hourly rate
((550 applications × 1.6 hours) – 1,200 hours) × $5 = $1,600 adverse

Labour rate:

(standard rate – actual rate) × actual hours
($5 – $4.25) × 1,200 = $900 favourable

Note that the three component variances add up to $400 favourable.

In this case, the separation of the labour cost variance into operational and planning components indicates a larger problem in the area of labour efficiency than might otherwise have been indicated. The operational variances are based on the revised (ex-post) standard and this gives a more meaningful performance benchmark than the original (ex-ante) standard.

Example 3

Operating statement

	$	$
Budgeted contribution		52,000
Sales volume contribution variance		–
Sales price variance		116,000 F
		168,000

		Favourable	Adverse	
Cost variances				
Direct material price	(\$10 × 10,800) – \$194,000		86,400	
Direct material usage	(10,000 – 10,800) × \$10		8,000	
Direct labour rate	(\$8 × 5,800) – \$69,600)		23,200	
Direct labour efficiency	(6,000 – 5,800) × \$8	1,600		
		1,600	117,600	116,000 A
Actual contribution				52,000

As the managing director states, and the above analysis shows, the overall variance for the company was zero: the adverse cost variances exactly offset the favourable sales price variance.

However, this analysis does not clearly indicate the efficiency with which the company operated during the period, as it is impossible to tell whether some of the variances arose from the use of inappropriate standards, or whether they were due to efficient or inefficient implementation of those standards. In order to determine this, a revised ex post plan should be constructed, setting out the standards that, with hindsight, should have been in operation during the period. These revised ex post standards are shown under (B) below.

	(A) *Original plan*	\$	**(B)** *Revised ex ante plan*	\$	**(C)** *Actual result*	\$
Sales	(1,000 × \$200)	200,000	(1,000 × \$330)	330,000	(1,000 × \$316)	316,000
Materials	(10,000 × \$10)	100,000	(10,000 × \$17)	170,000	(10,800 × \$18)	194,400
Labour	(6,000 × \$8)	48,000	(6,000 × \$12.50)	75,000	(5,800 × \$12)	69,600

	$	$
Planning variances (A – B)		
Sales price	130,000 F	
Materials price	70,000 A	
Labour rate	27,000 A	
		33,000 F
Operational variances		
Sales price (B – C)	14,000 A	
Materials price (10,800 × $1)	10,800 A	
Materials usage (800 × $17)	13,600 A	
Labour rate (5,800 × $0.50)	2,900 F	
Labour efficiency (200 hrs × $12.50)	2,500 F	
		33,000 A

A comparison of (B) and (C) produces operational variances, which show the difference between the results that were actually achieved and those that might legitimately have been achievable during the period in question. This gives a very different view of the period's operations. For example, on the cost side, the labour rate variance has changed from adverse to favourable, and the material price variance, while remaining adverse, is significantly reduced in comparison to that calculated under the traditional analysis; on the sales side, the sales price variance, which was particularly large and favourable in the traditional analysis, is transformed into an adverse variance in the revised approach, reflecting the fact that the company failed to sell at prices that were actually available in the market.

A comparison of the original plan (A) with the revised plan (B) allows the planning variances to be identified. As noted at the beginning of this section, these variances are uncontrollable by operating, staff, and may or may not have been controllable by the original standard-setters at the start of the budget period. Where a revision of standards is required due to environmental changes that were not foreseeable at the time the budget was prepared, the planning variances are truly uncontrollable. However, standards that failed to anticipate known market trends when they were set will reflect faulty standard-setting: it could be argued that these variances were controllable (avoidable) at the planning stage.

Test your understanding 1

Material A usage variance

AQ SP = 1,000 × $4 = $4,000

Variance = $2,400 F

SQ SP = (160 units × 10 kg/unit) × $4 = $6,400

Material B usage variance

AQ SP = 1,460 × $6 = $8,760

Variance = $10,440 F

SQ SP = (160 units × 20 kg/unit) × $6 = $19,200

Total usage variance = $2,400 + $10,440 = $12,840

Material mix variance

Material	Std mix	Actual material usage (kgs)	Actual usage @ std mix (kgs)	Mix variance (kgs)	Std cost per kg ($)	Mix variance ($)
A	10/30	1,000	820	180 A	4	720 A
B	20/30	1,460	1,640	180 F	6	1,080 F
		2,460	2,460	0	–	360 F

Material yield variance

Material	Std usage for actual output (kgs)	Actual usage @ std mix (kgs)	Yield variance (kgs)	Std cost per kg ($)	Yield variance ($)
A	160 × 10 kg = 1,600	820	780 F	4	3,120 F
B	160 × 20 kg = 3,200	1,640	1,560 F	6	9,360 F
	4,800	2,460	2,340 F	–	12,480 F

Alternatively, the material yield variance can be calculated in total using the following method:

(1)	Total input = 1,000 kgs + 1,460 kgs = 2,460 kgs.	
	This should produce (÷ 30 kgs)	82 units of output
(2)	2,460 kgs did produce	160 units of output
(3)	Difference = yield variance in units	78 units F
(4)	Value at the standard cost of	$160 per unit
(5)	Yield variance	$12,480 F

Total mix and yield variance = $12,480 F + $360 F = $12,840 F (as per the usage variance)

Test your understanding 2

Individual units mix variance

		Skilled Labour Hrs	**Unskilled Labour Hrs**		**Total** Hrs
1	Actual input	5,250	5,250		10,500 ⇓
2	Actual input in std proportions 6:4	6,300	4,200	⇐	10,500
3	Difference in quantity	1,050 F	1,050 A		
4	× Std price	× 12	× 7		
5	Mix variance	$12,600 F	$7,350 A		$5,250F

Weighted average method

$$\text{Weighted average std rate} = \frac{6 \times \$12 + 4 \times \$7}{6\text{ hours} + 4\text{ hours}} = \$10 \text{ per hour}$$

Weighted average mix variance

		Skilled Labour	Unskilled Labour	Total
		Hrs	Hrs	Hrs
1	Actual input	5,250	5,250	10,500 ⇓
2	Actual input in std proportions 6:4	6,300	4,200	⇐ 10,500
3	Difference in hours	–1,050	1,050	
4	× Difference in rate (weighted average std rate – individual labour std rate)			
	× (10 – 12)	× –2		
	× (10 – 7)		× 3	
5	Mix variance	$2,100 F	$3,150 F	$5,250 F

Yield variance (same answer for both methods)

$$\text{Std cost per unit of output} = \frac{6 \times \$12 + 4 \times \$7}{1\text{ unit}} = \$100 \text{ per unit}$$

		Hrs
1	Std yield $10{,}500\text{ hours} \times \frac{1\text{ unit}}{10\text{ hours}}$	1,050
2	Actual yield	1,000
3		50 A
4	× Std price/cost per kg of output	× 100
	Yield variance	$5,000 A

Test your understanding 3

Average number of drinks per passenger = 25/10 = 2.5

Weighted standard average cost per drink = $17.25/25 = $0.69

	Drinks
300 passengers should consume (× 2.5 drinks)	750
They did consume	850
Yield variance in number of drinks	100 (A)
× weighted standard average cost per drink	$0.69
Yield variance	$69 (A)

	Actual usage	**Standard mix**	**Mix variance**	**Standard cost per drink**	**Mix variance**
	Drinks	Drinks	Drinks		$
Low cost	215 (5)	170	45 (A)	$0.25	11.25 (A)
Medium cost	280 (8)	272	8 (A)	$0.50	4.00 (A)
High cost	355 (12)	408	53 (F)	$1.00	53.00 (F)
	850	850			**37.75 (F)**

Alternatively, using the weighted average method

	Mix variance	**Weighted average cost per drink**	**Standard cost per drink**	**Difference in price**	**Mix variance**
	Drinks				$
Low cost	45 (A)	$0.69	$0.25	$0.44	19.80 (F)
Medium cost	8 (A)	$0.69	$0.50	$0.19	1.52 (F)
High cost	53 (F)	$0.69	$1.00	-$0.31	16.43 (F)
					37.75 (F)

Test your understanding 4

Mix and yield variances

Actual output was 960; therefore the standard input material quantity (with an expected loss of 20%) is 960/0.8 = 1,200 kg (to be mixed 50% X, 30% Y and 20% Z).

The standard cost per litre of input was

Material	Input	Standard price	Total cost
	kg	$	$
X	500	5.00	2,500
Y	300	6.00	1,800
Z	200	7.00	1,400
	1,000		5,700

Standard price per kg = $5.70

(i) *Yield variance*

Standard input	1,200	
Actual input	1,280	
Variance	80 kg	Adverse
Standard price per kg of input	$5.70	
Yield variance	$456.00	Adverse

(ii) *Mix variance*

Material	Standard mix	Actual mix	Mix variance	Standard price	Mix Variance
	kg			$	$
X	640	600	40 F	5.00	200 F
Y	384	380	4 F	6.00	24 F
Z	256	300	44 A	7.00	308 A
	1,280 kg	1,280 kg			84 A

Test your understanding 5

(a) **Sales quantity profit variance**

It is apparent that the overall sales volume profit variance for the period is $40 adverse (that is (20 units adverse of Standard times $5) plus (10 units favourable of Deluxe times $6).

We can split this into a sales quantity profit variance (effectively a yield variance) and a sales mix profit variance. The sales quantity profit variance is calculated as follows:

(Actual units – budgeted units) × weighted average profit per unit

(500 units budget – 490 units actual) × $5.60 average profit = $56 A

(b) **Sales mix profit variance (using the individual units method)**

	Standard mix	**Actual mix**	**Variance (treatments)**	**Profit per treatment ($)**	**Variance ($)**
Standard	196	180	16 (A)	5	80 (A)
Deluxe	294	310	16 (F)	6	96 (F)
Total	490	490			16 (F)

The standard mix is the total unit sales (490) multiplied by 2/5 to give X and 3/5 to give Y.

(c) **Sales mix profit variance (using the weighted average method)**

	Standard mix	Actual mix	Variance (treatments)	Profit per treatment ($)	Weighted average profit ($)	Difference ($)	Variance ($)
Standard	196	180	16 (A)	5	5.60	0.60 (A)	9.60 (F)
Deluxe	294	310	16 (F)	6	5.60	0.40 (F)	6.40 (F)
Total	490	490					16.00 (F)

The Standard variance is favourable overall because, although the company sold less of that treatment than the standard mix, this is the less profitable treatment.

This perhaps explains the superiority of the weighted average method overall. Overall we have sold more of the more profitable treatment and less of the least profitable treatment so that it can be argued that both variances are in the company's favour and should be favourable.

Note: The example used relates to the sales volume profit variance, but exactly the same procedure can be used for its contribution and revenue variance alternatives.

Test your understanding 6

Material mix variance

The material mix variance is not affected by the material wastage and should be calculated in the normal way:

Material	Std mix	Actual material usage (kgs)	Actual usage @ std mix (kgs)	Mix variance (kgs)	Std cost per kg ($)	Mix variance ($)
S1	8/16	8,284	9,576.5	1,292.5 F	0.30	387.75 F
S2	5/16	7,535	5,985.3	1,549.7 A	0.50	774.85 A
S3	3/16	3,334	3,591.2	257.2 F	0.40	102.88 F
		19,153	19,153	0	–	284.22 A

Material yield variance

The yield variance will take account of the material wastage of 10%:

Material	Std usage for actual output (kgs)	Actual usage @ std mix (kgs)	Yield variance (kgs)	Std cost per kg ($)	Yield variance ($)
S1	8/16 = 8,560	9,576.5	1,016.5 A	0.30	304.95 A
S2	5/16 = 5,350	5,985.3	635.3 A	0.50	317.65 A
S3	3/16 = 3,210	3,591.2	381.2 A	0.40	152.48 A
	15,408 × 100/90 = 17,120	19,153	2,033 A	–	775. 08 A

Material usage variance

Total = $775.08 A + $284.22 A = $1,059.3 A

Test your understanding 7

Conventional approach

				$	
SHSR 5 hrs/unit x 250 units	x	$10/hr	=	12,500	Efficiency $2,000 A
AHSR 1,450 hrs	x	$10/hr	=	14,500	
AHAR			=	13,050	$1,450 F Rate

Planning and operational approach

Planning variance

Efficiency (5 hrs/unit – 6 hrs/unit) x 250 units x $10/hr $2,500 A

Operational variances

				$	
SHSR 6 hrs/unit x 250 units	x	$10/hr	=	15,000	Efficiency $500 F
AHSR 1,450 hrs	x	$10/hr	=	14,500	
AHAR			=	13,050	$1,450 F Rate

Test your understanding 8

(a) **Traditional variances**

Actual quantity × Actual price =		$41,500	
		Price variance	$2,500 F
Actual quantity × Standard price =	11,000 × $4 =	$44,000	
		Usage variance	$4,800 A
Standard quantity × Standard price =	1,400 × 7 × $4 =	$39,200	

(b) **Planning variances**

Revised standard quantity × Revised standard price =	1,400 × 8 × $3.80 =	$42,560	
		Planning variance	$3,360 A
Original standard quantity × Original standard price =	1,400 × 7 × $4 =	$39,200	

(c) **Operational variances**

AQ × AP =		$41,500	$300 F
		Price variance	
AQ × RSP =	11,000 × $3.80 =	$41,800	
		Usage variance	$760 F
RSQ × RSP =	1,400 × 8 × $3.80=	$42,560	

Test your understanding 9

(a) **Budgeted and actual profits**

Budget	**Kitchens**	**Bathrooms**	**Total**
	$m	$m	$m
Sales	40	14	54
Direct costs	(22)	(6)	(28)
Central services	(10)	(5)	(15)
Budgeted profit	8	3	11

Actual	**Kitchens**	**Bathrooms**	**Total**
	$m	$m	$m
Sales	33.8	15.25	49.05
Direct costs	(20.8)	(6.75)	(27.55)
Central services	(6.5)	(6.25)	(17.50)
Actual profit	6.5	2.25	4.00

(b) **Sales variances**

Sales price variance	**Kitchens**	**Bathrooms**	**Total**
	$	$	$
Standard sales price	10,000	7,000	
Actual sales price	13,000	6,100	
Variance	3,000 F	900 A	
Actual sales quantity	× 2,600	× 2,500	
Sales price variance	7,800,000 F	2,250,000 A	5,550,000 F

Sales mix profit variances

	Standard mix	Actual mix	Variance (units)	Profit per unit ($)	Variance ($m)
Kitchens	3,400	2,600	800 (A)	$2,000	1.60 (A)
Bathrooms	1,700	2,500	800 (F)	$1,500	1.20 (F)
Total	5,100	5,100			0.40 (F)

Sales quantity profit variances

	Standard mix	Budgeted sales	Variance (units)	Profit per unit ($)	Variance ($m)
Kitchens	3,400	4,000	600 (A)	$2,000	1.20 (A)
Bathrooms	1,700	2,000	300 (A)	$1,500	0.45 (A)
Total	5,100	6,000			1.65 (A)

Check

Sales volume variances

Kitchens (4,000 – 2,600) × $2,000 = $2.8m A

Bathrooms (2,000 – 2,500) × $1,500 = $0.75m F

Total $2.05m

Sales volume variance = mix variance + quantity variance
= $0.4m A + $1.65m A = $2.05 m

(c) **Reconciliation of profits**

	Favourable ($m)	Adverse ($m)	$m	
Budgeted profit (from part a)			11.00	
Sales mix variance (from part b)				
– kitchens		1.60		
– bathrooms	1.20			
Sales quantity variance (from part b)				
– kitchens		1.20		
– bathrooms				
Sales price variances (from part b)				
– kitchens	7.80			
– bathrooms		2.25		
Direct costs (W1)				
– kitchens		6.50		
– bathrooms	0.75			
Central services (W2)				
– volume (kitchens)		3.50		
– volume (bathrooms)	1.25			
– expenditure		2.50		
	11.00	18.00	7	A
Actual profit (from part a)			4	

Workings

(W1) **Direct cost variances:**

Kitchens 2,600 × (5,500 – 8,000) = $6.5m A
Bathrooms 2,500 × (3,000 – 2,700) = $0.75m F

(W2) **Central services volume variances:**

Kitchens (4,000 – 2,600) × $2,500 = $3.5m A
Bathrooms (2,500 – 2,000) × $2,500 = $1.25m F
Central services expenditure variance = $15m – $17.5m = $2.5m A

(d) **Performance of the company for the year**

(Actual profit at $4m is $7m below budgeted profit, a shortfall of 64%). The main causes are as follows:

- an overall fall in the total volume of sales resulting in a sales quantity variance of $1.65m A. The lower than expected volume has also resulted in central services costs being under absorbed as shown by the volume variances (net impact $2.25A).
- the sales mix has also switched from more profitable kitchens to less profitable bathrooms and this is reflected in the sales mix variance of $0.4m A.
- the impact of the lower volume of kitchen sales has been partially offset by the favourable price variance for kitchens. It is possible that a higher proportion of jobs are of the highly customised category rather than the 'off the shelf' packages. This has led to higher average prices being charged but also higher direct costs being incurred. The opposite seems to have occurred with bathrooms.
- Central services costs have exceeded budget by $2.5m. This may be due to higher costs incurred designing customised jobs.

It would be worth investigating whether the extra price charged for customised designs is covering all of the additional costs incurred. Higher prices may be necessary or better control of costs.

Tutorial note: For part (a): The information given in the question suggests that an OAR of $2,500 per job is used to absorb central services costs. This means that there is under absorbed central services cost of 17.5 – 6.5 – 6.25 = $4.75m. There is no indication that this is charged to the other divisions, but total costs must be shown to arrive at total profit.

Test your understanding 10

Operating statement for ATS

		$	$
Original budgeted contribution	1,200 × $26		31,200
Sales volume contribution variance	(1,000 – 1,200) × $26		5,200 A
			–––––
Budgeted contribution on actual sales			26,000
Planning variances			
Sales price	($110 – $130) × 1,000	20,000 F	
Material price	($3 – $4.50) × 8 × 1,000	12,000 A	
		–––––	
			8,000 F
			–––––
Revised contribution on actual sales			34,000
Operational variances			
Sales price	($130 – $135) × 1,000	5,000 F	
Material price	($4.50 – $4) × 7,800	3,900 F	
Material usage	(8,000 – 7,800) × $4.50	900 F	
Labour rate	($10 – $10.40) × 6,250	2,500 A	
Labour efficiency	(6,000 – 6,250) × $10	2,500 A	
		–––––	
			4,800 F
			–––––
Actual contribution			38,800
			–––––

Test your understanding 11

In this example, since the change in both the material usage and material price are inter-related, the total planning variance only is reported in the operating statement below.

	$
Budgeted profit	18,000
Budgeted fixed costs	30,000
Budgeted contribution	48,000
Planning variance	16,800 (A)
Revised budgeted contribution	31,200
Sales volume contribution variance	9,600 (F)
Budgeted contribution on actual sales	40,800
Operational variances	
Sales price	5,000 (A)
Materials usage	900 (A)
Direct labour rate	750 (A)
Direct labour efficiency	1,800 (A)
Actual contribution	32,350
Budgeted fixed costs	30,000
Fixed cost expenditure variance	2,000 (A)
Actual profit	350

Operational variances

Materials price	$
12,300 kilos should cost (× $3)	36,900
They did cost	36,900
Direct materials price variance	0

Materials usage	*Kilos*
2,400 units of product should use (× 5 kilos)	12,000
They did use	12,300
Direct materials usage variance (in kilos)	300 (A)
Standard price per kilo (ex post)	$3
Direct materials usage variance	$900

Labour rate	$
7,500 hours should cost (× $6)	45,000
They did cost	45,750
Direct labour rate variance	750 (A)
Labour efficiency	*Hours*
2,400 units of product should take (× 3 hours)	7,200
They did take	7,500
Direct labour efficiency variance (in hours)	300 (A)
Standard rate per hour	$6
Direct labour efficiency variance	$1,800 (A)
Sales price	$
2,400 units should sell for (× $50)	120,000
They did sell for	115,000
Sales price variance	5,000 (A)
Fixed overhead expenditure	$
Budgeted fixed costs	30,000
Actual fixed costs	32,000
Fixed cost expenditure variance	2,000 (A)
Sales volume	*Units*
Budgeted sales	2,000
Actual sales	2,400
Sales volume variance (in units)	400 (F)
Standard contribution per unit	$24
Sales volume contribution variance	$9,600 (F)

Planning variances

Material costs	**$/unit**
Ex ante standard per unit (4 kilos × $2)	8.0
Ex post standard per unit (5 kilos × $3)	15.0
Planning variance per unit	7.0 (A)
Actual units produced	× 2,400
Total planning variance	$16,800 (A)

Test your understanding 12

A performance reporting and management control system depends on both reliable planning as well as control over operating activities.

Some planning variances might be caused by factors that could not have been foreseen in advance. However, some planning variances might be caused by weaknesses in the planning process. If so, they can be significant and indicate the need for better planning procedures in the future.

Test your understanding 13

Key answer tips

The planning variances may be based upon budget or actual level of activity, depending upon at what point the sales volume variance was calculated. It is most common in the exam to base the planning variance on the actual units produced.

The mix variance may be calculated using either the individual units method or the weighted average price method. The total result, which is the important figure in this question, will be the same.

	$000	$000
Original budgeted contribution (10,000 × $158)		1,580
Planning variances		
Material A price ($25 – $21) × 5 kg × 9,000	180 F	
Material B price ($22 – $19) × 3 kg × 9,000	81 F	
		261 F
Sales volume variance (9,000 – 10,000) × $158		158 A
Revised contribution on actual sales		1,683

Note: If the planning variances were calculated based on actual sales (this method is not commonly used in exam questions but is shown here for completeness), the first part of the answer would appear as follows:

	$000	$000
Original budgeted contribution (10,000 × $158)		1,580
Planning variances		
Material A price ($25 – $21) × 5 kg × 10,000	200 F	
Material B price ($22 – $19) × 3 kg × 10,000	90 F	
		290 F
Sales volume variance (9,000 – 10,000) × $187 (W1)		187 A
Revised contribution		1,683

Operational variances

Selling price ($400 – $495) × 9,000	855 F	
Material A price (35,000 × $21) – $910,000	175 A	
Material B price (50,000 × $19) – $1,050,000	100 A	
Mix variance (W2)	36 F	
Yield variance (W3)	263 A	
Direct labour rate (30,000 hr × $10) – $385,000	85 A	
Direct labour efficiency (9,000 × 3 – 30,000) × $10	30 A	
Variable overhead expenditure (30,000 hr × $7) – $230,000	20 A	
Variable overhead efficiency (9,000 × 3 – 30,000) × $7	21 A	
	——	
Total operational variances		197 F
		——
		1,880
		——

The above variances can also be calculated as follows:

Material A variance

					$	
AQSP	35,000 kg	×	$21 / kg	=	735,000	$175,000 A Price
AQAP				=	910,000	

Material B variance

					$	
AQSP	50,000kg	×	$19 / kg	=	950,000	$100,000 A Price
AQAP				=	1,050,000	

Labour variances

					$	
SHSR	3 hrs / unit × 9,000 units	×	$10 / hr	=	270,000	Efficiency $30,000 A
AHSR	30,000 hrs	×	$10 / hr	=	300,000	
AHAR				=	385,000	$85,000 A Rate

Variable overhead variances

					$	
SHSR						
3 hrs / unit × 9,000 units	×	$7 / hr	=		189,000	Efficiency $21,000 A
AHSR						
30,000 hrs	×	$7 / hr	=		210,000	
AHAR						$20,000 A Rate
			=		230,000	

Sales price variance

	$
Std selling price	400
Actual selling price $4,455,000/9,000 units	495
	95 F
× Actual no of units sold	× 9,000
	$855,000 F

Workings

(W1) **Revised contribution per unit**

	$
Selling price	400
Material A 5 kg × $21	(105)
Material B 3 kg × $19	(57)
Direct labour 3 hr × $10	(30)
Variable overhead 3 hr × $7	(21)
Contribution	187

(W2) **Mix variance**

Note: A method is not specified. Use individual units method if given a choice as it is quicker and easier than the weighted average price method.

Material	Standard mix	Actual mix	Difference	@ Standard price	Variance
	000s	000s	000s		$000
A	53.125	35	18.125 F	$21	380.625 F
	31.875	50	18.125 A	$19	344.375 A
B	85	85	Nil		36.25 F

Standard mix of A : B is 5 kg : 3 kg

Hence, standard mix of actual input is:

$$A = 85 \times \frac{5}{8} = 53.125$$

$$A = 85 \times \frac{3}{8} = 31.875$$

(W3) **Yield variance**

Standard yield from actual input 85,000 kg ÷ 8 kg pu	10,625	units
Actual yield (output)	9,000	units
	1,625	units
@ Average price per unit of **output** (5 kg × $21) + (3 kg × $19)	$162	
Variance	$263,250	A

(W4)

	$000
Sales revenue	4,455
Less: Material A	(910)
Material B	(1,050)
Labour cost	(385)
Variable overhead	(230)
	1,880

(b) **Planning and operational variances**

The actual contribution is $300,000 higher than budget, despite sales volume falling from 10,000 units to 9,000 units. At first this appears to be an extraordinarily strong result. However, by calculating planning variances a new perspective emerges.

Both materials A and B were originally budgeted at prices that were quite substantially higher than the general market prices that emerged during the period. Material A could be bought at $4 less per kg than originally planned. This reduction in general market price immediately leads to a saving of $180,000 on the original budgeted cost. This is a significant saving. Similarly, material B's reduction in market price lead to a saving in the budget of $81,000. Planning variances indicate this large uncontrollable saving experienced by FB.

Once the budget is amended to reflect the new standard costs of the materials, actual results can be compared to the new budget. This exercise involves calculating operational variances. The operational variances for FB are quite revealing. There was a selling price variance of $855,000 favourable. However, virtually all the other variances were adverse. This would seem to indicate that FB did not perform particularly well in the latest period.

Planning and operational variances are useful for several reasons:

(1) They permit actual results to be compared to realistic up-to-date standards.

(2) The system is likely to provide more useful information for management.

(3) Operational staff may be more motivated by the feedback information, as their performance is judged against realistic standards.

(4) The importance of the planning function is emphasised – poor forecasting may be highlighted.

Mix and yield variances

The mix variance was $36,250 favourable. This was due to a far smaller proportion of the more expensive material A being used than was standard. The standard stated that 62.5% of material input should be material A. During the period, however, only 41% of input was material A. This is a significant difference. In each case the balance of material was material B (cheaper than A).

It is possible for FB to vary the input mix of raw materials. As this is the case, it would seem to be a useful exercise to examine how a deviation of the actual material mix from the expected mix has had an impact on costs.

Perhaps because of this mix variance there has been a massive drop in expected output. 85,000 kg of input should have produced 10,625 units of output. During the period only 9,000 units of output were produced. This is 15% below expectations. This has given rise to an adverse variance of $263,250 adverse. FB should investigate this significant variance and discover whether this variance was partly caused by the unusual mix in the period. It is probably important that FB correct the problems behind the yield variance and avoid it recurring in the future.

chapter

11

The budgeting framework

Chapter learning objectives

Lead	Component
B1. Explain the purposes of forecasts, plans and budgets.	(a) Explain the purposes of budgets, including planning, communication, co-ordination, motivation, authorisation, control and evaluation.
B3. Discuss budgets based on forecasts.	(a) Prepare a budget for any account in the master budget, based on projections/forecasts and managerial targets. (b) Discuss alternative approaches to budgeting.
B5. Analyse performance using budgets, recognising alternative approaches and sensitivity to variable factors.	(a) Analyse the consequences of "what if" scenarios.

1 Chapter overview diagram

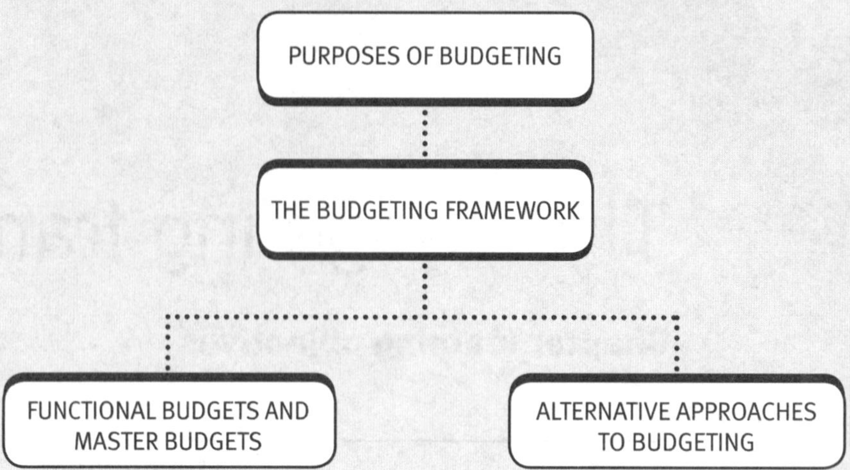

2 Budget

A quantitative or financial plan relating to the future. It can be for the company as a whole or for departments or functions or products or for resources such as cash, materials, labour, etc. It is usually for one year or less.

3 Purposes of budgeting

Budgets have several different purposes:

(1) planning

(2) control and evaluation

(3) co-ordination

(4) communication

(5) motivation

(6) authorisation.

Purposes of budgets explained

Budgets have several different purposes:

(1) **Planning**

Budgets **compel** planning. The budgeting process forces management to look ahead, set targets, anticipate problems and give the organisation purpose and direction. Without the annual budgeting process the pressures of day-to-day operational problems may tempt managers not to plan for future operations. The budgeting process encourages managers to anticipate problems before they arise, and hasty decisions that are made on the spur of the moment, based on expediency rather than reasoned judgements, will be minimised. Corporate planners would regard budgeting as an important technique whereby long-term strategies are converted into shorter-term action plans.

(2) **Control and evaluation**

The budget provides the plan against which actual results can be compared. Those results which are out-of-line with the budget can be further investigated and corrected. The performance of a manager is often evaluated by measuring his success in achieving his budgets. The budget might quite possibly be the only quantitative reference point available.

(3) **Co-ordination**

The budget serves as a vehicle through which the actions of the different parts of an organisation can be brought together and reconciled into a common plan. Without any guidance managers may each make their own decisions believing that they are working in the best interests of the organisation. A sound budgeting system helps to co-ordinate the different activities of the business and to ensure that they are in harmony with each other.

(4) **Communication**

Budgets communicate targets to managers. Through the budget, top management communicates its expectations to lower-level management so that all members of the organisation may understand these expectations and can co-ordinate their activities to attain them.

(5) **Motivation**

The budget can be a useful device for influencing managerial behaviour and motivating managers to perform in line with the organisational objectives.

(6) **Authorisation**

A budget may act as formal authorisation to a manager for expenditure, the hiring of staff and the pursuit of the plans contained in the budget.

The **budget period** is the time for which the budget is prepared. This is typically 1 year which reflects the fact that the financial reports for most organisations cover 1 year periods. But a budget can be for any length of time that suits management purposes.

Each budget period is normally split into control periods known as **budget intervals**. The budget interval is normally 3 months or 1 month. The 1 year budget is split into component parts for each budget interval and a budgetary control report is prepared at the end of each interval in which the budget and actual results are compared.

4 Functional budgets and the master budget

A **master budget** for the entire organisation brings together the departmental or activity budgets for all the departments or responsibility centres within the organisation.

The structure of a budget depends on the nature of the organisation and its operations. In a manufacturing organisation, the budgeting process will probably consist of preparing several **functional budgets**, beginning with a sales budget (assuming this is the 'principal budget factor').

The budget committee and the budget manual

The process of preparing and using budgets will differ from organisation to organisation. However there are a number of key requirements in the budgetary planning and control process.

The budget committee

The need for coordination in the planning process is paramount. For example, the purchasing budget cannot be prepared without reference to the production budget. The best way to achieve this coordination is to set up a budget committee. The budget committee should comprise representatives from all functions in the organisation.

The budget committee should meet regularly to review the progress of the budgetary planning process and to resolve problems that have arisen. These meetings will effectively bring together the whole organisation in one room, to ensure a coordinated approach to budget preparation.

The budget manual

Effective budgetary planning relies on the provision of adequate information to the individuals involved in the planning process.

A budget manual is a collection of documents which contains key information for those involved in the planning process.

Principal budget factor

When a key resource is in short supply and affects the planning decisions, it is known as the **principal budget factor** or **limiting budget factor**.

It is usually assumed in budgeting that sales demand will be the key factor setting a limit to what the organisation can expect to achieve in the budget period.

When the principal budget factor has been determined this should be the starting point for all other budgets.

Other limiting factors

In most organisations the principal budget factor is sales demand: a company is usually restricted from making and selling more of its products because there would be no sales demand for the increased output at a price which would be acceptable and/or profitable to the company.

Occasionally, however, there might be a shortage of a key resource, such as cash, raw material supplies, skilled labour or equipment. If a resource is in restricted supply, and the shortage cannot be overcome, the budget for the period should be determined by how to make the best use of this key budget resource, rather than by sales demand.

Principles such as linear programming, key factor analysis and throughput accounting could then be used to determine production plans.

These stages in budgeting are illustrated in the following diagram.

Budget preparation

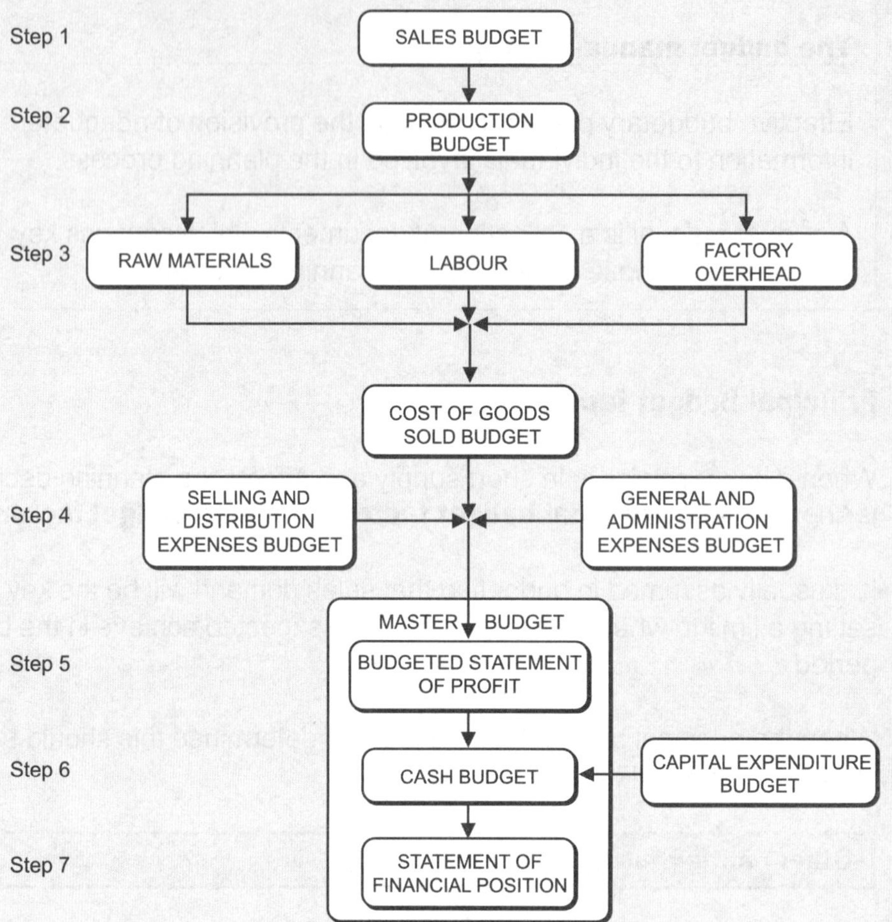

Explanation of each budget

You can see from this that the principal budget factor is the starting point in the process. It is generally sales, as shown in the diagram.

Step 1: The sales budget considers how many units can be sold.

Step 2: The production budget considers how many units must be produced to meet the budgeted sales level.

Note: The difference between the sales and the production budgets is the inventory of finished goods.

Step 3: The material, labour and overhead budgets can be established, based on the production budget.

Note: The material budget is generally calculated in two parts, firstly the quantity of material required in production, then the quantity of material required to be purchased. The difference between these will be the inventory of raw materials.

Material losses in production and idle time must be taken account of in the material and labour budgets.

Step 4: Non-production budgets. Budgets for non-production costs, such as selling and distribution costs, must also be considered.

Steps 5, 6 and 7: The master budget, comprising the statement of profit or loss, cash budget and statement of financial position can be pulled together from the individual budgets.

More specifics on each budget:

- **Sales budget**. Budget for future sales, expressed in revenue terms and possibly also in units of sale. The budget for the organisation as a whole might combine the sales budgets of several sales regions.
- **Production budget**. A production budget follows on from the sales budget, since production quantities are determined by sales volume. The production volume will differ from sales volume by the amount of any planned increase or decrease in inventories of finished goods (and work-in-progress).

In order to express the production budget in financial terms (production cost), subsidiary budgets must be prepared for materials, labour and production overheads. Several departmental managers could be involved in preparing these subsidiary budgets.

- **Direct materials usage budget**. This is a budget for the quantities and cost of the materials required for the planned production quantities.
- **Materials purchases budget**. This is a budget for the cost of the materials to be purchased in the period. The purchase cost of direct materials will differ from the material usage budget if there is a planned increase or decrease in direct materials inventory. The purchases budget should also include the purchase costs of indirect materials.
- **Direct labour budget**. This is a budget of the direct labour costs of production. If direct labour is a variable cost, it is calculated by multiplying the production quantities (in units) by the budgeted direct labour cost per unit produced. If direct labour is a fixed cost, it can be calculated by estimating the payroll cost.

- **Production overheads**. Budgets can be produced for production overhead costs. Where a system of absorption costing is used, overheads are allocated and apportioned, and budgeted absorption rates are determined.
- **Administration and sales and distribution overheads**. Other overhead costs should be budgeted.
- **Budgeted statement of profit or loss, cash budget and balance sheet**. Having prepared budgets for sales and costs, the master budget can be summarised as an statement of profit or loss for the period, a cash budget and a balance sheet (or statement of financial position) as at the end of the budget period.

If the budgeted profit, cash position or balance sheet are unsatisfactory, the budgets should be revised until a satisfactory planned outcome is achieved.

Example 1

Newton Ltd manufactures three products; the expected sales for each product are shown below.

	Product 1	Product 2	Product 3
Sales in units	3,000	4,500	3,000

Opening inventory is expected to be:

Product 1	500 units
Product 2	700 units
Product 3	500 units

Management have stated their desire to reduce inventory levels and closing inventories are budgeted as:

Product 1	200 units
Product 2	300 units
Product 3	300 units

Three types of material are used in varying amounts in the manufacture of the three products. Material requirements per unit are shown below:

	Product 1	Product 2	Product 3
Material M1	2 kg	3 kg	4 kg
Material M2	3 kg	3 kg	4 kg
Material M3	6 kg	2 kg	4 kg

The opening inventory of material is expected to be:

Material M1	4,300 kg
Material M2	3,700 kg
Material M3	4,400 kg

Management are keen to reduce inventory levels for materials as well and closing inventories are to be much lower. Expected levels are shown below:

Material M1	2,200 kg
Material M2	1,300 kg
Material M3	2,000 kg

Material prices are expected to be 10% higher than this year and current prices are $1.10/kg for material M1, $3.00/kg for material M2 and $2.50/kg for material M3.

Two types of labour are used in producing the three products. Standard hours per unit are shown below:

	Product 1	Product 2	Product 3
Skilled labour	3	1	3
Semi-skilled labour	3	3	4

Skilled labour are to be paid at the rate of $6/hour and semi-skilled labour at the rate of $4/hour.

Required:

Prepare budgets for:

(a) production (in quantity)

(b) materials usage (in quantity)

(c) materials purchases (in quantity and value)

(d) labour (in hours and value).

Cash budgets and cash flow forecasts

A **cash forecast** is an estimate of cash receipts and payments for a future period under existing conditions.

A **cash budget** is a commitment to a plan for cash receipts and payments for a future period after taking any action necessary to bring the forecast into line with the overall business plan.

Cash budgets are used to:

- assess and integrate operating budgets
- plan for cash shortages and surpluses
- compare with actual spending.

There are two different techniques that can be used to create a cash budget:

- a receipts and payments forecast
- a balance sheet forecast.

Receipts and payments forecast

This is a forecast of cash receipts and payments based on predictions of sales and cost of sales and the timings of the cash flows relating to these items.

Preparing forecasts from planned receipts and payments

Every type of cash inflow and receipt, along with their timings, must be forecast. Note that cash receipts and payments differ from sales and cost of sales in the statement of profit or loss because:

- not all cash receipts or payments affect the statement of profit or loss, e.g. the issue of new shares or the purchase of a non-current asset
- some statement of profit or loss items are derived from accounting conventions and are not cash flows, e.g. depreciation or the profit/loss on the sale of a non-current asset
- the timing of cash receipts and payments does not coincide with the statement of profit or loss accounting period, e.g. a sale is recognised in the statement of profit or loss when the invoice is raised, yet the cash payment from the receivable may not be received until the following period or later
- irrecoverable debts will never be received in cash and an allowance for irrecoverable debts may not be received at all. When you are forecasting the cash receipts from customers you must remember to adjust for these items.

The following approach is a comprehensive step-by-step guide to how a management accountant might go about preparing a full cash budget. Understanding this process should help you in your understanding and interpretation of cash budgets, but you will not be required to prepare a full cash budget in an examination.

Step 1 – Layout

There is no definitive layout that should be used for a cash budget. However, it will typically include the following:

(i) A clear distinction between the cash receipts and cash payments for each control period. Your budget should not consist of a jumble of cash flows. It should be logically arranged with a subtotal for receipts and a subtotal for payments.

(ii) A figure for the net cash flow for each period. It could be argued that this is not an essential feature of a cash budget. However, you will find it easier to prepare and use a cash budget in an examination if you include the net cash flow. Also, managers find in practice that a figure for the net cash flow helps to draw attention to the cash flow implications of their actions during the period.

(iii) The closing cash balance for each control period. The closing balance for each period will be the opening balance for the following period.

The following is a typical layout:

Month:	1	2	3	4
	$	$	$	$
Receipts (few lines)				
Sub total				
Payments (Many lines)				
Sub total				
Net cash flow				
Opening balance				
Closing balance				

Step 2 – Fill in the simple figures

Some payments need only a small amount of work to identify the correct figure and timing and can be entered straight into the proforma. These would usually include:

- wages and salaries
- fixed overhead expenses
- dividend payments
- purchase of non-current assets.

Step 3 – Work out the more complex figures

The information on sales and purchases can be more time consuming to deal with, e.g.:

- timings for both sales and purchases must be found from credit periods
- variable overheads may require information about production levels
- purchases may require calculations based on production schedules and inventory balances.

Example 2

The forecast sales for an organisation are as follows:

	January	February	March	April
	$	$	$	$
Sales	6,000	8,000	4,000	5,000

All sales are on credit and receivables tend to pay in the following pattern:

	%
In month of sale	10
In month after sale	40
Two months after sale	45

The organisation expects the rate of irrecoverable debts to be 5%.

Calculate the forecast cash receipts from receivables in April.

Interpretation of a cash budget

Examples of factors to consider when interpreting a cash budget include:

- Is the balance at the end of the period acceptable/matching expectations?
- Does the cash balance become a deficit at any time in the period?
- Is there sufficient finance (e.g. an overdraft) to cover any cash deficits? Should new sources of finance be sought in advance?
- What are the key causes of cash deficits?
- Can/should discretionary expenditure (such as asset purchases) be made in another period in order to stabilise the pattern of cash flows?
- Is there a plan for dealing with cash surpluses (such as reinvesting them elsewhere)?
- When is the best time to make discretionary expenditure?

Example 3

HT has prepared a cash budget for the first three months of the year as follows:

	January	February	March
	$	$	$
Receipts			
From sales	56,000	58,000	54,000
Payments			
Capital expenditure	–	–	30,000
For direct materials	21,000	17,500	16,500
For direct labour (30% × prod'n cost)	15,000	16,500	9,750
For fixed production overheads	2,000	2,000	2,000
For variable production overheads	13,000	10,600	8,800
For admin/selling overhead	15,000	–	–
Total outflow	66,000	46,600	67,050
Net cash flow for month	(10,000)	11,400	(13,050)
Opening balance	(5,000)	(15,000)	(3,600)
Closing balance	(15,000)	(3,600)	(16,650)

Required:

Explain the usefulness of this budget to the business and the issues that it raises.

5 Sensitivity analysis

There is always a significant degree of uncertainty concerning many of the elements incorporated within a business plan or budget. The budget officer is often required to report on such uncertainty in some way. There are various approaches to this issue and one of the most widely used is 'sensitivity analysis'.

A sensitivity analysis exercise involves revising the budget on the basis of a series of varied assumptions. **One assumption can be changed at a time** to determine the impact on the budget overall. For example, if sales quantities were to be changed the impact on profits, cash flow etc. could be observed.

When changing more than one variable at a time it may be better to use spreadsheets to simplify and speed up the process.

Example of sensitivity analysis

An organisation has a budget for the first quarter of the year as follows:

	$
Sales: 100 units @ $40 per unit	4,000
Variable costs: 100 units @ $20 per unit	(2,000)
Fixed costs	(1,500)
Profit	500

There is some uncertainty over the variable cost per unit and that cost could be anywhere between $10 and $30, with $20 as the 'expected' outcome. We are required to carry out a sensitivity analysis on this.

One approach to this would be to present the budget shown above as an 'expected' case but with two other cases as 'worst' and 'best' possible outcomes.

Worst-case budget ($30 unit variable cost)

	$
Sales: 100 units @ $40 per unit	4,000
Variable costs: 100 units @ $30 per unit	(3,000)
Fixed costs	(1,500)
Profit	(500)

Best-case budget ($10 unit variable cost)

	$
Sales: 100 units @ $40 per unit	4,000
Variable costs: 100 units @ $10 per unit	(1,000)
Fixed costs	(1,500)
Profit	1,500

This gives managers a range of possible outcomes and allows them to make decisions accordingly. In practice they may build in targets and monitoring points during the period to determine which budget is appearing most likely. This would allow them to take further action during the period rather than wait until the end of the quarter when it may be too late.

The effect of the change in variable costs on the statement of financial position can also be determined.

Let's assume that the opening position at the start of the quarter was as follows:

	$
Non-current assets	5,000
Receivables	1,500
Cash/(overdraft)	500
Net assets	7,000
Equity	5,000
Profit and loss reserve	2,000
Capital	7,000

Sales are all on 6 weeks credit and all expenses are paid for immediately they are incurred. Three alternative budgeted statements of financial position at the end of quarter 1 can be produced as follows:

	Expected	**Worst**	**Best**
Non-current assets	5,000	5,000	5,000
Receivables	2,000	2,000	2,000
Cash/(overdraft)	500	(500)	1,500
Net assets	7,500	6,500	8,500
Equity	5,000	5,000	5,000
Profit and loss reserve	2,500	1,500	3,500
Capital	7,500	6,500	8,500

Calculation of the individual figures should be fairly obvious. But, let us consider *the worst case* cash balance as an example:

	$	
Cash inflow from sales	2,000	(being 50% of sales)
Cash outflow for expenses	(4,500)	
Cash inflow from opening debtors	1,500	
Opening cash balance	500	
Closing cash balance	(500)	

In practical budgeting, there may be uncertainty concerning a large number of factors within the budget, and sensitivity analysis may consist of a series of complex 'what if?' enquiries – reworking the budget, on the basis of a range of different scenarios. In large organisations with complicated budgets, such exercises may be very demanding. In the pre-computer era, the relevant calculations were all carried out manually. This could be a time-consuming and error-prone exercise.

Using spreadsheets to aid sensitivity analysis

Computer spreadsheets have made the task much easier. However, the spreadsheet has to be designed carefully in order to facilitate sensitivity analysis exercises. A well-designed spreadsheet allows a single correction (on a unit price or an hourly wage rate) to update the whole budget. Spreadsheet modelling is one of the most critical of the practical skills required by management accountants.

6 Periodic vs rolling budgets

Periodic budget

A periodic budget shows the costs and revenue for one period of time, e.g. a year and is updated on a periodic basis, e.g. every 12 months.

Rolling budgets (continuous budgets)

A rolling budget is a 'budget continuously updated by adding a further accounting period (month or quarter) when the earliest accounting period has expired' *(CIMA Official Terminology)*. Rolling budgets are also called 'continuous budgets'. Rolling budgets are for a fixed period, but this need not be a full financial year.

Reasons for rolling budgets

The reason for preparing rolling budgets is to deal with the problem of uncertainty in the budget, when greater accuracy and reliability are required. A common example is **cash budgeting.** Cash management is often a critical element of financial management in organisations, and it is essential to have reasonably reliable forecasts of cash flows, especially over the course of the next few days, weeks or months. An organisation might therefore produce rolling budgets (= revised forecasts) for cash flow. The cash budget period might be three or six months, and rolling cash budgets might be prepared monthly.

Illustration 1

If rolling annual budgets are prepared quarterly, four rolling budgets will be prepared each year, each for a 12-month period. A new quarter is added at the end of the new budget period, to replace the current quarter just ending:

- One budget might cover the period 1 January – 31 December Year 1.
- The next rolling budget will cover 1 April Year 1 to 31 March Year 2.
- The next rolling budget will cover 1 July Year 1 to 30 June Year 2.
- The next quarterly rolling budget will cover 1 October Year 1 to 30 September Year 2, and so on.

Reasons for rolling budgets

The reason for preparing rolling budgets is to deal with the problem of uncertainty in the budget, when greater accuracy and reliability are required. A common example is **cash budgeting.** Cash management is often a critical element of financial management in organisations, and it is essential to have reasonably reliable forecasts of cash flows, especially over the course of the next few days, weeks or months. An organisation might therefore produce rolling budgets (= revised forecasts) for cash flow. The cash budget period might be three or six months, and rolling cash budgets might be prepared monthly.

Another example is budgeting in conditions subject to rapid financial change. When a budget is prepared, the forecasts on which it is based might be uncertain due to the probability of significant financial changes during the budget period. For example:

- The forecast rate of cost inflation/price inflation might be high
- The business might be affected by changes in an exchange rate, such as the sterling/US dollar rate and the exchange rate might be extremely volatile and subject to large movements within relatively short periods of time
- When there is a large amount of uncertainty in the budget, it might be appropriate to prepare rolling budgets at regular intervals, in order to have plans that are reasonably realistic and achievable.

Advantages and disadvantages of rolling budgets

Advantages

- They reduce uncertainty in budgeting.
- They can be used for cash management.
- They force managers to look ahead continuously.
- When conditions are subject to change, comparing actual results with a rolling budget is more realistic than comparing actual results with a fixed annual budget.

Disadvantages

- Preparing new budgets regularly is time-consuming.
- It can be difficult to communicate frequent budget changes.

Rolling budgets in practice

For years, senior managers at REL Consultancy Group handled budgeting and revenue forecasting much the way most other companies do. As year-end approached, they would evaluate performance, set sales targets for the upcoming year and then work to see that everyone met or exceeded the goals.

Unfortunately, the process didn't always produce the intended results.

'Invariably,' recalls Stephan Payne, president of the London-based global management consulting firm, 'one of the account directors would land a couple of good clients early in the year and make his annual budget well before the year closed. More often than not, he'd then take his foot off the gas and coast.' To make the budgeting process more timely and relevant, the firm embraced a more complex, albeit intuitive, approach to financial forecasting – the **rolling budget**. Rather than creating an annual financial forecast that remains static for the year, he and his colleagues now produce an 18-month budget and then update projections every month – in effect, recalculating the whole budget. As the firm's actual sales figures come in each month, directors plug them into their forecasting model in place of what they had projected, then roll the budget forward one more month.

No more free rides

The result: an always-current financial forecast that reflects not only the company's most recent monthly results but also any material changes to its business outlook or the economy. In addition, it provides fewer opportunities for account directors to ride the coattails of past performance.

'Now, even the guy who booked a million dollars' worth of business in one month can't sit still because 30 days later, we're going to have an entirely new forecast,' Payne says, adding, 'It's a dynamic process that makes a lot more sense.'

Although traditional 1-year budgets are still the norm at most companies large and small, many accountants argue that rolling budgets can be a far more useful tool. Unlike static budgets, they encourage managers to react more quickly to changing economic developments or business conditions. They discourage what is too often a fruitless focus on the past ('Why didn't we meet our numbers?') in favour of a realistic focus on the future. And they produce forecasts that, over the near term, are never more than a few months old, even when companies are rolling them forward on a quarterly basis – the more common approach – rather than REL's monthly basis.

'A static budget simply doesn't reflect the pace of business today,' says Jill Langerman, CPA, president and CFO of the accounting firm Fair, Anderson & Langerman in Las Vegas. 'If at mid-year you add a new product to your line-up, you want to calculate the costs and profit margins associated with that and reflected those calculations in your budget OSC to reflect the impact that it will have on your remaining product lines. That way, you can set an accurate performance target and make informed decisions about whether you're now free to invest more in the remaining product lines or perhaps add a new line. If you're not incorporating these new analyses into your budget, it becomes a rather useless document.'

Implementing rolling budgets doesn't necessarily require any fundamental change in the way a company has been doing its budgets – except, of course, it no longer does the job just once a year. However, companies that decide to step up to rolling budgets may want to take advantage of the decision to make a change and consider what else they can do to improve the process. After all, if a company can get everyone on board to make such a fundamental change, a further nudge to make the process more effective and efficient in other ways may be possible, too.

Taken from:

'Budgets on a roll: recalculating a business's outlook several times a year'

Randy Myers, Journal of Accountancy, December 2001. © 2001. Reprinted with permission of AICPA

7 Alternative approaches to budgeting

Incremental budgeting

The traditional approach to budgeting is to take the previous year's budget and to add on a percentage to allow for inflation and other cost increases. In addition there may be other adjustments for specific items such as an extra worker or extra machine.

Further explanation

- Fairly small changes are made to the current year's budget. For example, adjustments might be made to allow for a planned increase or decline in sales volume, and for inflationary increases in sales prices and costs.
- A check is then made to ensure that the budget produced in this way meets the performance targets of the organisation. For example, the company might have a target of keeping the operating costs to sales ratio at less than, say, 60%.

In a static business environment, incremental budgets are little more than 'last year's budget plus a percentage amount for inflation'.

Advantages and disadvantages of incremental budgeting

Advantages	Disadvantages
• simple	• backward looking
• cheap	• builds on previous inefficiencies
• suitable in stable environments	• doesn't remove waste/inefficiencies
• most practical	• unsuited to changing environments
	• targets are too easy
	• activities are not justified
	• encourages over-spending

Further explanation

The advantage of incremental budgeting is that it is an easy, quick and cheap method of preparing budgets for what may be many cost centres in a large organisation. However, the traditional approach has severe disadvantages.

Advantages

(1) It is a simple, low-cost budgeting system.

(2) If the business is fairly stable, the budgets produced by this method might be sufficient for management needs.

(3) There are some items of cost where an incremental budgeting approach is probably the most practical. For example, the easiest way of budgeting telephone expenses for the next year might be to base the planned cost on the previous year's budget (or possibly actual costs in the current year).

Disadvantages

(1) The main disadvantage is that it assumes that all current activities should be continued at the current level of operations and with the same allocation of resources.

(2) It is backward-looking in nature, since next year's budget is based on what has happened in the past. In a dynamic and rapidly-changing business environment, this approach to planning is inappropriate.

(3) It is often seen as a desk-bound planning process, driven by the accounts department.

(4) The performance targets in the budget are often unchallenging, based on past performance. Incremental budgeting does not encourage managers to look for ways of improving the business.

(5) When there are excessive costs in the budget for the current year, these will be continued in the future. Incremental budgeting is not a planning system for cutting out waste and overspending.

(6) Consideration will not be given to the justification for each activity. They will be undertaken merely because they were undertaken the previous year.

(7) Different ways of achieving the objective will not be examined.

(8) Past inefficiencies will be continued.

(9) Managers know that if they fail to spend their budget, it is likely to be reduced next period. They therefore try to spend the whole budget, regardless of whether or not the expenditure is justified.

ZBB is one method which may be used to overcome these problems.

Zero-based budgeting

ZBB may be defined as:

'A method of budgeting whereby all activities are re-evaluated each time a budget is formulated. Each functional budget starts with the assumptions that the function does not exist, and is at zero cost. Increments of costs are compared with increments of benefits, culminating in the planned maximum benefit for a given budgeted cost.'

Zero-based budgeting (ZBB) is a radical alternative to incremental budgeting. In ZBB, all activities and costs are budgeted from scratch (a zero base). For every activity, managers look at its costs and its purpose, and consider whether there are alternative ways of doing it. Inessential activities and costs are identified and eliminated, by removing them from next year's budget.

ZBB in practice

Implementing ZBB

All activities are subjected to the most basic scrutiny, and answers sought to such fundamental question as:

(a) Should the activity be undertaken at all?

(b) If the company undertakes the activity, how much should be done and how well should it be done (e.g. should an economy or a deluxe service level be provided)?

(c) How should the activity be performed – in-house or subcontracted?

(d) How much would the various alternative levels of service and provision cost?

In order to answer these questions, all existing and potential organisational activities must be described and evaluated in a series of 'decision packages', giving the following four-step process to a ZBB exercise:

(1) Determine the activities that are to be used as the object of decision packages – the provision of home support for the elderly or provision of catering facilities for the workforce, for example – and identify the manager responsible for each activity.

(2) Request the managers identified in (1) above to prepare a number of alternative decision packages for those individual activities for which they are responsible. (At least three packages are normally requested: one that sets out what could be delivered with funding maintained at the current level; one for a reduced level of funding, e.g. 80% of the current level; and one for an enhanced level of funding, e.g. 120% of the current level.)

(3) Rank the decision packages in order of their contribution towards the organisation's objectives.

(4) Fund the decision packages according to the ranking established under (3) above until the available funds are exhausted.

Adoption of ZBB

ZBB has been adopted more widely in the public sector than the private, although examples of organisations regularly adopting a full ZBB approach are rare. Full-scale ZBB is so resource-intensive that critics claim that its advantages are outweighed by its implementation costs. However, it is not necessary to apply ZBB to the whole of an organisation; benefits can be gained from its application to specific areas. For example, in the public sector, a decision could be made regarding the overall size of the childcare budget, and ZBB could be applied to allocate resources within that particular field; similarly, in a business organisation, ZBB could be applied to individual divisions on a rotational basis. This selective application ensures that a thorough reappraisal of activities is undertaken regularly, but not so regularly that the process itself is a major drain on organisational resources.

Notwithstanding the criticisms, the main plank of the ZBB approach – the rejection of past budgets as a planning baseline – is being increasingly accepted.

Illustration 2

A company is conducting a ZBB exercise, and a decision package is being prepared for its materials handling operations.

- The manager responsible has identified a base package for the minimum resources needed to perform the materials handling function. This is to have a team of five workers and a supervisor, operating without any labour-saving machinery. The estimated annual cost of wages and salaries, with overtime, would be $375,000.
- In addition to the base package, the manager has identified an incremental package. The company could lease two fork lift trucks at a cost of $20,000 each year. This would provide a better system because materials could be stacked higher and moved more quickly. Health and safety risks for the workers would be reduced, and there would be savings of $5,000 each year in overtime payments.
- Another incremental package has been prepared, in which the company introduces new computer software to plan materials handling schedules. The cost of buying and implementing the system would be $60,000, but the benefits are expected to be improvements in efficiency that reduce production downtime and result in savings of $10,000 each year in overtime payments.

The base package would be considered essential, and so given a high priority. The two incremental packages should be evaluated and ranked. Here, the fork lift trucks option might be ranked more highly than the computer software.

In the budget that is eventually decided by senior management, the fork lift truck package might be approved, but the computer software package rejected on the grounds that there are other demands for resources with a higher priority.

Advantages and disadvantages of ZBB

Advantages

- creates an environment that accepts change
- better focus on goals
- forward looking
- improves resource utilisation
- better performance measures
- focuses managers to examine activities

Disadvantages

- time-consuming
- expensive
- encourages short-termism
- management may lose focus on the true cost drivers
- managers require new budgeting skills
- can result in arbitrary decisions

Further explanation

Advantages

- It helps to create an organisational environment where change is accepted.
- It helps management to focus on company objectives and goals. It moves budgeting away from number-crunching, towards analysis and decision-making.
- It focuses on the future rather than on the past.
- It helps to identify inefficient operations and wasteful spending, which can be eliminated.
- Establishing priorities for activities provides a framework for the optimum utilisation of resources. This assists decision-makers when some expenditures are discretionary.
- It establishes a measure of performance for each decision package. This measure can be used to monitor actual performance and compare actual with budget.

- It involves managers in the budgeting process. Unlike incremental budgeting, it is not a desk-bound exercise driven by the accounting department. Preparation of the decision packages will normally require the involvement of many employees, and thus provides an opportunity for their view to be considered. This involvement may produce useful ideas, and promote job satisfaction among the wider staff.

Disadvantages

- It is a time-consuming exercise. It is unlikely that an organisation will have the time to carry out a ZBB exercise every year.
- There is a temptation to concentrate on short-term cost savings at the expense of longer-term benefits.
- It might not be useful for budgeting for production activities or service provision, where costs and efficiency levels should be well-controlled, so that budgets can be prepared from forecasts of activity volume and unit costs.
- In applying ZBB, 'activities' may continue to be identified with traditional functional departments, rather than cross-functional activities, and thus distract the attention of management from the real cost-reduction issues. For example, it could be argued that the costs incurred in a warranty department are largely a function of the reliability of products, which itself is a function of actions and decisions taken elsewhere. If the warranty department is treated as an activity under ZBB, the focus of the decision packages is likely to be on providing the same level of customer service at reduced cost, or enhancing the level of customer service for the same cost. The main driver behind the department's cost – product reliability – may remain unaddressed in ZBB, as it is with the blanket cut approach.
- It might require skills from management that the management team does not possess.
- The ranking process can be difficult, since widely-differing activities cannot be compared on quantitative measures alone. For example, it might be difficult to rank proposals for spending on better service quality, improvements in safety in the work place or more spending on new product development.

Activity-based budgeting

Introduction

In a manufacturing business, budgeting for direct costs is relatively straightforward. The costs of direct materials and direct labour are assumed to vary with production, and once production levels have been estimated, budgeting the direct costs of production is a matter of simple arithmetic.

Budgeting for overhead costs is not so simple. Traditionally, there has been a tendency to take an incremental approach in budgeting for overhead costs, and prepare next year's budget by simply adding a percentage to the current year budget, to allow for inflation. Zero-based budgeting is one method of bringing greater discipline to the process of budgeting for overhead activities and costs. Another method is activity-based budgeting.

As its name should suggest, activity-based budgeting (ABB) takes a similar approach to activity-based costing. ABB is defined as: 'a method of budgeting based on an activity framework and utilising cost driver data in the budget-setting and variance feedback processes' (CIMA *Official Terminology*).

Whereas ZBB is based on budgets (decision packages) prepared by responsibility centre managers, ABB is based on budgeting for activities.

In its simplest form, ABB is simply about using costs determined via ABC to prepare budgets for each activity. The basic approach of ABB is to budget the costs for each cost pool or activity as follows:

(1) The cost driver for each activity is identified. A forecast is made of the number of units of the cost driver that will occur in the budget period.

(2) Given the estimate of the activity level for the cost driver, the activity cost is estimated. Where appropriate, a cost per unit of activity, known as the **cost driver rate**, is calculated.

(There will also be some general overhead costs that are not activity-related, such as factory rental costs and the salary cost of the factory manager. General overhead costs are budgeted separately.)

e.g

Illustration 3

Consider the following example:

Septran operates two rail services. The Northern line operated for 20,000 hours last year. It had 200 full time staff. The Southern line operated for 39,000 hours last year. It had 300 full time staff. Eight train staff are needed for each journey on both lines. The total overhead for indirect wages was $39m.

Next year the government want to promote greater use of train services in the north of the country. Septran expect this to result in approximately 10,000 more journey hours for the Northern line. Because of transfers between services and other knock on effects, this is also likely to result in an extra 5,000 journey hours for the Southern line.

The company want to use an ABB approach to budget for the indirect wages cost next year.

Step 1

Firstly, the company need to determine how costs should be allocated to each service (each service effectively becomes a 'cost pool'). This might be the number of journeys or the number of full time employees. For indirect wages Septran believe that the number of full time staff would be the most appropriate way to allocate costs to each cost pool.

Step 2

The total overheads are then allocated to each cost pool on this basis.

	Northern line	**Southern line**	**Total**
	$m	$m	$m
Indirect wage cost – split 200:300	15.6	23.4	39.0

Step 3

The company then need to determine the cost driver. Semptrap believe that the cost is driven by the number of journey hours in operation.

	Northern line	**Southern line**
Indirect wage cost – split 20:30	$15.6m	$23.4m
Number of journey hours	20,000	39,000
Cost driver rate	$780 per journey hour	$600 per journey hour

Step 4

These established cost drivers will then be used to prepare the budget for next year:

	Northern line	Southern line
Cost driver rate	$780 per journey hour	$600 per journey hour
Budgeted level of activity	30,000 hours	44,000 hours
Budgeted indirect wage cost	$23.4m	$26.4m

The total budgeted indirect wage cost for next year will be $49.8m.

Advantages and disadvantages of ABB

Advantages

- useful when overheads are significant
- better cost control
- better information for management
- useful for TQM environments

Disadvantages

- expensive to implement
- only suited to ABC users

Further explanation

The advantages of ABB are similar to those provided by activity-based costing.

- It draws attention to the costs of 'overhead activities'. This can be important where overhead costs are a large proportion of total operating costs.
- It provides information for the control of activity costs, by assuming that they are variable, at least in the longer term.
- It provides a useful basis for monitoring and controlling overhead costs, by drawing management attention to the actual costs of activities and comparing actual costs with what the activities were expected to cost.
- It also provides useful control information by emphasising that activity costs might be controllable if the activity volume can be controlled.

- ABB can provide useful information for a total quality management (TQM) programme, by relating the cost of an activity to the level of service provided (for example, stores requisitions processed) – Do the user departments feel they are getting a cost-effective service?

The system however does have some disadvantages:

- It is an expensive system to implement. New information systems are required and managers need to be trained in its use.
- It will also rely on the use of activity based costing (ABC) as the standard costing system.

8 Chapter summary

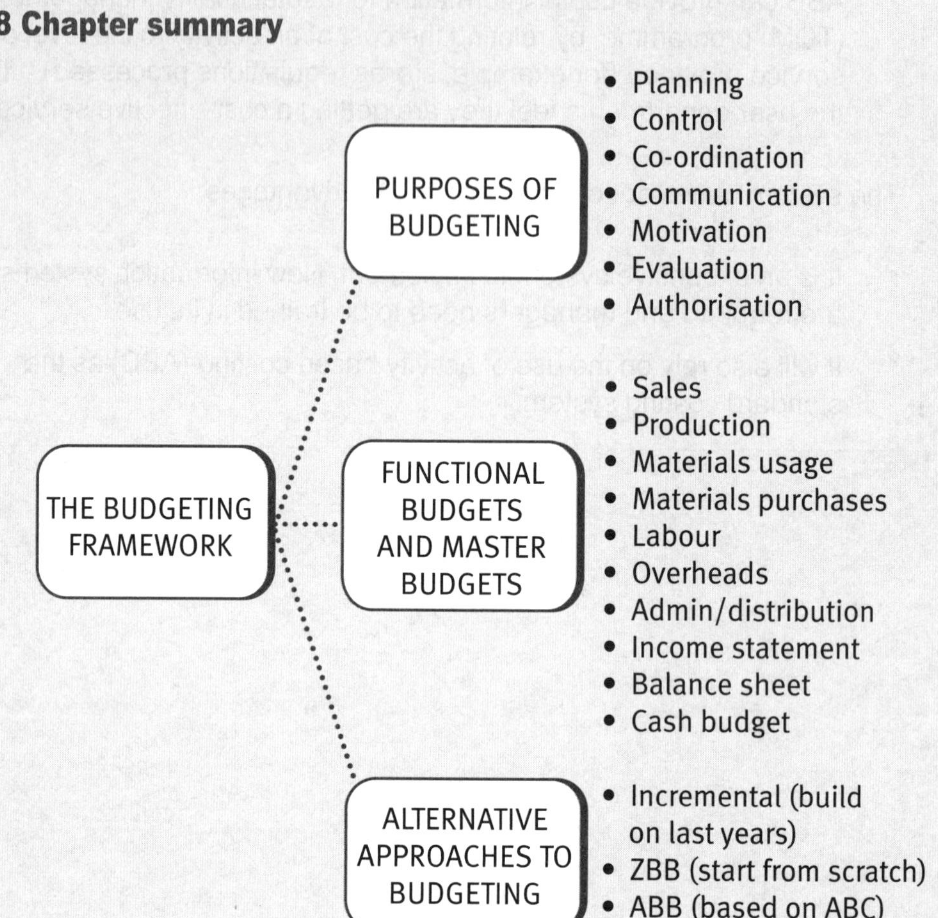

9 Practice questions

Test your understanding 1

Hopper manufactures two products, X and Y. Budgeted information for the next financial year is as follows:

	Product X	*Product Y*
	Units	*Units*
Budgeted sales	4,000	6,000
Budgeted closing inventory	500	300
Opening inventory	200	400
Direct materials requirements	*Kg per unit*	*Kg per unit*
Material DM1	1.2	2.0
Material DM2	0.8	–

	Material DM1	*Material DM2*
	Kg	*Kg*
Budgeted closing inventory	1,000	200
Opening inventory	3,000	600
Standard price per kg	$0.80	$0.50

Required:

In the boxes below, enter the purchase quantities and cost for both materials from a materials purchases budget for the year.

	Material DM1	*Material DM2*
Budgeted purchase quantities (kgs)		
Budgeted cost of purchases ($)		

Test your understanding 2

Scenario

You are employed as a management accountant by SRW. The company makes two similar products, the Alpha and Beta, and operates a five-day week for both production and sales. Both products use the same material and labour, but Beta requires more labour and materials than the Alpha. The company divides its year into five-week periods for budgetary purposes. One of your responsibilities is to prepare budgets for the Alpha and the Beta.

You are given the following information to help you prepare the production and resource budgets for period 8.

Forecast sales volumes (units)	*Days in period*	*Alpha*	*Beta*
Period 8	25	8,460	9,025
Period 9	25	10,575	12,635

Finished inventories

- There will be 1,692 Alphas and 3,610 Betas in finished inventory at the beginning of Period 8.
- The closing inventory of both Alphas and Betas depends on the forecast sales in period 9.
- Period 8's closing inventory of Alphas must equal 5 days sales of Alphas in period 9.
- Period 8's closing inventory of Betas must equal 10 days sales of Betas in period 9.
- The first-in-first-out inventory valuation method is used to value closing inventory.

Production and failure rates

- 10% of Alpha finished production and 5% of Beta finished production is faulty and has to be destroyed. This faulty production has no value.
- The faulty production arises from the production technology and is only discovered on completion. The cost of faulty production is part of the cost producing fault-free Alphas and Betas.

Materials

- Each Alpha produced requires 20 kg of materials and each Beta produced requires 40 kg of materials.
- The opening inventory of materials at the beginning of period 8 is 64,800 kg.
- The closing inventory of materials at the end of period 8 must be 52,600 kg.
- The material costs 50c per kilogram.

Labour

- Each Alpha produced requires two labour hours and each Beta produced requires three labour hours.
- SRW employs 300 production staff who work 35 hours per five-day week.
- The hourly rate per employee is $10 and if any overtime is required the overtime premium is $3 per employee per hour of overtime.
- Any overtime premium is charged to factory overheads and not to the cost of production.

Factory overheads

- Budgeted overheads are charged to production on the basis of labour hours.
- For Alpha, the budgeted factory overheads are $62 per labour hour. For Beta, they are $58 per labour hour.

Tasks:

(a) Prepare the following information for Period 8:

(i) Production budgets for Alpha and Beta

(ii) Material purchases budget in kilograms and $

(iii) Budgeted labour hours to be worked, including any overtime hours

(iv) Labour cost budget

(v) Total (full) cost of production budget for Alpha and Beta

(vi) Full cost of GOOD production per unit for Alpha and Beta

(Time allowed for part a: 30 minutes)

The Sales Director has just informed you that the Alpha sales in period 8 will be 2,000 units more than originally forecast. You are told the following:

- SRW production employees can work up to a maximum of 5,000 overtime hours in any five-week period.
- The material used in Alpha and Beta production can only be made by one company and SRW is the only user of the material. Currently there is a shortage of the material and the maximum additional material that can be obtained is 34,000 kg.
- The demand for Beta in period 8 will remain at 9,025 units.

(b) (i) Prepare calculations to show whether it is the material or labour hours that limits the extra production of Alpha in period 8.

(ii) Prepare a revised production budget in units for Alphas in period 8.

(iii) Calculate the shortfall in the planned extra sales of Alpha caused by the limit in extra production.

(iv) Suggest three ways how this shortfall may be overcome.

(Time allowed for part b: 30 minutes)

Test your understanding 3

A manufacturing business makes and sells widgets. Each widget requires two units of raw materials, which cost $3 each. Production and sales quantities of widgets each month are as follows:

Month	**Sales and production units**
December (actual)	50,000
January (budget)	55,000
February (budget)	60,000
March (budget)	65,000

In the past, the business has maintained its inventories of raw materials at 100,000 units. However, it plans to increase raw material inventories to 110,000 units at the end of January and 120,000 units at the end of February. The business takes one month's credit from its suppliers.

Required:

In the following boxes, enter the forecast payments to suppliers each month, for raw material purchases.

	January	February	March
	$	$	$
Payment to suppliers			

Test your understanding 4

Twenty per cent of a company's sales are made to cash customers. The records show that the credit customers settle their bills as follows:

Paid in the month following the sale 60%

Paid two months after the sale 38%

Bad debts 2%

Credit customers paying in the month following the sale receive a 3% discount.

Budgeted sales for the forthcoming period are as follows:

January	*February*	*March*
$20,400	$29,500	$26,800

Required:

Calculate the amount to be shown as receipts from sales in the cash budget for March.

Test your understanding 5

Scenario

A company makes and sells two products, X and Y, for which the budgeted sales price and variable costs per unit are:

	Product X	*Product Y*
Variable cost	$2	$4
Sales price	$5	$8

Budgeted fixed costs are $140,000. Budgeted sales are 30,000 units of Product X and 15,000 units of Product Y.

Tasks

(a) Calculate the budgeted profit.

(b) Calculate how profit would be affected in each of the following separate circumstances:

(i) if the variable cost of Product Y were 25% higher than expected

(ii) if sales of Product X were 10% less than budgeted

(iii) if sales of Product X were 5% less than budgeted and unit variable costs of X were 10% higher than budgeted

(iv) if total sales revenue is the same as in the original budget, but the sales mix (by revenue) is 50% of Product X and 50% of Product Y.

(Time allowed: 20 minutes)

Test your understanding 6

Scenario

For a number of years, the research division of Z has produced its annual budget (for new and continuing projects) using incremental budgeting techniques. The company is now under new management and the annual budget for 20X4 is to be prepared using zero based budgeting techniques.

Tasks:

(a) Explain the differences between incremental and zero based budgeting techniques.

(b) Explain how Z could operate a zero based budgeting system for its research projects.

The operating divisions of Z have in the past always used a traditional approach to analysing costs into their fixed and variable components. A single measure of activity was used which, for simplicity, was the number of units produced. The new management does not accept that such a simplistic approach is appropriate for budgeting in the modern environment and has requested that the managers adopt an activity-based approach to their budgets for 20X4.

Tasks:

(c) (i) Briefly explain activity-based budgeting (ABB).

(ii) Explain how activity-based budgeting would be implemented by the operating divisions of Z.

(Time allowed: 40 minutes)

Test your understanding 7

AW Inc produces two products, A and C. In the last year (20X4) it produced 640 units of A and 350 units of C incurring costs of $672,000. Analysis of the costs has shown that 75% of the total costs are variable. 60% of these variable costs vary in line with the number of A produced and the remainder with the number of C.

The budget for the year 20X5 is now being prepared using an incremental budgeting approach. The following additional information is available for 20X5:

- All costs will be 4% higher than the average paid in 20X4.
- Efficiency levels will remain unchanged.
- Expected output of A is 750 units and of C is 340 units.

Required:

Calculate the budgeted total variable cost of products A and C for the full year 20X5?

(Time allowed: 10 minutes)

Test your understanding 8

Identify which of the following budgets is likely to be the most time consuming to construct and manage?

A A periodic budget based on incremental budgeting principles

B A periodic budget based on ZBB principles

C A rolling budget based on incremental budgeting principles

D A rolling budget based on ZBB principles

Test your understanding 9

Identify which of the following statements is correct regarding the benefits to be gained from using ABB?

A If there is much inefficiency within the operations of a business then ABB will identify and remove these areas of inefficiency

B In a highly direct labour intensive manufacturing process, an ABB approach will assist management in budgeting for the majority of the production costs

C In an organisation currently operating efficiently, where the next period will be relatively unchanged from the current one, then ABB will make the budgeting process simpler and quicker

D If an organisation produces many different types of output using different combinations of activities then ABB can provide more meaningful information for budgetary control

Test your understanding 10

Branch makes and sells two products, P and Q. The following budget has been prepared:

	Product P	*Product Q*
Sales price per unit	€3	€6
Variable cost per unit	€2	€3

Budgeted fixed costs are €140,000. Budgeted sales are 20,000 units of Product P and 50,000 units of Product Q.

Tasks:

(a) Calculate the budgeted profit.

(b) Calculate by how much the profit would be reduced if the variable cost of Product P were 15% higher than budgeted and the variable cost of Product Q were 10% higher than budgeted.

(c) Calculate by how much the profit would be reduced or increased if total sales revenue is the same as in the original budget, but the sales mix (by revenue) is one-third Product P and two-thirds Product Q.

(Time allowed: 15 minutes)

Test your understanding answers

Example 1

(a) **Production budget**

	Product 1	**Product 2**	**Product 3**
	units	units	units
Sales	3,000	4,500	3,000
+ Cl. inventory	200	300	300
	3,200	4,800	3,300
– Op. inventory	500	700	500
Production qty	2,700	4,100	2,800

(b) **Material usage budget**

	Material M1	**Material M2**	**Material M3**
	Kg	Kg	Kg
Production requirement			
2,700 Product 1	5,400	8,100	16,200
4,100 Product 2	12,300	12,300	8,200
2,800 Product 3	11,200	11,200	11,200
Usage qty	28,900	31,600	35,600

(c) **Material purchases budget**

	Material M1	**Material M2**	**Material M3**
	Kg	Kg	Kg
Usage qty	28,900	31,600	35,600
+ Cl. inventory	2,200	1,300	2,000
	31,100	32,900	37,600
– Op. inventory	4,300	3,700	4,400
Purchase qty	26,800	29,200	33,200
	× $1.21	× $3.30	× $2.75
	$32,428	$96,360	$91,300

(d) **Labour budget**

	Skilled	**Semi-skilled**
	hrs	hrs
Production requirement		
2,700 Product 1	8,100	8,100
4,100 Product 2	4,100	12,300
2,800 Product 3	8,400	11,200
Usage qty	20,600	31,600
	× $6/hr	× $4/hr
	$123,600	$126,400

Example 2

Cash from:		$
April sales:	10% × $5,000	500
March sales:	40% × $4,000	1,600
February sales:	45% × $8,000	3,600
		5,700

Example 3

Interpretation of the cash budget

The company will be overdrawn throughout the three-month period, therefore it is essential that it should have access to borrowings to cover the shortfall. The bank might already have agreed an overdraft facility, but this should be at least $16,650 and ideally higher, to allow for the possibility that the actual cash flows will be even worse than budgeted.

The business may decide to delay the purchase of the capital equipment for one month in order to allow the cash position to move to a positive one before the investment is made. Alternatively, an extension of the overdraft facilities may be arranged for the appropriate period.

If it is decided that overdraft facilities are to be arranged, it is important that due account is taken of the timing of the receipts and payments within each month.

For example, all of the payments in January may be made at the beginning of the month but receipts may not be expected until nearer the end of the month. The cash deficit could then be considerably greater than it appears from looking only at the month-end balance.

If the worst possible situation arose, the overdrawn balance during January could become as large as $5,000 (Opening balance) minus $66,000 (January payments) = $71,000 before the receipts begin to arise. If management had used the month-end balances as a guide to the overdraft requirement during the period then they would not have arranged a large enough overdraft facility with the bank. It is important, therefore, that they look in detail at the information revealed by the cash budget, and not simply at the closing cash balances.

Test your understanding 1

Materials purchases budget

	Material DM1	*Material DM2*
	Kg	*Kg*
To make 4,300 units of X	5,160	3,440
To make 5,900 units of Y	11,800	0
Required for production	16,960	3,440
Budgeted closing inventory	1,000	200
	17,960	3,640
Opening inventory	3,000	600
Budgeted purchase quantities	14,960	3,040
Standard price per kg	$0.80	$0.50
Budgeted cost of purchases	$11,968	$1,520

Test your understanding 2

(a) (i) **Production budget (Period 8)**

	Alpha	*Beta*
Sales budget	8,460 units	9,025 units
Add: Closing inventory	2,115 units (W1)	5,054 units (W1)
Less: Opening inventory	(1,692 units)	(3,610 units)
Good production	8,883 units	10,469 units
Wastage	987 units	551 units
Total production	9,870 units	11,020 units

Working 1 – Closing inventory

Alpha

$$\frac{5}{25} \times 10{,}575 = 2{,}115 \text{ units}$$

Beta

$$\frac{10}{25} \times 12{,}635 = 5{,}054 \text{ units}$$

(ii) **Materials purchases**

	Kilograms	$
Alpha 9,870 × 20 kgs	197,400	98,700
Beta 11,020 × 40 kgs	440,800	220,400
	638,200	319,100
Add: Closing	52,600	
Less: Opening	(64,800)	
Purchases	626,000	313,000

(iii) **Labour hours**

	Hours
Alpha 9,870 × 2	19,740
Beta 11,020 × 3	33,060
	52,800
Normal hours 300 × 35 × 5 weeks	52,500
Overtime hours	300

(iv) **Labour cost budget**

Direct labour cost	52,800 × $10 =	$528,000
Overtime premium (OH)	300 × $3 =	$900

(v) **Full production cost**

	Alpha	*Beta*
Direct material	$98,700	$220,400
Direct labour	$197,400	$330,600
Overhead: 19,740 hours × $62	$1,223,880	
Overhead: 33,060 hours × $58		$1,917,480
	$1,519,980	$2,468,480
÷ Good units	÷ 8,883	÷ 10,469
Full cost per unit	$171.11	$235.79

(b) (i)

Increase in demand		2,000 units
		÷ 0.90
Therefore, increase in production		2,223 units
Hours required	2,223 units × 2 hours	4,446 hours
Overtime hours available	(5,000 hours – 300 hours)	4,700 hours

Therefore, labour hours are not a scarce resource.

Kilograms of material required	2,223 units × 20 kgs =	44,460 kgs
Available		34,000 kgs

Therefore, material is a scarce resource.

(ii)

Allowable increase in production: $\frac{34{,}000 \text{ hours}}{20}$ = 1,700 units

New production budget: 9,870 + 1,700 = 11,570 units

(iii) New production budget: = 11,570 units

The extra production = new production – existing production = 11,570 – =9,87z 1,700 units

Good units produced: (1,700 × 90%) = 1,530 units

Shortfall (when compared to the increase in demand of 2,000 units) = 470 units

(iv)
- Reduce planned closing inventory levels
- Improve wastage rate
- Reduce production of Beta

Test your understanding 3

When inventories of raw materials are increased, the quantities purchased will exceed the quantities consumed in the period.

Figures for December are shown because December purchases will be paid for in January, which is in the budget period.

Quantity of raw material purchased in units:

		Material (@ 2 units per widget)			
	Units of widgets produced	**December**	**January**	**February**	**March**
	Units	Units	Units	Units	Units
December	50,000	100,000			
January	55,000		110,000		
February	60,000			120,000	
March	65,000				130,000
Increase in inventories		–	10,000	10,000	–
Total purchase quantities		100,000	120,000	130,000	130,000
At $3 per unit		300,000	360,000	390,000	390,000

Having established the purchases each month, we can go on to budget the amount of cash payments to suppliers each month. Here, the business will take one month's credit.

	January	February	March
	$	$	$
Payment to suppliers	300,000	360,000	390,000

At the end of March, there will be payables of $390,000 for raw materials purchased, which will be paid in April.

Test your understanding 4

March sales = 20% for cash ($26,800 × 0.2)	5,360
February credit sales = 80% × 60% received less 3% discount ($29,500 × 0.6 × 0.97)	13,735.20
January credit sales = 80% × 38% received ($20,400 × 0.38)	6,201.60
	25,296.80

Test your understanding 5

The original budget and 'what if' budgets can be constructed quickly using a marginal costing approach.

	Product X	*Product Y*	*Total*
	$	$	$
Budgeted sales	150,000	120,000	270,000
Variable costs	60,000	60,000	120,000
Contribution	90,000	60,000	150,000
Fixed costs			140,000
Budgeted profit			10,000

(b) (i)	Product X		Product Y	Total
	$		$	$
Budgeted sales	150,000		120,000	270,000
Variable costs	60,000	(+25%)	75,000	135,000
Contribution	90,000		45,000	135,000
Fixed costs				140,000
Budgeted loss				(5,000)

(ii)		Product X	Product Y	Total
		$	$	$
Budgeted sales	(–10%)	135,000	120,000	255,000
Variable costs	(–10%)	54,000	60,000	114,000
Contribution		81,000	60,000	141,000
Fixed costs				140,000
Budgeted profit				1,000

(iii)		Product X	Product Y	Total
Sales units		28,500	15,000	
		$	$	$
Budgeted sales	(at $5)	142,500	120,000	262,500
Variable costs	(at $2.20)	62,700	60,000	122,700
Contribution		79,800	60,000	139,800
Fixed costs				140,000
Budgeted loss				(200)

(iv)

		Product X		Product Y	**Total**
Sales units	(135,000/5)	27,000	(135,000/8)	16,875	
		$		$	$
Budgeted sales	(50%)	135,000	(50%)	135,000	270,000
Variable costs	(at $2)	54,000	(at $4)	67,500	121,500
Contribution		81,000		67,500	148,500
Fixed costs					140,000
Budgeted profit					8,500

In practice, budget models are usually much more detailed and complex, but 'what if' analysis can be carried out simply and quickly.

In the example above, the 'what if' scenarios show that profit might be less than expected if actual results are less favourable than the assumptions and forecasts in the budget. If any of these results are unacceptable, management would need to consider alternative budget strategies for improving budgeted performance or reducing the risk.

Test your understanding 6

(a) An incremental budget starts off with last year's budget or last year's actual results and adds on a certain percentage to take account of expected inflation and/or any expected changes in the level of activity. It is a very simple, quick and cheap budget to produce, but it does not promote a questioning attitude. Activities are undertaken without thought. They are simply incorporated into the next budget because they were in the last budget and nobody has given any thought as to whether the activity is still really worthwhile.

With ZBB, each manager sets out what he or she wishes to accomplish over the forthcoming period. For each activity they want to undertake, they look at different ways of achieving the objective and they look at providing the service at different levels. They estimate the costs and benefits and the activity only takes place if the benefits exceed the costs. Also once all the activities have been evaluated, they can be ranked against each other and the company's resources directed to the best activities.

(b) The managers/researchers responsible for each project should decide which projects they wish to undertake in the forthcoming period. These projects will be a mixture of continued projects and new projects. For the projects which have already been started and which the managers want to continue in the next period, we should ignore any cash flows already incurred (they are sunk costs), and we should only look at future costs and benefits. Similarly, for the new projects we should only look at the future costs and benefits. Different ways of achieving the same research goals should also be investigated and the projects should only go ahead if the benefit exceeds the cost. Once all the potential projects have been evaluated if there are insufficient funds to undertake all the worthwhile projects, then the funds should be allocated to the best projects on the basis of a cost-benefit analysis.

ZBB is usually of a highly subjective nature. (The costs are often reasonably certain, but usually a lot of uncertainty is attached to the estimated benefits.) This will be even truer of a research division where the researchers may have their own pet projects which they are unable to view in an objective light.

(c) (i) Activity based budgeting is where the budget is based upon a number of different levels of activity, i.e. on a number of different cost drivers, rather than being based on just one level of activity such as machine hours or output in units.

The activity based budget will be based upon the number of units of the cost driver multiplied by the cost per unit of cost driver. The cost driver is that factor which actually causes the cost and therefore should lead to a more accurate budget as the budgeted cost will be based on the thing that should influence that cost. The alternative is to use absorption costing and assume that all overheads vary with output or machine hours or labour hours or that they are fixed.

(ii) Z may employ an outside specialist such as a management consultant who will investigate the business and determine what activities the business undertakes during the course of its operations.

The consultant will discuss matters with the staff and the process will normally be time consuming. For each activity, efforts will be made to determine the factor which is most closely related to the costs of that activity, i.e. the cost driver. The investigation may bring to light non-value-added activities which can then be eliminated. It should improve the understanding of all those involved as to the true relationship between cost and level of activity.

Managers would then estimate the expected incidence of their cost drivers and multiply by the budgeted cost driver rate to get the budget for the forthcoming period. ABB would be more complicated than a traditional budget and the overheads would be broken down into many activities such as set-up costs, materials, handling costs, etc rather than expenses such as rent, heating, depreciation, etc.

With ABB the majority of the overhead costs would be perceived as variable rather than fixed. Of course it is not necessary to employ an outside consultant. The company may feel that they have their own managers with sufficient skills and time to undertake the exercise.

Test your understanding 7

	Total variable cost	Variable cost per unit
20X4:		
Product A	$672,000 × 75% × 60% = $302,000	$302,000 ÷ 640 units = $472.50
Product C	$672,000 × 75% × 40% = $201,600	$201,600 ÷ 350 units = $576
20X5:		
Product A	$472.50 × 1.04 × 750 units = $368,550	n/a
Product C	$576 × 1.04 × 340 units = $203,674	n/a

Test your understanding 8

D

Rolling budgets are more time consuming to manage than periodic budgets as they must be update more regularly. ZBB is a more expensive system to manage than incremental budgeting as every item must be fully justified and investigated before being included in the budget.

Test your understanding 9

D

Situation A would be best suited by implementing Zero Base Budgeting.

Situation B does not require ABB since it has relatively low overheads.

Situation C would be suitable for incremental budgeting. ABB will certainly not be quicker.

Test your understanding 10

Part (a)

The budgeted profit is €30,000

	Product P	*Product Q*	*Total*
	€	€	€
Budgeted sales	60,000	300,000	360,000
Variable costs	40,000	150,000	190,000
Contribution	20,000	150,000	170,000
Fixed costs			140,000
Budgeted profit			30,000

Part (b)

The profit would fall by €21,000.

	Product P	*Product Q*	*Total*
	€	€	€
Budgeted sales	60,000	300,000	360,000
Variable costs (+15%)	46,000 (+10%)	165,000	211,000
Contribution	14,000	135,000	149,000
Fixed costs			140,000
Revised profit			9,000
Original budgeted profit			30,000
Reduction in profit			21,000

Part (c)

The profit would fall by €10,000.

	Product P	*Product Q*	*Total*
Sales units	40,000	40,000	
	€	€	€
Budgeted sales (at €3)	120,000 (at €6)	240,000	360,000
Variable costs (at €2)	80,000 (at €3)	120,000	200,000
Contribution	40,000	120,000	160,000
Fixed costs			140,000
Revised profit			20,000
Original budgeted profit			30,000
Reduction in profit			10,000

chapter

12

Budgetary control

Chapter learning objectives

Lead	Component
B1. Explain the purposes of forecasts, plans and budgets.	(a) Explain how the purposes of budgets may conflict.
B4. Discuss the principles that underlie the use of budgets for control.	(a) Discuss the concept of the budget as a control system and the use of responsibility accounting and its importance in the construction of functional budgets that support the overall master budget.

1 Session Content Diagram

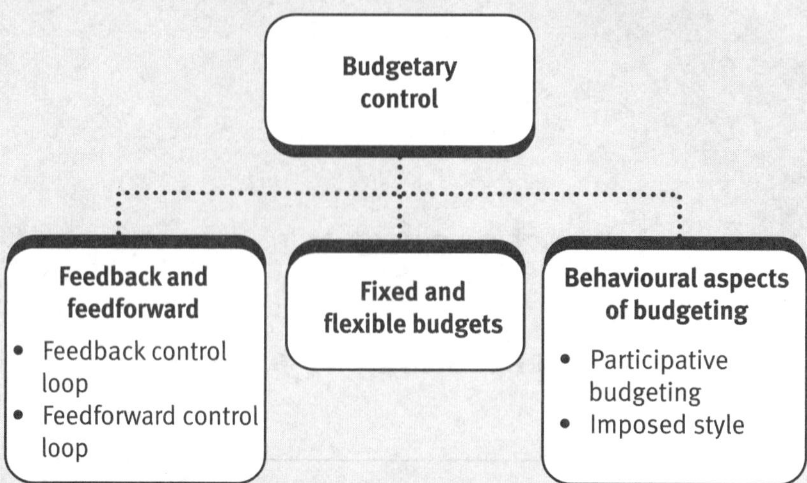

2 The meaning of budgetary control

Budgetary control is about assessing actual performance against budgeted performance and taking corrective action when necessary.

The control system is a systematic approach which tells managers whether or not they are achieving what they planned to achieve.

It focuses on total costs for a department or business unit, and responsibility for these total costs is allocated to an individual (this is known as responsibility accounting). If there are any differences between actual and budgeted performance (known as a variance), the responsible individual can act to either correct the budget or to take action to bring the cost back under control (whichever is most appropriate).

Effective budgetary control

Atrill and McLaney identify a number of characteristics that are common to businesses with effective budgetary control:

- a serious attitude is taken to the system
- clear demarcation between areas of managerial responsibility
- budget targets that are challenging yet achievable
- established data collection, analysis and reporting techniques
- reports aimed at individual managers
- fairly short reporting periods
- timely variance reports
- action being taken to get operations back under control if they are shown to be out of control.

3 Feedback and feedforward control

There are two main types of control system:

- **feedback control** – in this system the aim is to correct *problems that have been discovered* at the period end when the actual results are compared with the budget.

More details on feedback control

Feedback control is the comparison of actual results against expected results and if there is a significant difference, then it is investigated and if possible and desirable it is corrected.

It is defined as:

'Measurement of differences between planned outputs and actual outputs achieved, and **the modification of subsequent action** and/or plans to achieve future required results. Feedback control is an integral part of budgetary control and standard costing systems.' (CIMA Official Terminology)

Corrective action that brings actual performance closer to the target or plan is called *negative feedback*.

Corrective action that increases the difference between actual performance and the target or plan is called *positive feedback.*

Feedback control in budgeting

- An organisation prepares a budget, and commits resources to achieving the budget targets.
- The business uses its resources to make products or provide services. Private sector organisations sell their output.
- Outputs from the system are measured. In budgetary control, output measurements will be quantities of products made or services provided, costs incurred, revenues earned, and profits and return. Some non-financial performance measurements might also be taken.
- The measurements provide feedback information to management, who compare actual results with the budget.
- Where a need for control action is identified, the manager responsible takes suitable control action.

With negative feedback, the control action is intended to bring actual performance back into line with the budget. For example, if actual costs are higher than budget, control action might be taken to cut costs. Similarly, if actual sales volume is lower than budgeted sales, action might be taken to boost sales.

With positive feedback, control action would be intended to increase the differences between the budget and actual results. For example, if actual sales are higher than budget, control action might be taken to make this situation continue. Similarly, when actual costs are less than budget, measures might be taken to keep costs down.

The manner in which a feedback control loop might work in the context of a budgetary control system may be illustrated by the following diagram:

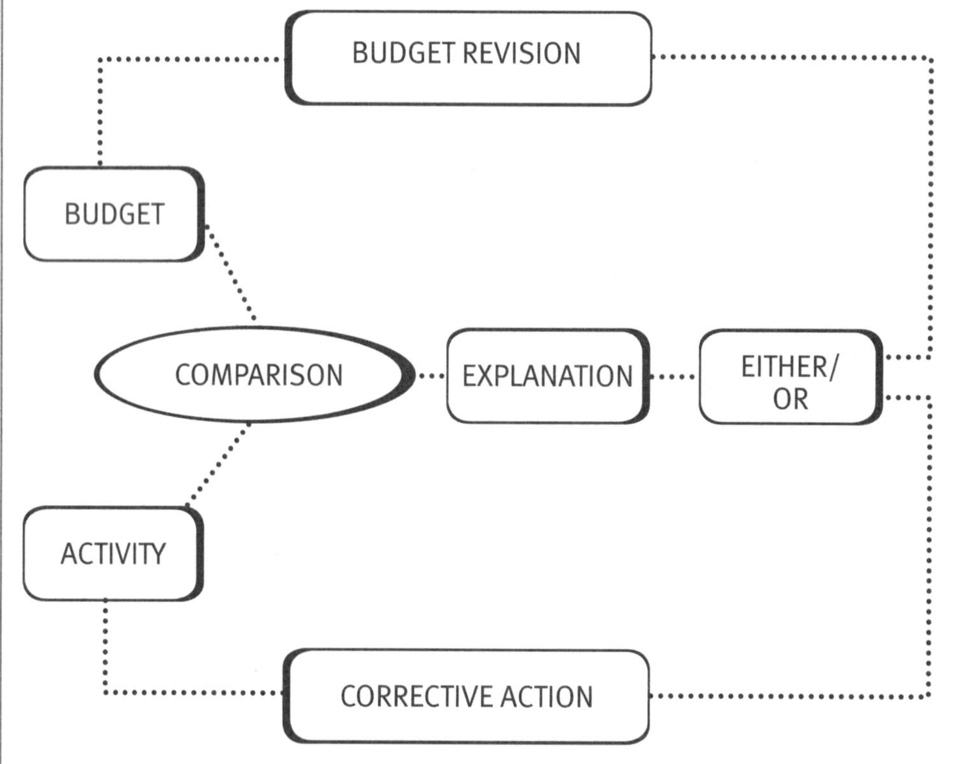

- **feedforward control** – in this system the aim is to *anticipate problems* with the aim of preventing them from occurring. Feedforward control should be used in conjunction with feedback control.

More details on feedforward control

Feedforward

Feedforward is the comparison of the results that are currently expected in the light of the latest information and the desired results. If there is a difference, then it is investigated and corrected.

Feedback happens after the event and discovers that something **has** gone wrong (or right). It is obviously too late to affect the result that has just happened, but the idea is that if we can understand what went wrong in the previous period, then we can stop the problem from recurring.

Feedforward is more proactive and aims to **anticipate** problems and prevent them from occurring.

It is defined as the 'forecasting of differences between actual and planned outcomes and the implementation of actions before the event, to avoid such differences' (CIMA Official Terminology).

Whereas feedback is based on a comparison of historical actual results with the budget for the period to date, feedforward looks ahead and compares:

- the target or objectives for the period, and
- what actual results are now forecast.

Advantages and problems with feedforward control

Feedforward control reporting offers the key advantage that it is forward-looking. It informs management what is likely to happen unless control measures are taken. Management can compare their targets for the period with current expectations.

In contrast, feedback control is backward-looking, and historical variances or differences from plan are not necessarily a guide to what will happen over the full budget period.

A problem with feedforward control is that control reports should be produced regularly, which means that forecasts must be updated regularly. To implement an efficient feed-forward control system, it is therefore necessary to have an efficient forecasting system. Forecasts might be prepared using computer models, with revisions to the forecast each month based on updated information about actual results to date, and where appropriate by making alterations to the basic assumptions in the model.

Illustration 1

A departmental manager is responsible for the cash budget for the department for the year. The organisation uses feedforward control systems.

The cash budget at the start of the year stated that there would be a cash balance of $400,000 at the beginning of June and that a piece of capital equipment costing $320,000 was to be purchased in the month.

Two months earlier, in April, using the feedforward control systems in the organisation, the manager responsible for the budget realises that the cash budget was optimistic and that, because some credit customers are paying later than was expected, the expected cash balance will be only $220,000 at the start of June.

Feedforward control

Feedback control has two elements here. Firstly, it has been used to identify a problem in advance (i.e. in April). The manager can see that the department will not have enough cash in June to purchase the machine as planned.

Secondly, having anticipated the potential problem if the machine is purchased, it allows the manager to take steps to eliminate the problem before it occurs:

- the department could simply delay the purchase of the machine for 1 or 2 months
- or it could negotiate with the supplier of the equipment to see if they would be willing to accept installments
- or it could speak to the bank manager and obtain a temporary overdraft, etc.

Control reports

Feedback control reports and feedforward control reports might be presented at the same time but they will have a different, layout, present different information and have different uses in that:

- the feedback control report will look backwards at the performance for the period and consider any difference from the planned performance for that period
- the feedforward control report will look forward and create expectations about expected future performance with the aim of identifying potential future issues for resolution.

e.g

Illustration 2

A sales manager receives monthly control reports about sales values. The budgeted sales for the year to 31 December are $600,000 in total. At the end of April the manager might receive the following feedback control report.

Feedback control report

Sales report for April

	Month			*Cumulative*		
	Budget	*Actual*	*Variance*	*Budget*	*Actual*	*Variance*
Product	$000	$000	$000	$000	$000	$000
P1	35	38	3 (F)	90	94	4 (F)
P2	20	14	6 (A)	50	39	11 (A)
P3	25	23	2 (A)	50	45	5 (A)
Total	80	75	5 (A)	190	178	12 (A)

The aim of this report is to assess performance in April. The sales manager can see that product P3 has had a poor month of sales and has achieved $2,000 less sales than expected. The manager can also see that product P3 is now $5,000 below where it should have been at this point in the year. The manager might want to take some corrective action at this point such as replacing some of the sales team for P3 or reducing performance related pay for that product.

Feedforward control report

Alternatively, the sales manager might be presented with a feedforward control report, as follows:

Sales report, April

	Budget	*Current forecast*	*Variance*
Product	$000	$000	$000
P1	240	250	10 (F)
P2	150	120	30 (A)
P3	210	194	16 (A)
Total	600	564	36 (A)

This report compares the expected year end totals for each product against the original budget for the year. For example, P2 was budgeted to achieve sales by the end of the year of $150,000, but a revised budget for the year now suggest that P2 will only achieve $120,000 of sales by the end of December.

The manager can react to this by seeking ways to make up the deficit in sales in P2 before the year end (for example, by improving the marketing of P2 or by motivating the sales staff to sell more of P2 before the year end).

4 Fixed and flexible budgets

A **fixed** budget contains information on costs and revenues for one level of activity.

A **flexible** budget shows the same information, but for a number of different levels of activity. Flexible budgets are useful for both planning purposes and control purposes.

(1) When preparing a flexible budget, managers are forced to consider the different scenarios and their responses to them. Thus for a number of different situations, managers will have calculated their costs and revenues. If an unexpected event does occur, changing the level of activity, management will be better prepared.

(2) Budgetary control is the comparison of actual results against budget. Where the actual level of activity is different to that expected, comparisons of actual results against a fixed budget can give misleading results.

In budgetary control systems managers should always compare performance against a flexed budget.

Illustration 3

A company manufactures a single product and the following data show the actual results for costs for the month of April compared with the budgeted figures.

Operating statement for April

	Budget	*Actual*	*Variance*
Units produced	1,200	1,000	(200)
	$	$	$
Direct material	19,200	16,490	2,710
Direct labour	13,200	12,380	820
Production overhead	24,000	24,120	(120)
Administration overhead	21,000	21,600	(600)
Selling overhead	16,400	16,200	200
Total cost	93,800	90,790	3,010

Note: Variances in brackets are *adverse*.

Looking at the costs incurred in April, a cost saving of $3,010 has been made compared with the budget. However, the number of units produced was 200 less than budget so some savings in expenditure might be expected. It is not possible to tell from this comparison how much of the saving is due to efficient cost control, and how much is the result of the reduction in activity.

The type of budget being used here is a **fixed budget**. A fixed budget is one which remains **unchanged regardless of the actual level of activity.** In situations where activity levels are likely to change, and there is a significant proportion of variable costs, it is difficult to control expenditure satisfactorily with a fixed budget.

If costs are mostly fixed, then changes in activity levels will not cause problems for cost comparisons with fixed budgets.

A **flexible budget** can help managers to make more valid comparisons. It is designed to show the allowed expenditure for the actual number of units produced and sold. Comparing this flexible budget with the actual expenditure, it is possible to distinguish genuine efficiencies and inefficiencies.

Preparing a flexible budget

Before a flexible budget can be prepared, managers must identify the cost behaviour, i.e. which costs are fixed, which are variable and which are semi-variable. The allowed expenditure on variable costs can then be increased or decreased as the level of activity changes. You will recall that fixed costs are those costs which will not increase or decrease over the relevant range of activity. The allowance for these items will therefore remain constant. Semi-variable costs have both a fixed and a variable element.

We can now continue with the example.

Management has identified that the following budgeted costs are fixed:

	$
Direct labour	8,400
Production overhead	18,000
Administration overhead	21,000
Selling overhead	14,000

It is now possible to identify the expected variable cost per unit produced.

	Original budget	*Fixed cost*	*Variable cost*	*Variable cost per unit*
	(a)	*(b)*	*(c) = (a) – (b)*	*(c) ÷ 1,200*
Units produced	1,200			
	$	$	$	$
Direct material	19,200	–	19,200	16
Direct labour	13,200	8,400	4,800	4
Production overhead	24,000	18,000	6,000	5
Administration overhead	21,000	21,000	–	–
Selling overhead	16,400	14,000	2,400	2
	93,800	61,400	32,400	27

From this you can see that:

- administration overhead is fixed
- direct material is variable
- direct labour, production overhead and selling and distribution overheads are semi-variable.

Now that managers are aware of the fixed costs and the variable costs per unit it is possible to 'flex' the original budget to produce a budget cost allowance for the actual 1,000 units produced.

The budget cost allowance (or flexed budget) for each item is calculated as follows:

Budget cost allowance = Budgeted fixed cost + (number of units produced × variable cost per unit)

The budget cost allowances can be calculated as follows:

Direct material = 0 + (1,000 × 16) = $16,000

Direct labour = 8,400 + (1,000 × 4) = $12,400

Production overhead = 18,000 + (1,000 × 5) = $23,000

Administration overhead = 21,000 + 0 = $21,000

Selling overhead = 14,000 + (1,000 × 2) = $16,000

A flexible budget statement can now be produced:

Flexible budget comparison for April

	Cost allowance	*Actual cost*	*Variance*
	$	$	$
Direct material	16,000	16,490	(490)
Direct labour	12,400	12,380	20
Production overhead	23,000	24,120	(1,120)
Administration overhead	21,000	21,600	(600)
Selling overhead	16,000	16,200	(200)
Total cost	88,400	90,790	(2,390)

Note: Variances in brackets are adverse.

This revised analysis shows that in fact the cost was $2,390 higher than would have been expected from a production volume of 1,000 units.

The cost variances in the flexible budget comparison are almost all adverse. These overspendings were not revealed when the fixed budget was used and managers may have been under the false impression that costs were being adequately controlled.

The total budget variance

If we now produce a statement showing the fixed budget, the flexible budget and the actual results together, it is possible to analyse the total variance between the original budget and the actual results.

	Fixed budget	*Flexible budget*	*Actual results*	*Expenditure variances*
	$	$	$	$
Direct material	19,200	16,000	16,490	(490)
Direct labour	13,200	12,400	12,380	20
Production overhead	24,000	23,000	24,120	(1,120)
Administrative overhead	21,000	21,000	21,600	(600)
Selling and distribution overhead	16,400	16,000	16,200	(200)
	93,800	88,400	90,790	(2,390)

5,400 Volume variance (fixed budget to flexible budget)

(2,390) Expenditure variance (flexible budget to actual results)

3,010 Total variance

The total variance is therefore made up of two parts:

(1) the volume variance of $5,400 favourable, which is the expected cost saving resulting from producing 200 units less than budgeted

(2) the expenditure variance of $2,390 adverse, which is the net total of the over- and under-expenditure on each of the costs for the actual output of 1,000 units.

Notice that the volume variance is the saving in standard variable cost: 200 units × $27 per unit = $5,400.

When you looked at standard costing, you learned how some of the expenditure variances can be analysed between their price and usage elements – for example, how much of the variance is caused by paying a different price per hour of labour (the labour rate variance), or per kilogram of material (the material price variance), and how much is caused by using a different quantity of material or labour (the usage and efficiency variances).

Using flexible budgets for planning

You should appreciate that while flexible budgets can be useful for control purposes they are not particularly useful for planning. The original budget must contain a single target level of activity so that managers can plan such factors as the resource requirements and the product pricing policy. This would not be possible if they were faced with a range of possible activity levels, although managers will of course consider a range of possible activity levels before they select the target budgeted activity level.

The budget can be designed so that the fixed costs are distinguished from the variable costs. This will facilitate the preparation of a budget cost allowance (flexed budget) for control purposes at the end of each period, when the actual activity is known.

5 Responsibility accounting and controllability of costs

A key aspect of budgetary control is responsibility accounting – that is, making managers account for the costs (and/or revenues) for which they have responsibility. However this will only work effectively if managers are appraised only on the costs which they can control. The success of responsibility accounting relies on the ability of the organisation to correctly identify the costs that a manager can control.

Controllable costs are costs which can be influenced by the budget holder and are generally considered to be those which are:

- variable or
- directly attributable fixed costs.

Uncontrollable costs are costs that cannot be influenced (i.e. their value can neither be increased nor decreased) by management action.

Further details

Most variable costs within a department are thought to be controllable in the short term because a manager can influence the efficiency with which resources are used, even if they cannot do anything to raise or lower price levels. So costs such as direct labour costs and material costs in a manager's department are said to be controllable by that manager.

Many fixed costs are uncontrollable (or committed) in the short term (such as insurance etc.) and these are not normally treated as controllable costs. But some fixed costs are directly attributable to a department in that, although they are fixed (in the short term) within the relevant range of output, a drastic reduction in the department's output, or closure of the division entirely, would reduce or remove these costs. This might include costs such as supervisors' salaries, department rent etc.

A useful distinction can be made between **committed** fixed costs, which are costs that are uncontrollable in the short term, but are controllable over the longer term; and **discretionary** fixed costs, which are costs treated as fixed cost items that can nevertheless be controlled in the short term, because spending is subject to management discretion. Examples of discretionary fixed costs are advertising expenditure, and executive travel and subsistence costs, and these would normally be included as directly attributable fixed costs.

Example 1

The manager of the purchasing department is given responsibility for the total expenditure in her department for the year. In calculating the organisation's budgeted profit for the year, the accountant in the organisation included the following total costs for the purchasing department:

	Total
	$
Direct materials	1,165,000
Direct labour	28,000
Indirect fixed labour cost	80,000
Other fixed overheads	100,000
Share of central overheads	67,000
Total costs	1,440,000

It has been determined that the indirect fixed labour cost and 40% of the other fixed overheads are directly attributable to the department.

When assessing the total cost variance for the department, what total cost should be used as the budgeted controllable cost for the manager?

A $1,313,000

B $1,333,000

C $1,373,000

D $1,440,000

Recharging uncontrollable costs

Focusing solely on controllable costs, however, can bring in some further complications in that it may mean that uncontrollable costs are ignored by all managers. In order to rectify this, some organisations decide that even uncontrollable costs should be charged to departments.

Illustration

A summarised report for the profit centres of an organisation might be:

	Centre A	*Centre B*	*Centre C*	*Total*
	$	$	$	$
Revenue	300,000	260,000	420,000	980,000
Variable costs	170,000	100,000	240,000	510,000
Directly attributable costs	70,000	120,000	80,000	270,000
Controllable costs	**240,000**	**220,000**	**320,000**	**780,000**
Attributable gross profit	60,000	40,000	100,000	200,000
Other overhead costs				**(180,000)**
Net profit				20,000

A criticism of the controllability accounting principle is that managers are not encouraged to think about costs for which they are not responsible. In the example above, there are $180,000 of costs not attributable to any profit centre. These might be head office costs, for example, or marketing overheads.

- Within a system of responsibility accounting, there should be cost centre managers accountable for these costs.
- Even so, these overhead costs might be caused to some extent by the demands placed on head office administration or marketing services by the profit centre managers.
- When these costs are high, a further problem is that profit centre profits need to be large enough to cover the general non-allocated overhead costs.

An argument could therefore be made that profit centre managers should be made accountable for a share of overhead costs that are not under their control, and a share of these costs should be charged to each profit centre. Profit reporting would therefore be as follows:

	Centre A	*Centre B*	*Centre C*	*Total*
	$	$	$	$
Revenue	300,000	260,000	420,000	980,000
Variable costs	170,000	100,000	240,000	510,000
Directly attributable costs	70,000	120,000	80,000	270,000
Controllable costs	**240,000**	**220,000**	**320,000**	**780,000**
Attributable gross profit	60,000	40,000	100,000	200,000
Other overhead costs	(50,000)	(50,000)	(80,000)	**(180,000)**
Net profit	10,000	(10,000)	20,000	20,000

Pros and Cons

The advantages of this approach to responsibility accounting are:

- business unit managers are made aware of the significance of other overhead costs
- business unit managers are made aware that they need to earn a sufficient profit to cover a fair share of other overhead costs.

The disadvantages of this approach are that:

- business unit managers are made accountable for a share of other overhead costs, but they can do nothing to control them
- the apportionment of other overhead costs between business units, like overhead apportionment generally, is usually a matter of judgement, lacking any economic or commercial justification.

6 The behavioural aspects of budgetary control

Senior managers will often get less junior managers and other members of staff involved in creating budgets. This helps satisfy one of the purposes of budgeting in that it can aid motivation. But it can have a detrimental impact on the other purposes such as distorting the evaluation of actual performance if managers incorporate 'slack' into the budget in order to make it easier to achieve.

Distorting the purposes of budgeting

Involving managers in the completion of a budget can help achieve some of the purposes of budgets but may distort others.

Some of the purposes that are **enhanced** by manager involvement are:

- **Planning.** Planning is taking place at many levels, and should be more accurate than if it simply takes place at a high level, by individuals who are not familiar with the day to day needs of the business. More junior managers will have better information as they are 'closer to the action' and this should improve the quality of budgets overall.
- **Communication.** There should be more communication across all levels of management. It might also make it possible to communicate overall strategic goals to managers by explaining to them the purpose of the budget being prepared and how it fits in to overall budgets and organisational goals.
- **Motivation.** Managers often want to take on extra responsibilities and get further involved in the decision making process. Giving them the power to set budgets might achieve this goal. Managers might also take more personal ownership of achieving budget goals which they have set and be more motivated to achieve what they have promised in the budget.

Whilst the following purposes might be **distorted**:

- **Co-ordination.** This may become more complicated and slower. This is because, not only does there need to be co-ordination between departments but there also has to be co-ordination between the different levels of management within each department. Managers will have to co-ordinate with each other and it may be that inaccuracies occur in budgets if individual manager cannot see the overall ('big') picture or do not understand fully the organisation's goals for the budget period.
- **Evaluation.** In some instances managers might build 'slack' into a budget that they control. This means that they will make it more easily achievable by overstating target costs and/or understating target revenues (if these are included in their budget). This will make it easier for them to achieve the budget targets and associated rewards. But it will make the evaluation of budget performance less useful for senior managers. For example, the variance system might only generate favourable variances because the original plan or standard was understated.

- **Authorisation.** It may be harder to control the authorisation of budget items if there are no checks on the manager. It may also be that managers disagree over budget responsibility and try to allocate costs to other managers rather than take responsibility for themselves.

But there this will not always be the case. Every manager and every company will react differently to a budgetary control system. For example, involvement of managers in one firm might lead to better motivation, but other managers may be reluctant to get involved and therefore become dissatisfied if they are asked to get involved in the process.

Conflicts between the goals of budgeting

These behavioural aspects help explain that many of the goals of budgeting are contradictory. One the one side we want to be able to fairly evaluate the performance of managers. But we also want to motivate managers and therefore, even if managers are not involved in the process, managers may find the budget too challenging and therefore reduce their effort. That in turn would distort any evaluation.

Likewise, we want budgets to act as a way of communicating organisational goals. But the budget themselves may distort the goals as they will be very short-term, be focused on cost reduction rather than, say, quality aspects, and they will solely focus on financial aspects of the organisation's goals. There is therefore a conflict between aiming to achieve financial control and communicating the organisation's goals.

Furthermore, the budget is designed to act as a plan for a manager or department. The manager may therefore follow this plan at the expense of other critical success factors that arise in the internal or external environment of the firm. For example, a production manager may continue to use the planned materials mix even if the sales department are indicating that customers would prefer a different product design and the purchasing department have adjusted their purchases accordingly. The production manager then has to choose between the plan and inter-departmental co-ordination.

Many of the conflicts arise due to the human nature of a budgetary control system. Managers do not always follow organisational goals, they do not always think long term, they may be wary of moving away from the plan etc. This provides a conflict between many of the goals of a budgetary control system which needs to be considered at a strategic level when implementing such a system.

7 Behavioural aspects of budgeting

Choosing the level of participation in budgeting

These behavioural aspects are influenced by the amount of participation that is given to managers in the preparation of the budget. It results in organisations choosing between two extremes of budgetary participation:

- **The imposed style.** In this style of budgeting the budget is set centrally with little involvement by the budget holder. This reduces the scope for slack in the budget, improves co-ordination and avoids some of the goal congruence issues identified with budgetary participation.
- **The participative style.** In this style the budget holder is involved in setting the budget. This should make the budget more accurate and better motivate the budget holder to achieve it.

Further details

Imposed style

An imposed/top-down budget is defined in CIMA's *Official Terminology* as 'A budget allowance which is set without permitting the ultimate budget holder to have the opportunity to participate in the budgeting process'

Advantages of imposed style

There are a number of reasons why it might be preferable for managers not to be involved in setting their own budgets:

(1) Involving managers in the setting of budgets is more time consuming than if senior managers simply imposed the budgets.

(2) Managers may not have the skills or motivation to participate usefully in the budgeting process.

(3) Senior managers have the better overall view of the company and its resources and may be better-placed to create a budget which utilises those scarce resources to best effect.

(4) Senior managers also are aware of the longer term strategic objectives of the organisation and can prepare a budget which is in line with that strategy.

(5) Managers may build budgetary slack or bias into the budget in order to make the budget easy to achieve and themselves look good.

(6) Managers cannot use budgets to play games which disadvantage other budget holders.

(7) By having the budgets imposed by senior managers, i.e. someone outside the department, a more objective, fresher perspective may be gained.

(8) If the participation is only pseudo-participation and the budgets are frequently drastically changed by senior management, then this will cause dissatisfaction and the effect will be to demotivate staff.

Participative style

Participative/bottom up budgeting is a 'budgeting system in which all budget holders are given the opportunity to participate in setting their own budgets'. (CIMA *Official Terminology*)

Advantages of participative budgets

(1) The morale of the management is improved. Managers feel like their opinion is listened to, that their opinion is valuable.

(2) Managers are more likely to accept the plans contained within the budget and strive to achieve the targets if they had some say in setting the budget, rather than if the budget was imposed upon them. Failure to achieve the target that they themselves set is seen as a personal failure as well as an organisational failure.

(3) The lower level managers will have a more detailed knowledge of their particular part of the business than senior managers and thus will be able to produce more realistic budgets.

Other behavioural aspects of budgeting

Other aspects that managers may have to incorporate into a budgetary control system include:

- incorporating the achievement of personal goals in order to motivate the budget holder
- achieving goal congruence between the budget holder's goals and the organisation's goals
- avoiding budget holders seeing the budget as a pot of cash that must be spent
- negotiating budgets with the budget holder
- coping with conflicts with the accounting treatment of some costs
- allowing the budget holder to have some freedom and not to feel too constrained by the budget
- setting the correct level of 'difficulty' in a budget.

Further details

Achieving personal goals

To be fully effective, any system of financial control must provide for motivation and incentive. If this requirement is not satisfied, managers will approach their responsibilities in a very cautious and conservative manner.

Personal goals and ambitions are, in theory, strongly linked to organisational goals. These personal goals may include a desire for higher income and higher social standing. To simultaneously satisfy the goals of the organisation and the goals of the individual there must be 'goal congruence'. That is, the individual manager perceives that his or her own goals are achieved by his or her acting in a manner that allows the organisation to achieve its goals. The problem is that reliance on budgetary control systems does not always result in goal congruence.

The success of a budgetary control system depends on the people who operate and are affected by it. They must work within the system in an understanding and co-operative manner. This can only be achieved by individuals who have a total involvement at all stages in the budget process. However, it is often found that

(1) A budget is used simply as a pressure device. If the budget is perceived as 'a stick with which to beat people', then it will be sabotaged in all sorts of subtle ways.

(2) The budgeting process and subsequent budgetary control exercises induce competition between individual departments and executives. Managers may be induced to do things in order to 'meet budget' that are not in the best interests of the business as a whole.

(3) Adverse variances attract investigation and censure but there is no incentive to achieve favourable variances.

(4) Failure to distinguish controllable from uncontrollable costs in budgetary control can alienate managers from the whole process.

Failure of goal congruence

It has been seen that an essential element in budgetary control is performance evaluation. Actual results are compared with budget or standard in order to determine whether performance is good or bad. What is being evaluated is not just the business operation but the managers responsible for it. The purpose of budgetary control is to induce managers to behave in a manner that is to the best advantage of the organisation. Compliance with budget is enforced by a variety of negative and positive sanctions.

When adverse variances are reported for operations then this implies poor performance by the managers of the operations. If they are unable to correct or explain away the adverse variances, then they may suffer negative sanctions. They may have forgo salary increases, or they may be demoted to a less prestigious post. Other more subtle negative sanctions are possible that anyone who has ever worked for a large organisation will be aware of.

Positive inducements may be offered to encourage managers to avoid adverse variances. A manager who meets budget may be granted a performance-related salary bonus, promotion, a new company car or use of the executive dining room.

Consequently, the manager has a considerable incentive to ensure that the department or operation he/she is responsible for achieves its budgeted level of performance. However, there are a variety of ways of doing this that might not be to the advantage of the organisation as a whole.

For example, the manager of a production line can cut costs and hence improve its reported performances by reducing quality controls. This may result in long-term problems concerning failure of products in service, loss of customer goodwill and rectification costs – but these are not the concern of the production line manager. This is a clear failure of goal congruence.

The control system is capable of distorting the process it is meant to serve – or 'the tail wags the dog'. The enforcement of a budgetary control system requires sensitivity if this is not to happen.

The budget as a pot of cash

In some environments managers may come to consider the budget as a sum of money that has to be spent. This arises particularly in service departments or public sector organisations, the performance of which is gauged mainly through comparison of actual and budget spending.

The manager of a local authority 'street cleaning' department may be given an annual budget of £120,000 to clean the streets. The manager knows that she will be punished if she spends more than £120,000 in the year. She also knows that if she spends less than £120,000 in the year then her budget will probably be reduced next year. Such a reduction will involve a personal loss of status in the organisation and will make her job more difficult in the next year.

In order to ensure that she does not overspend her annual budget in the current year the manager may spend at a rate of £9,000 per month for the first 11 months of the year. This can be achieved by reducing the frequency of street cleaning and using poor-quality materials. It allows a contingency fund to be accumulated in case of emergencies.

However, in the final month of the year the manager has to spend £21,000 if she wishes to ensure that her whole budget is fully used. She might achieve this by using extra labour and high-quality materials.

Does this behaviour make sense? Of course it does not. The whole pattern of behaviour is distorted by the control system. It means that local residents have a substandard service for 11 months of the year and money is wasted in the 12th month.

It is, however, a fact that suppliers to government departments and local councils often experience a surge in orders towards the end of the financial year. This surge is caused by managers placing orders at the last moment in order to ensure that their full budget for the year is committed.

Budget negotiation

Budgets are normally arrived at by a process of negotiation with the managers concerned. A budget may actually be initiated by departmental managers and then corrected as a result of negotiation with the budget officer.

Clearly, a manager has an incentive to negotiate a budget that is not difficult to achieve. This produces a phenomenon known as 'padding the budget' or 'budgetary slack'. A manager will exaggerate the costs required to achieve objectives. This has the following results:

(1) If the manager succeeds in padding his budget, then the whole control exercise is damaged. Comparison of actual with budget gives no meaningful measure of performance and the manager is able to include inefficiencies in his operation if he wishes.

(2) A successful manager becomes one who is a hard negotiator. The problem with this is that the negotiations in question are between colleagues and not with customers. 'Infighting' may become entrenched in the management process.

(3) A great deal of time and energy that could be directed to the actual management of the business is distracted by what are essentially administrative procedures.

These are all examples of a control system distorting the processes they are meant to serve.

Influence on accounting policies

Any management accountant who has been engaged in the preparation of financial control reports will be familiar with attempts by managers to influence the accounting policies that are used. For example, the apportionment of indirect costs between departments often contains subjective elements. Should security costs be apportioned on the basis of floor space or staff numbers?

The manner in which the indirect costs are apportioned can have a considerable impact on how the performance of individual departments is perceived. This position creates the scope and incentive for managers to argue over accounting policies.

If a manager perceives that her department's performance is falling below budget, then he/she may sift through the costs charged to his/her department and demand that some be reclassified and charged elsewhere. The time and energy that goes into this kind of exercise has to be diverted from that available for the regular management of the business.

Budget constrained management styles

When the performance of a manager is assessed by his ability to meet budget, then he is likely to adopt a conservative approach to new business opportunities that appear. The immediate impact of new business ventures is likely to be a rise in capital and operating costs – with an adverse impact on current period profit. The benefits of such ventures may only be felt in the long term. Hence, when a new opportunity appears, the manager evaluating it may only perceive that its acceptance will result in below-budget performance in the current period – and turn it down on this ground alone. Another consideration is that reliance on budgetary control is an approach to management that involves sitting in an office and reading financial reports. Such an approach (in conjunction with features such as executive dining rooms) may result in an unsatisfactory corporate culture based on hierarchies and social divisions. Large organisations that rely heavily on budgetary control systems often take on an 'ossified' character.

Yet another consideration is that a reliance on budgetary planning may induce managers to favour projects and developments that are most amenable to the construction of budgets. Projects that involve little uncertainty and few unknowns are easy to incorporate in budgets and hence managers may be more inclined to adopt such projects than the alternatives. Projects that involve significant uncertainties may be attractive if they incorporate some combination of high expected returns and low cost interim exit routes – but a budget constrained manager may be disinclined to adopt such projects simply because they are difficult to incorporate in budgets. Some writers suggest that the budgetary approach may be particularly inappropriate in a dynamic and turbulent business environment.

The general conclusion concerning this and previous points is that good budgetary control can offer certain benefits. However, when budgetary control is enforced in a rigid or insensitive manner it may end up doing more harm than good.

Setting the difficulty level of targets

Much of the early academic work on budgets concerned the extent to which the 'tightness' or looseness' of a budget acted as an incentive or disincentive to management effort. This was the issue of 'budget stretch'. Seminal works in this general area included studies by A.C. Stedry (see his 1960 text 'Budget Control and Cost Behaviour') and G.H. Hofstede (see his 1968 text 'The Game of Budget Control').

The main thrust of the findings that emerged from these studies was:

(1) Loose budgets (i.e. ones easily attainable) are poor motivators

(2) As budgets are tightened, up to a point they become more motivational

(3) Beyond that point, a very tight budget ceases to be motivational.

The role of budget participation and the manner in which aspirations and objectives are stated was also explored in certain studies. It was suggested that the participation of managers in budget setting was a motivational factor – but see earlier discussion concerning budget padding and negotiation.

8 Chapter summary

Budgetary control

Feedback & feedforward

- Feedback: aimed at correcting problems
- Feedforward: aimed at preventing problems

Fixed & flexible budgets

- Fixed budget information on costs and revenues for one level of activity
- Flexible budget shows the same information, but for a number of different levels of activity.

Behavioural aspects

- Responsibility accounting: making managers account for the costs for which they have responsibility and can control
- A choice needs to be made between an imposed or participative style of budgeting.

9 Practice questions

Test your understanding 1

The following fixed and flexible budgets have been prepared:

	Fixed budget 100% level	*Flexible budget 90% level*
	$	$
Sales	750,000	675,000
Direct variable costs	420,000	378,000
Overheads	230,000	216,800
Total costs	650,000	594,800
Profit	100,000	80,200

Actual sales for the period were $700,000 and there was an adverse sales price variance of $5,000 (A).

Required:

Prepare a flexible budget for the actual level of sales.

Test your understanding 2

An office manager uses the high-low method to establish the expected costs for office expenses, based on the following data for monthly expenses:

	Costs for 6,000 labour hours	*Costs for 8,000 labour hours*
	$	$
Heating and lighting	17,000	18,000
Telephones	7,200	8,400
Sundry expenses	29,400	33,400

Variable costs are assumed to vary with the number of labour hours worked in the office during the period.

In the most recent month, 7,700 labour hours were worked and actual costs were as follows:

	$
Heating and lighting	17,600
Telephones	8,750
Sundry expenses	32,600

Required:

Calculate the cost variances for the month.

Test your understanding 3

Extracts from the budgets of B Ltd are given below:

Sales and inventory budgets (units)

	Period 1	*Period 2*	*Period 3*	*Period 4*	*Period 5*
Opening inventory	4,000	2,500	3,300	2,500	3,000
Sales	15,000	20,000	16,500	21,000	18,000

Cost budgets ($000)

	Period 1	*Period 2*	*Period 3*
Direct materials	108.0	166.4	125.6
Direct labour	270.0	444.0	314.0
Production overheads (excluding depreciation)	117.5	154.0	128.5
Depreciation	40.0	40.0	40.0
Administration overhead	92.0	106.6	96.4
Selling overhead	60.0	65.0	61.5

The following information is also available:

(i) Production above 18,000 units incurs a bonus in addition to normal wages rates

(ii) Any variable costs contained in the selling overhead are assumed to vary with sales. All other variable costs are assumed to vary with production.

Required:

(a) Calculate the budgeted production for periods 1 to 4

(b) Prepare a suitable cost budget for period 4.

In period 4 the inventory and sales budgets were achieved and the following actual costs recorded:

	$000
Direct material	176
Direct labour	458
Production overhead	181
Depreciation	40
Administration overhead	128
Selling overhead	62
	1,045

Required:

(c) Show the budget variances from actual

(d) Criticise the assumptions on which the cost budgets have been prepared.

Test your understanding 4

A company has prepared an activity-based budget for its stores department. The budgeted costs are:

	Cost driver	*Budgeted cost*
Receiving goods	Number of deliveries	$80 per delivery
Issuing goods from store	Number of stores requisitions	$40 per requisition
Ordering	Number of orders	$25 per order
Counting inventory	Number of inventory counts	$1,000 per count

Keeping records – $24,000 each year

Supervision – $30,000 each year

Actual results for April were:

	Activity	Actual cost
		$
Receiving goods	45 orders delivered	3,450
Issuing goods	100 requisitions	4,400
Ordering	36 orders	960
Counting	2 inventory counts	1,750
Record keeping		1,900
Supervision		2,700
Total costs		15,160

Required:

Prepare a variance report for the month.

Test your understanding 5

Scenario

The materials purchasing manager is assessed on:

- total material expenditure for the organisation
- the cost of introducing safety measures, regarding the standard and the quality of materials, in accordance with revised government legislation
- a notional rental cost, allocated by head office, for the material storage area.

Task:

Discuss whether these costs are controllable by the manager and if they should be used to appraise the manager.

(Time allowed: 10 minutes)

Test your understanding 6

Explain whether a production manager should be accountable for direct labour and direct materials cost variances.

(Time allowed: 10 minutes)

Test your understanding answers

Example 1

The correct answer is answer A.

The shared central overheads should not be included as a controllable cost as the manager cannot normally influence costs which are incurred elsewhere. All of the variable (direct) costs should be included as being controllable by the manager. In terms of the fixed costs, all of the indirect fixed labour cost and 40% of the other fixed overheads are directly attributable to the department and should be included as a controllable cost.

Therefore the total controllable costs are = \$1,165,000 + \$28,000 + \$80,000 + (40% × \$100,000) = \$1,313,000.

Test your understanding 1

(W1) **Actual sales at budgeted prices**

	$
Actual sales at actual prices	700,000
Sales price variance	5,000 (A)
Actual sales at budgeted prices	705,000

Actual sales are therefore at the (705/750) 94% activity level.

(W2) **Fixed and variable overheads**

	$
Overheads at 100% activity level	230,000
Overheads at 90% activity level	216,800
Variable overheads for 10% activity	13,200

	$
Total overheads at 100% activity level	230,000
Variable overheads at 100% activity level	132,000
Fixed overheads	98,000

Flexed budget 94% activity

	$	$
Sales		705,000
Direct variable costs (420,000 × 94%)		394,800
Variable overhead (13,200 × 94/10)		124,080
Fixed overhead		98,000
Total overheads		222,080
Total costs		616,880
Profit		88,120

Test your understanding 2

	Heating and lighting	*Telephones*	*Sundry expenses*
	$	$	$
Total cost for 8,000 hours	18,000	8,400	33,400
Total cost for 6,000 hours	17,000	7,200	29,400
Variable cost for 2,000 hours	1,000	1,200	4,000
Variable cost per hour	$0.50	$0.60	$2.00

	Heating and lighting	*Telephones*	*Sundry expenses*
	$	$	$
Total cost for 8,000 hours	18,000	8,400	33,400
Variable cost for 8,000 hours	4,000	4,800	16,000
Fixed costs	14,000	3,600	17,400

For 7,700 hours

	Heating and lighting	*Telephones*	*Sundry expenses*
	$	$	$
Expected fixed costs	14,000	3,600	17,400
Expected variable cost	3,850	4,620	15,400
Expected total cost	17,850	8,220	32,800
Actual cost	17,600	8,750	32,600
Cost variance	**250 (F)**	**530 (A)**	**200 (F)**

Test your understanding 3

(a)

	Period 1	*Period 2*	*Period 3*	*Period 4*	*Period 5*
Sales	15,000	20,000	16,500	21,000	18,000
Add: Closing inventory	2,500	3,300	2,500	3,000	
Less: Opening inventory	(4,000)	(2,500)	(3,300)	(2,500)	(3,000)
Production	13,500	20,800	15,700	21,500	–

(b) In Period 4, Production = 21,500 units

		$000
Direct materials	(W1)	172.0
Direct labour	(W2)	465.0
Production overhead	(W3)	157.50
Depreciation		40.0
Administration overhead	(W4)	108.0
Selling overhead	(W5)	66.0
		1,008.50

Working 1

$$\frac{\$108{,}000 \text{ (Period 1)}}{13{,}500 \text{ units}} = \$8 \times 21{,}500 = \$172{,}000$$

Working 2

Normal wage $\dfrac{\$270{,}000}{13{,}500} = \$20$ per unit

Bonus (Period 2) = \$444,000 – (20,800 × \$20) = \$28,000 premium

Premium rate: $\dfrac{\$28{,}000}{2{,}800 \text{ units above } 18{,}000} = \$10$ per unit

in Period 4, (21,500 × \$20) + (3,500 × \$10) = \$465,000

Working 3

Variable cost per unit $= \dfrac{154 - 117.5}{20.8 - 13.5} = \dfrac{36.5}{7.3} = \$5$ per unit

Working 4

Variable cost per unit $= \dfrac{106.6 - 92.0}{20.8 - 13.5} = \dfrac{14.6}{7.3} = \$2$ per unit

Working 5

Variable cost per unit $= \dfrac{65.0 - 60}{20.0 \text{ sales} - 15.0} = \$1$ per unit

Fixed cost = \$60,000 – (\$1 × 15,000) = \$45,000

In Period 4, \$1 × 21,000 + \$45,000 = \$66,000

	P4 Budget	*P4 Actual*	*Variance*	Adverse/Favourable
Material	172.0	176.0	4.0	Adverse
Labour	465.0	458.0	7.0	Favourable
Production overhead	157.5	181.0	23.5	Adverse
Depreciation	40.0	40.0	0.0	–
Administration overhead	108.0	128.0	20.0	Adverse
Selling overhead	66.0	62.0	4.0	Favourable
	1,008.50	1,045.0	36.5	Adverse

(d)

- Linear costs
- No Incremental fixed costs
- Variable cost per unit is constant
- Volume the only factor to affect total costs.

Test your understanding 4

Activity	*Expected cost*	*Actual cost*	*Variance*
	$	$	$
Receiving goods 45 orders delivered	3,600	3,450	150 (F)
Issuing goods 100 requisitions	4,000	4,400	400 (A)
Ordering 36 orders	900	960	60 (A)
Counting 2 inventory counts	2,000	1,750	250 (F)
Record keeping	2,000	1,900	100 (F)
Supervision	2,500	2,700	200 (A)
	15,000	15,160	160 (A)

Test your understanding 5

The total material expenditure for the organisation will be dependent partly on the prices negotiated by the purchasing manager and partly by the requirements and performance of the production department. If it is included as a target for performance appraisal the manager may be tempted to purchase cheaper material which may have an adverse effect elsewhere in the organisation.

The requirement to introduce safety measures may be imposed but the manager should be able to ensure that implementation meets budget targets.

A notional rental cost is outside the control of the manager and should not be included in a target for performance appraisal purposes.

Test your understanding 6

- The production manager will be responsible for managing direct labour and direct material usage.
- However, the manager may not be able to influence:
  - the cost of the material
  - the quality of the material
  - the cost of labour
  - the quality of labour.
- Performance should be measured against the element of direct cost which the manager can control.

chapter

13

Forecasting techniques

Chapter learning objectives

Lead	**Component**
B2. Prepare forecasts of financial results.	(a) Calculate projected product/service volumes, revenue and costs employing appropriate forecasting techniques and taking account of cost structures.

1 Chapter overview diagram

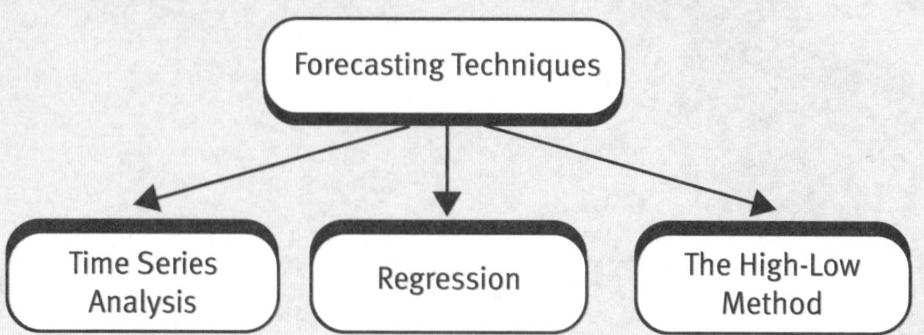

Forecasts in budgeting

Budgets are based on forecasts. Forecasts might be prepared for:

- the volume of output and sales
- sales revenue (sales volume and sales prices)
- costs.

The purpose of forecasting in the budgeting process is to establish realistic assumptions for planning. Forecasts might also be prepared on a regular basis for the purpose of feedforward control reporting.

A forecast might be based on simple assumptions, such as a prediction of a 5% growth in sales volume or sales revenue. Similarly, budgeted expenditure might be forecast using a simple incremental budgeting approach, and adding a percentage amount for inflation on top of the previous year's budget.

On the other hand, forecasts might be prepared using a number of forecasting models, methods or techniques. The reason for using these models and techniques is that they might provide more reliable forecasts.

This chapter describes:

- the high-low method
- the uses of linear regression analysis
- techniques of time series analysis.

Forecasting can also be carried out using a diagram (known as a scatter diagram). The data is plotted on a graph. The y-axis represents the *dependent* variable, i.e. that variable that depends on the other. The x-axis shows the *independent* variable, i.e. that variable which is not affected by the other variable. From the scatter diagram, the line of best fit can be estimated. The aim is to use our *judgement* to draw a line through the middle of data with the same slope as the data. Because it is based on judgement it is potentially less accurate than some of the more mathematical approaches used in this chapter.

More complex models might be used in practice, but these are outside the scope of the syllabus.

2 The high-low method

This is a method of breaking semi-variable costs into their two components. A semi-variable cost being a cost which is partly fixed and partly variable.

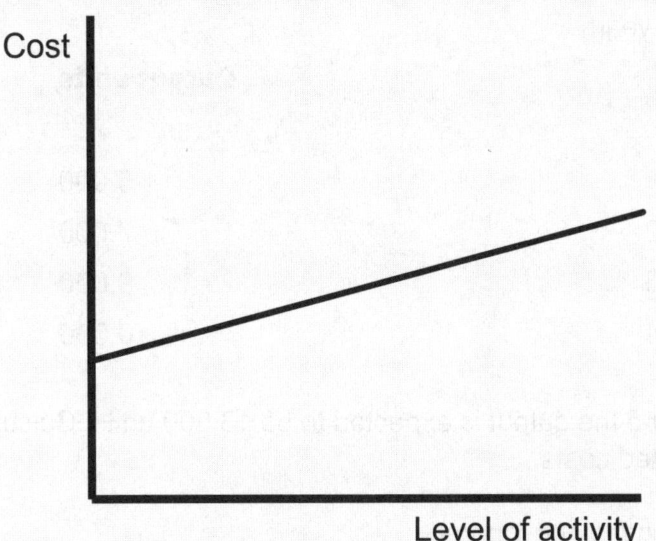

In the exam in computational questions, semi-variable costs must be broken down into their 2 components using the *high-low method.*

Step 1 Determine the variable costs

It is important that we start with the **highest and lowest output** (activity) and their associated costs.

$$\text{Variable cost per unit} = \frac{\text{Increase in cost}}{\text{Increase in activity}}$$

Choose either the highest or lowest output and multiply it by the variable cost per unit just calculated. This will tell us the total variable costs at that output.

Step 2 Find the fixed cost

A semi-variable cost consists of two components. We have found the variable component. What is left must be the fixed component. If we take the total cost and deduct the variable costs (just calculated) then we are left with the fixed costs.

Step 3 Calculate the expected cost

Once the variable cost per unit and the total fixed costs are known, these can be used to predict future cost levels. The total expected future costs will be:

= total fixed costs (from step 2) + [forecast production (in units) × variable cost per unit (from step 1)]

Example 1

Great Auk Limited has had the following output and cost results for the last 4 years:

	Output units	Cost
		$
Year 1	5,000	26,000
Year 2	7,000	34,000
Year 3	9,000	42,000
Year 4	10,000	46,000

In year 5 the output is expected to be 13,000 units. Calculate the expected costs.

Inflation may be ignored.

The high-low method with stepped fixed costs

Sometimes fixed costs are only fixed within certain levels of activity and increase in steps as activity increases (i.e. they are stepped fixed costs).

The high/low method can still be used to estimate fixed and variable costs. Simply choose two activity levels where the fixed cost remains unchanged.

Adjustments need to be made for the fixed costs based on the activity level under consideration.

Illustration

An organisation has the following total costs at three activity levels:

Activity level (units)	4,000	6,000	7,500
Total cost	$40,800	$50,000	$54,800

Variable cost per unit is constant within this activity range and there is a step up of 10% in the total fixed costs when the activity level exceeds 5,500 units.

What is the total cost at an activity level of 5,000 units?

Calculate the variable cost per unit by comparing two output levels where fixed costs will be the same:

Variable cost per unit = [(54,800 – 50,000)/(7,500 – 6,000)] = $3.20

Total fixed cost above 5,500 units = [54,800 – (7,500 × 3.20)] = $30,800

Total fixed cost below 5,500 units = 30,800/110 × 100 = $28,000

Total cost for 5,000 units = [(5,000 × 3.20) + 28,000] = $44,000

3 Regression analysis

The high-low method only takes account of two observations – the highest and the lowest. To take account of all observations a more advanced calculation is used known as **linear regression** which uses a formula to estimate the linear relationship between the variables as follows:

The equation of a straight line is:

$$y = a + bx$$

where y = dependent variable
a = intercept (on y-axis)
b = gradient
x = independent variable

and $$b = \frac{n\Sigma xy - \Sigma x \Sigma y}{n\Sigma x^2 - (\Sigma x)^2}$$

where n = number of pairs of data

and $$a = \bar{y} - b\bar{x}$$

Example 2

Marcus Aurelius Ltd is a small supermarket chain, that has 6 shops. Each shop advertises in their local newspapers and the marketing director is interested in the relationship between the amount that they spend on advertising and the sales revenue that they achieve. She has collated the following information for the 6 shops for the previous year:

Shop	**Advertising expenditure**	**Sales revenue**
	\$000	\$000
1	80	730
2	60	610
3	120	880
4	90	750
5	70	650
6	30	430

She has further performed some calculations for a linear regression calculation as follows:

- the sum of the advertising expenditure (x) column is 450
- the sum of the sales revenue (y) column is 4,050
- when the two columns are multiplied together and summed (xy) the total is 326,500
- when the advertising expenditure is squared (x^2) and summed, the total is 38,300, and
- when the sales revenue is squared (y^2) and summed, the total is 2,849,300.

Calculate the line of best fit using regression analysis.

Detailed proof of totals in example 2

Advertising expenditure $000	**Sales** $000			
x	y	xy	x^2	y^2
80	730	58,400	6,400	532,900
60	610	36,600	3,600	372,100
120	880	105,600	14,400	774,400
90	750	67,500	8,100	562,500
70	650	45,500	4,900	422,500
30	430	12,900	900	184,900
450	4,050	326,500	38,300	2,849,300

Interpretation of the line

Mathematical interpretation (No good! No marks!)

If x = 0, then y = 300 and then each time x increases by 1 y increases by 5

Business interpretation (This is what the examiner wants.)

If no money is spent on advertising then sales would still be $300,000. Then for every additional $1 increase in advertising sales revenue would increase by $5.

Linear regression in budgeting

Linear regression analysis can be used to make forecasts or estimates whenever a linear relationship is assumed between two variables, and historical data is available for analysis.

Two such relationships are:

- **A time series and trend line.** Linear regression analysis is an alternative to calculating moving averages to establish a trend line from a time series. (Time series is explained later in this chapter)
  - The independent variable (x) in a time series is time.
  - The dependent variable (y) is sales, production volume or cost etc.

- **Total costs, where costs consist of a combination of fixed costs and variable costs** (for example, total overheads, or a semi-variable cost item). Linear regression analysis is an alternative to using the high-low method of cost behaviour analysis. It should be more accurate than the high-low method, because it is based on more items of historical data, not just a 'high' and a 'low' value.
  - The independent variable (x) in total cost analysis is the volume of activity.
  - The dependent variable (y) is total cost.
  - The value of a is the amount of fixed costs.
  - The value of b is the variable cost per unit of activity.

Regression analysis is concerned with establishing the relationship between a number of variables. We are only concerned here with linear relationships between 2 variables.

When a linear relationship is identified and quantified using linear regression analysis, values for a and b are obtained, and these can be used to make a forecast for the budget. For example:

- a sales budget or forecast can be prepared, or
- total costs (or total overhead costs) can be estimated, for the budgeted level of activity.

Forecasting

The regression equation can be used for predicting values of y from a given *x* value.

Example 2 – CONTINUED

Marcus Aurelius Ltd has just taken on 2 new stores in the same area and the predicted advertising expenditure is expected to be $150,000 for one store and $50,000 for the other.

(a) Calculate the predicted sales revenues.

(b) Explain the reliability of the forecasts.

Correlation

Regression analysis attempts to find the linear relationship between two variables. Correlation is concerned with establishing how strong the relationship is.

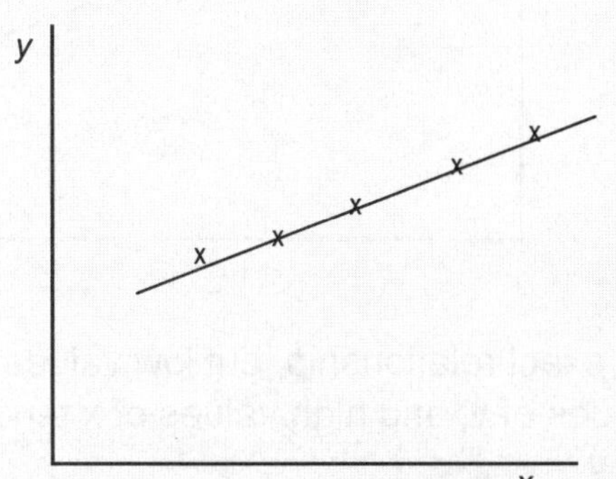

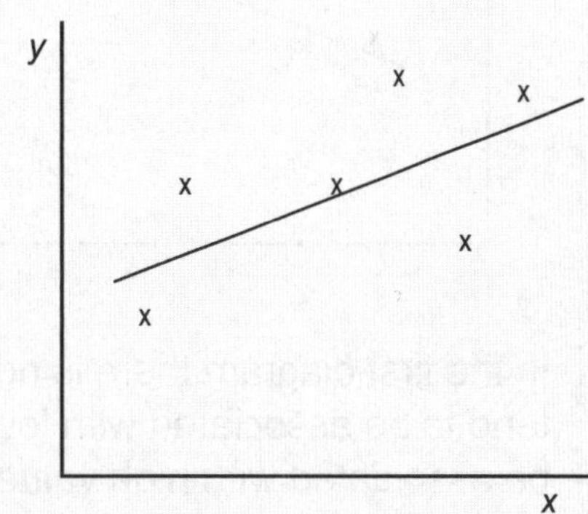

Clearly in the first diagram, the regression line would be a much more useful predictor than the regression line in the second diagram.

Degrees of correlation

Two variables might be:

(a) perfectly correlated
(b) partly correlated
(c) uncorrelated.

Different types of correlation explained

Perfect correlation

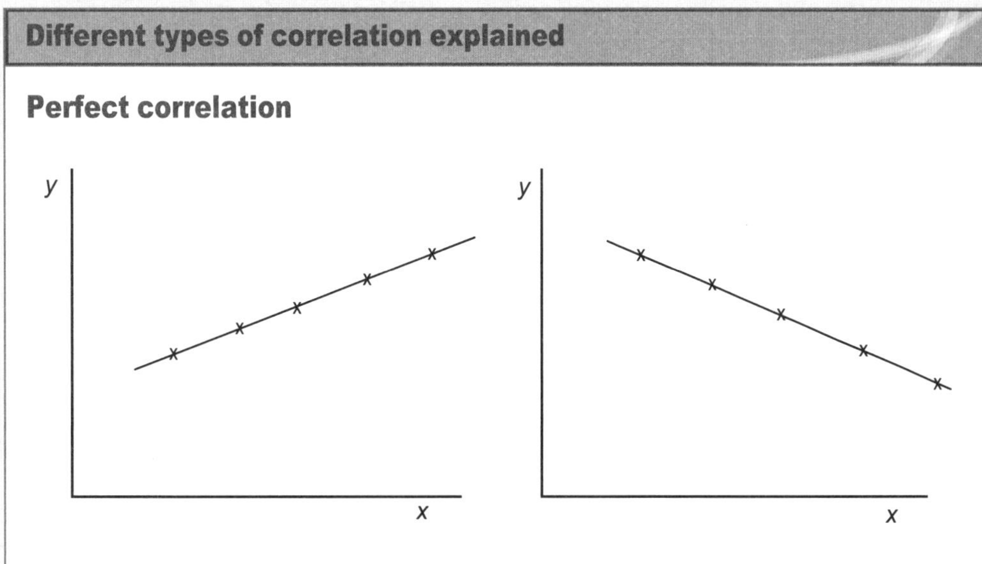

All the pairs of values lie on a straight line. There is an exact linear relationship between the two variables.

Partial correlation

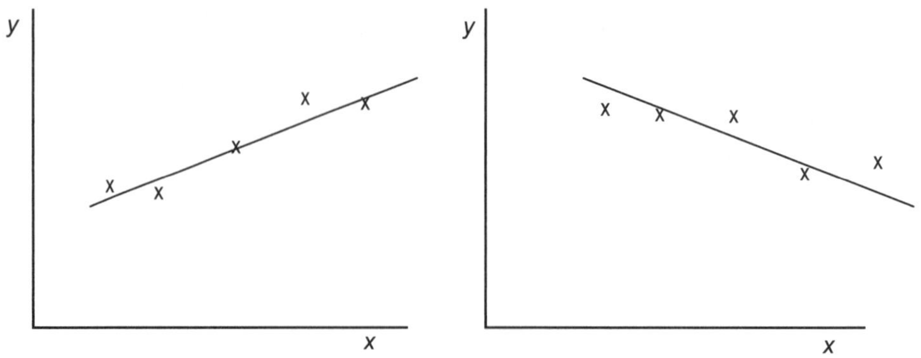

In the first diagram there is not an exact relationship, but low values of *x* tend to be associated with low values of y, and high values of *x* tend to be associated with high values of y.

In the second diagram again there is not an exact relationship, but low values of *x* tend to be associated with high values of y and vice versa.

No correlation

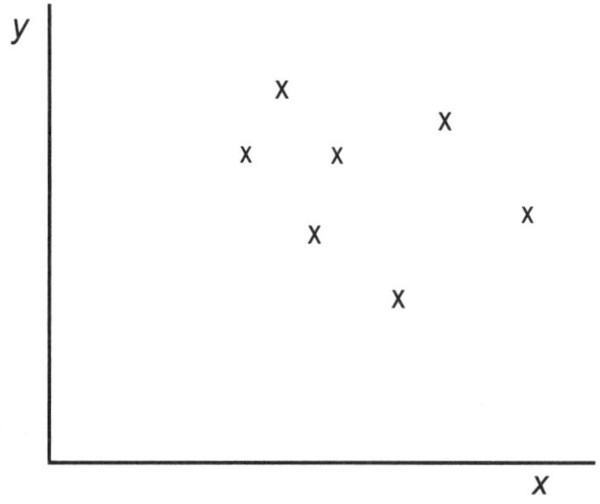

The values of the two variables seem to be completely unconnected.

Positive and negative correlation

Correlation can be positive or negative.

Positive correlation means that high values of one variable are associated with high values of the other and that low values of one are associated with low values of the other.

Negative correlation means that low values of one variable are associated with high values of the other and vice versa.

The correlation coefficient

The degree of correlation can be measured by the Pearsonian correlation coefficient, r (also known as the product moment correlation coefficient).

r must always be between –1 and +1.

If r = 1, there is perfect positive correlation
If r = 0, there is no correlation
If r = –1, there is perfect negative correlation

For other values of r, the meaning is not so clear. It is generally taken that if r > 0.8, then there is strong positive correlation and if r < –0.8, there is strong negative correlation, however more meaningful information can be gathered from calculating the coefficient of determination, r^2.

$$r = \frac{n\sum xy - \sum x \sum y}{\sqrt{\left(n\sum x^2 - \left(\sum x\right)^2\right)\left(n\sum y^2 - \left(\sum y\right)^2\right)}}$$

The coefficient of determination

This measures how good the estimated regression equation is, designated as r^2 (read as r-squared). The higher the r-squared, the more confidence one can have in the equation. Statistically, the coefficient of determination represents the proportion of the total variation in the y variable that is explained by the regression equation. It has the range of values between 0 and 1.

For example, if we read the following statement "factory overhead is a function of machine-hours with $r^2 = 0.80$," can be interpreted as "80% of the total variation of factory overhead is explained by the machine hours and the remaining 20% is accounted for by something other than machine-hours." The 20% is referred to as the error term.

Limitations of simple linear regression

(1) Assumes a linear relationship between the variables.

(2) Only measures the relationship between two variables. In reality the dependent variable is affected by many independent variables.

(3) Only interpolated forecasts tend to be reliable. The equation should not be used for extrapolation.

(4) Regression assumes that the historical behaviour of the data continues into the foreseeable future.

(5) Interpolated predictions are only reliable if there is a significant correlation between the data.

Interpolation and extrapolation

(1) If the value of x is within the range of our original data, the prediction is known as *Interpolation*.

(2) If the value of x is outside the range of our original data, the prediction is known as *Extrapolation*.

In general, interpolation is much safer than extrapolation.

4 Adjusting forecasts for inflation

The accuracy of forecasting is affected by the need to adjust historical data and future forecasts to allow for price or cost inflation.

- When historical data is used to calculate a trend line or line of best fit, it should ideally be adjusted to the same index level for prices or costs. If the actual cost or revenue data is used, without adjustments for inflation, the resulting line of best fit will include the inflationary differences.
- When a forecast is made from a line of best fit, an adjustment to the forecast should be made for anticipated inflation in the forecast period.

Example 3

Production overhead costs at company BW are assumed to vary with the number of machine hours worked. A line of best fit will be calculated from the following historical data, with costs adjusted to allow for cost inflation over time.

Year	Total production overheads	Number of machine hours	Cost index
	$		
20X1	143,040	3,000	192
20X2	156,000	3,200	200
20X3	152,320	2,700	224
20X4	172,000	3,000	235

Required:

(a) Reconcile the cost data to a common price level, to remove differences caused by inflation.

(b) If the line of best fit, based on current (20X4) prices, is calculated as:

$y = 33{,}000 + 47x$

where y = total production overhead costs in $ and x = the number of machine hours:

calculate the expected total overhead costs in 20X5 if expected production activity is 3,100 machine hours and the expected cost index is 250.

The high-low method with inflation

The high low method may be distorted in the presence of inflation. The best technique is to strip out the inflation, perform the technique as usual and then re-apply the inflation.

Illustration

A hotel cleaning department uses a combination of salaried staff (which are a fixed cost paid an annual fixed salary) supplemented at busy periods (such as at the weekend) with part-time staff (seen to be a variable cost). It has gathered the following information on wage cost over the last two months.

	Visitors	Total wages ($)
Month 1	260	7,600
Month 2	300	8,610

Month 2 corresponded with a wage review. At the start of that month all staff received a 5% pay rise.

The restaurant wants to determine the estimated wage cost for the next month when it is expected to have 340 visitors.

Solution

Firstly we should strip out the 5% inflation included in the Month 2 cost so that the uninflated wage cost would be $8,200 (i.e. $8,610/1.05).

Now we can apply the usual high-low technique:

Variable cost per visitor = [(8,200 – 7,600)/(300 – 260)] = $15

Total fixed cost for 560 visitors = [$7,600 – (260 × $15)] = $3,700

Now we can inflate these estimates for the Month 2 pay rise:

Revised variable cost per visitor = $15 × 1.05 = $15.75

Revised total fixed cost = $3,700 × 1.05 = $3,885

The total estimated cost for 340 visitors will be:

= $3,885 + (340 × $15.75) = $9,240.

5 Time series analysis

A time series is a series of figures recorded over time, e.g. unemployment over the last 5 years, output over the last 12 months, etc.

A graph of a time series is called a *histogram*.

Examples of a time series

Examples of time series might include the following:

- quarterly sales revenue totals over a number of years
- annual overhead costs over a number of years
- daily production output over a month.

Where the item being measured is subject to 'seasonal' variations, time series measurements are usually taken for each season. For example, if sales volume varies in each quarter of the year, a time series should be for quarterly sales. Similarly, if the sales in a retail store vary according to the day of the week, a time series might measure daily sales.

A time series has 4 components:

(1) The trend (T)
(2) Seasonal variations (S)
(3) Cyclical variations (C)
(4) Residual variations (R)

We are primarily interested in the first two – the trend and the seasonal variation.

Time series analysis is a term used to describe techniques for analysing a time series, in order to:

- identify whether there is any **underlying historical trend** and if there is, measure it
- use this analysis of the historical trend to forecast the trend into the future
- identify whether there are any **seasonal variations** around the trend, and if there is measure them
- apply estimated seasonal variations to a trend line forecast in order to prepare a forecast season by season.

In other words, a trend over time, established from historical data, and adjusted for seasonal variations, can then be used to make predictions for the future.

The trend

Most series follow some sort of long term movement – upwards, downwards or sideways. In time series analysis the trend is measured.

Seasonal variations

Seasonal variations are short-term fluctuations in value due to different circumstances which occur at different times of the year, on different days of the week, different times of day, etc e.g.:

- Ice cream sales are highest in summer
- Sales of groceries are highest on Saturdays
- Traffic is greatest in the morning and evening rush hours.

Illustration 1

A business might have a flat trend in sales, of $1 million each six months, but with sales $150,000 below trend in the first six months of the year and $150,000 above trend in the second six months. In this example, the sales would be $850,000 in the first six months of the year and $1,150,000 in the second six months.

- If there is a straight-line trend in the time series, seasonal variations must cancel each other out. The total of the seasonal variations over each cycle should be zero.
- Seasonal variations can be measured:
  - in units or in money values, or
  - as a percentage value or index value in relation to the underlying trend.

Cyclical and residual factors

Cyclical variations

Cyclical variations are medium-term to long term influences usually associated with the economy. These cycles are rarely of consistent length. A further problem is that we would need 6 or 7 full cycles of data to be sure that the cycle was there.

Residual or random factors

The residual is the difference between the actual value and the figure predicted using the trend, the cyclical variation and the seasonal variation, i.e. it is caused by irregular items, which could not be predicted.

Calculation of the trend

There are three main methods of finding the underlying trend of the data:

(1) *Inspection*. The trend line can be drawn by eye with the aim of plotting the line so that it lies in the middle of the data.

(2) *Least squares regression analysis*. The *x* axis represents time and the periods of time are numbers, e.g. January is 1, February is 2, March is 3, etc.

(3) *Moving averages*. This method attempts to remove seasonal or cyclical variations by a process of averaging.

Calculating a moving average

A moving average is in fact a series of averages, calculated from time series historical data.

- The first moving average value in the series is the average of the values for time period 1 to time period n. (So, if n = 4, the first moving average in the series would be the average of the historical values for time period 1 to time period 4.)
- The second moving average value in the series is the average of the values for time period 2 to time period (n + 1). (So, if n = 4, the second moving average in the series would be the average of the historical values for time period 2 to time period 5.)
- The third moving average value in the series is the average of the values for time period 3 to time period (n + 2). (So, if n = 4, the third moving average in the series would be the average of the historical values for time period 3 to time period 6.)

The moving average value is associated with the mid-point of the time periods used to calculate the average.

The moving average time period

When moving averages are used to estimate a trend line, an important issue is the choice of the number of time periods to use to calculate the moving average. How many time periods should a moving average be based on?

There is no definite or correct answer to this question. However, where there is a regular cycle of time periods, it would make sense to calculate the moving averages over a full cycle.

- When you are calculating a moving average of daily figures, it is probably appropriate to calculate a seven-day moving average.
- When you are calculating a moving average of quarterly figures, it is probably appropriate to calculate a four-quarter moving average.
- When you are calculating a moving average of monthly figures, it might be appropriate to calculate a 12-month moving average, although a shorter-period moving average might be preferred.

The seasonal variation

Once the trend has been found, the seasonal variation can be determined. A seasonal variation means that some periods are better than average (the trend) and some worse. Then the model can be used to predict future values.

Measuring seasonal variations

The technique for measuring seasonal variations differs between an additive model and a multiplicative model. The additive model method is described here.

- Seasonal variations can be estimated by comparing an actual time series with the trend line values calculated from the time series.
- For each 'season' (quarter, month, day etcetera), the seasonal variation is the difference between the trend line value and the actual historical value for the same period.
- A seasonal variation can be calculated for each period in the trend line. When the actual value is higher than the trend line value, the seasonal variation is positive. When the actual value is lower than the trend line value, the seasonal variation is negative.
- An average variation for each season is calculated.

- The sum of the seasonal variations has to be zero in the additive model. If they do not add up to zero, the seasonal variations should be adjusted so that they do add up to zero.
- The seasonal variations calculated in this way can be used in forecasting, by adding the seasonal variation to the trend line forecast if the seasonal variation is positive, or subtracting it from the trend line if it is negative.

When a multiplicative model is used to estimate seasonal variations, the seasonal variation for each period is calculated by expressing the actual sales for the period as a percentage value of the moving average figure for the same period.

The additive model

The additive model. Here the seasonal variation is expressed as an absolute amount to be added on to the trend to find the actual result, e.g. ice-cream sales in summer are good and in general we would expect sales to be $200,000 above the trend.

Actual/Prediction = T + S + C + R

In exam questions we would not be required to calculate the cyclical variation, and the random variations are by nature random and cannot be predicted and also ignored. The equation simplifies to:

Prediction = T + S

Example of the calculation

A small business operating holiday homes in Scotland wishes to forecast next year's sales for the budget, using moving averages to establish a straight-line trend and seasonal variations. Next year is 20Y0. The accountant has assumed that sales are seasonal, with a summer season and a winter season each year.

Seasonal sales for the past seven years have been as follows:

	Sales	
	Summer	**Winter**
	$000	$000
20X4	124	70
20X5	230	180
20X6	310	270
20X7	440	360
20X8	520	470
20X9	650	

Required:

(a) Calculate a trend line based on a two-season moving average.

(b) Use the trend line to calculate the average increase in sales each season.

(c) Calculate the adjusted seasonal variations in sales.

(d) Use this data to prepare a sales forecast for each season in 20Y0.

Solution

(a)

Season and year	Actual sales	Two-season moving total	Seasonal moving average	Centred moving average (Trend)	Seasonal variation
	(A)			(B)	= (A) – (B)
	$000	$000	$000	$000	$000
Summer 20X4	124				
		194	97		
Winter 20X4	70			123.5	– 53.5
		300	150		
Summer 20X5	230			177.5	+ 52.5
		410	205		
Winter 20X5	180			225.0	– 45.0
		490	245		
Summer 20X6	310			267.5	+ 42.5
		580	290		
Winter 20X6	270			322.5	– 52.5
		710	355		
Summer 20X7	440			377.5	+ 62.5
		800	400		
Winter 20X7	360			420.0	– 60.0
		880	440		
Summer 20X8	520			467.5	+ 52.5
		990	495		
Winter 20X8	470			527.5	– 57.5
		1,120	560		
Summer 20X9	650				

The trend line is shown by the centred moving averages.

(b) The average increase in sales each season in the trend line is:

($527,500 – $123,500)/8 seasons = $50, 500 each season

(c) Seasonal variations need to add up to zero in the additive model. The seasonal variations calculated so far are:

Year	Summer	Winter
	$000	$000
20X4		– 53.5
20X5	+ 52.5	– 45.0
20X6	+ 42.5	– 52.5
20X7	+ 62.5	– 60.0
20X8	+ 52.5	– 57.5
Total variations	+ 210.0	– 268.5

	Summer	Winter	Total
Number of measurements	4	5	
Average seasonal variation	+ 52.5	– 53.7	– 1.2
Reduce to 0 (share equally)	+ 0.6	+ 0.6	+ 1.2
Adjusted seasonal variation	+ 53.1	– 53.1	0.0

The seasonal variations could be rounded to + $53,000 in summer and – $53,000 in winter.

(d) To predict the sales in 20Y0 we first need to extrapolate the trend line into 20Y0 and then adjust it for the expected seasonal variation.

	Expected trend (W1)	Adjusted seasonal variation	Forecast sales
Summer 20X9	578.0		
Winter 20X9	628.5		
Summer 20Y0	679.0	+ 53.0	732.0
Winter 20Y0	729.5	– 53.0	676.5

(W1)

If the actual trend in Winter 20X8 was 527.5, then we can expect the next trend figure to be 578 (527.5 plus the average increase in trend calculated in part (b) of 50.5). We can continue this process for each trend figure over the next few periods.

The multiplicative model

Here the seasonal variation is expressed as a ratio/proportion/ percentage to be multiplied by the trend to arrive at the actual figure, e.g. ice-cream sales in summer are good and in general we would expect sales to be 50% more than the trend

Actual/Prediction = T × S × C × R

Again this simplifies to:

Prediction = T × S

Illustration 2

Consider a business with the following actual results in a year:

Year	Quarter	Units sold
20X1	1	65
20X1	2	80
20X1	3	70
20X1	4	85

The trend is expected to increase by 10 units per month and has been calculated as 60 units for the first quarter. This provides the following table:

Year	Quarter	Units sold	Trend
20X1	1	65	60
20X1	2	80	70
20X1	3	70	80
20X1	4	85	90

Required:

How might these figures be used to develop a time series model in order to forecast unit sales in each quarter of year 2, using

(a) an additive modelling approach, and

(b) a multiplicative modelling approach?

Solution

The point of departure is to take the actual unit sales and compare the trend figures with the actual figures for year 1 in order to determine the seasonal variation for each quarter. This variation can be expressed as (a) a lump sum for each quarter (the additive model) or (b) an index representing the percentage of trend (the multiplicative, or proportional, model).

Year	Quarter	Units sold	Trend	(a) Variation	(b) var %
20X1	1	65	60	5	+8.33
20X1	2	80	70	10	+14.29
20X1	3	70	80	–10	–12.50
20X1	4	85	90	–5	–5.56

Notes:

(1) The multiplicative model season variations may be expressed in several different ways. For example, the quarter 3 factor may be expressed as an indexation 87.5% or 0.875.

(2) In the multiplicative model the total seasonal variations should add to zero (or 0%). In this scenario we are looking only at an abstract of a longer trend and therefore it does not add to 0% here.

One may then apply these variation figures to trend projections in order to produce a quarterly forecast for unit sales in Year 2. The two modelling approaches produce two alternative forecasts under headings (a) and (b).

Year	Quarter	Trend	Additive (forecast)	Multiplicative (forecast)
20X2	5	100	105	108
20X2	6	110	120	126
20X2	7	120	110	105
20X2	8	130	125	123

Note that this is the simplest possible example. In particular, we are basing our analysis on only one set of observations (those for this particular year). In practice, one would prefer to calculate the seasonal variations on the basis of the average of two or three sets of observations. Thus, if one observed quarter 1 variations from trend (additive model) of 6 (year A), 5 (year B) and 7 (year C) then one would adopt the average of the three (6) as the quarter 1 seasonal variation. The averaging process has the effect of 'ironing out' the impact of random variations over the past period you are considering.

Advantages and disadvantages

The advantages of forecasting using time series analysis are that:

- forecasts are based on clearly-understood assumptions
- trend lines can be reviewed after each successive time period, when the most recent historical data is added to the analysis; consequently, the reliability of the forecasts can be assessed
- forecasting accuracy can possibly be improved with experience.

The disadvantages of forecasting with time series analysis are that:

- there is an assumption that what has happened in the past is a reliable guide to the future
- there is an assumption that a straight-line trend exists
- there is an assumption that seasonal variations are constant, either in actual values using the additive model (such as dollars of sales) or as a proportion of the trend line value using the multiplicative model.

None of these assumptions might be valid.

However, the reliability of a forecasting method can be established over time. If forecasts turn out to be inaccurate, management might decide that they are not worth producing, and that different methods of forecasting should be tried. On the other hand, if forecasts prove to be reasonably accurate, management are likely to continue with the same forecasting method.

6 Chapter summary

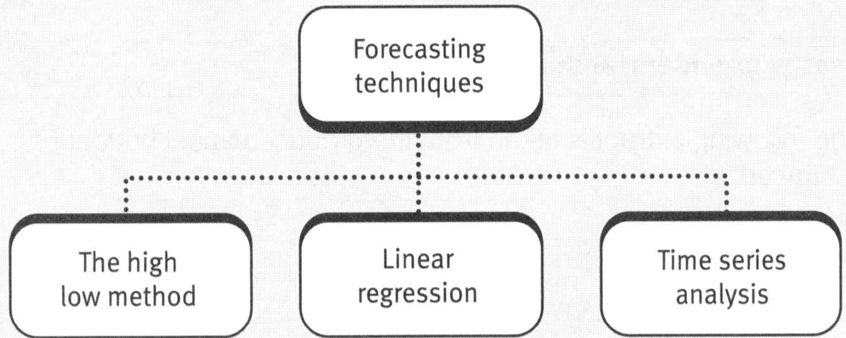

The high low method

- The key is to use the highest and lowest output
- Calculate variable costs first
- Watch out for inflation and steps in fixed costs

Linear regression

- Assumes a linear relationship between two variables
- a = fixed costs
- b = the variable cost
- Variables must be correlated

Time series analysis

- Takes account of inflation
- The trend is calculated using a moving average
- Forecasts need to be adjusted for seasonal variations

7 Practice questions

Test your understanding 1

The following extract is taken from the production cost budget of S Limited:

Production (units)	2,000	3,000
Production cost ($)	11,100	12,900

The budget cost allowance for an activity level of 4,000 units would be $______.

Test your understanding 2

The following data have been extracted from the budget working papers of BL Limited.

Production volume	*1,000*	*2,000*
	$/unit	$/unit
Direct materials	4.00	4.00
Direct labour	3.50	3.50
Production overhead – department 1	6.00	4.20
Production overhead – department 2	4.00	2.00

Identify the total fixed cost and variable cost per unit *(circle the correct figure in each column)*

Total fixed cost	**Variable cost per unit**
3,600	7.50
7,600	9.90

Test your understanding 3

A company will forecast its quarterly sales units for a new product by using a formula to predict the base sales units and then adjusting the figure by a seasonal index.

The formula is BU = 4,000 + 80Q

Where BU = Base sales units and Q is the quarterly period number.

The seasonal index values are:

Quarter 1	105%
Quarter 2	80%
Quarter 3	95%
Quarter 4	120%

Identify the forecast increase in sales units from Quarter 3 to Quarter 4:

A 25%

B 80 units

C 100 units

D 1,156 units

Test your understanding 4

W plc is preparing its budgets for next year.

The following regression equation has been found to be a reliable estimate of W plc's deseasonalised sales in units:

y = 10x + 420

Where *y* is the total sales units and *x* refers to the accountancy period. Quarterly seasonal variations have been found to be:

Q1	Q2	Q3	Q4
+10%	+25%	–5%	–30%

In accounting period 33 (which is quarter 4) identify the forecast seasonally adjusted sales units:

A 525

B 589

C 750

D 975

Test your understanding 5

A company has achieved the following sales levels of its key product, article B, over the last four years:

Sales of article B ('000 units)

	Q1	Q2	Q3	Q4
20X3	24.8	36.3	38.1	47.5
20X4	31.2	42.0	43.4	55.9
20X5	40.0	48.8	54.0	69.1
20X6	54.7	57.8	60.3	68.9

(a) Explain what sort of trend and seasonal pattern would be expected to emerge from the analysis of this data?

(b) Numbering 20X3 Q1 as $t = 1$, through to 20X6 Q4 as $t = 16$, calculate the equation of the trend (T) as a linear regression line.

(c) Forecast the trend in sales for the four quarters of 20X7.

(d) Calculate the seasonal component (S) using the multiplicative model. Adjust your average seasonal variations so that they add to 4.

(e) Forecast the sales of B for the four quarters of 20X7.

(f) If actual sales for this company in the first quarter of the next year were 60,000 units, seasonally adjust this figure to estimate the underlying trend line in the first quarter.

The calculations so far have been based on the use of linear regression in order to determine the trend line. Let's look at this same question but this time using time series analysis.

(g) Calculate the trend for the sales of article B as a centred four-point moving average.

(h) Evaluate the seasonal component for each quarter based on the moving average trend.

(i) Forecast the sales of B for the four quarters of 20X7 using trend forecasts of 66.7, 68.8, 70.9 and 73.

Note: This is a very long question and an exam question will not involve all of these components. However, it should act as a way for you to test your understanding of all of the forecasting techniques considered in this scenario.

Test your understanding answers

Example 1

Step 1: Calculate the variable cost per unit

$$\text{Variable cost per unit} = \frac{\text{Increase in cost}}{\text{Increase in level of activity}}$$

$$= \frac{\$46,000 - \$26,000}{10,000 \text{ units} - 5,000 \text{ units}}$$

$$= \$4 \text{ per unit}$$

Step 2: Find the fixed cost

The fixed cost can be determined either at the high level or the low level.

	High level	**Low level**
	$	$
Semi-variable cost	46,000	26,000
Variable costs		
$4 per unit × 10,000 units	40,000	
$4 per unit × 5,000 units		20,000
Fixed cost	6,000	6,000

Step 3: Calculate the expected cost

Therefore cost for 13,000 units = (13,000 units × $4 per unit) + $6,000 = $58,000

Example 2

$$b = \frac{n\Sigma xy - \Sigma x \Sigma y}{n\Sigma x^2 - (\Sigma x)^2}$$

$$= \frac{6 \times 326{,}500 - 450 \times 4{,}050}{6 \times 38{,}300 - 450^2}$$

$$= \frac{136{,}500}{27{,}300} \quad = \quad 5$$

$$a = \overline{y} - b\overline{x}$$

$$a = \frac{4{,}050}{6} - 5 \times \frac{450}{6} \quad = \quad 300$$

The regression equation is $y = 300 + 5x$

Example 2 – CONTINUED

(a)

			$000
Sales revenue	= $300k + (5 × $150k)	=	1,050
Sales revenue	= $300k + (5 × $50k)	=	550

(b) The second prediction is the more reliable as it involves interpolation. The first prediction goes beyond the original data upon which the regression line was based and thus assumes that the relationship will continue on in the same way, which may not be true.

Example 3

(a) As the line of best fit is based on 20X4 prices, use this as the common price level. Costs should therefore be adjusted by a factor:

$$\frac{\text{Index level to which costs will be adjusted}}{\text{Actual index level of costs}}$$

Year	Actual overheads	Cost index	Adjustment factor	Costs at 20X4 price level
	$			$
20X1	143,040	192	× 235/192	175,075
20X2	156,000	200	× 235/200	183,300
20X3	152,320	224	× 235/224	159,800
20X4	172,000	235	× 235/235	172,000

(b) If the forecast number of machine hours is 3,100 and the cost index is 250:

Forecast overhead costs = [$33,000 + ($47 × 3,100 hours)] × (250/235)

= $178,700 × (250/235)

= $190,106

Test your understanding 1

The high-low method

Step 1 Calculate the variable cost per unit

$$\text{Variable cost per unit} = \frac{\text{Increase in cost}}{\text{Increase in level of activity}}$$

$$= \frac{\$12,900 - \$11,100}{3,000 \text{ units} - 2,000 \text{ units}}$$

= $1.80 per unit

Step 2 Find the fixed cost

A semi-variable cost has only got 2 components – a fixed bit and a variable bit. We now know the variable part. The bit that's left must be the fixed cost. It can be determined either at the high level or the low level.

	High level	**Low level**
	$	$
Semi-variable cost	12,900	11,100
Variable part		
$1.80/unit × 3,000 units	5,400	
$1.80/unit × 2,000 units		3,600
Fixed cost	7,500	7,500

Therefore cost for 4,000 units = 4,000 units × $1.80 per unit + $7,500 = $**14,700**.

Test your understanding 2

We know the cost per unit. We need to multiply by the number of units so that we can find the total cost for 1,000 units and 2,000 units. Then we can apply the high-low method.

Production volume	**1,000**	**2,000**
	$/unit	$/unit
Direct materials	4.00	4.00
Direct labour	3.50	3.50
Production overhead – department 1	6.00	4.20
Production overhead – department 2	4.00	2.00
	17.50	13.70
× No of units	× 1,000	× 2,000
Total cost	17,500	27,400

Now we can do the high-low method.

The high-low method

Step 1 Calculate the variable cost per unit

$$\text{Variable cost per unit} = \frac{\text{Increase in cost}}{\text{Increase in level of activity}}$$

$$= \frac{\$27{,}400 - \$17{,}500}{2{,}000\text{ units} - 1{,}000\text{ units}}$$

= **$9.90 per unit**

Step 2 Find the fixed cost

A semi-variable cost has only got 2 components – a fixed bit and a variable bit. We now know the variable part. The bit that's left must be the fixed cost. It can be determined either at the high level or the low level.

	High level	**Low level**
	$	$
Semi-variable cost	27,400	17,500
Variable part		
$9.90/unit × 2,000 units	19,800	
$9.90/unit × 1,000 units		9,900
Fixed cost	**7,600**	7,600

Test your understanding 3

D

Sales in quarter 3 (Q = 3)			
Base = 4,000 + (80 × 3)	=	4,240	
Seasonal adjustment		95%	
Actual sales	=	4,028	
Sales in quarter 4 (Q = 4)			
Base = 4,000 + (80 × 4)	=	4,320	
Seasonal adjustment		120%	
Actual sales	=	5,184	
Overall increase in sales	=	5,184 – 4,028	= 1,156 units

Test your understanding 4

A

y = 10x + 420

We are told that x refers to the accountancy period, which is 33, therefore:

y = 420 + (33 × 10) = 750

This is the trend, however and we need to consider the seasonal variation too. Accounting period 33 is quarter 4. Quarter 4 is a bad quarter and the seasonal variation is –30%, therefore the expected results for period 33 are 30% less than the trend.

Expected sales = 750 × 70% = 525 units

Test your understanding 5

(a) For every quarter, each year shows an increase in sales, so an increasing trend is expected. Also, there is a regular seasonal pattern with a steady increase in sales from Q1 to Q4.

(b) Letting $x = t$ and $y = T$, the necessary summations are n = 16; Σx = 136; Σy = 772.8; Σxy = 7,359.1; Σx^2 = 1,496.

$$b = \frac{n\Sigma xy - \Sigma x \Sigma y}{n\Sigma x^2 - (\Sigma x)^2} = \frac{(16 \times 7{,}359.1) - (136 \times 772.8)}{(16 \times 1{,}496) - 136^2} = 2.3244 \text{ (to 4 dp)}$$

$$a = \bar{y} - b\bar{x} = \frac{772.8}{16} - 2.324411765 \times \frac{136}{16} = 28.54 \text{ (to 2dp)}$$

The trend equation is thus:

$T = 28.54 + 2.3244t$

(c) In 20X7, t takes values 17 to 20, giving trend forecasts as follows:

Q1	$t = 17$	$T = 28.54 + 2.3244 \times 17 = 68.0548$
Q2	$t = 18$	$T = 70.3792$
Q3	$t = 19$	$T = 72.7036$
Q4	$t = 20$	$T = 75.028$

(d)

Year	*Quarter*	*t*	*T*	*Sales, Y*	*Y/T*
20X3	1	1	30.8669	24.8	0.8034
	2	2	33.1913	36.3	1.0937
	3	3	35.5157	38.1	1.0728
	4	4	37.8401	47.5	1.2553
20X4	1	5	40.1646	31.2	0.7768
	2	6	42.4890	42.0	0.9885
	3	7	44.8134	43.4	0.9685
	4	8	47.1378	55.9	1.1859

20X5	1	9	49.4622	40.0	0.8087
	2	10	51.7866	48.8	0.9423
	3	11	54.1110	54.0	0.9979
	4	12	56.4354	69.1	1.2244
20X6	1	13	58.7599	54.7	0.9309
	2	14	61.0843	57.8	0.9462
	3	15	63.4087	60.3	0.9510
	4	16	65.7331	68.9	1.0482

Year	*Q1*	*Q2*	*Q3*	*Q4*	
20X3	0.8034	1.0937	1.0728	1.2553	
20X4	0.7768	0.9885	0.9685	1.1859	
20X5	0.8087	0.9423	0.9979	1.2244	
20X6	0.9309	0.9462	0.9510	1.0482	
Total	3.3198	3.9707	3.9902	4.7138	*Total*
Average	0.8300	0.9927	0.9976	1.1785	3.9988
+	0.0003	0.0003	0.0003	0.0003	0.0012
Comp.	0.8303	0.9930	0.9979	1.1788	4.0000

Quite a few rounding errors will have built up by now, so do not worry if your results differ a little from these. *Note: to improve accuracy and minimise the presence of rounding errors, in calculating T you should use all the decimal places in your regression line equation from part b, i.e.* $T = 28.5425 + 2.324411765 \times t$.

To two decimal places, the seasonal components are

0.83	0.99	1.00	1.18

(e) The model is $Y = T \times S$ so the forecast sales *(Y)* in '000 units are given by multiplying the trend forecasts *(T)* by the seasonal factors (S).

Using a regression equation and seasonal components to create the forecast:

Forecast trend	68.0548	70.3792	72.7036	75.028
Seasonal	0.8303	0.993	0.9979	1.1788
Forecast sales	56.5	69.9	72.6	88.4

(f) The seasonally adjusted figure is an estimate of the trend and so is given by Y/S = 60,000/0.8303 = 72,263 units.

(g)

Year	Quarter	Sales (Y)	Four-point moving total	Eight-point moving total	Four-point moving ave. trend (T)
20X3	1	24.8			
	2	36.3			
			146.7		
	3	38.1		299.8	37.4750
			153.1		
	4	47.5		311.9	38.9875
			158.8		
20X4	1	31.2		322.9	40.3625
			164.1		
	2	42.0		336.6	42.0750
			172.5		
	3	43.4		353.8	44.2250
			181.3		
	4	55.9		369.4	46.1750
			188.1		
20X5	1	40.0		386.8	48.3500
			198.7		
	2	48.8		410.6	51.3250
			211.9		
	3	54.0		438.5	54.8125
			226.6		
	4	69.1		462.2	57.7750
			235.6		
20X6	1	54.7		477.5	59.6875
			241.9		
	2	57.8		483.6	60.4500
			241.7		
	3	60.3			
	4	68.9			

(h) Calculating *Y/T* and arranging the values according to their quarters gives:

	Q1	**Q2**	**Q3**	**Q4**	
20X3			1.017	1.218	
20X4	0.773	0.998	0.981	1.211	
20X5	0.827	0.951	0.985	1.196	
20X6	0.916	0.956			
Total	2.516	2.905	2.983	3.625	**Total**
Average	0.839	0.968	0.994	1.208	4.009
–	0.002	0.002	0.002	0.002	0.008
Comp.	0.837	0.966	0.992	1.206	4.001

Rounding to two decimal places gives seasonal components of:

0.84 0.97 0.99 1.21

(i) Forecast for 20X7

	Q1	**Q2**	**Q3**	**Q4**
Trend	66.70	68.80	70.90	73.00
Comp.	0.84	0.97	0.99	1.21
Sales	56.028	66.736	70.191	88.33

Hence the sales forecasts for the four quarters of 20X7 are (in '000 units):

56 67 70 88

chapter

14

The treatment of uncertainty and risk in decision making

Chapter learning objectives

Lead	Component
D1. Analyse information to assess risk and its impact on short-term decisions.	(a) Discuss the nature of risk and uncertainty and the attitudes to risk by decision makers. (b) Analyse risk using sensitivity analysis, expected values, standard deviations and probability tables. (c) Apply decision models to deal with uncertainty in decision making.

1 Chapter overview diagram

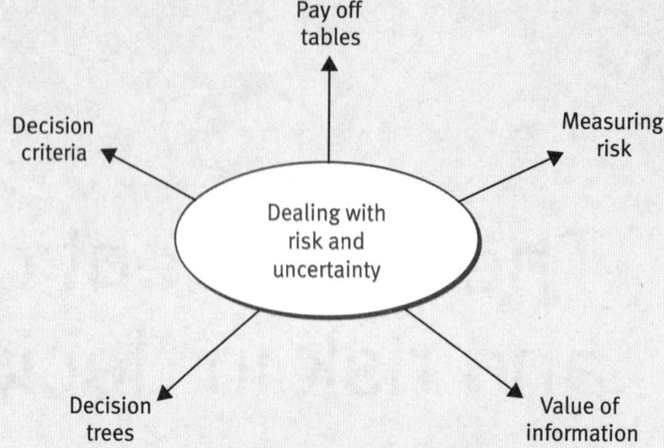

Topic overview

Many business decisions will involve an element of risk and uncertainty. This chapter looks at how risk and uncertainty can be built into the decision making process. This is often achieved by building in probabilities for expected outcomes and using expected values and decision trees to assess the problem.

Forecasting and decision making often include an element of risk or uncertainty. Because they look to the future they often involve estimates of future costs and benefits. In this chapter we look at how these risks and uncertainty can be built into the decision making process.

Decision making involves making decisions now about what will happen in the future. Events in the future can be predicted, but managers can rarely be 100% confident that these predicted future events will actually arise. As actual results emerge managers are likely to discover that they have achieved better or worse results than those predicted originally.

There are several ways of dealing with this variability of outcomes. In this session we will consider several different possible outcomes that may arise. It is common in practice to consider three possible outcomes; the most likely outcome, the pessimistic (worst possible) outcome and the optimistic (best possible) outcome. Analysts may consider more than these three possibilities, but more information will become more complicated and cumbersome to analyse and understand.

Examination questions will generally provide all the different possible outcomes that may arise, together with the associated chance (probability) of the outcome occurring. It is our task to analyse the information given, recommend an appropriate strategy for management to follow and finally to highlight the potential risk involved in the various choices.

2 Risk and uncertainty

The difference between risk and uncertainty

When making decisions, a decision maker will aim to account for risk but may struggle to account for uncertainty.

- **risk** – quantifiable – possible outcomes have associated probabilities, thus allowing the use of mathematical techniques
- **uncertainty** – unquantifiable – outcomes cannot be mathematically modelled.

Illustration on risk and uncertainty

Risk: there are a number of possible outcomes and the probability of each outcome is known.

For example, based on past experience of digging for oil in a particular area, an oil company may estimate that they have a 60% chance of finding oil and a 40% chance of not finding oil.

Uncertainty: there are a number of possible outcomes but the probability of each outcome is not known.

For example, the same oil company may dig for oil in a previously unexplored area. The company knows that it is possible for them to either find or not find oil but it does not know the probabilities of each of these outcomes.

One possible approach to dealing with risk is to deploy sophisticated modelling techniques in an attempt to improve the reliability of business forecasts. The use of trend analysis, encountered earlier in this text, is one possibility. Within this chapter we will look at how a simpler expected value technique may be of use.

3 Probabilities and expected values

An expected value summarises all the different possible outcomes by calculating a single weighted average. It is the long run average (mean).

The expected value is not the most likely result. It may not even be a possible result, but instead it finds the average outcome if the same event was to take place thousands of times.

Expected value formula

EV = Σpx **LEARN**

where x represents the future outcome

and p represents the probability of the outcome occurring

Illustration 1

An organisation is considering launching a new product. It will do so if the expected value of the total revenue is in excess of $1,000. It is decided to set the selling price at $10. After some investigation a number of probabilities for different levels of sales revenue are predicted; these are shown in the following table:

Units sold	Revenue	Probability	Pay-off
	$		$
80	800	0.15	120
100	1,000	0.50	500
120	1,200	0.35	420
		1.00	EV = 1,040

The expected sales revenue at a selling price of $10 per unit is $1,040, that is [800 × 0.15] + [1,000 × 0.50] + [1,200 × 0.35]. In preparing forecasts and making decisions management may proceed on the assumption that it can expect sales revenue of $1,040 if it sets a selling price of $10 per unit. The actual outcome of adopting this selling price may be sales revenue that is higher or lower than $1,040. And $1,040 is not even the most likely outcome; the most likely outcome is $1,000, since this has the highest probability.

Histograms

Probability data may be presented diagrammatically in the form of a histogram. The information given in the illustration immediately above might be presented as follows:

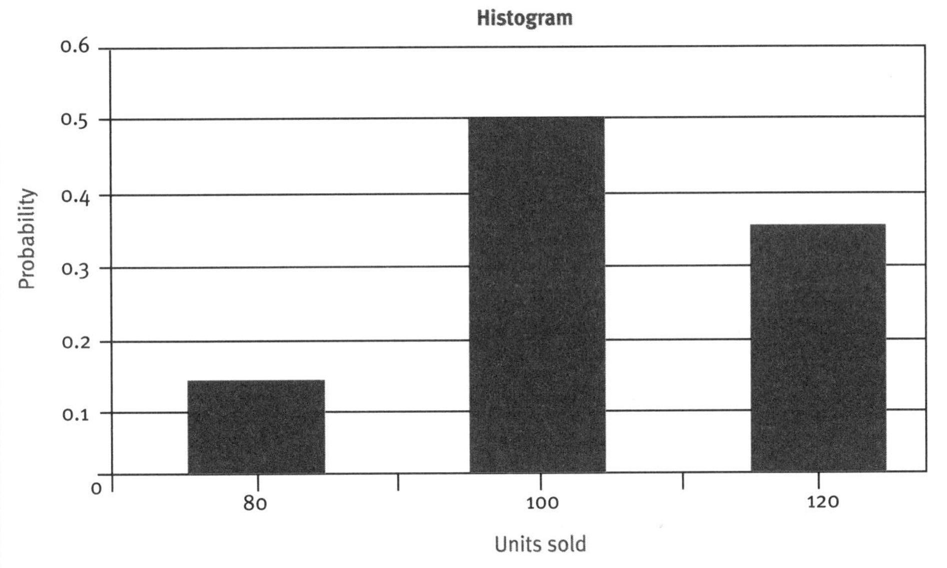

The single figure of the expected value of revenue can hide a wide range of possible actual results.

Example 1 – Calculating an expected value

A company has identified four possible outcomes from a new marketing strategy as follows:

Outcome	Profit ($)	Probability
A	100,000	0.10
B	70,000	0.40
C	50,000	0.30
D	–20,000	0.20

Calculate the expected outcome of this strategy.

Furthermore, not all decision-makers will have the same attitude towards risk. There are three main types of decision-maker.

- **Risk neutral** decision-makers consider all possible outcomes and will select the strategy that maximises the expected value or benefit.
- **Risk seekers** are likely to select the strategy with the best possible outcomes, regardless of the likelihood that they will occur. They will apply the maximax criteria (covered later).
- **Risk averse** decision-makers try to avoid risk. They would rather select a lower, but certain, outcome than risk going for a higher pay-off which is less certain to occur. They will apply the maximin criterion or the minimax regret approach (both covered later).

Illustration 2

For instance, after investigation in the previous illustration the predicted revenues might have been different. They might have been as follows:

Units sold	Revenue $	Probability	Pay-off $
40	400	0.15	60.00
100	1,000	0.50	500.00
137	1,370	0.35	479.50
		1.00	EV= 1039.50

Both situations give rise to the same expected sales revenue of $1,040 (to the nearest $), but the two situations are not the same. The second involves a wider dispersal of possible outcomes; hence it involves higher risk. If the decision-makers are risk averse they will judge the range of possible outcomes described in the second situation to be worse than the first. If the decision-makers are risk seekers they may prefer the second situation, because of the higher outcome in the best possible situation. However, in this case, the dire downside of $400 may put them off. Whatever the case it can be seen that the evaluation of the options solely on the basis of their expected value may not always be appropriate.

Utility theory

Utility is another important aspect of risk and uncertainty. The basis of the theory is that an individual's attitude to certain risk profiles will depend on the amount of money involved. For example, most people would accept a bet on the toss of a coin, if the outcome were that they would win $6 if it came down heads and if it came down tails they would pay $4. The average person would be happy to play secure in the knowledge that they would win if the game were repeated over a long enough period; if not it would still be a good bet. But if the stakes were raised so that the win was $6,000 on a single toss coming down heads and a loss of $4,000 if it came down tails, the average person might think twice and reject the bet as being too risky. Utility theory attaches weights to the sums of money involved; these are tailor-made to the individual's attitude towards winning and losing certain sums of money.

Therefore, considering a proposed option solely on the basis of its expected value ignores the range of possible outcomes.

Further expected value examples

Situation 1

A company buys in sub-assemblies in order to manufacture a product. It is reviewing its policy of putting each sub-assembly through a detailed inspection process on delivery, and is considering not inspecting at all. Experience has shown that the quality of the sub-assembly is of acceptable standard 90 per cent of the time. It costs $10 to inspect a sub-assembly and another $10 to put right any defect found at that stage. If the sub-assembly is not inspected and is then found to be faulty at the finished goods stage the cost of rework is $40.

Required:

Advise the company whether or not they should change their policy.

Solution

Four outcomes are possible:

(i) Inspect and find no problems – cost $10.

(ii) Inspect and find problems – cost $20.

(iii) Do not inspect and no problems exist – no cost.

(iv) Do not inspect and problems do exist – cost $40.

If sub-assemblies achieve the required standard 90 per cent of the time then there is a 10 per cent chance that they will be faulty.

The expected value of the cost of each policy is as follows:

Inspect	[0.9 × $10] + [0.1 × $20] = $11
Do not inspect	[0.9 × $0] + [0.1 × $40] = $4

Taken over a long enough period of time, a policy of not carrying out an inspection would lead to a saving in cost of $7 per sub-assembly. On a purely quantitative analysis, therefore, this is the correct policy to adopt.

However, in the real world such a high level of failures is incompatible with a requirement for a 'quality product', and the concept of continuous improvement. It would be more useful to ask the supplier some basic questions regarding his quality management, in order to bring about a fundamental shift towards outcome (iii), rather than simply implementing a policy on the basis of such an uncritical analysis of the situation.

Situation 2

An individual is considering backing the production of a new musical in the West End. It would cost $100,000 to stage for the first month. If it is well received by the critics, it will be kept open at the end of the first month for a further 6 months, during which time further net income of $350,000 would be earned. If the critics dislike it, it will close at the end of the first month. There is a 50:50 chance of a favourable review.

Required:

Should the individual invest in the musical?

Solution

The expected value of backing the musical is:

[0.5 × $250,000] – [0.5 × $100,000] = $75,000

As this provides a positive return it would be accepted on the basis of expected values as the alternative yields zero. However, the expected value can be misleading here as it is a one-off situation and the expected profit of $75,000 is not a feasible outcome. The only feasible outcomes of this project are a profit of $250,000 or a loss of $100,000.

While almost everybody would welcome a profit of $250,000, not many individuals could afford to sustain a loss of $100,000 and they would place a high utility on such a loss. Many investors would be risk averse in such a situation because they would not consider that a 50 per cent chance of making $250,000 was worth an equal 50 per cent risk of losing $100,000; the loss might bankrupt them. On the other hand, if the individual were a multi-millionaire the return of 250 per cent would be very appealing and the loss of a mere $100,000 would have a low utility attached to it.

The two exercises have only had single-point outcomes, that is conformity or otherwise with a pre-set quality standard and a successful show or a flop. It is obvious that the two outcomes of the first exercise represent the only possible alternatives and so quantification of the related pay-offs along the lines of the example appears reasonable. It is also obvious that the profit of $250,000 predicted for a successful show in the case of the second exercise is far too precise a figure. It would be more realistic to assume a range of possible successful pay-offs, which will vary, according to the number of seats sold and the price of the seats. If probabilities are attached to each estimate, the expected value of a successful outcome will take account of the range of possible outcomes, by weighting each of them by its associated probability.

The range of possible outcomes might be as follows:

Profit ($)	**Probability**	**Expected value** ($)
(100,000)	0.500	(50,000)
200,000	0.175	35,000
250,000	0.200	50,000
300,000	0.075	22,500
350,000	0.050	17,500
	1.000	75,000

The statement of a range of possible outcomes and their associated probabilities is known as a probability distribution. Presenting the distribution to management allows two further useful inferences to be drawn:

- *The most likely successful outcome.* That is the successful outcome with the highest probability (a profit of $250,000).
- *The probability of an outcome being above or below a particular figure.* The particular figure will either be the expected value or a figure of consequence, such as zero profit, where a lesser outcome might have dire consequences. By summing the probabilities for pay-offs of $200,000 and $250,000, it can be concluded that there is a 37.5 per cent probability that profits will be $250,000 or less if the musical is successful. By summing those for $300,000 and $350,000 it can be determined that the probability of a profit of $300,000 or more in the event of success is only 12.5 per cent.

Advantages and disadvantages of EVs

Advantages	Disadvantages
• takes account of risk	• subjective
• easy decision rule	• not useful for one-offs
• simple	• ignores attitudes to risk
	• answer may not be possible

Further explanation

Advantages:

- Takes risk into account by considering the probability of each possible outcome and using this information to calculate an expected value.
- The information is reduced to a single number resulting in easier decisions.
- Calculations are relatively simple.

Disadvantages:

- The probabilities used are usually very subjective.
- The EV is merely a weighted average and therefore has little meaning for a one-off project.
- The EV gives no indication of the dispersion of possible outcomes about the EV, i.e. the risk.
- The EV may not correspond to any of the actual possible outcomes.

Standard deviations

In order to measure the risk associated with a particular project, it is helpful to find out how wide ranging the possible outcomes are. The conventional measure is the standard deviation. The standard deviation compares all the actual outcomes with the expected value (or mean outcome). It then calculates how far on average the outcomes deviate from the mean. It is calculated using a formula.

The basic idea is that the standard deviation is a measure of volatility: the more that actual outcomes vary from the average outcome, the more volatile the returns and therefore the more risk involved in the investment/decision.

Further details on standard deviations

The standard deviation is calculated using the following formula:

$$\sigma = \sqrt{\frac{\sum (x - \overline{x})^2}{n}}$$

σ = standard deviation
$\sum$ = sum of
x = each value in the data set
$\overline{x}$ = mean of all values in the data set
n = number of value in the data set

Let's examine how standard deviations are calculated and used by considering the following illustration.

Illustration

A company is considering whether to make product X or product Y. They cannot make both products. The estimated sales demand for each product is uncertain and the following probability distribution of the expected profits for each product has been identified.

Product X

Profits ($)	**Probability**	**Expected value** ($)
3,000	0.10	300
3,500	0.20	700
4,000	0.40	1,600
4,500	0.20	900
5,000	0.10	500
	1.00	4,000

Product Y

Profits ($)	**Probability**	**Expected value** ($)
2,000	0.05	100
3,000	0.10	300
4,000	0.40	1,600
5,000	0.25	1,250
6,000	0.20	1,200
	1.00	4,450

Using an expected value approach the company's decision would be to produce product Y. However, let's consider the standard deviation calculations for each product:

Product X

Profit Deviation from Expected value	**Squared deviation**	**Probability**	**Weighted amount** ($)
3,000 – 4,000 = –1,000	1,000,000	0.10	100,000
3,500 – 4,000 = –500	250,000	0.20	50,000
4,000 – 4,000 = 0	0	0.40	0
4,500 – 4,000 = 500	250,000	0.20	50,000
5,000 – 4,000 = 1,000	1,000,000	0.10	100,000
	Sum of weighted squared deviation		300,000
	Standard deviation		547.72
	Expected value		4,000

Product Y

Profit Deviation from Expected value	Squared deviation	Probability	Weighted amount ($)
2,000 – 4,450 = –2,450	6,002,500	0.05	300,125
3,000 – 4,450 = –1,450	2,102,500	0.10	210,250
4,000 – 4,450 = –450	202,500	0.40	81,000
5,000 – 4,450 = 550	302,500	0.25	75,625
6,000 – 4,450 = 1,550	2,402,500	0.20	480,500
	Sum of weighted squared deviation		1,147,500
	Standard deviation		1,071.21
	Expected value		4,450

The expected profit for each product gives us an average value based upon the probability associated with each possible profit outcome. If profit is used for decision-making, then on that basis Product Y would be produced as it yields the highest return.

However, the profit for each product does not indicate the range of profits that may result. By calculating the standard deviation, this allows us to identify a range of values that could occur for the profit for each product. Product Y has a higher standard deviation than Product X and is therefore more risky. There is not a significant difference in profit for each of the products. However, Product X is less risky than Product Y and therefore the final selection will depend on the risk attitude of the company.

The coefficient of variation

If we have two probability distributions with different expected values their standard deviations are not directly comparable. We can overcome this problem by using the coefficient of variation (the standard deviation divided by the expected value) which measures the relative size of the risk.

For example, the standard deviation of the numbers 2, 7 and 9 is 2.94. The mean is 6 {(2 + 7 + 9)/3}. The standard deviation is calculated by taking the squares of the three deviations from the mean (16 + 1 + 9 = 26) and then calculating the square root of their average ($\sqrt{(26/3)}$ = 2.94). In this case, equal weighting is given to the three figures. The coefficient of variation is the standard deviation of the series divided by its mean which is 0.49 in this case (2.94/6).

The standard deviation of a range of numbers gives a measure of the associated level of uncertainty. The measure is an absolute one and in order to allow comparison of two different series where the mean values of the two differ significantly, then the coefficient of variation is used.

Expected values, standard deviations or coefficient of variations are used to summarise the outcomes from alternative courses of action however it must be remembered that they do not provide all the relevant information to the decision maker. The probability distribution will provide the decision maker with all of the information they require. It would be appropriate to use expected values, standard deviations or coefficient of variations for decision making when there are a large number of alternatives to consider i.e. where it is not practical to consider the probability distributions for each alternative.

Normal distributions

In the exam CIMA provides a table of the normal distribution. These are based on the principles of the normal distribution curve.

The normal distribution curve

Normal distributions were introduced in paper C03 at the Certificate level. To understand distribution we have to introduce the idea of the random variable. For example, if when tossing a coin we know the outcome will either be heads or tails, and the probability of each is 50%, but we do not know how many times the coin will be tossed, then the number of tosses will be the random variable.

If we toss the coin 50 times, we expect 25 heads and 25 tails, but this may not be the actual outcome. If we repeat the exercise, we may get a slightly different set of results.

Each set of results would follow a normal distribution. Many random variables follow a normal distribution, e.g. the height or the IQ of the population. A normal distribution is often drawn as a "bell shaped" curve, with its peak at the mean in the centre, as shown:

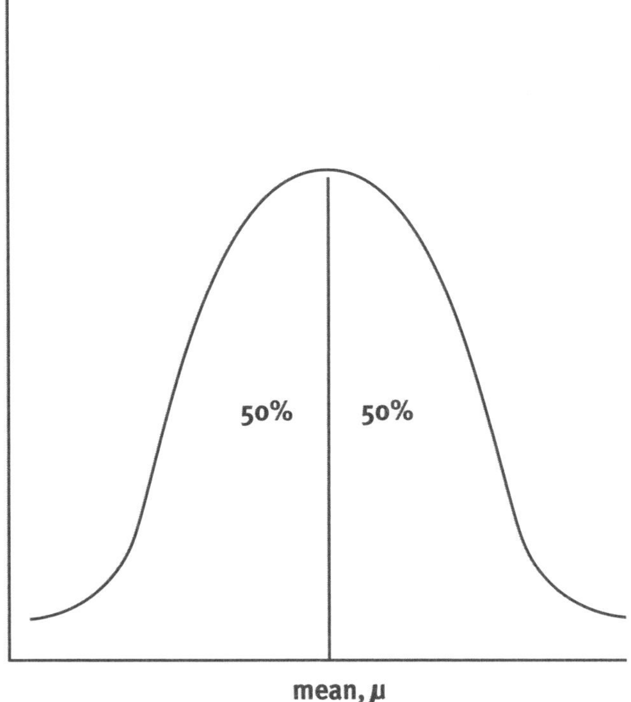

Characteristics of the normal distribution curve

- Normal distribution is a continuous probability distribution.
- Probabilities are represented by areas under the curve.
- The total area under the curve is 1.
- The curve is symmetrical and bell shaped.
- The width of the curve is measured in terms of standard deviation.
- The mean, median and mode are at the centre of the curve.

The number given in the normal distribution tables is known as the z score. The z score allows us to calculate the proportion of the distribution meeting certain criteria for any normal distribution.

Example 2

In a particular country the height of adult males is normally distributed with a mean of 175 cm and a standard deviation of 5cm.

Required:

Calculate the probability of a man in this country being shorter than 168cm?

4 Pay off tables and decision criteria

When evaluating alternative courses of action, management's decision will often depend upon their attitude towards the risk. To consider the risk borne by each alternative it is necessary to consider ALL the different possible profits/losses that may arise. A pay off table is simply a table that illustrates all possible profits/losses.

Two way data tables

Two way data tables are used to represent inter-related data in an easy to understand manner.

For example, consider a company who are unsure about both selling price and variable cost. They believe that selling price may be either $40 or $50 depending on differing market conditions, and that variable production cost will be either $20 or $30 depending on wage negotiations currently taking place.

The company has therefore got a number of potential contributions per unit that could be represented in a two way table as follows:

	Selling price	
	$40	$50
Variable production cost		
$20	$20	$30
$30	$10	$20

A user can interpret the table quickly and easy. It can be seen, for example, that if selling price is $40 and variable production costs are $30, then the contribution per unit will be $10.

Two way data tables can be expanded to calculate expected contribution from different volume levels. This will be explored further in the following illustration.

Illustration 3

Geoffrey Ramsbottom runs a kitchen that provides food for various canteens throughout a large organisation. A particular salad is sold to the canteen for $10 and costs $8 to prepare. Therefore, the contribution per salad is $2.

Based upon past demands, it is expected that, during the 250-day working year, the canteens will require the following daily quantities:

On 25 days of the year	40 salads
On 50 days of the year	50 salads
On 100 days of the year	60 salads
On 75 days	70 salads
Total 250 days	

The kitchen must prepare the salad in batches of 10 meals and it has to decide how many it will supply for each day of the forthcoming year.

Constructing a pay-off table:

- If 40 salads will be required on 25 days of a 250-day year, the probability that demand = 40 salads is:

P(Demand of 40) = 25 days ÷ 250 days

P(Demand of 40) = 0.1

- Likewise, P(Demand of 50) = 0 .20; P(Demand of 60 = 0.4) and P (Demand of 70 = 0.30).
- Now let's look at the different values of profit or losses depending on how many salads are supplied and sold. For example, if we supply 40 salads and all are sold, our profits amount to 40 × $2 = 80.
- If however we supply 50 salads but only 40 are sold, our profits will amount to 40 × $2 – (10 unsold salads x $8 unit cost) = 0.
- Note too that there is an upper limit to the potential profit in some instances. If, for example, we supply 60 salads then the maximum we can sell is 60 salads with a profit of $2 per unit (and $120 overall). If demand reaches 70 salads we can still only sell 60 salads and therefore the maximum profit we can make from supplying 60 salads is $120.

Solution

The pay off table would appear as follows:

			Daily Supply			
		Probability	**40 salads**	**50 salads**	**60 salads**	**70 salads**
Daily demand	40 salads	0.10	$80	$0	($80)	($160)
	50 salads	0.20	$80	$100	$20	($60)
	60 salads	0.40	$80	$100	$120	$40
	70 salads	0.30	$80	$100	$120	$140

This could then be used to determine the expected value from each daily supply level:

EV (of supplying 40 salads) = 0.10(80) + 0.20(80) + 0.40(80) + 0.30 (80) = 80

EV (of supplying 50 salads) = 0.10(0) + 0.20(100) + 0.40(100) + 0.30 (100) = 90

EV (of supplying 60 salads) = 0.10(–80) + 0.20(20) + 0.40(120) + 0.30 (120) = 80

EV (of supplying 70 salads) = 0.10(–160) + 0.20(–60) + 0.40(40) + 0.30 (140) = 30

On the basis of expected values, the best strategy would be to supply 50 salads and gain an EV of 90.

Example 3

- Hofgarten Newsagents stocks a weekly magazine which advertises local second-hand goods. Marie, the owner, can:
  - buy the magazines for 15c each
  - sell them at the retail price of 25c.
- At the end of each week unsold magazines are obsolete and have no value.
- Marie estimates a probability distribution for weekly demand which looks like this:

Weekly demand in units	Probability
10	0.20
15	0.55
20	0.25
	1.00

Required:

(i) Calculate the expected value of demand?

(ii) If Marie is to order a fixed quantity of magazines per week, calculate how many should that be. Assume no seasonal variations in demand.

5 Maximax, maximin and minimax regret

When probabilities are not available, there are still tools available for incorporating uncertainty into decision making.

Maximax

The maximax rule involves selecting the alternative that maximises the maximum pay-off achievable.

This approach would be suitable for an optimist who seeks to achieve the best results if the best happens.

Illustration 4 – The 'Maximax' rule

Let's apply the maximax rule to the previous illustration on Geoffrey Ramsbottom

Geoffrey Ramsbottom's table looks as follows:

		Probability	Daily Supply 40 salads	50 salads	60 salads	70 salads
Daily demand	40 salads	0.10	$80	$0	($80)	($160)
	50 salads	0.20	$80	$100	$20	($60)
	60 salads	0.40	$80	$100	$120	$40
	70 salads	0.30	$80	$100	$120	$140

The manager who employs the maximax criterion is assuming that whatever action is taken, the best will happen; he/she is a risk-taker.

Here, the highest maximum possible pay-off is $140. We should therefore decide to supply 70 salads a day.

Example 4

A company is choosing which of three new products to make (A, B or C) and has calculated likely pay-offs under three possible scenarios (I, II or III), giving the following pay-off table.

Profit (loss) Scenario	Product chosen A	B	C
I	20	80	10
II	40	70	100
III	50	(10)	40

Required:

Using maximax, which product would be chosen?

Maximin

The maximin rule involves selecting the alternative that maximises the minimum pay-off achievable.

This approach would be appropriate for a pessimist who seeks to achieve the best results if the worst happens.

Illustration 5 – The 'Maximin' rule

Geoffrey Ramsbottom's table looks as follows:

			Daily Supply			
		Probability	**40 salads**	**50 salads**	**60 salads**	**70 salads**
Daily demand	40 salads	0.10	$80	$0	($80)	($160)
	50 salads	0.20	$80	$100	$20	($60)
	60 salads	0.40	$80	$100	$120	$40
	70 salads	0.30	$80	$100	$120	$140

If we decide to supply 40 salads, the minimum pay-off is $80.

If we decide to supply 50 salads, the minimum pay-off is $0.

If we decide to supply 60 salads, the minimum pay-off is ($80).

If we decide to supply 70 salads, the minimum pay-off is ($160).

The highest minimum payoff arises from supplying 40 salads.

Example 4 continued

Required:

Using the information from Example 4, apply the maximin rule to decide which product should be made.

The minimax regret rule

The minimax regret strategy is the one that minimises the maximum regret. It is useful when probabilities for outcomes are not available or where the investor is risk averse and wants to avoid making a bad decision. Essentially, this is the technique for a 'sore loser' who does not wish to make the wrong decision.

'Regret' in this context is defined as the opportunity loss through having made the wrong decision.

Illustration 6 – The 'Minimax Regret' rule

Following up from the pay-off table example, Geoffrey Ramsbottom's table looks as follows:

			Daily Supply			
		Probability	**40 salads**	**50 salads**	**60 salads**	**70 salads**
Daily demand	40 salads	0.10	$80	$0	($80)	($160)
	50 salads	0.20	$80	$100	$20	($60)
	60 salads	0.40	$80	$100	$120	$40
	70 salads	0.30	$80	$100	$120	$140

If the minimax regret rule is applied to decide how many salads should be made each day, we need to calculate the 'regrets'. This means we need to find the biggest pay-off for each demand row, then subtract all other numbers in this row from the largest number.

For example, if the demand is 40 salads, we will make a maximum profit of $80 if they all sell. If we had decided to supply 50 salads, we would achieve a nil profit. The difference, or 'regret' between that nil profit and the maximum of $80 achievable for that row is $80.

Regrets can be tabulated as follows:

		Daily Supply			
		40 salads	**50 salads**	**60 salads**	**70 salads**
Daily demand	40 salads	$0	$80	$160	$240
	50 salads	$20	$0	$80	$160
	60 salads	$40	$20	$0	$80
	70 salads	$60	$40	$20	$0

Conclusion

If we decide to supply 40 salads, the maximum regret is $60. If we decide to supply 50 salads, the maximum regret is $80. For 60 salads, the maximum regret is $160, and $240 for 70 salads. A manager employing the minimax regret criterion would want to minimise that maximum regret, and therefore supply 40 salads only.

Example 4 continued

Required:

Using the information from Example 4, apply the minimax regret rule to decide which product should be made.

Perfect and imperfect information

In many questions the decision makers receive a forecast of a future outcome (for example a market research group may predict the forthcoming demand for a product). This forecast may turn out to be correct or incorrect. The question often requires the candidate to calculate the value of the forecast.

Perfect information The forecast of the future outcome is always a correct prediction. If a firm can obtain a 100% accurate prediction they will always be able to undertake the most beneficial course of action for that prediction.

Imperfect information The forecast is usually correct, but can be incorrect. Imperfect information is not as valuable as perfect information. Imperfect information may be examined in conjunction with Decision Trees (see later in this chapter).

The value of information (either perfect or imperfect) may be calculated as follows:

Expected profit (outcome) WITH the information

minus

Expected profit (outcome) WITHOUT the information

Illustration 7 – The value of information

A new ordering system is being considered, whereby customers must order their salad online the day before. With this new system Mr Ramsbottom will know for certain the daily demand 24 hours in advance. He can adjust production levels on a daily basis. How much is this new system worth to Mr Ramsbottom?

	X	**P**	
Supply = demand	Pay off	Probability	px
40	$80	0.1	8
50	$100	0.2	20
60	$120	0.4	48
70	$140	0.3	42
			118

E.V. with perfect information	= $118
E.V. without perfect information (from the original EV calculation)	= $90
Value of perfect information	$28 per day

Example 4 continued

Following on from the data provided in Example 4, the company has made an estimate of the probability of each scenario occurring as follows:

Scenario	Probability
I	20%
II	50%
III	30%

However, an external consultant has some information about each likely scenario and can say with certainty which scenario will arise.

Calculate the value of the external consultants information.

6 Decision trees and multi-stage decision problems

A decision tree is a diagrammatic representation of a decision problem, where all possible courses of action are represented, and every possible outcome of each course of action is shown. Decision trees should be used where a problem involves a series of decisions being made and several outcomes arise during the decision-making process. In some instances it may involve the use of joint probabilities – where the outcome of one event depends of the outcome of a preceding event.

Joint probabilities

So far only a very small number of alternatives have been considered in the examples. In practice a greater number of alternative courses of action may exist, uncertainty may be associated with more than one variable and the values of variables may be interdependent, giving rise to many different outcomes.

The following exercise looks at the expected value of a manufacturing decision, where there are three alternative sales volumes, two alternative contributions, and three alternative levels of fixed cost. The number of possible outcomes will be 3 × 2 × 3 = 18.

Example

A company is assessing the desirability of producing a souvenir to celebrate a royal jubilee. The marketing life of the souvenir will be 6 months only. Uncertainty surrounds the likely sales volume and contribution, as well as the fixed costs of the venture. Estimated outcomes and probabilities are:

Units sold	Probability	Cont'n per unit $	Probability	Fixed cost $	Probability
100,000	0.3	7	0.5	400,000	0.2
80,000	0.6	5	0.5	450,000	0.5
60,000	0.1			500,000	0.3
	1.0		1.0		1.0

The next table shows the expected value of the net contribution to be $49,000. Totalling up the joint probabilities for each set of sales shows the project has a 56.5 per cent chance of making a net contribution, a 33 per cent chance of making a loss, and a 10.5 per cent chance of making neither a net contribution nor a loss. (For example, to calculate the probability of making a loss: we can see from the next table that a loss will arise in 7 situations. So if we add the overall probability of this happening we add up the joint probabilities associated with each of these outcomes – 0.150 + 0.090 + 0.025 + 0.015 + 0.010 + 0.025 + 0.015 = 0.33).

Units sold	Cont'n per unit $	Total Cont'n $ a	Fixed Cost $ b	Probability	Joint Prob. c	EV of net cont. $ (a-b) x c
100,000	7	700,000	400,000	0.3×0.5×0.2=	0.030	9,000
	7	700,000	450,000	0.3×0.5×0.5=	0.075	18,750
	7	700,000	500,000	0.3×0.5×0.3=	0.045	9,000
	5	500,000	400,000	0.3×0.5×0.2=	0.030	3,000
	5	500,000	450,000	0.3×0.5×0.5=	0.075	3,750
	5	500,000	500,000	0.3×0.5×0.3=	0.045	0
80,000	7	560,000	400,000	0.6×0.5×0.2=	0.060	9,600
	7	560,000	450,000	0.6×0.5×0.5=	0.150	16,500
	7	560,000	500,000	0.6×0.5×0.3=	0.090	5,400
	5	400,000	400,000	0.6×0.5×0.2=	0.060	0
	5	400,000	450,000	0.6×0.5×0.5=	0.150	–7,500
	5	400,000	500,000	0.6×0.5×0.3=	0.090	–9,000
60,000	7	420,000	400,000	0.1×0.5×0.2=	0.010	200
	7	420,000	450,000	0.1×0.5×0.5=	0.025	–750
	7	420,000	500,000	0.1×0.5×0.3=	0.015	–1,200
	5	300,000	400,000	0.1×0.5×0.2=	0.010	–1,000
	5	300,000	450,000	0.1×0.5×0.5=	0.025	–3,750
	5	300,000	500,000	0.1×0.5×0.3=	0.015	–3,000
			1.0		1.0	49,000

Decisions like this can be quite hard to visualise and it may be more useful to use a decision tree to express the situation.

In an examination you will not be asked to create a decision tree, but you may want to use one as an aid to answering more complex risk questions. You may also be asked to interpret or use decision trees in examination questions and understanding how they are created should make this easier.

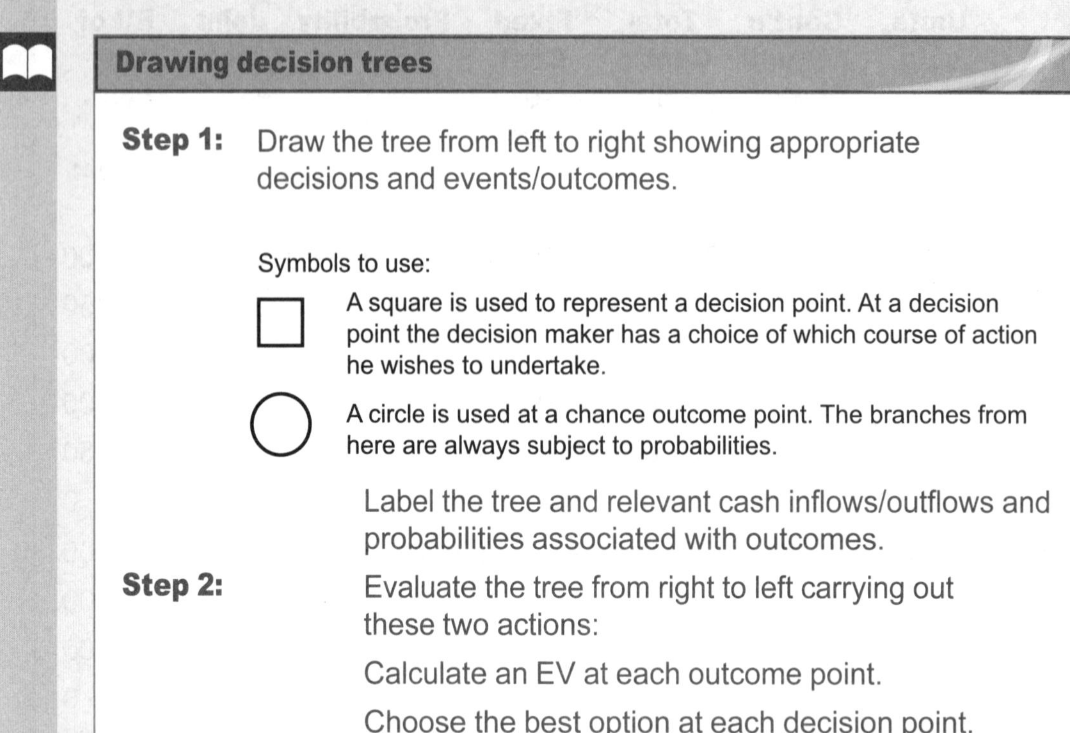

Drawing decision trees

Step 1: Draw the tree from left to right showing appropriate decisions and events/outcomes.

Symbols to use:

□ A square is used to represent a decision point. At a decision point the decision maker has a choice of which course of action he wishes to undertake.

○ A circle is used at a chance outcome point. The branches from here are always subject to probabilities.

Label the tree and relevant cash inflows/outflows and probabilities associated with outcomes.

Step 2: Evaluate the tree from right to left carrying out these two actions:

Calculate an EV at each outcome point.

Choose the best option at each decision point.

Step 3: Recommend a course of action to management.

Example 5 – Decision trees

A business is considering launching a product that will have development costs of $6m. There is a 60% chance that the development of the product will be successful. If the launch is not successful then the product will be abandoned and the development costs will be lost.

If the development is a success then the company will continue on to marketing the product. There is a 70% chance that the marketing will be successful and make a profit of $20m. If the marketing campaign is unsuccessful a profit of only $1m is expected. Both profit figures are stated after taking account of marketing costs but before development costs.

The expected value of the development and marketing plan is $____m *(round to two decimal places)*

More on decision trees

Decision trees force the decision maker to consider the logical sequence of events. A complex problem is broken down into smaller, easier-to-handle sections. The financial outcomes and probabilities are shown separately, and the decision tree is 'rolled back' by calculating expected values and making decisions. In the examination ensure that only relevant costs and revenues are considered.

Consider the following example:

A company is planning on drilling for oil. It can either drill immediately (at a cost of $50m) or carry out some preliminary tests (cost ($10m). Alternatively, the company could sell the rights to the site to another company for $40m.

If it decides to drill now there is a 55% chance that it will find oil and extract it (with a value of $150m).

If further tests are carried out first there is a 70% chance that they will indicate the presence of oil. The sales rights would then be worth $65m. Alternatively, the company could drill for oil itself at a cost of $50m. There is then an 80% chance that oil extraction (worth $150m) is successful.

If further tests are carried out and indicate that no oil is present the value of any sales rights would fall to $15m. The company could still decide to drill for oil itself- but there is only a 20% chance that it would successfully find and extract oil at that point.

A decision tree for this problem would look as follows:

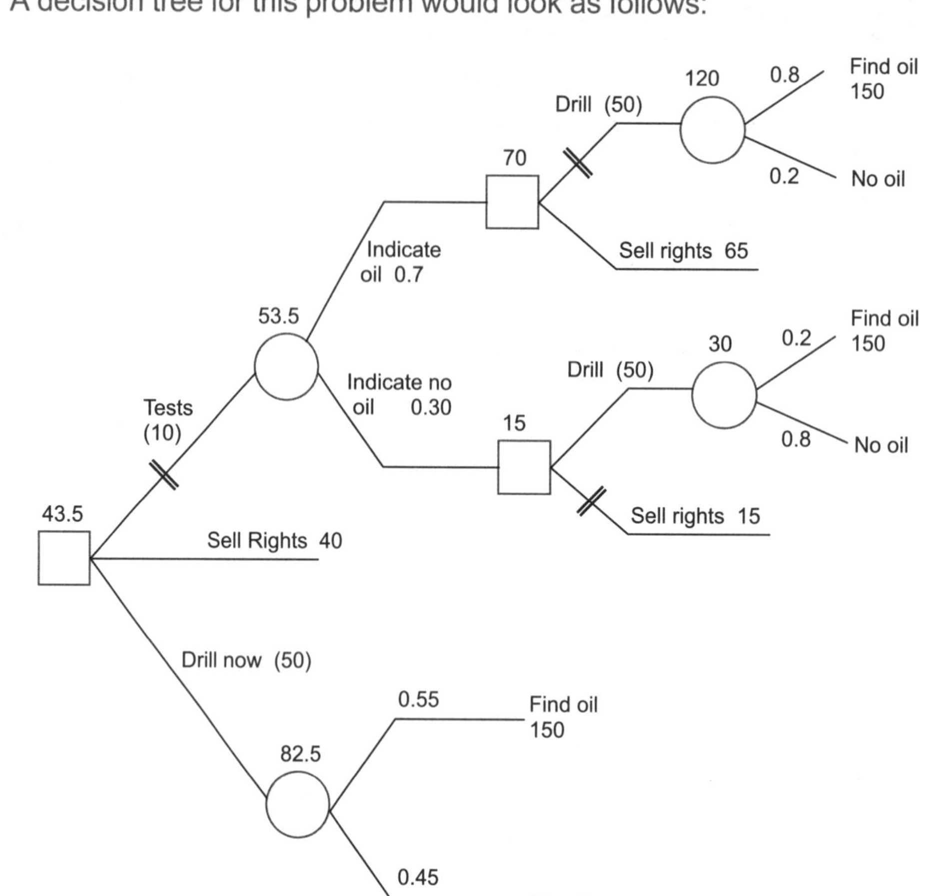

Explanation

It is easier to start at the bottom of the tree. The first box shows the first decision to be made – to test, to drill or to sell the rights. If we follow the 'drill' line/branch, we come a 'chance' point (represented by a circle). This shows that if we drill there are two possible outcomes – there is a 55% that we find oil and make a positive net return of $150m. There is also a 45% that no oil is found and that no return is made. The figure on the circle of $82.5m is the expected value calculated from these two outcomes. However, the drill line has a cost of $50m so that the overall net expected return would be $32.5m – and it is this figure that should be used to compare the drill option against the other options.

The middle branch of the tree shows the expected value from selling the rights – $40m.

The top branch shows the analysis of the testing decision. It can be seen that there are many more possible outcomes and also further decisions to made based on whether or not the tests indicate the presence of oil. Lines that have a double cross marking on them show the best choice to be made based on expected values.

Advice

The company should undertake geological tests. If the tests indicate that oil is present then a drilling programme should be carried out. However, if the tests indicate that there is no oil then the company should sell the drilling rights.

This strategy will maximise expected returns at £43.5m.

Benefits and problems

The main value of a decision tree is that it maps out clearly all the decisions and uncertain events and exactly how they are interrelated. They are especially beneficial where the outcome of one decision affects another decision. For example in the above, the probability of eventual success changes depending on the test outcomes. The analysis is made clearer by annotating the tree with probabilities, cash flows, and expected values so that the optimum decisions (based on expected values) can be clearly seen.

However, drawing a tree diagram is only one way of undertaking a decision. It is based on the concept of expected value and as such suffers from the limitations of this technique. For example, in this example, if the test drilling proves positive, the tree indicated the company should drill, as opposed to selling the rights. But if it does there is a 20% chance of it losing £50 million. A risk-averse company may well decide to accept the safer option and sell the rights and settle for £65 million.

A number of other factors should be taken into account when considering decision tree-type problems:

- *Assumes risk neutrality.* As mentioned under probability, some decision-makers do not choose options which give the greatest expected value, because they are either risk seekers or risk averse.
- *Sensitivity analysis.* The analysis depends very much on the values of the probabilities in the tree. The values are usually the subjective estimates of the decision-makers, and, no matter how experienced the people involved are, the values must be open to question. Sensitivity analysis can be used to consider 'break-even' positions for each variable – i.e. the value for a variable (such as probability) at which the decision would change. Sensitivity analysis is covered later in this chapter.
- *Oversimplification.* In order to make the tree manageable, the situation has often to be greatly simplified. This makes it appear far more discrete than it really is. In practice, it is much more likely that the outcomes would form a near continuous range of inflows and outflows. This cannot be shown on a decision tree, and so any decision tree usually represents a simplified situation.

7 Sensitivity analysis

Sensitivity analysis takes each uncertain factor in turn, and calculates the change that would be necessary in that factor before the original decision is reversed.

By using this technique it is possible to establish which estimates (variables) are more critical than others in affecting a decision.

The process in calculating sensitivities

The process is as follows:

- Best estimates for variables are made and a decision arrived at. For example, a profit calculation may indicate accepting a project.
- Each of the variables is analysed in turn to see how much the original estimate can change before the original decision is reversed. For example, it may be that the estimated selling price can fall by 5% before the profit becomes negative and the project would be rejected.
- Estimates for each variable can then be reconsidered to assess the likelihood of the decision being wrong. For example, what is the chance of the selling price falling by more than 5%?

Illustration 8

A manager is considering a make v buy decision based on the following estimates:

	If made in-house	**If buy in and re-badge**
	$	$
Variable production costs	10	2
External purchase costs	–	6
Ultimate selling price	15	14

Identify the sensitivity of the decision to the external purchase price.

Step 1: What is the original decision?

Comparing contribution figures, the product should be bought in and re-badged:

	If made in-house	**If buy in and re-badge**
	$	$
Contribution	5	6

Step 2: Calculate the sensitivity (to the external purchase price)

For indifference, the contribution from outsourcing needs to fall to $5 per unit. Thus the external purchase price only needs to increase by $1 per unit (or $1/$6 = 17%).

If the external purchase price rose by more than 17% the original decision would be reversed.

Example 6 – Sensitivity analysis

A manager has identified the following two possible outcomes for a process

Outcome	**Probability**	**Financial implications ($000s)**
Poor	0.4	Loss of 20
Good	0.6	Profit of 40

The expected value has been calculated as EV = (0.4 × –20) + (0.6 × 40) = +16. This would suggest that the opportunity should be accepted.

Required:

(a) Suppose the likely loss if results are poor has been underestimated. What level of loss would change the decision? In effect we want a break-even estimate.

(b) Suppose the probability of a loss has been underestimated. What is the break-even probability?

Strengths and weaknesses

Strengths of sensitivity analysis

- There is no complicated theory to understand.
- Information will be presented to management in a form which facilitates subjective judgement to decide the likelihood of the various possible outcomes considered.
- It identifies areas which are crucial to the success of the project. If the project is chosen, those areas can be carefully monitored.

Weaknesses of sensitivity analysis

- It assumes that changes to variables can be made independently, e.g. material prices will change independently of other variables. Simulation allows us to change more than one variable at a time.
- It only identifies how far a variable needs to change; it does not look at the probability of such a change.
- It provides information on the basis of which decisions can be made but it does not point to the correct decision directly.

8 Chapter summary

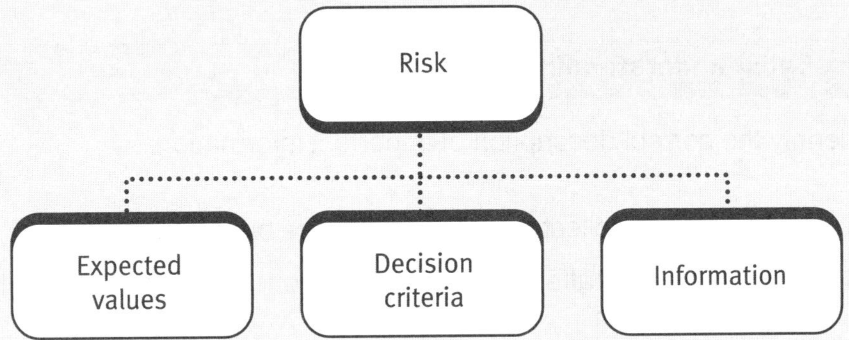

Expected values

- Multiply the probability and expected outcome
- Provides an 'average' of possibilities
- Relies on accuracy of the information
- Use decision trees for complex problems

Decision criteria

- Risk neutral = choose the highest EV
- Risk averse = use maximin
- Risk seeker = use maximax
- Worried about bad decisions = use minimax regret

Information

- Compare the EV with the information and without

9 Practice questions

Test your understanding 1

Identify the correct description of imperfect information:

A costs more to collect than its value to the business

B is available only after preliminary decisions on a business venture have been taken

C does not take into account all factors affecting a business

D may contain inaccurate predictions

Test your understanding 2

A company is considering investing in one of the following projects.

Project	**Expected value** $000	**Standard deviation** $000
A	850	500
B	1,200	480
C	150	200
D	660	640

If the company wishes to select the project with the lowest risk factor (coefficient of variation) it select will select Project _ *(Enter the letter of the preferred project)*

Test your understanding 3

Scenario

Three investors are considering the same investments. The net returns from the investments depend on the state of the economy and are illustrated as follows:

State of the economy	Returns from investment			Probability of economic state
	A $	**B** $	**C** $	
Good	6,000	14,000	3,000	0.1
Fair	5,000	3,000	5,000	0.4
Poor	4,000	500	8,000	0.5

Details on the attitudes to risk of the three investors is as follows:

- Micah is risk neutral
- Zhang is a risk seeker
- Jill is risk averse and typically follows a minimax regret strategy with her investments.

Task

Discuss which investment would be best suited to each investor's risk attitude *(calculations must be provided to support your answer)*.

(Time allowed: 10 minutes)

Test your understanding 4

PT has $8m of debt, on which it pays annual interest of 4%. The company's operating cash inflow in the coming year is forecast to be $600,000, and currently the company has $80,000 cash on deposit. The company has no other lines of credit available.

Required:

Given that the annual volatility (standard deviation) of the company's cash flows (measured over the last 5 years) has been 40%, the probability that Villa Co will default on its interest payment within the next year is ____% *(fill in the number to the nearest 1 decimal place)*

Test your understanding 5

For the past 20 years a charity organisation has held an annual dinner and dance with the primary intention of raising funds.

This year there is concern that an economic recession may adversely affect both the number of persons attending the function and the advertising space that will be sold in the programme published for the occasion.

Based on past experience and current prices and quotations, it is expected that the following costs and revenues will apply for the function:

			$
Cost:	Dinner and dance:	Hire of premises	700
		Band and entertainers	2,800
		Raffle prizes	800
		Photographer	200
		Food at $12 per person (with a guarantee of 400 persons minimum)	
	Programme:	A fixed cost of $2,000 plus $5 per page	

Revenues:	Dinner and dance:	Price of tickets	$20 per person
		Average revenue from:	
		Raffle	$5 per person
		Photographs	$1 per person
	Programme:	Average revenue from advertising	$70 per page

A sub-committee, formed to examine more closely the likely outcome of the function, discovered the following from previous records and accounts:

Number of tickets sold	**Number of past occasions**
250 to 349	4
350 to 449	6
450 to 549	8
550 to 649	2

Number of programme pages sold	**Number of past occasions**
24	4
32	8
40	6
48	2

Required:

Calculate the expected value of the profit to be earned from the dinner and dance this year.

Test your understanding 6

A company can make either of two new products, X and Y, but not both. The profitability of each product depends on the state of the market, as follows:

Market state	Profit from product		Probability of market state
	X $	**Y** $	
Good	20,000	17,000	0.2
Fair	15,000	16,000	0.5
Poor	6,000	7,000	0.3

The expected value of perfect information as to the state of the market is _______ (*insert the correct figure)*

Test your understanding 7

An organisation is making a decision on which of two products to launch. Future profit outcomes for each product will either be high or low.

It has created the following decision tree to summarise the problem:

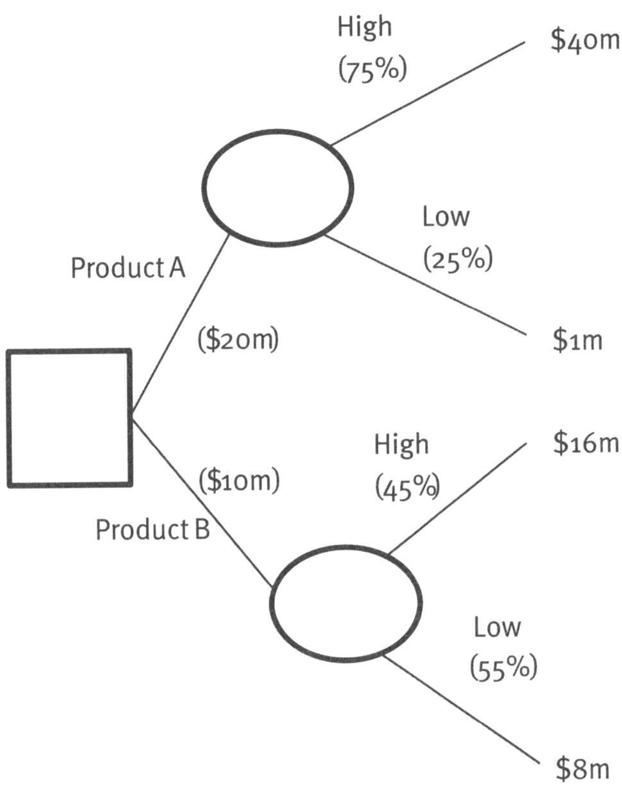

The expected value from the optimal decision is:

A $1.6m

B $10.25m

C $11.6m

D $30.25m

Test your understanding 8

An organisation is considering launching one of two new products and has created the following decision tree to represent its decision:

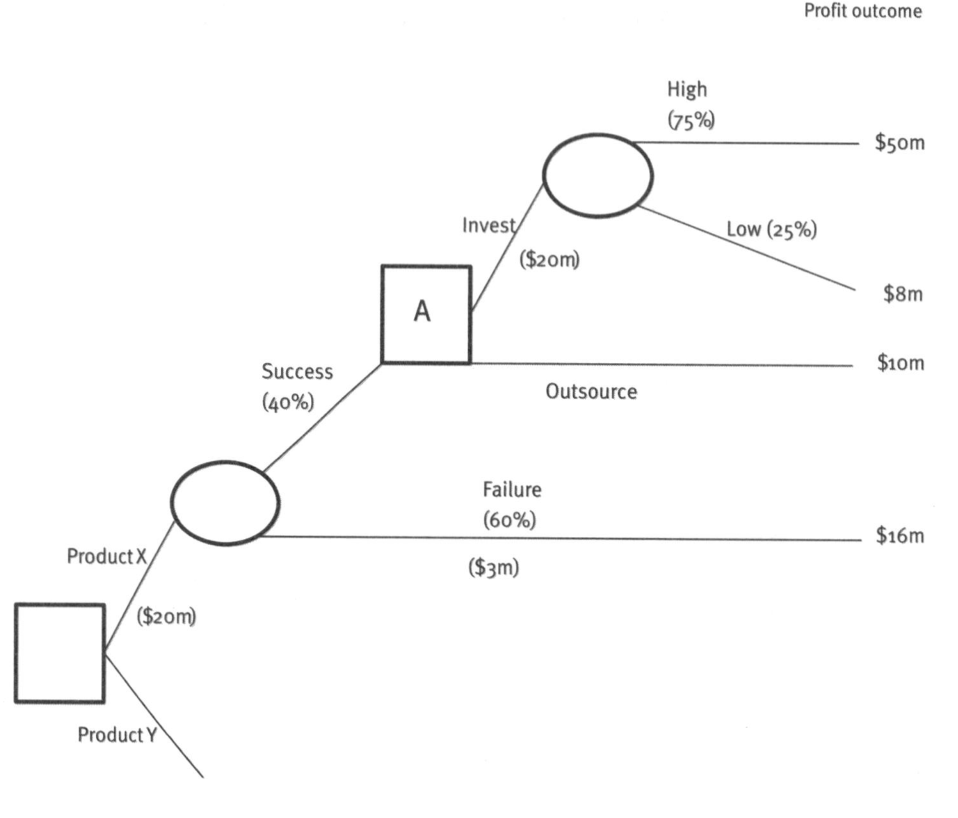

The maximum expected value of profit at decision point A is $_____

Test your understanding 9

Scenario

The Venus Department Store operates a customer loan facility. If one of its new customers requests a loan then Venus either refuses it, gives a high loan limit, or gives a low loan limit. From a number of years past experience the probability that a new customer makes a full repayment of a loan is known to be 0.95, whilst the probability of non-repayment is 0.05 (these probabilities being independent of the size of loan limit). The average profit in $, per customer made by Venus is given by the following table.

	Loan Limit	
	High	**Low**
Full-repayment	50	20
Non-repayment	–200	–30

The junior accountant at the store has created a decision tree to summarise the store's position on providing credit to customers:

(a)

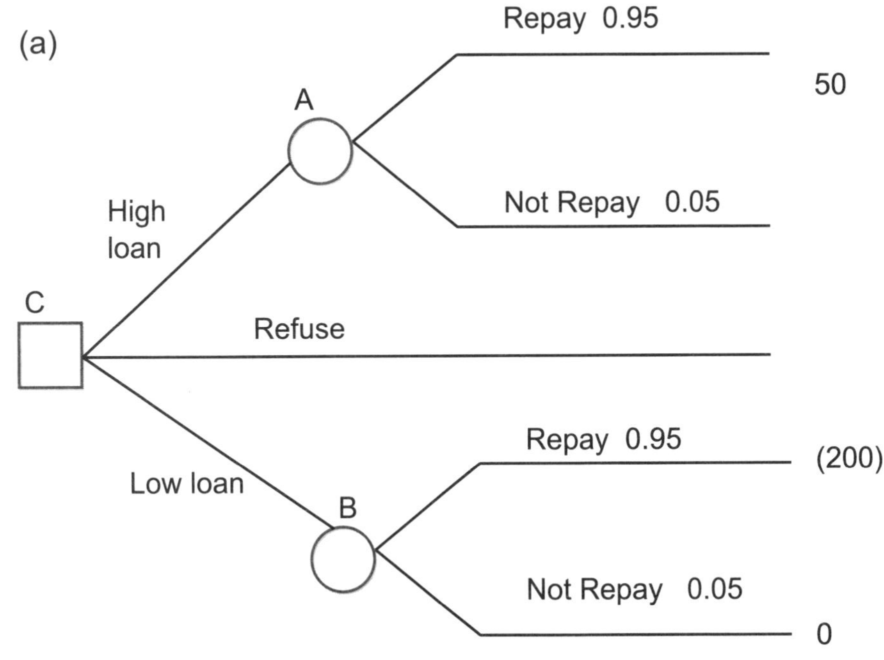

At points A and B calculate Expected Values:

At A	EV = (0.95 × 50) + (0.05 × (200))	= **37.5**
At B	EV = (0.95 × 20) + (0.05 × (30))	= **17.5**

Task:

Explain the decision tree to the store's management and recommend whether or not credit should be offered to customers.

(Time allowed: 10 minutes)

The junior accountant has also prepared the following information regarding the use of a credit agency who would assess customers before any decision was taken. Analysis of the last 1,000 customer ratings by this agency have been used in the construction of the following decision tree:

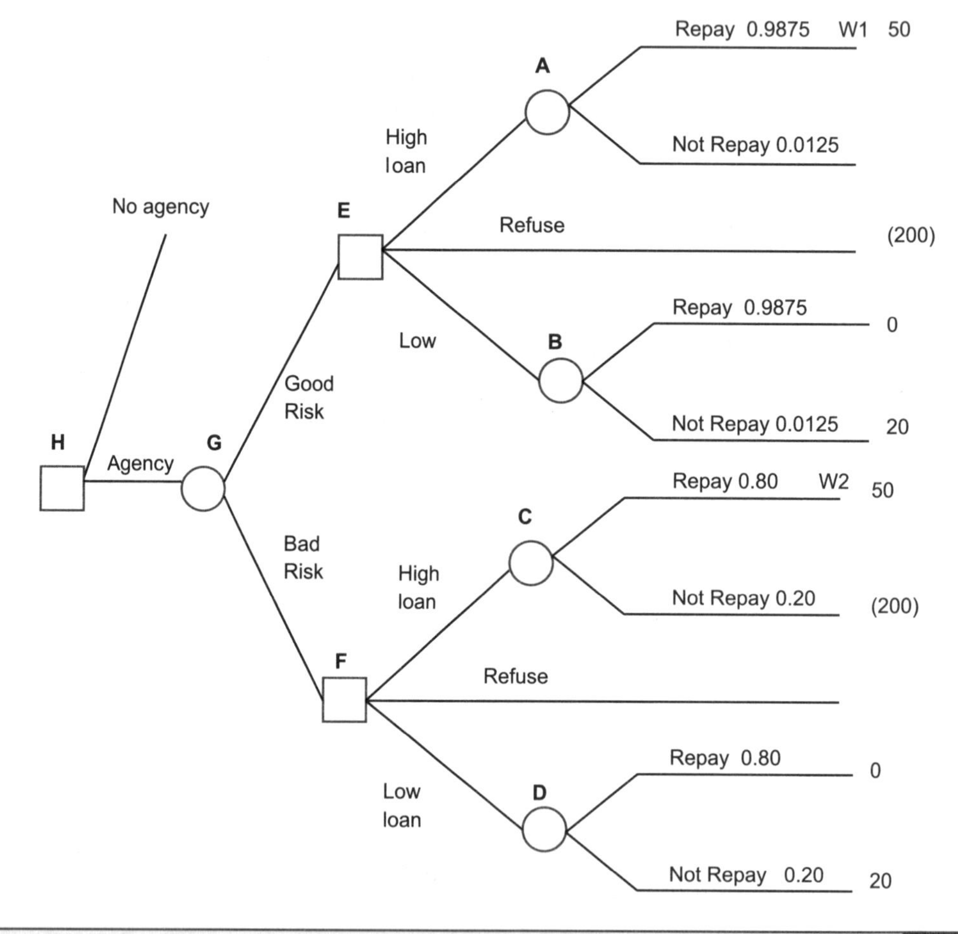

Workings

(W1) A sample of 800 customers have been assessed by the agency as being a good risk. Of these 790 did repay the loan. This represents 98.75% (790 ÷ 800) of the good risk customers.

Hence, the remaining 1.25% of the good risk customers did not repay the loan. (10 ÷ 800).

(W2) In a similar way to (W1), 160 out of the 200 bad risk customers did repay the loan, i.e. 80%.

40 out of the 200 bad risk customers did not repay the loan, i.e. 20%.

Expected values

At A	(0.9875 × 50) + (0.0125 × (200))	=	$46.875
At B	(0.9875 × 20) + (0.0125 × (30))	=	$19.375
At C	(0.8 × 50) + (0.2 × (200))	=	0
At D	(0.8 × 20) + (0.2 × (30))	=	$10.00
At G	(0.8 × 46.875) + (0.2 × 10.00)	=	$39.50

Expected return with perfect information = $47.50

Tasks:

- Explain the difference between imperfect and perfect information.
- Explain how this applies to the department store's decision and recommend whether a credit agency should be used by the store.

(Time allowed: 20 minutes)

Test your understanding answers

Example 1 – Calculating an expected value

Expected value calculation

Outcome	Profit ($)	Probability	Profit x Probability ($)
A	100,000	0.10	10,000
B	70,000	0.40	28,000
C	50,000	0.30	15,000
D	–20,000	0.20	–4,000
Expected value			49,000

Expected profit is $49,000.

Example 2

The mean is 175cm. 168cm is 7cm away from the mean.
This represents 7/5 = 1.40 standard deviations. This is the z score.

From tables, on the left hand column, look up the z score to one decimal place, i.e. 1.4. Look along this row until it meets the column with the 2nd decimal place (0.00). The table gives us 0.4192. The normal distribution table used has a maximum value of 0.5. We want to determine the percentage of people who are MORE than 1.4 standard deviations away from the mean and this is therefore calculated as 0.5 – 0.4192 = 0.0808. This can then be converted into a percentage by multiplying by 100 = 8.08%

Hence, the probability of a man being shorter than 168cm is 8.08% (approximately 8%).

Example 3

(i) EV of demand = (10 × 0.20) + (15 × 0.55) + (20 × 0.25) = 15.25 units per week.

(ii) The first step is to set up a decision matrix of possible strategies (numbers bought) and possible demand, as follows:

Outcome	**Strategy (number bought)**		
(number demanded)	10	15	20
10			
15			
20			

The 'pay-off' from each combination of action and outcome is then computed:

No sale: cost of 15c per magazine.

Sale: profit of 25c – 15c = 10c per magazine.

Pay-offs are shown for each combination of strategy and outcome.

Probability	**Outcome (number demanded)**	**Decision (number bought)**		
		10	15	20
0.20	10	100	25	(50)
0.55	15	100	150	75
0.25	20	100	150	200
1.00	EV	100c	125c	81.25c

Conclusion: The strategy which gives the highest expected value is to stock 15 magazines each week.

Workings

(i) If 10 magazines are bought, then 10 are sold no matter how many are demanded and the payoff is always 10 × 10c = 100c.

(ii) If 15 magazines are bought and 10 are demanded, then 10 are sold at a profit of 10 × 10c = 100c, and 5 are scrapped at a loss of 5 × 15c = 75c, making a net profit of 25c.

(iii) The other contributions are similarly calculated.

Example 4

Using maximax, an optimist would consider the best possible outcome for each product and pick the product with the greatest potential.

Here C would be chosen with a maximum possible gain of 100.

Example 4 continued

- Using maximin, a pessimist would consider the poorest possible outcome for each product and would ensure that the maximum pay-off is achieved if the worst result were to happen.
- Therefore, product A would be chosen resulting in a minimum pay-off of 20 compared to a minimum pay-off of (10) for product B and 10 for product C.

Example 4 continued

In the pay-off matrix above, if the market state had been scenario I:

The correct decision would have been:	B (net income $80)
If A had been chosen instead:	The company would have been out of pocket by $60 (i.e. 80 – 20)
If C had been chosen:	It would have been out of pocket by $70 (i.e. 80 – 10)

- The opportunity loss associated with each product is: A = $60, B =$0, C = $70.

Scenario II and III can be considered in the same way and the results can be summarised in a regret table.

The completed opportunity loss ('regret') table is thus as follows.

	Decision		
State	**A**	**B**	**C**
I	60	0	70
II	60	30	0
III	0	60	10
Maximum regret	60	60	70

The maximum regret value for:

A = \$60

B = \$60

C = \$70

The minimum value of these is \$60, hence the minimax regret strategy would be either A or B.

B would probably be adopted because its second-highest regret outcome (\$30) is lower than the second-highest for A (\$60).

Example 4 continued

Firstly, we have to calculate the expected value without the information.

EV (A) = 0.2(20) + 0.5(40) + 0.3(50) = 39

EV (B) = 0.2(80) + 0.5(70) + 0.3(–10) = 48

EV (C) = 0.2(10) + 0.5(100) + 0.3(40) = 64

So the company would choose project C, with an expected pay-off of 64.

If the company had perfect information it would act as follows:

Scenario indicated by perfect information	Company's decision*	Pay-off
I	Invest in product B	80
II	Invest in product C	100
III	Invest in product A	50

* this will be based on the highest expected pay-off in that scenario. For example, if scenario I is predicted the company will face a pay-off of 20 from product A, 80 from product B, and 10 from product C. It will therefore decide to invest in product B.

The expected value from these decisions would be:

EV (C) = 0.2(80) + 0.5(100) + 0.3(50) = 81

This is 17 higher than the expected value (64) when the company had no information. Therefore the information has a value of 17.

Example 5 – Decision trees

The situation can be summarised in a decision tree as follows:

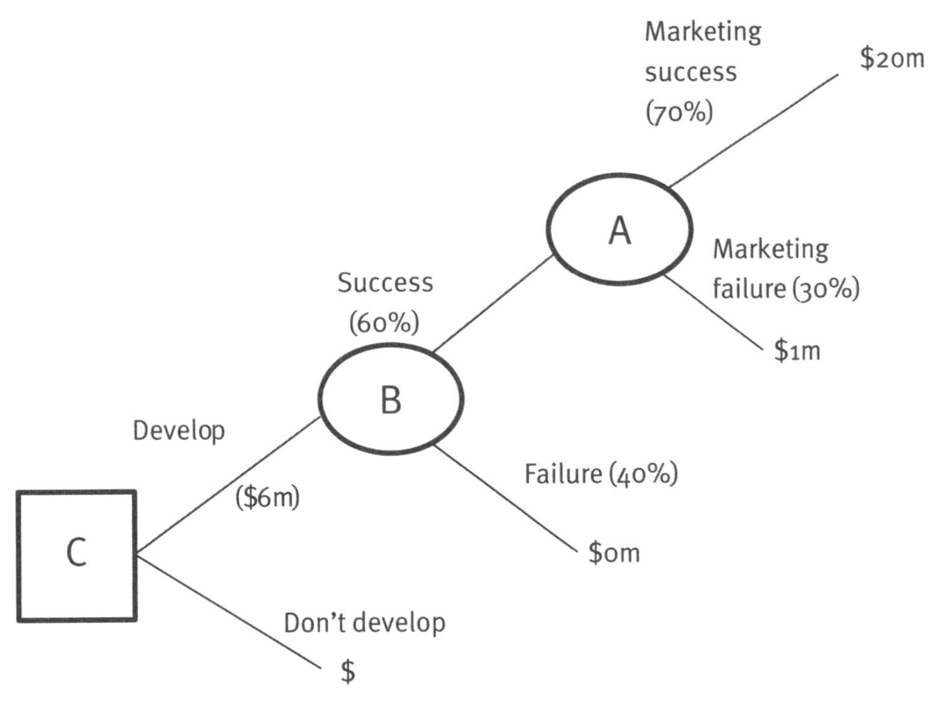

The expected value at point A = (0.7 × \$20m) + (0.3 × \$1m) = \$14.3m

The expected value at point B = (0.6 × \$14.3m) + (0.4 × \$0k) = \$8.58m

The value of the development (point C) = \$8.58m – \$6m = \$2.58m

When compared to the \$0 returns from not developing it is better to develop the product

The expected value of the development and marketing plan is \$**2.58** m.

Example 6 – Sensitivity analysis

(a) The EV would have to decrease by $16,000 before the original decision is reversed, i.e. this is the break-even point.

– Let the loss be L

Currently, EV = (0.4 × L) + (0.6 × 40)

If EV falls to zero:

EV of 0 = (0.4 × L) + (0.6 × 40)

0 = 0.4L + 24

– 24 = 0.4L

– 24/0.4 = L

L = – 60

– The loss would have to increase from $20,000 to $60,000 before the decision is reversed. This is a 200% increase in the loss.

(b) The EV would have to decrease by $16,000 before the original decision is reversed, i.e. this is the break-even point.

– Let the probability of a loss be P and the probability of a profit be 1 – P.

Currently, EV = (P × –20) + (1 – p × 40)

If EV falls to zero:

EV of 0 = (P × –20) + (1 – p × 40)

0 = –20P + 40 –40P

60P = 40

P = 40/60

P = 0.67

– The probability of a loss would have to increase to 0.67 from 0.4 before the decision is reversed.

Test your understanding 1

D

Perfect information is certain to be right about the future. Imperfect information may predict wrongly.

Test your understanding 2

If the company wishes to select the project with the lowest risk factor (coefficient of variation) it select will select Project **B**

Project	**Expected value** $000	**Standard deviation** $000	**Coefficient of variation**
A	850	500	0.59
B	1,200	480	0.40
C	150	200	1.33
D	660	640	0.97

Test your understanding 3

Micah

As a risk neutral investor Micah will base his decision on the expected value of each investment. These are calculated as follows:

Investment A = ($6,000 × 0.1) + ($5,000 × 0.4) + ($4,000 × 0.5) = $4,600

Investment B = ($14,000 × 0.1) + ($3,000 × 0.4) + ($500 × 0.5) = $2,850

Investment C = ($3,000 × 0.1) + ($5,000 × 0.4) + ($8,000 × 0.5) = $6,300

Micah will therefore choose to invest in Investment C as it has the highest overall expected value.

Zhang

As a risk seeker Zhang will ignore the expected values and probabilities, and she will focus solely on the payouts. She will apply the maximax criteria and consider where the highest payout might arise. The highest possible return is the $14,000 that arises in a good market state for Investment B. Zhang will therefore choose to invest in Investment B.

Jill

To apply the minimax regret criteria Jill will have to create a regret table as follows:

State of the economy		**Regret**	
	A $	**B** $	**C** $
Good	8,000	0	11,000
Fair	0	2,000	0
Poor	4,000	7,500	0
Maximum regret	8,000	7,500	11,000

If Jill were to invest in Investment A and the economy was in a good state she would receive $6,000. However, if she had instead gone for Investment B then she could have received $14,000 – $8,000 more than she will get from Investment A. This represents the regret. The maximum regret in each column is summarised in the final row. The minimax regret strategy is to choose the lowest of these figures – the $7,500 from Investment B. Jill will therefore choose to invest in B as this has the lowest amount of possible regret.

Test your understanding 4

PT will have expected cash of $600,000 + $80,000 = $680,000. It has an interest commitment (outgoing) of $320,000 (= 4% on $8m). If receipts fall by $360,000 ($680,000 – $320,000) the organisation will default on its interest commitment.

So we need to calculate the probability that the cash available will fall by $360,000 over the next year.

Assuming that the annual cash flow is normally distributed, a volatility (standard deviation) of 40% on a cash flow of $600,000 represents a standard deviation of 0.40 × $600,000 = $240,000.

Thus, our fall of $360,000 represents 360,000/240,000 = 1.50 standard deviations.

From the normal distribution tables, the area between the mean and 1.50 standard deviations = 0.9332. Hence, there must be a 1.000 – 0.9332 = 0.0668 chance of the cashflow being insufficient to meet the interest payment. i.e. the probability of default is approximately **6.7**%.

Test your understanding 5

Revenue per person = $20 + $5 + $1

Number of tickets	Probability	Revenue	Food cost	Net benefit	Prob. × benefit
		$	$	$	$
300	0.2	7,800	(4,800)	3,000	600
400	0.3	10,400	(4,800)	5,600	1,680
500	0.4	13,000	(6,000)	7,000	2,800
600	0.1	15,600	(7,200)	8,400	840
	1.0		**Expected value = 5,920**		

Number of pages	Probability	Contribution $65 per page	Prob. × contribution
		$	$
24	0.2	1,560	312
32	0.4	2,080	832
40	0.3	2,600	780
48	0.1	3,120	312
	1.0		**Expected value = 2,236**

Total contribution	$5,920 + $2,236	=	$8,156
Less fixed costs		=	($6,500)
Expected profit			$1,656

Test your understanding 6

Without information, the expected profits are:

Product X: $20,000 × 0.2 + $15,000 × 0.5 + $6,000 × 0.3 = $13,300

Product Y: $17,000 × 0.2 + $16,000 × 0.5 + $7,000 × 0.3 = $13,500

So without information, product Y would be selected.

With perfect information, product X would be selected if the market was good, and product Y in the other two cases. The expected value would then be:

$20,000 × 0.2 + $16,000 × 0.5 + $7,000 × 0.3 = $14,100

The expected value of perfect information is therefore $14,100 – $13,500 = $**600**

Test your understanding 7

The expected value from each product is:

Product A: ($40m × 0.75) + ($1m × 0.25) – $20m = $10.25m

Product B: ($16m × 0.45) + ($8m × 0.55) – $10m = $1.6m

So Product A would be selected, and the expected value would be $10.25m (**Option B**).

Test your understanding 8

Decision point A appears to represent a decision between the following two outcomes:

		Value
Outsource		\$10m
Invest	(\$50m × 0.75) + (\$8m × 0.25) – \$20m	\$19.5m

The option to invest would appear to be the optimal decision at point A as it has the highest expected value.

The maximum expected value of profit at decision point A is \$**19.5m**

Test your understanding 9

First decision tree

The decision tree provides information on the three possible decisions available to the business:

- the upper most line shows the returns from offering customers a high loan limit. It shows that there is a 95% chance of repayment and a respective return of \$50. There is also a 5% chance of default with a loss of \$200. The expected value calculated at point A illustrates that this would have an average overall value to the business of \$37.50.
- the lowest line provides similar information on the returns from offering a low loan limit. The expected value at point B shows that this would have an average overall value to the business of \$17.50.
- the middle line shows that if a loan limit is refused to the customer then the expected return is \$0.

The three values can be compared at point C and the highest expected return (\$37.50) comes from offering customers a high loan limit. This therefore instructs the store as to its optimal decision policy – if a new customer asks for credit, he/she should be offered a high loan limit.

Second decision tree

There are two types of information presented in the junior accountant's analysis:

Perfect information	This assumes that the credit agency's prediction on whether a customer is a good or bad risk is always 100% accurate. In reality, this is unlikely to be achievable.
Imperfect information	This recognises that the credit agency will not always get their prediction correct. Sometimes good risk customers will be classed as bad risk customers (and vice versa). This becomes a more complex problem and the decision tree summarises the information used to come to a decision on the value of this information.

- The uppermost line shows the decision making process if the credit agency indicates that a new customer will be a good credit risk (i.e. they are more than likely to repay the loan). This takes the store to decision point E where it must decide between offering a high loan limit (the expected value (EV) shows at point A that this would generate an average profit of $46.875), refusing credit (the EV is $0) and offering a low loan limit (EV = $19.375). So at point E, the best decision would be to offer a high loan limit if the agency indicates that the new customer is a good credit risk and this would have an EV of $46.875.
- The line stretching towards decision point F illustrates a similar analysis would take place if the agency indicated that the new customer was a bad credit risk. The optimal policy would be to follow along path D where the EV is $10. So if the agency indicates a bad credit risk for a new customer a low credit loan should be offered with an EV of $10.
- To bring all of this analysis together, points E and F are then compared at point G. This takes account of the probability of the agency indicating either good risk or bad risk and builds in the presence of imperfect information. The EV at point G ($39.50) indicates the overall profit to the business in the presence of this imperfect information.

The business is therefore left with three important pieces of information:

- in the absence of any information, the store can expect to make a profit of $37.50
- in the presence of imperfect information from the agency, the store can expect to make a profit of $39.50
- if perfect information could be achieved, the store can expect to make a profit of $47.50.

So the value of the information has a maximum value of $10 ($47.50 – $37.50). The value of the agency's information is $2 ($39.50 – $37.50). The store should therefore use the credit scoring agency provided that they charge less than $2 for each credit assessment.

Index

A

B

C

Index

Index

Index

Index

V

W

Y

Z

Index